T0309495

Innovative Applications of Ambient Intelligence:

Advances in Smart Systems

Kevin Curran
University of Ulster, UK

Information Science
REFERENCE

Managing Director:	Lindsay Johnston
Senior Editorial Director:	Heather Probst
Book Production Manager:	Sean Woznicki
Development Manager:	Joel Gamon
Development Editor:	Hannah Abelbeck
Acquisitions Editor:	Erika Gallagher
Typesetters:	Milan Vracarich, Jr.
Print Coordinator:	Jamie Snavely
Cover Design:	Nick Newcomer

Published in the United States of America by
Information Science Reference (an imprint of IGI Global)
701 E. Chocolate Avenue
Hershey PA 17033
Tel: 717-533-8845
Fax: 717-533-8661
E-mail: cust@igi-global.com
Web site: http://www.igi-global.com

Copyright © 2012 by IGI Global. All rights reserved. No part of this publication may be reproduced, stored or distributed in any form or by any means, electronic or mechanical, including photocopying, without written permission from the publisher. Product or company names used in this set are for identification purposes only. Inclusion of the names of the products or companies does not indicate a claim of ownership by IGI Global of the trademark or registered trademark.

Library of Congress Cataloging-in-Publication Data

Innovative applications of ambient intelligence : advances in smart systems / Kevin Curran, editor.
    p. cm.
  Summary: "This book provides perspectives on the convergence of ubiquitous computing, intelligent systems research, and context awareness with the aim of encouraging the further development of ambient intelligence frameworks and research"-- Provided by publisher.
  Includes bibliographical references and index.
  ISBN 978-1-4666-0038-6 (hardcover) -- ISBN 978-1-4666-0039-3 (ebook) -- ISBN 978-1-4666-0040-9 (print & perpetual access) 1. Ambient intelligence. I. Curran, Kevin, 1969-
  QA76.9.A48I56 2012
  004.01'9--dc23
                                    2011039617

British Cataloguing in Publication Data
A Cataloguing in Publication record for this book is available from the British Library.

All work contributed to this book is new, previously-unpublished material. The views expressed in this book are those of the authors, but not necessarily of the publisher.

Table of Contents

Detailed Table of Contents

Chapter 1
Cristiano Castelfranchi, Istituto di Scienze e Tecnologie della Cognizione, CNR, Italy
Giovanni Pezzulo, Istituto di Scienze e Tecnologie della Cognizione, Italy & Istituto di Linguistica
Computazionale, CNR, Italy
Luca Tummolini, Istituto di Scienze e Tecnologie della Cognizione, CNR, Italy

A crucial part of the intelligence that smart environments should display is a specific form of social intelligence: the ability to read human behavior and its traces in terms of underlying intentions and assumptions. Such ability is crucial to enable human users to tacitly coordinate and negotiate with smart and proactive digital environments. In this paper, the authors argue that the necessary tool for this ability is behavioral and stigmergic implicit (i.e. non-conventional) communication. The authors present a basic theory of such a fundamental interactive means—the theory of Behavioral Implicit Communication (BIC).

Chapter 2
Declan Traynor, University of Ulster, UK
Ermai Xie, University of Ulster, UK
Kevin Curran, University of Ulster, UK

Ambient Intelligence (AmI) deals with the issue of how we can create context-aware, electronic environments which foster seamless human-computer interaction. Ambient Intelligence encompasses the fields of ubiquitous computing, artificially intelligent systems, and context awareness among others. This paper discusses context-awareness and examines how discoveries in this area will be key in propelling the development of true AmI environments. This will be done by examining the background and reasoning behind this particular strand of AmI research along with an overview of the technologies being explored alongside possible applications of context awareness in computing as well as technological and socio-ethical challenges in this field.

In this paper, we present the interpretation and generation processes of a spoken dialogue interface for ambient intelligence. The interface is automatically created for each specific environment and the interpretation and generation vary depending on the environment and its context. These processes rely on a dialogue tree structure. Several modules process the tree structure and the context information to produce specific dialogues for the current environment state. The interface has been implemented and evaluated in an ambient intelligence environment. Satisfactory objective and subjective evaluation results are shown at the end of the paper.

The recognition of human behaviour from sensor observations is an important area of research in smart homes and ambient intelligence. In this paper, we introduce the idea of spatio-temporal footprints, which are local patterns in space and time that should be similar across repeated occurrences of the same behaviour. We discuss the spatial and temporal mapping requirements of these footprints, together with how they may be used.

iCampus is a prototype multi-agent system whose goal is to provide the ambient intelligence required to connect people in a university campus and make that campus inclusive and accessible. Software agents called guides run on mobile phones to help students with information about people, places, and events, thus providing people real-time, location-based advice that makes them more aware of what is going on in the campus. The work outlines how to specify iCampus in the Ambient Event Calculus and implement it using the agent environment GOLEM to deploy guide agents over a campus network. The work is illustrated by showing how iCampus improves the mobility of blind or partially sighted students within a campus, which has been the main motivation behind the work.

Since the appearance of the Ambient Intelligence paradigm, as an evolution of the Ubiquitous Computing, a great deal of the research efforts in this field have been mainly aimed at anticipating user actions and needs, out of a prefixed set. However, Ambient Intelligence is not just constrained to user behaviour pattern matching, but to wisely supervise the whole environment, satisfying those unforeseen requirements or needs, by means of rational decisions. This work points at the lack of commonsense reasoning, as the main reason underlying the existance of these idiots savant systems, capable of accomplishing very specific and complex tasks, but incapable of making decisions out of the prefixed behavioral patterns. This work advocates for the integration of the commonsense reasoning and understanding capabilities as the key elements in bridging the gap between idiot savant systems and real Ambient Intelligence systems.

Interaction is a core concept in the fields of Ubiquitous computing, Ambient systems design, and generally in the fields of HCI and Interaction Design. Despite this, a lack of knowledge about the fundamental character of interaction still exists. Researchers have explored interaction from the viewpoints of user-centered design and design of graphical user interfaces, where interaction stands for the link between technology and humans or denotes the use aspect. A framework is proposed for exploring interaction as a design space in itself between a human and the technology. It is proposed that this framework for interaction as a design space for Interaction Design, in which the very form of the in-between, the interaction, be explicitly targeted. It is an opportunity to go beyond user and usability studies to seek answers to fundamental questions concerning the form and character of interaction as implemented in today's interactive systems. Moreover, this framework is an opportunity to expand and explain a new design space for Interaction Design. The proposed framework, anchored in two exemplifying cases, illustrates the character and the form of interaction as it situates itself in online, ubiquitous and everyday IT use.

With auditory augmentation, the authors describe building blocks supporting the design of data representation tools, which unobtrusively alter the auditory characteristics of structure-borne sounds. The system enriches the structure-borne sound of objects with a sonification of (near) real time data streams. The object's auditory gestalt is shaped by data-driven parameters, creating a subtle display for ambient data streams. Auditory augmentation can be easily overlaid to existing sounds, and does not change prominent auditory features of the augmented objects like the sound's timing or its level. In a peripheral monitoring situation, the data stay out of the users' attention, which thereby remains free to focus on a primary task. However, any characteristic sound change will catch the users' attention. This article describes the principles of auditory augmentation, gives an introduction to the *Reim* Software Toolbox, and presents the first observations made in a preliminary long-term user study.

This paper describes a methodology and lessons learned from collecting datasets in Ambient Intelligence Environments. The authors present considerations on how to setup an experiment and discuss decisions taken at different planning steps, ranging from the selection of human activities over sensor choices to issues of the recording software. The experiment design and execution is illustrated through a dataset involving 150 recording sessions with 28 sensors worn on the subject body and embedded into tools and the environment. The paper also describes a number of unforeseen problems that affected the experiment and useful considerations that help other researchers recording their own ambient intelligence datasets.

Mobile devices offer convenient communication capabilities and have the potential to create intermediary support for ergonomically challenged users. With the global proliferation of increasing longevity, assisting the elderly and those living with impediments through human engineering and computing technology is pivotal to biotechnological attainment. To remain independently empowered, seamless integrations through efficient affable interfaces are required to provide sedulous location-independent and appliance-sensitive media viewing for the user. The Ambient Interface Design (AID) system assists with finding personal preferences and provides a synchronisation framework, coordinating connectivity across various environmentally distributed devices via sensor data mapping. Cooperative interface communication coupled with context awareness will be abstracted to a representation that facilitates optimisation and customisation to these displays. To overcome personal challenges in the efficient selection and acquisition of online information, AID mediates between the needs of the user and the constraints of the technology to provide a singular customised encapsulation of 'ability preference and device' for each authenticated member. A particular emphasis is the application of a human-centered design ethos.

To envision the future of technology, we would do well to first look to the past. The past provides a vocabulary of possibilities which can be rearranged and supplemented with fresh ideas and technology to craft not just new opportunities, but a new language of experience. If the future consists of virtual, augmented or mixed reality events in pervasive, ambient or ubiquitous computing spaces, much inspiration and practical guidance may be gained through the examination of principles and practices associated with contemporary and traditional live performance.

    Hayat Al Mushcab, University of Ulster, Northern Ireland
    Kevin Curran, University of Ulster, Northern Ireland
    Jonathan Doherty, University of Ulster, Northern Ireland

Obesity is rising at an alarming rate. A great challenge facing the health community is introducing population-wide approaches to weight management as existing health and medical provisions do not have the capacity to cope. Technology is fast becoming an important tool to combat this trend. The use of activity monitors is becoming more common in health care as a device to measure everyday activity levels of patients as activity is often linked to weight. This paper outlines a research project where Bluetooth technology can be used to connect a commercial wrist-worn activity monitor with a Windows Mobile device to allow the user to upload the activity data to a remote server.

    Michael O'Grady, University College Dublin, Ireland
    Gregory O'Hare, University College Dublin, Ireland
    Rem Collier, University College Dublin, Ireland

Delivering multimedia services to roaming subscribers raises significant challenges for content providers. There are a number of reasons for this; however, the principal difficulties arise from the inherent differences between the nature of mobile computing usage, and that of its static counterpart. The harnessing of appropriate contextual elements pertaining to a mobile subscriber at any given time offers significant opportunities for enhancing and customising service delivery. Dynamic content provision is a case in point. The versatile nature of the mobile subscriber offers opportunities for the delivery of content that is most appropriate to the subscriber's prevailing context, and hence is most likely to be welcomed. To succeed in this endeavour requires an innate understanding of the technologies, the mobile usage paradigm and the application domain in question, such that conflicting demands may be reconciled to the subscriber's benefit. In this paper, multimedia-augmented service provision for mobile subscribers is considered in light of the availability of contextual information. In particular, context-aware pre-caching is advocated as a means of maximising the possibilities for delivering context-aware services to mobile subscribers in scenarios of dynamic contexts.

    Rich Picking, Glyndwr University, UK
    Vic Grout, Glyndwr University, UK
    John McGinn, Glyndwr University, UK
    Jodi Crisp, Glyndwr University, UK
    Helen Grout, Glyndwr University, UK

This paper describes the user interface design, and subsequent usability evaluation of the EU FP6 funded Easyline+ project, which involved the development of ambient assistive technology to support elderly and disabled people in their interaction with kitchen appliances. During this process, established usability design guidelines and principles were considered. The authors' analysis of the applicability of these has led to the development of a new set of principles, specifically for the design of ambient computer systems. This set of principles is referred to as *SCUFF*, an acronym for *simplicity, consistency, universality, flexibility* and *familiarity*. These evaluations suggest that adoption of the SCUFF principles was successful for the Easyline+ project, and that they can be used for other ambient technology projects, either as complementary to, or as an alternative to more generic and partially relevant principles.

    Vasiliki Theodoreli, Athens Information Technology, Greece
    Theodore Petsatodis, Athens Information Technology, Greece
    John Soldatos, Athens Information Technology, Greece
    Fotios Talantzis, Athens Information Technology, Greece
    Aristodemos Pnevmatikakis, Athens Information Technology, Greece

The emerging surface computing trend is a key enabler for a wide range of ergonomic interfaces and applications. Surface computing interfaces are considered appropriate toward facilitating elderly interaction with ICT devices and services. In this paper, the authors present the development of an innovative low-cost multi-surface device and its application in elderly cognitive training. The multi-touch device has been designed and implemented as a cost-effective motivating environment for elderly cognitive training. Along with the implementation of the device and the bundled services, this paper also presents a number of cognitive training exercises that have been developed on the device.

    Roberto Speicys Cardoso, INRIA, France
    Mauro Caporuscio, Politecnico di Milano, Italy

Ambient computing requires the integration of multiple mobile heterogeneous networks. Multi-path communication in such scenarios can provide reliability and privacy benefits. Even though the properties of multi-path routing have been extensively studied and a number of algorithms proposed, implementation of such techniques can be tricky, particularly when resource-constrained nodes are connected to each other through hybrid networks with different characteristics. In this paper, the authors discuss the challenges involved in implementing multipath communication on a middleware for hybrid mobile ad hoc networks. The authors present the PLASTIC middleware, several compelling applications of multi-path communication and the main issues concerning their implementation as a primitive middleware-provided communication.

Sonia Ben Mokhtar, LIRIS CNRS, France
Pierre-Guillaume Raverdy, INRIA, France
Aitor Urbieta, IKERLAN-IK4, Spain
Roberto Speicys Cardoso, INRIA, France

The inherent heterogeneity of ambient computing environments and their constant evolution requires middleware platforms to manage networked components designed, developed, and deployed independently. Such management must also be efficient to cater for resource-constrained devices and highly dynamic situations due to the spontaneous appearance and disappearance of networked resources. For service discovery protocols (SDP), one of the main functions of service-oriented architectures (SOA), the efficiency of the matching of syntactic service descriptions is most often opposed to the fullness of the semantic approach. As part of the PLASTIC middleware, the authors present an interoperable discovery platform that features an efficient matching and ranking algorithm able to process service descriptions and discovery requests from both semantic and syntactic SDPs. To that end, the paper defines a generic, modular description language able to record service functional properties, potentially extended with semantic annotations. The proposed discovery platform leverages the advanced communication capabilities provided by the PLASTIC middleware to discover services in multi-network environments. An evaluation of the prototype implementation demonstrates that multi-protocols service matching supporting various levels of expressiveness can be achieved in ambient computing environments.

Fabio Mancinelli, XWiki SAS, France

This paper explores the idea of what can be achieved by using the principles and the technologies of the web platform when they are applied to ambient computing. In this paper, the author presents an experience that realizes some of the goals of an Ambient Computing system by making use of the technologies and the common practices of today's Web Platform. This paper provides an architecture that lowers the deployment costs by maximizing the reuse of pre-existing components and protocols, while guaranteeing accessibility, interoperability, and extendibility.

Joos-Hendrik Böse, International Computer Science Institute Berkeley, USA
Jürgen Broß, Freie Universität Berlin, Germany

In this paper, the authors present a probabilistic model to evaluate the reliability of the atomic commit for distributed transactions in mobile ad-hoc networks (MANETs). This model covers arbitrary MANET scenarios as well as strict and semantic transaction models. The authors evaluate the approach to integrate a backup coordinator to reduce blocking risks. For the purpose of showing an example of a MANET scenario, the authors illustrate how the considered blocking probability is very low.

Chapter 20

    Vasileios Fotopoulos, University of Ioannina, Greece
    Apostolos V. Zarras, University of Ioannina, Greece
    Panos Vassiliadis, University of Ioannina, Greece

In this paper, the authors investigate the concept of designing user-centric transaction protocols toward achieving dependable coordination in AmI environments. As a proof-of-concept, this paper presents a protocol that takes into account the schedules of roaming users, which move from one AmI environment to another, avoiding abnormal termination of transactions when users leave an environment for a short time and return later. The authors compare the proposed schedule-aware protocol against a schedule-agnostic one. Findings show that the use of user-centric information in such situations is quite beneficial.

Preface

Figure 1. Nike application GPS update for Facebook

INTRODUCTION

There is one particular wall posting on my Facebook account which always seems to make me stop and daydream. It is a post from my Friend Debbie, or should I say, it is actually her automatic Nike application which 'posts' telling me when she is starting her run and when she has finished (Figure 1). All her friends can then monitor her times and actual distance run. We also have the option of sending her messages as she runs....as if...

Anyhow, I am aware of course for years about such devices/gadgets/GPS apps from the fitness world - but it is the integration of this particular application which always makes me think of futuristic scenarios when we can tag other everyday chores and actions around the house. What if the vacuum cleaner has a network connection and broadcasts to the world whenever we clean "Kevin Curran has started to vacuum the kitchen......Kevin Curran has started in the hallway.....Kevin Curran has emptied the vacuum cleaner...." or "Kevin Curran has filled the cats dish"...Kevin Curran has broken the vase...... Kevin Curran has finally taken a bath"....OK, we get the message. I guess what I wanted to bring into this piece is that data - even innocuous data such as this - even if we do not post it to social networking sites might actually be beneficial. I mean what would you call embedding a sensor in everyday objects? It really is a form of embedded business intelligence. Now, that term is overloaded in many ways, but such embedded broadcasting of activity could - if the right analytical tools/processes are applied - perhaps lead to addressing any inefficiencies in our life. Perhaps such data mining might really discover that we run our lives inefficiently. By embedding activity monitoring into our everyday objects.....perhaps we can indeed enrich our everyday lives.

There are some basic functions of Ambient Intelligence, one of which is context awareness. This is where the sensors are placed into the environment. They then communicate and help to identify movements and actions. For instance, audio, video, and data can be transferred wirelessly to devices within an Ambient Intelligent system, therefore enabling access to information and entertainment wirelessly. Finally, by doing everyday things such as talking, moving, and gestures, the users of an Ambient Intelligent environment can interact with their surroundings. By doing these daily activities, they are enabling a hands free type of interactivity with the surrounding environment (Aarts and Marzano, 2003).

The key to delivering ambient intelligence to users is being able to provide what is wanted, when, where, and how it is wanted. All aspects are important so that the user receives the right information, at the right time, and in the right way so that the person can make use of the information. Ambient Intelligence also can cater for those people who may have a disability such as the requirement of a hearing aid. However, user control is voluntary so they can decide what information they want and whether or not they want to receive it at any point (Basten et al., 2003).

Devices face temporary and unannounced loss of network connectivity when they move from one cell to another and are frequently required to react to changes in the environment, such as a change in context or a new location. The concepts of context and context-awareness have been central issues in Ambient Intelligent research for the last decade (Oh et al., 2007). Context-awareness has emerged as an important idea for achieving automatic behaviours in pervasive and predictive systems. For example, a system that senses a user's condition, location, or physical actions and adapts to maximise user convenience is utilising context awareness. Initial research began by looking at context-aware systems more generally and independently of specific applications, including context middleware and toolkits from Dey et al. (1999). Everyday objects are being enhanced with sensing, processing, and communication abilities, and as a result, our everyday living is moving towards a higher degree of complexity. There is a need for context-aware Ambient Systems to continuously and implicitly adapt the environment to meet evolving user expectations. Up-to-date valid context information is the key requirement for successful transparent interaction. Methods of representing context awareness, context modeling, and acquisition techniques are of critical importance in the development of Context-Aware Ambient Systems. In fact, semantic technologies represent a very promising approach to solving many problems in ambient applications.

AMBIENT INTELLIGENCE AND TECHNOLOGY IN TODAY'S WORLD

Ubiquitous multimedia computing has awakened the passions of many of the research labs of the world due in part to the flourishing of wireless communication infrastructures such as 3G, WiMax, LTE, and RFID. So it was with great interest that I came across the article *Trends in Ubiquitous Multimedia Computing* (Lee and Chen, 2009). The focus of their research was to sift through surveys on various ubiquitous multimedia computing related topics in order to trace the latest development in this particular field. Factor Analysis, PFNeT, and context-based ontology were used (which is similar to Author Co-citation Analysis (ACA)). So in the resultant top 10 research trends in the UMC field by factor analysis, they found that #5 was *Context-aware workflow language based on Web services* and #6 was *Ambient intelligent systems.* (It may be worth noting that instead of searching all the papers in the citation index database, they limited the search to literature published in the citation data from ISI web in 2008. The initial citation graph contained 15,708 document nodes and 17,292 citation arcs, and they removed papers with less than 3 citations so the graph was eventually built from 1,506 papers.)

The Context Aware trends in UMC that were discovered were m-health, which includes health information systems, clinical bioinformatics, ubiquitous computing in health care, clinical decision support, patient access medical records, smart house for older persons, and more. Other context aware areas included context-awareness applications, context-aware computing technology in intelligent decision-making, context-aware product bundling architecture, context-aware comparative shopping, context-management services, context-aware adaptive information system, context aware proactive service, and context-aware migratory service.

The reason I highlight the areas above is because I believe context awareness and ambient intelligence will move up the top 10 trends chart should this exercise be repeated year on year. In fact, it is obvious just from this issue alone, the importance of context in our ambient intelligent platforms. As we are aware, "Context refers to the conditions in which something exists or occurs," and what better area of computer science to address this than the world of ambient intelligence?

While still talking about context: jokes rely on context. There are gags that a comedian would never tell on TV but go down as a treat on stage to live audiences. Also, the jokes you share with your friends on the bus may not be appreciated as much in front of the church on a Sunday morning. Yes, context… In fact, there was a recent attempt quantify the funniest joke ever told. The most interesting outcome was the differences revealed along cultural, age, and gender lines. Men tended to enjoy more aggressive jokes, along with the so-called dirty joke featuring sexual or scatological references, while women preferred clever wordplay or puns. They did reach a compromise with regards the funniest joke ever told and it went like this *"A couple of New Jersey hunters are out in the woods when one of them falls to the ground. He doesn't seem to be breathing; his eyes are rolled back in his head. The other guy whips out his cell phone and calls the emergency services. He gasps to the operator, "My friend is dead! What can I do?" The operator, in a calm soothing voice says, "Just take it easy. I can help. First, let's make sure he's dead." There is a silence, then a shot is heard. The guy's voice comes back on the line. He says: "OK, now what?"*

To be serious again for a moment, ambient, pervasive, and ubiquitous computing are seen as a drastic shift for computing systems. In reality, networked computing resources should become invisible to users and simply provide them with the right services at the right time. Latest evolutions in both the computing and the networking domains have been remarkable. Handheld user devices, such as smartphones, now embed computing resources that make them comparable to desktop computers of the previous decade. Wireless networks become ubiquitous and offer overlapping coverage and alternative attractive features. Sensors become embedded in most user devices but also in any imaginable object of the physical environment. While the above offer a powerful substrate, ambient computing has still a long way to go before becoming truly ad hoc (Georgantas and Issarny, 2010).

The significance that Ambient Intelligence (AmI) has acquired in recent years requires the development of innovative solutions. In this sense, the development of AmI-based systems requires the creation of increasingly complex and flexible applications. The use of context-aware technologies is an essential aspect in these developments in order to perceive stimuli from the context and react upon it autonomously (Alonso et al., 2011).

Another technology which is beginning to have a positive impact in Ambient Intelligence research is Augmented Reality. Augmented Reality (AR) is a technology that provides the user with a real time 3D enhanced perception of a physical environment with addition virtual elements either virtual scenery, information regarding surroundings, other contextual information, and also capable of hiding or replacing real structures. With Augmented Reality applications becoming more advanced, the ways the technology can be viably used is increasing. Augmented Reality has been used for gaming several times with varying results. AR systems are seen by some as an important part of the ambient intelligence landscape. It is also used to good effect in the domestic, industrial, scientific, medicinal, and military sectors, which may benefit future ambient intelligent systems (Curran et al., 2011).

Future smart environments will be able to observe behavior, and to understand and anticipate it. It has been less emphasized, however, that once this form of ambient intelligence will be achieved, humans will be able to exploit it in new ways: i.e. by performing actions while knowing and expecting that the environment will notice and understand what we are doing. Our behavior - and its physical traces - will thus become a "message," a "signal" sent to the environment itself in order to obtain collaboration, although remaining a concrete practical action, not symbolic gestures or mimics. The theory of this form of intentional (or functional, non-intended) communication is crucial for the future human-environment interaction (as for human-robot interaction (Castelfranchi et al., 2010).

There is currently a move towards integrating commonsense reasoning and understanding capabilities as the key elements in bridging the gap between idiot savant systems and real Ambient Intelligence systems. Since the appearance of the Ambient Intelligence paradigm, as an evolution of the Ubiquitous Computing, a great deal of the research efforts in this field have been mainly aimed at anticipating user actions and needs, out of a prefixed set. However, Ambient Intelligence is not just constrained to user behaviour pattern matching, but to wisely supervise the whole environment, satisfying those unforeseen requirements or needs, by means of rational decisions (Santofimia et al., 2010).

AMBIENT INTELLIGENCE AND THE FUTURE

Recently, some of the media picked up on the story of the Los Angeles-based woman who is claiming damages from Google because she was injured while taking a "safe" route recommended by Google Maps. Yes, you did read that correctly. According to her claim, she sustained injuries and "emotional suffering" from the accident, which occurred after she following directions on her BlackBerry. The Californian woman claimed she used Google Maps to chart an approximately two-mile course in an upscale Utah ski town and Google Maps led her to a four-lane highway without sidewalks that she claims was "not reasonably safe for pedestrians" and "as a direct and proximate cause of... Google's careless, reckless, and negligent providing of unsafe directions... was led onto a dangerous highway and was thereby stricken by a motor vehicle, causing her to suffer severe permanent physical, emotional and mental injuries..." Let me remind you that this woman is in her twenties. This was not a school kid.

One may believe this is an isolated incident and unlikely to reoccur.....but is it? In other words, are we as developers/architects of automated systems to think of every potential misuse of our systems in the future by people (however stupid they may appear)? The first thing that comes to mind after this incident is that the end-user license agreement (EULA) for any location determination technologies will now contain a significant number of extra lines. Even on that issue, does anyone read EULAs anymore? And were they ever even a waiver of responsibility anyhow? I mean, if someone writes a piece of code and then hides a line in the EULA which states that they can snoop at any time on the information contained in a person's online account, does that allow them to do this or do the data protection laws of that jurisdiction supersede those lines? Also, what about those lines of disclaimers added to email messages - what is that about?

What I am hoping to highlight here is the blind reliance on system output in lieu of common sense. This, in fact, could have major repercussions in the Ambient Intelligence world. Without stating the obvious, our systems' main focus is on supplementing human knowledge/assisting in daily living. Few of our systems output hard and fast "correct" decisions. No, our systems are aids in daily life, and therefore, are prone to misinterpretation. If we were to take the above case (which I must make clear has had no decision as yet in a court of law) as a marker for the future, then none of us could ever release a product out into the wild. Therefore, let us hope that common sense prevails in the ruling, and in the meantime, please do test that last module that you coded!

Cloud computing has still got traction behind it especially now with Apple moving into the arena with the iCloud service (Ihnatko, 2011). Cloud relies on distributed architectures which centralise server resources on a scalable platform so as to provide on demand computing resources and services. There still, however, remain concerns over security risks that have been highlighted in the last twelve months with sensational breaches of systems belonging to giants such as Sony.

In future multimedia systems, seamless access to application services on different devices available to users in their vicinity will be commonplace. The availability of these services will change as the mobile user moves, but current 3G multimedia systems do not support access to multiple applications operating on multiple different devices in the context of a session or indeed seamless device session handover.

THE NEED TO CLASSIFY DATA

Classifying data is becoming a critical IT activity for the purposes of implementing the optimal data solution to store and protect data throughout its lifetime. It could become an important aspect of future Ambient Intelligent Systems. Developing a data classification methodology for a business involves establishing criteria for classes of data or application based on its value to the business. Four distinct levels of classifying data or applications are commonly used: mission-critical data, vital data, sensitive data, and non-critical data. Determining these levels takes some cooperative effort within the business and when completed, enables the most cost-effective storage and data protection solutions to be implemented. Data classification levels also identify which backup and recovery or business resumption solution is best suited for each level to meet the RPO (Recovery Point Objective) and RTO (Recovery Time Objective) requirements. Other considerations include availability, length of data retention, service levels and performance requirements, and overall costs.

Information is an extremely valuable asset to any organization and like all valuable assets; it should be protected from threats. Data classification can be defined by its strategic role in enhancing the protection of information assets while enabling proper access to them and the resource components that must be engaged to ensure its effectiveness. Forward-looking organisations that align data classification schemes with enterprise objectives are more likely to translate this strategy into reduced costs of doing business, revenue enhancement, and ultimately, shareholder value. As a strategic process, data classification either protects an organization's information assets from harm, or enables access to information assets in a manner that supports the objectives of the organization.

Public organisations by tradition have understood the need for data classification as a tool for protecting information from outside interests. Sectors such as government departments (most of the time) have well established schemes of protective marking that applies from state secrets to information that would cause only embarrassment if lost. The problem, however, is that processes that have worked well in the past are failing to meet today's demands. A key problem is the sheer amount of information being generated and the ease by which this can be shared and distributed without ownership attributes attached. The mind-set of the "Facebook generation" is as widespread in the public sector as in the private, and they expect easy access to and sharing of data. For instance, in 2007, the loss of a HMRC CD containing the personal details of every person in Britain with a child under 16 went missing in the post. It was greeted with astonishment and anger by the public, however for those working in the sector, the only real amazement was that it did not happen earlier. Public sector data security policies have tended to prioritise confidentiality at the expense of availability and data integrity. This can often detract from system usability; however, there is also an increasing need to store personally identifiable information. A lot of this data has not fit within existing data classification regimes, and notably, there has been little tendency to consider the impact of the gathering of large quantities of such information. As a consequence, many systems at the lower end of data sensitivity have not had adequate safeguards in place. Those public sector data breaches, such as the HMRC incident, have provided a catalyst for widespread improvements. Many public sector bodies now place a premium on the establishment of a risk management culture aimed at rebuilding the public's confidence in the storage and management of their sensitive data. Personal data can now be expected to receive the same treatment previously reserved for higher levels of classification. The UK Government has recently published a Security Policy Framework that outlines a set of new minimum mandatory measures including reporting and compliance mechanisms, which supersedes the protectively marked Manual of Protective Security. This underlines a new level of openness, as well as illustrating the increasing similarity in data and risks to data across the public and private sectors. A public domain Information Assurance Maturity Model has also been published, which provides a practical framework for IA compliance consistent with and building upon existing standards and regulation relevant to the private sector, such as ISO 27001 and the UK Data Protection Act.

The implementation of Ambient Intelligent environments, other new technologies, and rapid connectivity to external parties has led to increased risks to an organisation's information assets. Information that is more valuable than ever before is more accessible and easier to divert. Organisations that fail to address the broader security issues that accompany this change will have insufficient controls in place to minimize risks. These risks could lead to significant financial, legal difficulties and reputation risk for these organisations. Appropriate preventive, detective, and corrective controls in the form of policies, standards, procedures, organisational structures, or software/technology functions, and monitoring mechanisms are therefore required to minimise the risks associated with the confidentiality, integrity, and availability of information assets within an organisation. These aspects of security should be the underpinnings of any ICT security program. The move to the cloud will be important. The move within the EU at present to enforce safe harbour and address the grey area of data domicile will usher in a greater awareness of data classification. It is also possible that due to the multi-tenant nature of a cloud platform, organisations will also pay greater attention to the data lifecycle phases and ensure that aspects such as data destruction is provided and auditable as part of the service. The very fact that an organisation is allowing confidential important information to leave the company network should lead them to examine how they can robustly protect that data and the answer can be simply an effective data classification strategy.

There are three main reasons to adopt data classification: 1) Tagging data allows it to be found more easily, 2) It helps to remove duplicated information, which helps to cut storage and backup costs, and 3) It can meet legal and regulatory requirements for retrieving specific information within a set timeframe, and this is often the motivation behind implementing data classification technology. Any organisation wishing to benefit from these 3 reasons is most likely to go down the data classification route. Consequently, any organisations that place little emphasis on information retrieval speeds, data duplication, and legal requirements are less likely to see the need to visit the arena of data classification. Common inhibitors to going down the data classification route are that the tools, processes, experience, and leadership are absent in many organisations to effectively classify data and to make potentially difficult choices. A policy-driven data classification approach provides an automated method to enforce the assignment of correct levels. There are various data classification tools available today, and each should be reviewed to determine their product focus meets the business requirements. In truth, modern organisations can be overwhelmed with redundant data, including relational and non-relational, much of which is redundant and varying in quality; therefore, plans must be in place to source most important data and document it along with business rules. Once this metadata is in place, then classification taxonomies can be used to tag assets of varying types, in terms of their business relevance.

Another danger is defining access requirements. It can be difficult for any organisation to understand exactly who has a clear need to use the information during regular business operations, who needs access only for support and maintenance purposes, and finally, who will periodically audit operations to prevent fraud and security incidents and detect performance anomalies. Industry standards recommend that the information owner should be ultimately accountable for whatever happens with the information. This therefore needs to be supported by a formal approval and authorization mechanism. Of course, unique requirements will be identified depending on how distributed each information system actually is, the different user profiles, and the selected access control solution. A single repository controlling global access is desirable, but not always viable from a business standpoint, while local groups granting access and synchronizing with each other periodically will require uniform approval criteria and validation procedures among the authorizing parties to ensure consistency.

A critical factor for success is that the classification scheme should clearly express the association between the data and their supporting business processes. Once meaningful terminology is employed in the classification scheme, a secondary capability should evolve seamlessly. This capability is the mapping and expression of security characteristics such as ownership, liability, and control of data. Here then, the security characteristics flow directly from the business process, rather than being derived from unrelated criteria. It is also critical that the business requirements start with a high-level business impact analysis so that they recognize critical business information. This can be done using questionnaires or interviewing key users to identify the business processes and unstructured information such as e-mails or spreadsheets that are most likely to impact the organisation. The key success factor in a data classification scheme is that classes of information are properly defined and related to process owners, easily communicated to all stakeholders, and clearly convey a business value to the organization, while expressing the need for hard, technical internal controls that IT understands.

Policies and processes are crucial. Ensuring that data classification schema are implemented requires storage administrators and end-users to agree on classification criteria. Policies can then be established to enforce the criteria on an on-going basis. A clear owner for the data classification process greatly facilitates the effort, class assignment process, and prioritization. Businesses can get bogged down in the assignment process if a clear leader is not established. With the advent of more advanced storage management tools and information lifecycle management initiatives, the classification of data and information becomes critical to establish initial data placement and on-going automated management. The ingredients for a successful data classification implementation include a policy-engine and a tiered storage hierarchy. It is important to educate the workforce that the classification of data and documents is essential to differentiate between that which is of little value and that which is highly sensitive and confidential. When data is stored, whether received, created, or amended, it should always be classified into an appropriate sensitivity level. For many organisations, a simple 5 scale grade with categories such as Top Secret, Highly Confidential, Proprietary, Internal Use Only, and Public should suffice. It can, in reality, be difficult to convince decision makers in an organisation of the wisdom of investment in security measures such as data classification. Most organisations, when implementing the necessary security and control mechanisms, face a number of issues as security investments are justified against hypothetical losses, and communicating risks and benefits of security investments to nontechnical stakeholders can be difficult.

CONCLUSION

Ambient Intelligence is an evolution of technology, communication, and awareness towards human-computer interaction. Ambient Intelligence is the environment of computing, networking technology, and interfaces. It has the awareness of specific characteristics of human presence and personality. It deals with the needs of users, should be capable of responding intelligently, and may even engage in intelligent dialogue. Ambient Intelligence should not be visible to the user unless necessary. It is also crucial that interaction should be of minimal effort to the user, easy to understand, and therefore an enjoyable experience. Ambient Intelligence is being adapted to build smart systems to guide human activities in critical domains, such as healthcare, ambient assisted living, and disaster recovery. However, the practical application to such domains generally calls for stringent dependability requirements, since the failure of even a single component may cause dangerous loss or hazard to people and machineries. Despite these concerns, there is still little understanding on dependability issues in Ambient Intelligent systems and on possible solutions. There is, however, some work underway to build innovative architectural solutions to such issues, based on the use of runtime verification techniques (Cinque et al., 2010).

The evolution and convergence of information, communication, and networking technologies has established a framework for the adoption of ambient, ubiquitous computing in every aspect of life. Ambient Intelligence offers the real possibility of a revolutionary change in the way services are delivered. The AmI vision imagines ambient environments, enriched with assistive technology that can make necessary resources available to users in everyday life. Access to accurate information is important, and the pervasive nature of AmI technology ensures that users have constant access to up-to-date information regardless of their location (Kosta et al. 2010).

Ambient intelligent systems are context-aware and adaptive, providing contextually relevant information that is personalised to the user. This allows people to quickly hone in on the information they need to make informed decisions in time-critical situations. Digital location maps, communication tools, and messaging services support the numerous interactions that occur within people's daily lives. The success of Ambient Intelligence will depend on how secure it can be made. Information retrieval must be user-led, and privacy must be protected to avoid any violations of the public's rights. Ambient intelligence should be invisible, unobtrusive, but still in our consciousness (Riva et al. 2005). The ultimate goal for

Ambient Intelligence must, therefore, be user empowerment with the creation of universally accessible services, supporting authorised users in a transparent and effective way. This new technology has the potential to radically energise existing services by harnessing information and using it to its best effect, empowering users, and allowing them to focus more on what is really important in their daily lives.

Kevin Curran
University of Ulster, UK

REFERENCES

Aarts, E., & Marzano, S. (2003). The new everyday: Visions of ambient intelligence. Rotterdam, The Netherlands: 010 Publishing.

Alonso, R., Tapia, D., & Corchado, J. (2011). SYLPH: A platform for integrating heterogeneous wireless sensor networks in ambient intelligence systems. *International Journal of Ambient Computing and Intelligence, 3*(2), 1–15.

Basten, T., Geilen, M., & de Groot, H. (2003). *Ambient intelligence: Impact on embedded system design.* Boston, MA: Kluwer Academic Publishers.

Curran, K., McFadden, D., & Devlin, R. (2011). The role of augmented reality within ambient intelligence. *International Journal of Ambient Computing and Intelligence, 3*(2), 16–33.

Dey, A. K., Salber, D., Futakawa, M., & Abowd, G. D. (1999). The conference assistant: Combining context-awareness with wearable computing. *Proceedings of the 3rd International Symposium on Wearable Computers* (ISWC '99), October 20-21, 1999, (pp. 21-28).

Georgantas, N., & Issarny, V. (2010). Ad-hoc ambient computing. *Special Issue on Ad hoc Ambient Computing* [IJACI]. *International Journal of Ambient Computing and Intelligence, 2*(4), iii–iv.

Ihnatko, A. (2011, July 11). MacBook Air is where the iCloud lives. *ComputerWorld.* Retrieved from http://www.computerworld.com/s/article /9218293/MacBook_Air_is_where_ the_iCloud_lives?taxonomyId=15

Kosta, E., Pitkänen, O., Niemelä, M., & Kaasinen, E. (2010). Mobile-centric ambient intelligence in health and homecare - Anticipating ethical and legal challenges. *Science and Engineering Ethics, 16*(2), 303–323. doi:10.1007/s11948-009-9150-5

Lee, I., & Chen, S. (2009). Trends in ubiquitous multimedia computing. *International Journal of Multimedia and Ubiquitous Engineering, 4*(2).

Oh, Y., Schmidt, A., & Woo, W. (2007). *Designing, developing, and evaluating context-aware systems.* *MUE2007* (pp. 1158–1163). IEEE Computer Society.

Riva, G., Vatalaro, F., Davide, F., & Alcaiz, M. (Eds.). (2005). *Ambient intelligence: The evolution of technology, communication and cognition towards the future of human-computer interaction.* Studies in New Technologies and Practices in Communication, vol. 6. Amsterdam, The Netherlands: IOS Press. Retrieved from: http://www.neurovr.org/emerging/volume6.html

Chapter 1
Behavioral Implicit Communication (BIC):
Communicating with Smart Environments via our Practical Behavior and Its Traces

Cristiano Castelfranchi
Istituto di Scienze e Tecnologie della Cognizione, CNR, Italy

Giovanni Pezzulo
Istituto di Scienze e Tecnologie della Cognizione, Italy & Istituto di Linguistica Computazionale, CNR, Italy

Luca Tummolini
Istituto di Scienze e Tecnologie della Cognizione, CNR, Italy

ABSTRACT

A crucial part of the intelligence that smart environments should display is a specific form of social intelligence: the ability to read human behavior and its traces in terms of underlying intentions and assumptions. Such ability is crucial to enable human users to tacitly coordinate and negotiate with smart and proactive digital environments. In this paper, the authors argue that the necessary tool for this ability is behavioral and stigmergic implicit (i.e. non-conventional) communication. The authors present a basic theory of such a fundamental interactive means—the theory of Behavioral Implicit Communication (BIC).

INTRODUCTION

It is widely acknowledged that a crucial part of the intelligence that we need in our smart environments is a specific form of social intelligence: the ability to "read" our behavior and its traces in terms of our intentions and assumptions (Augusto

& McCullagh, 2007; Storf & Becker, 2008). This is a necessary condition for an active environment to coordinate its activities and changes with our behavior in an effective way. This is true, not only to avoid the creation of interferences and obstacles to our situated activity, but possibly to be cooperative and even pro-active, and for favoring our activity by removing obstacles, and by creating the needed conditions for our goals to

DOI: 10.4018/978-1-4666-0038-6.ch001

Copyright © 2012, IGI Global. Copying or distributing in print or electronic forms without written permission of IGI Global is prohibited.

be achieved. Anticipating our steps in this way will enable new forms of cooperation and collaboration between users and smart environments. Ideally, this advanced capacity requires some capability of *mindreading* as part of its intelligence. The idea of mindreading, which has been developed in the philosophical and cognitive science communities, is used here to refer to *the estimation of an agent's (human's) hidden cognitive variables, such as her (1) beliefs, (2) proximal and distal intentions, and (3) action goals* (Csibra & Gergely, 2006; Iacoboni, 2008).

Indeed, it is almost a platitude that future smart environments should be able to observe our behavior, and to understand and anticipate it. It has been less emphasized, however, that once this form of ambient intelligence will be achieved, humans will be able to exploit it in new ways: i.e. by performing practical actions while knowing and expecting that the environment will notice and understand what we are doing. Our behavior—and its physical traces—will thus become a "message", a "signal" often intentionally sent to the environment itself in order to obtain collaboration, although remaining a concrete practical action, not symbolic gestures or mimics. The theory of this form of communication is crucial for the future human-environment interaction (as for human-robot interaction).

In what follows we clarify this form of *Behavioral Implicit Communication* (BIC) (not to be confused with "non verbal behavior or communication") both in its *direct* and *indirect* forms. We contend that such theory can be used to support an "explicit design" of more natural and effective forms of interaction between users and smart environments.

BIC COMMUNICATION: FROM OBSERVATIONS TO SIGNALS

Given the emphasis on the non-obstructive nature of the AmI applications in relation to the natural activities of humans, much of contemporary research is focused on approaches that minimize or do not rely at all on "explicit" interaction (Augusto & McCullagh, 2007). From our perspective, a paramount example of "explicit" interaction is the use of *linguistic* or *gestural communication* to support interaction between users and smart environments. However, beyond these two kinds of communication, there is a third one that we call *Behavioral Implicit Communication*, where there isn't any specialized signal (i.e. neither arbitrary acoustic symbols nor codified gestures), but *the practical behavior itself is the message*. BIC is very useful in a coordination context (see below), where *by simply performing an action we send a message to our partner(s) in the interaction*. This message may for example be intentional, i.e. the sender wants that the receiver knows that she is performing that action.

However, this message exchange presupposes a more primitive and basic substrate which is due to "observation": the unilateral capability of the agent to observe the other's behavior and to "read" it; to understand what she is doing, what she intends and plans to do (her goals), or at least to predict and expect her next position or action using this information, for instance (some sort of primitive "inference") for "anticipatory coordination" (Castelfranchi, 2006).

In other words, communication is based on and exploits "signification" (the semiotic ability of cognitive agents; for example the ability to take 'smoke' as a sign of 'fire', or to ascribe 'thirst' to a drinking agent) that goes beyond simple perception but it not necessarily used only for communication.

A COMPUTATIONAL FRAMEWORK FOR OBSERVATION AND MIND-READING

Below we sketch a computational framework to formalize the basic cognitive abilities that the

Figure 1. Computational (Bayesian) framework for mindreading. Human's actions (A), based on beliefs (B) and intentions (I), change the environmental state (S) and determine observable effects (O). The generative model permits to estimate the value of the latent cognitive variables (B, I, A) based on observations, i.e., to read an agent's behavior in terms of its underlying cognitive state. The same framework also allows predictions of future actions and intentions. See the main text for explanation.

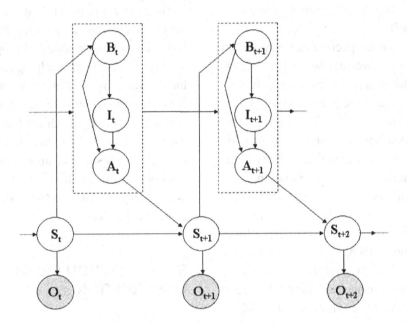

environment should display (see Figure 1). The framework adopts the formalism of graphical models, and in particular Dynamic Bayesian Networks (DBN) (Murphy, 2002; Pearl, 2000), which couples the power of a sound statistical formalism for reasoning under uncertainty, with the intuitiveness of graphical representations. Within the model, nodes indicate random variables (gray nodes are observable), with an associated probability distribution over possible states (e.g., environmental states S, or agent's actions A) and arrows indicate probabilistic relations between variables.

One peculiarity of our model is that it is *generative*. A classical example of generative model is in the domain of vision, where the task consists in using observations (O) for reconstructing the "true", non-observable (latent) state of the environment (S). An instance of this kind of problems is the ability to recognize an object (e.g., a glass)

despite the fact that, when seen from different viewpoints, it has different surface characteristics. In this case, the generative model is able to generate the different perceptual appearances (as a function of the object plus, say, its position and orientation), and so to capture the object invariance. The DBN formalism also captures the dynamical aspects of this situation; for instance, the environmental dynamics ($S_t \rightarrow S_{t+1}$), which could be determined by some latent process (e.g., the laws of physics).

We apply the same generative approach to the recognition of human's actions (A), which are themselves non-observable (latent), but determine observable effects (see Baker, Saxe & Tenenbaum 2009 for a similar approach). For example, the action "cleaning the kitchen" could determine a variety of observable effects in different conditions (e.g., movements of the human), but, even if executed in different ways, it is still the same action. Note that here we intend human actions as being *goal-directed*, and not simply regular patterns of movements. In this sense, action recognition implies the recognition of the action goal (e.g., "cleaning this kitchen now") rather than simply the classification of movements (e.g., "sweeping").

From a cognitive perspective, not only human actions (A) are goal-directed, but they are determined by the human's intentions (I) and beliefs (B). Again, the generative nature of the model can be exploited to support a deep *mindreading* behind human's surface movements, so to provide the intelligent environment with the ability to reconstruct her (latent) cognitive variables, namely beliefs (B), intentions (I), and actions (A), instead than simply monitoring the observable effects of her actions (O). In terms of the Bayesian model sketched in Figure 1, then, the task becomes one of estimating the human's hidden variables B, I, and A, which cause changes in S (and O), instead than simply monitoring O and reconstructing S. In other words, the intelligent agent observes the human, and tries to infer her actions, intentions, and beliefs, based on the observable effects of her actions (plus eventually extra knowledge such as the Bayesian *priors P(I) and P(A),* that is, the a-priori probability that she will select certain intentions and actions).

Within the Bayesian framework, efficient methods exist for estimating latent variables based on observations and prior knowledge, which could be adopted for inferring (the posterior probability of) the human's actions and intentions, or for predicting her future actions and intentions: $P(A_{t+1}|A)$ and $P(I_{t+1}|I)$. For technical reference, see Bishop (2006), which also describes possible learning algorithms. See also Baker, Saxe, and Tenenbaum (2009), Cuijpers, van Schie, Koppen, Erlhagen, and Bekkering (2006), and Verma and Rao (2006) for recent developments of mindreading and "inverse planning" methodologies within cognitive modeling and cognitive robotics.

There are two main advantages of this procedure from the point of view of intelligent ambient design. First, by estimating the hidden causes of the observables, the intelligent ambient can model and predict the human's behavior more efficiently, by finding deep regularities in the causal structure beyond her actions, instead than mere correlations at the level of observables. This opens up the possibility of (proactively) helping and facilitating the human's actions. In addition, and most importantly for our analysis, by knowing that the intelligent ambient is able to mindread her, the human can use her own behavior in such a way that her goals and intentions are well understood by the smart environment, to implicitly communicate that she needs help, to signal that she cannot achieve one of her goals, etc.

BIC EVOLUTION FROM OBSERVATION

Once the environment is endowed with a mindreading ability, humans will be able to exploit it in an adaptive way. In order to appreciate the kind of interactions that might be enabled, it is useful to offer a progression from "weak" to "strong" forms of Behavioral Implicit Communication.

In the weakest form of Behavioral Communication, the agent is not acting in order to let the environment understand what she is doing (this isn't one of her motivating intentions); she is simply aware of this possible result of her behavior, and lets it happen. This is a very weak form, because there is no real intention; the communicative result is just a known (not desired) side effect of the action. True BIC requires that the agent realize the communicative effect on purpose. The complete form occurs when an agent chooses and performs the practical action also *with the purpose to make another one see and understand.* The communicative effect is necessary (although not sufficient) for such action. This is full Behavioral Implicit Communication since communicating is part of the agent's aims and motivates the action. An additional step is when the behavior is performed *only* for communication and looses its practical purpose (or even the practical effect). In the last case, the act either is:

- just faked (simulation, bluff) (which is very important in conflict coordination), or
- it is just a ritual, i.e. the action has fully become a case of "Non Verbal Communication" or a conventional symbolic gesture with a practical origin (Castelfranchi, 2006).

We have presented here the 'intentional' path in BIC, when the communication is intentional. But there are also more primitive forms of BIC for sub-cognitive agents without true intentions. Both these varieties are applicable in smart environments populated by software agents. While the former is more suitable for agents that have a rich internal structure, such as BDI-like agents, the latter can be also implemented in simpler, reactive agents. We claim that in Human-Human, Human-Agent (Castelfranchi, 2005), Human-Robot (Giardini & Castelfranchi, 2004), Agent-Agent (Tummolini, Castelfranchi, Ricci, Viroli, & Omicini, 2004a, 2004b), Robot-Robot interaction, and in Human-Environment interaction, the possibility of communicating through actions is very interesting and could be the solution for several coordination problems, while being at the same time a natural and intuitive form of interaction.

Stigmergy: An Indirect Form of BIC

It is worth noting that not only behavioral implicit communication is possible by observing the "behavior" of an agent, but also by observing its "traces".

Trace-based communication is related to the notion of *stigmergy*, firstly introduced in the biological study of social insects (Grassé, 1959). The term has been introduced to characterize how termites (unintentionally) coordinate themselves in the construction of their nest, without sending direct messages to each other. Stigmergy has been considered either as a consequence of the effects produced in the local environment by previous behavior or as a form of indirect communication through the environment. Both these characterizations are however inadequate. The former, for instance, is not able to discriminate between simple signification and true communication, and between pro-social and antisocial behavior (i.e. it would cover prey-predator coordination as a form of stigmergy). The latter fails to acknowledge that any kind of communication exploits some environmental channel and some physical outcome of the act; any communication is "through the environment".

From our perspective, stigmergy is communication via long-term traces, physical practical outcomes, useful environment modifications, which are not specialized signals. We restrict stigmergy to a special form of BIC where the addressee does not perceive the behavior (during its performance) but perceives other post-hoc traces and outcomes of it. But in order a trace-based communication to be stigmergy it is necessary that the perceived "object" be also a practical one and the originating action be also for practical purposes (like nest building).

Moreover stigmergy is not only for insect, birds, or non-cognitive agents. There are very close examples also in human intentional behavior. Consider a sergeant that—while crossing a mined ground—says to his soldiers: "walk on my prints!". From that very moment any print is a mere consequence of a step, plus a stigmergic (descriptive "here I put my foot" and prescriptive "put your foot here!") message to the followers. Consider also the double function of guardrails: on the one side, they physically prevent cars from invading the other lane and physically constrain their way; on the other side, they communicate that "it is forbidden to go there" and also normatively prevent that behavior In this case, the communicative function is a parasitic effect of the practical act and of its long-term physical products. It is BIC, and stigmergic communication in particular.

'COORDINATION' NEEDS 'OBSERVATION' AND 'SIGNIFICATION'

Human and smart environment interaction is first of all an instance of "coordination". Coordination is that additional part or aspect of the activity of an agent specifically devoted to deal and cope with dynamic environment interferences, either positive or negative, i.e. with opportunities and dangers/obstacles. Living in a common world entails that there exists "interference" between the behaviors of the agents (the action of an Agent Y could affect the goal of another Agent X); interference can be either "negative" (Y's action creates obstacles to X's action or damage her goals) or "positive" (Y's actions realize X's goals or create opportunities for her actions). Thus X has to perceive (or infer) those 'interferences' in order to avoid or exploit them.

Coordination is not necessarily social (one can coordinate himself with a rolling stone); also when social, it is not necessarily mutual or cooperative as is usually assumed to be.

The basic forms of coordination are:

- *Unilateral*: X just coordinates her own behavior with Y's or environmental dynamics, ignoring Y's coordination or non-coordination activity.
- *Bilateral*: X coordinates his behavior with Y's observed behavior; and Y does the same. Bilateral but independent: X coordinates his behavior with Y's observed behavior; and Y does the same in an independent way.
- *Reciprocal*: X coordinates his behavior with Y's behavior by taking into account

the fact that Y is coordinating her behavior with X's behavior.
- *Mutual*: it is based on symmetric and interdependent intentions and mutual awareness (shared beliefs). Both X and Y wants the other to coordinates with his/her own behavior and understand that s/he intends to coordinate with the her/his own behavior.
  - Coordination can also be distinguished into (Castelfranchi, 2005):
- *Reactive*: is the coordination response to an already existing and perceive obstacle, for example after a first collision.
- *Anticipatory*: is the coordination in relation of a non yet perceived event, announced by some sign and foreseen by the agent.

As we have said, even when bilateral and reciprocal, coordination is not necessarily cooperative. Also in conflict and war there is coordination, and it clearly is not cooperative and not for cooperation. Prey and predator for example (consider a leopard following a gazelle) coordinate with each other: the leopard curves left and right and accelerates or decelerates on the basis of the observed path and moves of its escaping prey; but, at the same time the gazelle jumps left or right and accelerates or not in order to avoid the leopard and on the basis of the observed moves of it. Their coordination moves mainly are 'reactive' (just in response to the previous move of the enemy), and for sure nor cooperative, and neither mutual. Moreover, they obviously are not communicating to each other their own moves (although they are very informative and meaningful for the other). This is an observation based but not a communication-based (BIC) reciprocal coordination.

BIC for Coordination

Coordination is one of the main functions of observation for agents living in a common world inhabited by other agents. It is clear that in order to coordinate with a given event or action, an agent should perceive it or foresee it thanks to some perceptual cue (i.e. an "index" or a "sign"). In social coordination, in particular, an agent must observe the other agents' behaviors or traces for understanding what they are doing or intend to do. In sum coordination is based on observation and, more precisely, "signification".

However, a large part of the coordination activity (and social interaction) is not simply based on observation but is BIC-based. For example, in mutual coordination not just signification is needed but true BIC: i.e. since X wants that Y coordinates his behaviors by observing and understanding what she is doing, she is performing her action also with the goal that Y reads it, she is communicating to Y through her action—what she is doing or intends to do. In coordination the most important message conveyed by BIC is not the fact that I intend to do (and keep my personal or social commitments, which is crucial in cooperation), or my reasons and motives for acting, or the fact that I'm able and skilled, etc. It is more relevant communicating (informing) about when, how, where I'm doing my act/part in a shared environment, so that you can coordinate with my behavior while knowing time, location, shape, etc.

TACIT MESSAGES

Since reciprocal and mutual coordination is the kind of interaction that characterizes human and smart environments interaction, it is useful to deepen the proto-typical kinds of messages that might be exchanged in this context. In what follows we will provide a taxonomy of tacit messages organized around these seven categories. We consider this variety of possibilities the basic behavioral messages on top of which more complex ones can be exchanged.

An action is considered here as a goal-oriented modification (or forbearance from any modification) of the environment. For an action to happen, such a modification conceptually implies that (1)

an agent (2) intends to do the action, and (3) in presence of the right opportunities (4) and with the right skills, (5) she modifies (or forbears from modifying) the environment (6) in order that (7) a certain result is realized.

Informing Presence

The most basic message that an action or a trace can deliver is a sign of the presence of another agent: I inform you that: "I'm here"

Consider for example the habit of turning the lights on in one's house when one is going out. When a room is clearly visible from the outside, leaving a light on is a signal that is left for a possible intruder to mean that somebody is still at home. The light in itself has not a conventional meaning but the possible inferences that can be drawn by observing it are exploited to send a 'deceiving' message. Moreover, in this case, although the real goal of the practical action is informative, one does not want to be understood as communicating. This example is also useful to stress that sometimes it is not even desirable that the addressee understands that one is communicating. The light is intended to be understood as a simple trace and not as a trace intentionally emitted for some informative goal (the signal).

Informing Intention

From simple actions and traces, it is possible to extract also information about one's intention to do a given action. Here the relevant meaning is:

I inform you that: "I intend to do this action"

A lot of social relationships require, beyond explicit words and declarations, the practical 'demonstration' of a given attitude or decision.

In particular demonstration of trust can be used to support trust relationships. As an example consider the phenomenon of trust dynamics where the fact that an agent trusts another one increases the latter trustworthiness (for example the trustee's care or persistence). Knowing this, the trusting agent intentionally exploits this process for example by leaving on the desk of a subordinate a very critical file. In this case the trace is an implicit signal of the intention to trust and is also necessary to create trust because it is a presupposition of the dynamic process. The (communicative) action of trusting and delegating impacts on the beliefs of the trusting agent that are the bases for the "reliance" decision producing the external action of delegating in the first place.

Differently, this kind of meaning highlights also the possibility of warning without words. Mafia's "warnings" fall for example in this category. The traces of burning, destroying, killing and even of hacking a secured server are stigma of true practical actions and the harm is a real one. However the basic aim of these behaviors (burning, killing, etc.) is informative. It is aimed at intimidating, terrifying via a specific meaning: "I'm willing to do this" and also "I'm powerful and ready to act" (see next basic message). This meaning is what really matter and what induces the addressee (that not necessarily is already the victim) to give up or to fear a given agent. The trace is a show down of intentions and power: a "message" to be "understood".

Informing Ability

One of the most frequent messages sent by a normal behavior is very obvious but at the same time incredibly relevant:

I inform you that: "I'm able to do this"

When learning to do something for example under the supervision of a teacher, each action is also a message to the teacher of one's own improvements and acquired abilities. Similarly, by leaving a trace of one's action that is observable by others one can convey this specific message.

In many interactions, for example, a behavior is done or a trace is left also to increase trust and reputation. In fact, an agent knows that trust (for future interactions) depends on current behavior because the behavior will be read as a sign of competences and disposition (honesty, loyalty, persistence, etc.). Hence the agent can decide to give another one this impression and image for future interactions. But in fact, since the agent knows that the behavior is for the others a prognostic sign of one's own future behavior, with the current conduct it is also sent a message. If the agents need to choose each other as partners in teamwork activities, then the capacity to signal one's own ability on purpose is a crucial message that can be used to speed up partner choices.

Informing the Opportunity for Action

By mere practical behavior, it is also possible to inform about obstacles and opportunities. In this case the meaning is:

I inform you that: "These are the conditions for this action"

Lines at the post office provide a lot of information to the newcomer. First of all, lines are signs informing about which are the active counters (the condition for action). Although this is not an intentional message sent by those who are queuing, however, it acquires a communicative function, on which the staff relies. In fact, when new electronic information devices are installed, it must be explicitly signaled which are the working counters.

The queue line also informs about the fact that the others are waiting to act; the condition for acting is there but not already available. Observable waiting is clearly a message that at least the other clients in the line intend the newcomer understand. In this case this message is sent on purpose just by maintaining an ordered line (this is why they are accurate in this). By understanding the message and start waiting, the newcomer too sends the same message again; the line self-organizes and maintains its emerging structure. Moreover, the physical shape of the line informs also on who is the last waiting person, back to whom the newcomer has to wait.

Informing the Action Accomplishment

Another core and basic meaning is:

I inform you that: "I have done this"

This simple message is extremely important in interactions where, for example, a given behavior is expected by another agent. Consider for example, a child showing the mother that he is eating a given food, or a psychiatric patient showing to the nurse that he is drinking his drug. It is not the fact the one is able to eat or drink that is relevant here, but that, as expected, the eating and the drinking have been accomplished. It is this kind message is particularly important in the satisfaction of social commitments, expectations, and obligations.

Observable and perceivable actions and traces of action accomplishment are also used for coordination. Suppose that you have to move a heavy table with another agent: it is natural in this case to use the table itself as a coordination device, and to exploit the physical sensations (that you know that the table will transmit to the other and that the other will take into account for adjusting his behavior) as messages. Feeling the direction and the acceleration that you impose to the table, the other will adjust her behaviors on this basis. If one on the contrary had to rely on verbal instructions the process would be extremely more demanding and probably impossible. The messages might not be precise or fast enough. Moreover they should be decoded and interpreted at the symbolic level before being translated into motor-commands blocking the coordinated flow in the activity.

Informing the Goal

The next basic behavioral message is:

I inform you that: "I have this goal"

Consider for example two soccer players that need to coordinate in order to pass the ball and score a goal. To let the other understand that one intends to perform a specific action among the various alternatives, often a soccer player starts acting on the expectation that the other will understand in which direction to go. By kicking the ball in one direction, the first player is communicating with the other team member what kind of plan is to be performed. In this case, the trace of the action is the ball going in a specific direction that is observable by the partner and again in this case the communication is supported by a modification of the environment.

Informing the Result

The last basic behavioral message we are interested to point out is:

I inform you that: "This is the result"

Suppose for example that while cleaning the dishes, a glass is dropped and breaks into pieces. You decide not to remove the fragments in order to let your husband understand that, although he was convinced that they were unbreakable glasses, this glass being struck, it breaks. On this behavioral base, the husband can infer that actually the glasses are fragile. As it is clear from this example a trace can be an implicit signal not only when it is the result of an intentional action (as when you break something on purpose to send a message), but also a consequence of an intentional forbearance from acting (like in this case, when you abstain from cleaning).

THE COGNITIVE PREREQUISITES FOR BEHAVIORAL IMPLICIT COMMUNICATION

It is useful at this point to summarize the social and cognitive abilities required to enable this form of communication.

From the perspective of the sender X (i.e. the human) we have that:

1. X's goal in sending the BIC message is that Y believes that X is doing a certain action; moreover, X frequently intends that Y understands what X has in mind while doing the action: her beliefs or goals.
2. X assumes that Y does not already knows/believes the content of the message, and if the message is an 'imperative' does not already intend to do that action.
3. In Meta-BIC X also plans that Y realizes that X intends to communicate and that Y understands the message.

Thus X has (and bases her message on) a rather complex form of mind reading of Y, even a recursive one: "X wants/believes that Y believes that X wants/believes...."

On the side of the addressee Y (i.e. the smart environment), we have:

1. Y (even before BIC and as one of the conditions for its evolution) interprets X's behavior in mental terms: as due to given beliefs and goals. Y reacts to X's goals, intentions, and beliefs more than to X's observable movements, especially for anticipatory coordination.
2. Y is able to contextually interpret X's behavior as a message, i.e. as intentionally aimed at changing his own mental states ("X believes that I believe..... X intends that I believe...").

In order to enable behavioral implicit communication we need not only to have mind-reading abilities on both sides, but we also require goals about the mind of the other agent and we arrive to cooperation on such goals. We may consider that in BIC there are two goals/functions meeting each other: the communicator's goal (X's behavior has the goal or function that Y "understands", recognizes, and comes to believe something) and the interpreter's goal (Y has the goal/function of interpreting X's behavior in order to give it a meaning).

CONCLUSION

Let us draw some conclusions on this point.

Though coordination is possible without communication, usually coordination exploits communication. Since BIC is (i) a very economic (parasitic), (ii) a very spontaneous, (iii) a very practical and rather effective form of communication just exploiting side effects of acts, traces, and the natural disposition of agents to observe and interpret the behavior of the interfering others, a rather important prediction follows:

Humans interacting with a smart environments will use a lot of BIC and will spontaneously develop it.

Actually a very large part of communication for coordination in situated and embodied agent exploits reciprocal perception of behavior or of its traces and products; i.e. it is just BIC. Even more, (second prediction):

The interaction between humans and smart environments a lot of specialized (conventional or evolutionary) signs will derive from BIC behavior that have been ritualized.

This kind of observation-based, non-special-message-based communication should be much more exploited in CSCW and computer mediated interaction, in multi-robot coordination, in human-robot coordination, in MA systems, and, we argue in this paper, with the future smart environments. Ambient Intelligence will necessarily enable this form of communication. We will have not only to establish with our intelligent, proactive, cooperative environment a good 'understanding' of what we are doing and a good coordination, but we will tacitly negotiate agreements and conventions; for example, about the habitual location of people or objects, preferences, or habits and practices.

REFERENCES

Augusto, J. C., & McCullagh, P. (2007). Ambient Intelligence: Concepts and Applications. *International Journal of Computer Science and Information Systems*, *4*(1), 1–28..doi:10.2298/CSIS0701001A

Baker, C. L., Saxe, R., & Tenenbaum, J. B. (2009). Action understanding as inverse planning. Cognition.

Bishop, C. M. (2006). *Pattern Recognition and Machine Learning*. New York: Springer.

Castelfranchi, C. (2005). ToM and BIC: Intentional behavioral communication as based on the theory of mind. In Proceedings of the AISB Symposium on Social Virtual Agents (pp. 37).

Castelfranchi, C. (2006). SILENT AGENTS: From Observation to Tacit Communication. In J. Simão Sichman, H. Coelho, & S. O. Rezende (Eds.), Advances in Artificial Intelligence - Proceedings of IBERAMIA-SBIA 2006 (LNCS 4140). ISBN 3-540-45462.

Csibra, G., & Gergely, G. (2006). 'Obsessed with goals': Functions and mechanisms of teleological interpretation of actions in humans. Acta Psychologica, 124, 60–78. PubMed doi:10.1016/j.actpsy.2006.09.007

Cuijpers, R. H., van Schie, H. T., Koppen, M., Erlhagen, W., & Bekkering, H. (2006). Goals and means in action observation: A computational approach. Neural Networks, 19, 311–322. PubMed doi:10.1016/j.neunet.2006.02.004

Giardini, F., & Castelfranchi, C. (2004). Behavior Implicit Communication for Human-Robot Interaction. In Proceedings of the AAAI Fall Symposium 2004 on the Intersection of Cognitive Science and Robotics: From Interfaces to Intelligence) (pp. 91-96).

Grassé, P. P. (1959). La Reconstruction du Nid et les Coordinations Inter-individuelles chez Bellicosoitermes Natalensis et Cubitermes. La Théorie de la Stigmergie: Essai d'Interprétation du Comportement des Termites Constructeurs. *Insectes Sociaux*, *6*, 41–81. doi:10.1007/BF02223791

Iacoboni, M. (2008). *Mirroring people: The new science of how we connect with others*. New York: Farrar, Straus and Giroux.

Murphy, K. P. (2002). Dynamic Bayesian networks: Representation, inference and learning. Unpublished doctoral dissertation, University of California, Berkeley.

Pearl, J. (2000). *Causality: Models, Reasoning, and Inference*. Cambridge, UK: Cambridge University Press.

Pezzulo, G. (2008). Coordinating with the Future: The Anticipatory Nature of Representation. *Minds and Machines*, *18*, 179–225..doi:10.1007/s11023-008-9095-5

Storf, H., & Becker, M. (2008). A Multi-Agentbased Activity Recognition Approach for Ambient Assisted Living. Retrieved from http//www.aal-europe.eu

Tummolini, L., Castelfranchi, C., Ricci, A., Viroli, M., & Omicini, A. (2004). "Exhibitionists" and "Voyeurs" do it better: A Shared Environment for Flexible Coordination with Tacit Messages. In H. van Parunak & D. Weyns (Eds.), *Proceedings of the Workshop on Coordination in Emergent Societies* (E4MAS 2004).

Tummolini, L., Castelfranchi, C., Ricci, A., Viroli, M., & Omicini, A. (2004). What I See is What You Say: Coordination in a Shared Environment with Behavioral Implicit Communication. In G. Vouros (Ed.), *Proceedings of the Workshop on Coordination in Emergent Societies* (CEAS 2004).

Verma, D., & Rao, R. P. N. (2006). Planning and Acting in Uncertain Environments using Probabilistic Inference. In *Proceedings of IROS* (pp. 2382-2387).

This work was previously published in International Journal of Ambient Computing and Intelligence, Volume 2, Issue 1, edited by Kevin Curran, pp. 1-12, copyright 2010 by IGI Publishing (an imprint of IGI Global).

Chapter 2
Context–Awareness in Ambient Intelligence

Declan Traynor
University of Ulster, UK

Ermai Xie
University of Ulster, UK

Kevin Curran
University of Ulster, UK

ABSTRACT

Ambient Intelligence (AmI) deals with the issue of how we can create context-aware, electronic environments which foster seamless human-computer interaction. Ambient Intelligence encompasses the fields of ubiquitous computing, artificially intelligent systems, and context awareness among others. This paper discusses context-awareness and examines how discoveries in this area will be key in propelling the development of true AmI environments. This will be done by examining the background and reasoning behind this particular strand of AmI research along with an overview of the technologies being explored alongside possible applications of context awareness in computing as well as technological and socio-ethical challenges in this field.

INTRODUCTION

Context awareness can be defined as "...any information that can be used to characterize the situation of an entity. An entity is a person, place, or object that is considered relevant to the interaction between a user and an application, including the user and applications themselves" (Dey & Abowd, 2000). This definition makes no

DOI: 10.4018/978-1-4666-0038-6.ch002

assumptions about the types of information which are relevant to context such as time, location, identity and so on. Following the more open ended definition above caters for situations where the context may be derived from one, many or all of these types of information as well as other types of information which are not defined from the outset. This understanding of context is necessary in creating truly intelligent environments for the future which are extensible in order to keep up with the rapidly changing and increasingly diverse

Copyright © 2012, IGI Global. Copying or distributing in print or electronic forms without written permission of IGI Global is prohibited.

contexts in which human-computer interactions are taking place.

Context-Awareness in computing can be seen as the existence of computer systems and applications which can gather and make sense of "information about the immediate situation—the people, roles, activities, times, places, devices, and software that define the situation" (Vian et al., 2006) and then demonstrate the appropriate related behaviour based on the perceived context. Such behaviour might include the presentation of customised or specially formatted information or the performance of some action to avoid a potentially hazardous situation. Future revelations in the area of context-awareness have the potential to dramatically improve the way in which ubiquitous and intelligent computing environments support our everyday activities as well as provide richer experiences in human-computer interaction.

Ubiquitous computing expert Mark Weiser talked about a new wave of pervasive computing which he described as "the age of calm technology, when technology recedes into the background of our lives" and where computers would be "embedded in our daily lives and supporting them". Research into context-aware computing holds the key to realising this vision of seamless human-computer interaction where all information relevant to context will be gleaned automatically by intelligent systems. When discussing this point it is important to re-evaluate what environmental information is relevant to context. For example, information on the identity of users might be implicitly gathered by the application as the user approaches the computer or the point of interface. This could be done using facial recognition, for example. Alternatively, the user might explicitly provide identity information to the application via a more conventional log-in prompt. In both cases, the information on the user's identity provides context but in the latter case the system is not necessarily intelligent or context-aware. If we were to have computing devices embedded in our environments but we still had to interact

explicitly with them, then we would gain no real benefit from the ubiquitous computing paradigm. In fact, copious devices and computer applications which expect explicit user involvement would serve as more of an hindrance in carrying out our everyday activities rather than a means of supporting them. In order to achieve the sort of innovation discussed by Weiser and others, we must continue to investigate and develop truly context-aware applications which can gather and make sense of information relevant to the current context and then exhibit some behaviour depending on the context. Some of the possibilities for Ambient Intelligence to support our daily activities include working out quick routes for car journeys and applications which infer our shopping list by gathering information about the contents of our fridge and combining this with the information that you are having friends over for dinner (Shadbolt, 2003). In this sense, these applications must be truly context aware so that they integrate seamlessly into people's daily lives and avoid becoming "ubiquitous clutter" rather than useful pervasive computing services.

Context-aware computing might also hold the key to opening up communication between people and computers as people have an implicit understanding of context and how this enables rich person-to-person interaction as despite massive advances in both hardware and software interfaces, people still maintain an "impoverished mechanism" for interacting with computers (Dey & Abowd, 2000). Many researchers in the field of context-awareness are looking at how context-aware computing could lead to richer human computer interaction and the provision of more relevant and useful services to the end user. An example of this is a context-aware tour guide which could sense a user as they approach specific exhibitions. Such a guide could take information on location of a user and combine this with the exhibitions they have visited previously to form an understanding of the context and then present tailored information which will be relevant and interesting to the user in that instance. Another example might be a computer application which senses the presence and proximity of a user's mobile devices. Suppose the user had information about their business meetings stored on the device. A context aware application might be able to automatically discover such information and synchronise it with the user's calendar information on their home desktop. The application might be able to resolve conflicts in the user's timetables or automatically schedule reminders for future activities. Such automatic coordination of information to create more useful services is just one of the many examples of how context-aware computing could lead to more intuitive human-computer interaction.

CONTEXT AWARE WIRELESS ENABLING TECHNOLOGIES

This section presents a brief overview of some of the key enabling technologies for context-aware systems. These technologies, if integrated and used in the correct way, could provide a mechanism for computer systems to sense and make sense of situational information and then perform some actions depending on the current context. Vian et al. (2006) state that "the context awareness of the next decade will evolve out of the interaction of three key technologies " which they go on to define as wireless communications technologies, sensing technologies and semantic ("sense-making") technologies. Some of the individual technologies encompassed by these three general categories offer researchers in the field of context-awareness much promise in the way of creating truly context-aware environments. The area of wireless communications deals with the standards, devices and concepts to enable continuous interaction between the constantly growing number of computing devices that are becoming embedded in our society as we move towards the era of ubiquitous computing. The following information gives an overview of Personal Area Networks (PANs), the ZigBee communication standard and Mesh Networking.

Personal Area Networks (PANs)

A Personal Area Network (PAN) is a computer network which focuses on the communication and interaction between devices which are located on or surrounding one person. Such a network could facilitate communication between a user's mobile phone or PDA and their office computer, for example, to automatically synchronise important calendar events and memos stored on either device, as in the example discussed previously. Wireless Personal Networks (WPANs) are becoming increasingly more popular as the proposed method of achieving this sort of interaction between devices and are implemented with the use of technologies such as Bluetooth and the ZigBee protocol (discussed later). The use of Bluetooth in Wireless Personal Area Networking is commonly seen in the integration of one user's personal devices (e.g. a Bluetooth mouse connected to their PC) as well as in the communication between multiple users' devices (e.g. content sharing between mobile phones).

A recent arrival in the PAN area is Skinplex, developed by a German company, IDENT Technology. Skinplex implements a PAN whereby small electronic transmitters are worn or placed very close to a person d receivers which communicate with these transmitters may be integrated throughout that person's environment. Skinplex works by taking advantage of the human body's ability to transmit electric fields, using the subject's body itself as a transmission medium to provide some sense of context awareness in various situations involving a person's interaction with their environment. For example, this technology has been applied in systems to control electric windows and convertible roof systems in cars, where by sensors placed in the windows, doors and roof of a car may sense the electric field surrounding a person's hand and then take the appropriate action to avoid injury to that person.

Skinplex has also been employed in identification of individuals in order to key-less access systems in cars and buildings, for example. In this case, receivers are integrated in the handles of doors and small code generators are worn close to the subject's body. These generators transmit data via the person's skin so that when they touch a handle, an electronic ID is transmitted through the body, to the handle where it is decoded and, if verified, causes the door lock to open. Technologies such as Skinplex are often referred to within the PAN sub-category of Body Area Networking. Research into these sorts of innovatory technologies will enhance the seamlessness of interaction required between a user and the physical environment in a future of context-awareness and ambient intelligence. In a future of ubiquitous computing, truly context-aware environments will have to recognise and deal with the sporadic addition and removal of devices from a local environment as the presence of certain devices and people (possibly carrying implanted devices or as the subjects of their own Body Area Networks) will have an effect on the context of a given instance. For this reason, wireless mesh networking might play an important role in providing the backbone infrastructure for managing these constant and ever-changing connections.

ZigBee

ZigBee is an open global standard in wireless sensor technology which defines a set of protocols for use in Wireless Personal Area Networks (WPANs). It is particularly targeted towards wireless radio networking applications for use in the fields of environment monitoring and control and its specification is developed by the ZigBee Alliance, an international consortium of companies who wish to extend the use of ZigBee compliant technologies in real-world applications. The ZigBee Alliance designed and developed the standard to meet the need for a low-cost wireless radio networking technology which adhered to the principles of ultra-low power consumption, use of unlicensed radio bands, cheap and easy installation, provision of flexible and extendible networks and provision of some integrated intelligence for network organisation and message-routing

Three main types of ZigBee devices exist in a ZigBee network. These are the ZigBee Co-ordinator (ZC), ZigBee Router (ZR) and ZigBee End Device (ZED). Each ZigBee network contains only one ZigBee Co-ordinator. This device is mainly required upon initialisation of the network and carries out some key activities including scanning for quiet frequency channels and selecting the least busy channel for use by the network, initialising the network and then allowing other devices to connect to the network. In many cases, it also serves as the trust centre and repository for data which is critical to network security. ZigBee routers allow various ZigBee end-devices to connect to the network through them as well as providing a message relay service for these nodes. There can be many ZRs in a ZigBee network, depending on its size and topology. ZigBee End Devices are the most commonly found nodes in a ZigBee network. They are simple devices which support just enough functionality to transmit and receive small amounts of data and interface with some other device in the physical world. They cannot pass on messages for other nodes and other nodes cannot connect to the network through an end device. ZEDs are often battery-powered and have the ability to go into a power-saving "sleep" when not transmitting or receiving any data. The network functions through radio communication between the different nodes in the network. The end devices interface with the physical environment and send out transmissions to other end devices when an action is required. These transmissions are relayed throughout the network by the routers until they reach the destination device which then interfaces with some element or device in the physical environment to implement the required action. The fact that ZigBee End Devices are power-saving, wireless and perform only simple communications functions means that they are relatively inexpensive and unobtrusive to implement in a physical environment such as a home or workplace. ZigBee End Devices can be attached to the many interactive elements of an environment (computer screens, light switches, heating systems, ventilation systems etc...) to automate interaction depending on the context of a situation. The context will be determined by intelligent software agents (discussed later) however communications technologies such as ZigBee along with its support for Mesh Networking and ability to interface with other networks like PANs and BANs could provide the necessary underlying communications network to support this automatic interaction with the environment depending on context.

Radio Frequency Identification (RFID)

Radio Frequency Identification is the process of attaching a small wireless device to an object, be that a commercial product or a person's clothing, in order to identify and track that object using radio waves. The devices used in this process are commonly referred to as RFID tags. RFID tags typically consist of two core components: a microchip for information processing and storage as well as control of radio frequency modulation and an antenna for sending and receiving radio signals. RFID tags are mainly active or passive. Active RFID tags contain a battery which allows them to autonomously transmit signals. Passive tags have no independent power source and so only transmit when in range of a reader which powers them via electromagnetic induction and initiates the transmission. RFID tags are a prime example of the use of micro technology in sensor networks.

RFID is commonly used today in a range of applications from asset tracking by large product

manufacturers and distributors to increasing ID security in passports. In supply chain management, in particular, RFID seems set to replace the ubiquitous bar code in a few years. RFID tags can store a limited amount of data (around 2KB). In today's applications, this data is usually nothing more than a unique identification number and perhaps some general details about the product or person that the tag is intended to track. Most RFID sensing system (whether it uses active or passive tags) works in roughly the same way (see Figure 1):

- The microchip of an RFID tag stores some data which is waiting to be read by a reader.
- An RFID reader sends out an electromagnetic energy which is received by the antenna of a nearby RFID tag.
- In the case of passive tags, this electromagnetic energy powers the tag, initialising a radio frequency transmission from the tag of the data stored in that tag's microchip. Active tags perform the same transmission except they use the power stored in their own battery to autonomously begin sending data when a signal is received from the reader.
- The reader will then intercept the transmission and interpret the frequency transmitted as meaningful data.

In this case it is easy to see that the RFID readers act as the sensors and the tags are a means of electronically tagging objects in the physical world so that details about these objects (stored on the tags) can be collected and processed by computer systems. One fruitful application of RFID in context-aware systems is to identify individual persons. As an example, consider a key-less entry system for the front door of a context aware home or building. The door should recognise authorised inhabitants of the building and should unlock (and perhaps even open) the door as they approach.

Figure 1. RFID system components

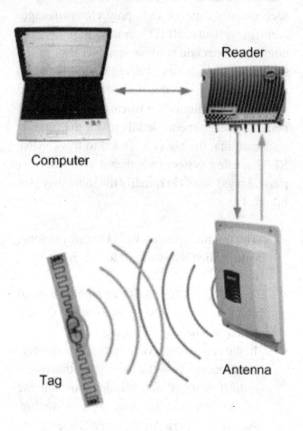

One method of distinguishing authorised persons from unauthorised ones in this scenario is to use RFID as the sensor technology. If each person had an RFID tag on their clothing or on an ID card which they carried with them, this tag could store a unique ID number or some distinguishing information about an individual. As a person approaches the door, an RFID reader placed on or near the door could request data from the person's tag and, if the ID number or details stored on the tag verifies that person as an authorised inhabitant, unlock the door.

A WISP is a sensing and computing device that is powered and read by off the shelf UHF RFID readers (WISP, 2009). A WISP takes the model of a passive RFID tag and integrates an on-board micro controller which is capable of taking samples from a variety of sensor devices. A WISP can combine passive RFID with such sensors as accelerometers, thermometers and light sensors to create a wirelessly-networked, battery-less sensor device. WISPs provide significant advantages over conventional RFID tags as they can gather, store and transmit much richer information which is obtained by their related sensors while still being powered and read by conventional RFID readers so they integrate easily and inexpensively with current standards. WISPs also provide increased data storage capabilities (up to 8KB) and the ability to transmit specific contextual data rather than fixed data as in conventional tags.

Motes and Smartdust

The concept of Motes and Smartdust represents a new paradigm in the area of distributed wireless sensor technology. It has evolved from significant developments in the fields of micro technology, wireless communications and computer interaction with the physical world. According to Warneke, Liebowitz, and Pister (2001), the goal of Smartdust research is to explore how *"an autonomous sensing, computing and communication system can be packed into a cubic-millimetre mote..."*. The name 'Mote' refers to a tiny device which integrates all of the fore-mentioned features and which has the capability of autonomously forming wireless connections with other nearby motes in order to establish an ad-hoc wireless sensor network. As the miniaturization of these devices evolves, the range of possible applications for them is continually expanding. The term Smartdust has arisen out of the expectation that, in years to come, these integrated wireless communication and sensor devices could be the size of a single speck of sand or dust.

At a general level, motes and the way in which they network with one another, in many ways resemble the ZigBee and Mesh Networking Standards discussed earlier. Motes, like ZigBee devices, are designed to be cheap and light on power consumption while maintaining flexible and reliable networking capabilities. There are also some key differences in the two which provide the experimental mote with a significant advantage over more slightly established technologies like ZigBee. Whereas a ZigBee network requires a number of ZigBee Router devices to route transmissions between End Devices, all motes are capable of autonomously and directly communicating with other neighbouring motes. This allows them to quickly self-form into large wireless networks. Much like the ZigBee Co-ordinator device, a mote network must, however, contain a "collection" mote which accepts data routed to it by all of the other motes in the network and then transmits this data on to some other network or location over larger geographical areas. Motes also contain integrated sensors, similar to the WISP discussed previously. Sensors such as accelerometers, vibration sensors, sensors for light, sound, temperature, liquid level have already are frequently integrated into motes. A mote may contain more than one type of sensor and so may monitor many elements of its surroundings. (although this will, naturally, increase its power consumption and cost.)

Motes could be used in analysing the structural integrity of buildings and bridges. The microscopic nature of motes allows them to be incorporated into poured concrete when building bridges, for example. Passively powered motes might be placed in the concrete and could contain sensors which monitor the salt levels in the concrete (salt decreases the structural integrity of concrete). Whenever necessary, a vehicle could drive across the bridge, outputting a powerful electromagnetic field which would cause the motes to power on and transmit the data read from their sensors. Using this information, structural engineers could take preventative action to increase the bridge's lifespan or avoid a collapse.

The Smartdust concept represents a culmination of the many wireless communications and sensor technologies mentioned in earlier sections. While it is still a largely experimental technology, mote devices could provide the kind of smart sensing needed in future context-aware environments. Almost any type of existing electronic sensor can be integrated into a mote device and they are some of the smallest known wireless sensor devices in existence, meaning that, like RFID and ZigBee devices, they can be unobtrusively embedded in our everyday environments. A home, workplace or even an entire city could be laden with these devices yet they will function out of sight of the human beings which they support. Such technologies really give life to Weiser's vision of computing systems acting as *"quiet, invisible servants"* within our environments.

SENSE MAKING TECHNOLOGIES

The following is a discussion of intelligent software agents and how their function can be tied to the advent of internet tagging and folksonomies and their use within the "semantic" web.

Intelligent Software Agents

A software agent is a self-contained program capable of controlling its own decision making and acting, based on its perception of its environment, in pursuit of one or more objective (Jennings & Woodridge, 1996). Such intelligence will be crucial in a context-aware system. Computer applications must be capable of determining and understanding the context of situations and then acting on this context before technologies like smart sensors can be of any real use to us in supporting our daily activities. Humans have an implicit understanding of context and state that people have capabilities which allow this such as Chen et al. (2003):

- Ontology Sharing – humans are able to share common languages and vocabularies
- Sensing – humans are able to perceive their environments through sensory organs

- Reasoning – humans are able to make sense out of what they have perceived based on what they already know

These capabilities in software will be essential to the practical realization of context-aware computing applications. (Wooldridge & Jennings, 1996). Ontology sharing deals with shared languages and vocabularies which foster a shared understanding of context within certain situations or relating to certain subjects. Ontological tagging has become a distinguishing feature of the Web 2.0 era, allowing internet users to co-ordinate and share information by assigning their own tags to different types of information based on its content, medium and relationships to other areas of interest for example (Vian et al., 2006). An application scarcely exists today which does not possess some ability to interface with the web. There are many applications, both commercial and community driven, which sift through the abundant "tag clouds" found on the semantic web and retrieve and present relative information to a user based on user requests or pre-defined user preferences. If intelligent software was able to autonomously elicit these preferences or trends in user activity, for example, then such software agents could prove very useful in providing a new generation of services to the human individual in a context-aware environment. Consider a context aware shopping centre where user's mobile devices are scanned as they enter and information about information they are interested in could be inferred and collated by intelligent software for the purpose of providing the customer with adverts for products available in the centre's stores that the software has determined they may be interested in. The software could do this by first gathering information about user preferences from sensors then collating this information, determining the context in which it should be understood and perhaps classifying this information with some sort of ontological tagging system. The software could compare this information with tag clouds

on the World Wide Web and cross reference this with information from the websites of retailers which it already knows have outlets at that centre. When it finds information on offers relevant to the user's tastes, it could trigger some action such as sending a text or multimedia message to that user's mobile phone with the offer information embedded and present the ability for the user to view further information (such as directions to the nearest outlet offering the deal). This is a simple example as to how such ontological information will improve the efficiency of software agents in determining context and ultimately increase the usefulness of the services which these agents provide. With regard to the sensing requirement, the challenge facing software developers in this field is creating robust and efficient interfaces at the lowest levels of their software for interfacing with the many sensors which will feature in a context-aware environment.

Finally, incorporating reasoning will involve the development of complex algorithms to correlate and make sense of the copious amounts of information processed by software agents in a world of ubiquitous computing. Constant data flows from sensors, the World Wide Web and data being output by other systems and agents will all have to be simultaneously processed by software agents and acted upon if necessary. In order to effectively resemble a human being's understanding of context, an agent will have to continually re-evaluate its perception of a situation. For instance, while processing one set of information and beginning to act upon the results of the processing, new flows of situational information can cause the context to change rapidly. Truly intelligent software agents will have to be able to deal with such a scenarió as a person would.

CONTEXT-AWARE APPLICATIONS

This section looks at some of the most promising possibilities for context-aware computing to make a difference in supporting the lives of people within two key environments; context-awareness in the home and context-awareness in healthcare.

Context-Aware Homes

Many scenarios exist describing how context-aware computing might play a role in the home environment. Among these are:

- Context-aware lights, chairs and tables which adjust as a family gathers in a room. These elements might reconfigure depending on locations, number and identities of the individuals entering the room as well as the tasks which they are expected to perform (one might read a book while another watches television and so on).
- Phones which only ring in rooms where the addressee of a call is actually present, preventing other people being disturbed by useless ringing.
- Security systems which are aware of a home's inhabitants and monitor activity around the perimeters of the house (people entering a back yard, driveway, opening a door or window and so on). Such a system would provide call out alarms or take preventative action in the case of a break-in, fire, or an elderly resident who is at risk of serious injury.
- Sensor technologies like motes could be used to monitor the various environmental parameters such as smoke levels, gas levels, room temperatures. Intelligent software could accept all of this information from the sensors and decide when action needs to be taken. This action might include alerting the home's inhabitants to a possible fire hazard, sending out an alert to authorities when an emergency has occurred or when unauthorised individuals have been detected within the home. (Meyer and Rakotonirainy, 2003).

With the increasing development and convergence of the communication and sensor technologies and intelligent software, the scope of these sorts of applications in the home will be bound only by their developer's imaginations.

Context-Awareness in Healthcare

There is growing interest in integrating hospital beds, medicine containers and trays and context-aware information and communication systems for hospital staff including:

- A context-aware hospital bed with integrated display for the patient's entertainment or for displaying information to a clinician depending on the situation. Such a bed "knows" which patient is currently occupying it and can interface with other technologies, such as a context-aware medicine tray, described below.
- A context-aware medicine tray, used by a nurse to make his/her rounds for administering medicines to all the different patients in a ward. The tray could interface with technologies like the bed described above in order to become aware of the patient which the nurse is currently treating. The tray's surface could light up the correct medicine container for that patient helping nurses in reducing the number of incidents where the wrong medicines are accidentally administered to a patient (Bricon-Souf & Newman, 2007).

Location tracking systems such as RFID can be used to tag important equipment in Accident and Emergency Units, such as beds, operating instruments, life-support machines, crash carts (defibrillators) and so on. When needed in an emergency, the locations of these objects can be quickly looked up or information on their location automatically presented to hospital staff by intelligent agents. These context-aware systems in hospitals have the potential to increase the speed and efficiency with which patients are helped. Many challenges face the development of context-aware computing and ambient intelligence going forward. These include both technological challenges and socio-ethical concerns which must be addressed.

CONCLUSION

In order to create an intelligent environment in which the underlying computer systems are mostly invisible to the user, technologies from different areas of speciality must be able to work together in a flexible and robust fashion. As well as developing new standards for wireless communication and networking, we must ensure that the various technologies that are part of a context aware system will be capable of complying with these standards and interfacing with each other in a seamless fashion. This will be a challenge as corporate competition in the current market for smart and mobile devices usually prevents certain services from interacting. This goes against the sort of open communications required in a pervasive computing environment. The increasing numbers of computing devices being used in everyday society naturally causes a significant increase in our need for energy to power these devices. A future of ubiquitous computing could potentially contain millions of devices in one local environment. Each of these devices will need a smart energy source so that they may function for long periods without explicit human interaction or maintenance. ZigBee and smart devices like motes aim to reduce power consumption by using simple integrated circuits and micro-controllers which can sleep when not needed, allowing them to operate unnoticed for many months or years depending on their application. The increased use of sensor and wireless network technologies calls for a revision of our attitudes to data security. With so much information about people being harvested

and transmitted over local networks, between networks and over geographical networks like the internet, we need to ensure that the correct encryption methods are in place to prevent this data being intercepted and possibly misused by rogue individuals or conglomerates. Current RFID tag models and smart wireless sensing devices contain only simple microprocessors and low amounts of main memory. For this reason, the computations which they can perform are limited and so the encryption techniques which they apply to the data they gather, store and transmit are much less sophisticated and secure than those commonly employed on larger, more capable machines today. As more sophisticated hardware is brought into the realm of miniaturization, however, this problem should begin to solve itself in tandem with the ongoing development of more and more reliable encryption algorithms and software.

Following on from the technological challenge of securing user data in context-aware and ubiquitous computing environments, we must consider the fact that many users will have questions about the integrity of those implementing pervasive systems. Many feel that an increase in the presence of sensor technologies in our everyday society could lead to an age of unseen surveillance where government and corporate agencies could use all of this information to control populations and/or influence our commercial choices by constantly "spamming" us with adverts deemed to be relevant to our interests or current situations. Our development of ever more futuristic and dramatic computing applications such as these may just be a case of life imitating art, however, we must be careful to ensure that such scenarios do not come to fruition as context-aware systems could become more of a hindrance to daily life than a means of supporting and improving it. If we look forward to a future of even more prevalent and pervasive computing systems where computers seamlessly support our every activity, the ramifications of such a system failure would be disastrous. Another point to consider is the redundancy of various human skills, particularly within the industrial sector. The rise of factory floor machinery has brought about a decline in the number of production line jobs in which humans are required. Even smarter and more efficient systems of computing could eventually lead to such industries and workplaces becoming completely automated with very little human supervision required. This could cause job losses unless properly controlled and strategically introduced to allow people to develop other skills which can only be performed by a human operator.

Finally, all of the points mentioned above come down to one thing: Do people really want context-aware applications to manage and support their daily activities? The answer to this question is unclear, but with the level of public interest in technology in society today, it is likely more and more automated and intelligent systems will creep into everyday life without little opposition.

REFERENCES

Bricon-Souf, N., & Newman, C. (2007). Context awareness in healthcare: A review. International Journal of Medical Informatics, 76(1), 2–12. PubMed doi:10.1016/j.ijmedinf.2006.01.003

Chen, H. (2003). Creating Context Aware Software Agents. In *Innovative Concepts for Agent-Based Systems*. Berlin, Germany: Springer. doi:10.1007/978-3-540-45173-0_15

Dey, A., & Abowd, G. (2000). Towards a Better Understanding of Context and Context- Awareness. Paper presented at the CHI 2000 Workshop on the What, Who, Where, When, and How of Context-Awareness.

Meyer, S., & Rakotonirainy, A. (2003). A Survey of Research on Context-Aware Homes. *Conferences in Research and Practice in Information Technology Series, 21,* 158–168.

Schilit, B., Adams, N., & Want, R. (1994). Context-Aware Computing Applications. In Proceedings of the IEEE Workshop on Mobile Computing Systems and Applications (pp. 85-90).

Shadbolt, N. (2003). Ambient Intelligence. *IEEE Intelligent Systems, 18*(4), 2–3..doi:10.1109/MIS.2003.1200718

Vian, K., Liebhold, M., & Townsend, A. (2006). The Many Faces of Context-Awareness: A Spectrum of Technologies, Applications and Impacts (Technology Horizons Program. Tech Rep. SR-1014). Retrieved from http://www.iftf.org

Warneke, B., Last, M., & Liebowitz, B. (2001). Smart Dust: Communicating with a Cubic-Millimetre. *IEEE Computing, 34*(3), 44–51.

WISP. (2009). WISP Wiki. Retrieved from http://wisp.wikispaces.com/

Wooldridge, M., & Jennings, N. (1996). Software Agents. *IEEE Review,* 17-20.

This work was previously published in International Journal of Ambient Computing and Intelligence, Volume 2, Issue 1, edited by Kevin Curran, pp. 13-23, copyright 2010 by IGI Publishing (an imprint of IGI Global).

Chapter 3
A Dynamic Spoken Dialogue Interface for Ambient Intelligence Interaction

Germán Montoro
Universidad Autónoma de Madrid, Spain

Pablo A. Haya
Universidad Autónoma de Madrid, Spain

Xavier Alamán
Universidad Autónoma de Madrid, Spain

ABSTRACT

In this paper, we present the interpretation and generation processes of a spoken dialogue interface for ambient intelligence. The interface is automatically created for each specific environment and the interpretation and generation vary depending on the environment and its context. These processes rely on a dialogue tree structure. Several modules process the tree structure and the context information to produce specific dialogues for the current environment state. The interface has been implemented and evaluated in an ambient intelligence environment. Satisfactory objective and subjective evaluation results are shown at the end of the paper.

1. INTRODUCTION

In recent years a new research area has appeared within the ubiquitous computing (Weiser, 1991) field under the name of active environments, intelligent environments or ambient intelligence. The aim of ambient intelligence is to provide a more natural interaction between the environment and its inhabitants. The environment must help people in their everyday life, offering more human-like ways of communication. Therefore classrooms, offices, laboratories and homes should be capable of assisting their occupants in their tasks. This interaction must be adapted to the task, the environment, its occupant and the available devices. This implies the offering for selection of a specific communication modality.

DOI: 10.4018/978-1-4666-0038-6.ch003

Copyright © 2012, IGI Global. Copying or distributing in print or electronic forms without written permission of IGI Global is prohibited.

Nevertheless, not all the projects related with ambient intelligence consider the necessity of deploying interaction interfaces. This is the case of some projects of the Housing department (Munguia Tapia et al., 2004), which employ low level sensors to recognize the activity of its occupants. A similar idea is shown by the MavHome project (Das & Cook, 2004). Other projects, like The Adaptive House (Mozer, 2005), do not consider appropriate the environment has any kind of new interface.

On the other hand, some projects try to obtain more natural forms of communication to integrate them with the environment. That is the case of Aire (Adler and Davis, 2004), which has studied the possibilities for combining sketching with speech for multimodal design. Another project that has explored the use of speech for interacting with the environment is Homey (Milward & Beveridge, 2004). This project aims to carry out research on an intelligent dialogue interface designed to develop a dialogue between a tele-medicine interface and a patient. Considering the environment characteristics, this dialogue interface requires dynamic adaptation. Furthermore, the interaction can be multimodal. One of the main contributions to this field was the project Smartkom (Wahlster, 2006). This interface recognized speech or gestures and generated text, graphics or speech. Users could employ any of these modalities in three different scenarios: at home or in the office, at a communications booth and on the move with mobile devices.

In this paper we present a Spanish spoken dialogue interface for ambient intelligence environments. A dialogue control structure is automatically created according to the specific environment and it allows to interact with the environment and control its devices by means of spoken language interaction. Adaptation occurs at the interface creation and interaction processes. In both cases the interface and its behaviour automatically vary depending on the environment and its state. Contextual information obtained from the environment is employed to assist dialogue processes such as simple pronominal anaphora resolution, sentence interpretation, or recognition error recovering.

The paper is organized as follows. In Section 2 we introduce the concept of spoken dialogue interfaces in ambient intelligence environments. Section 3 presents the implemented ambient intelligence environment. We provide an overview of the environment representation in Section 4 and of the dialogue representation in Section 5. In Section 6 we give a more concise description of the interpretation and generation algorithms. Section 7 provides real examples of interaction. The interface evaluation is explained in Section 8. Finally we give some conclusion in Section 9.

2. DIALOGUE INTERFACES IN AMBIENT INTELLIGENCE ENVIRONMENTS

Although the presence of sound is not an essential characteristic for an ambient intelligence environment, we consider that a spoken dialogue interface is an important aspect in the development of these environments. Speech is a common, spontaneous and simple mean of communication (Clark & Brennan, 1991). This way, although it cannot always be the best input mechanism, it is a powerful method for the development of person-computer communication environments (Karat et al., 1999). This kind of interaction provides ambient intelligence environments with a more natural and intuitive way of communication. A continuous interaction in a daily occupied highly interactive environment without the possibility of using the voice could be a considerable effort and decrease significantly the capabilities of its occupants.

Moreover, a field research study carried out with real subjects to know their expectations about ambient intelligence environments shows that people prefer to employ their voice to control the home devices and, when they can choose between different modalities, they mainly choose oral communication (Brumitt & Cadiz, 2001).

Most of the spoken dialogue interfaces developed so far have focussed on the desktop classic environment or telephone-based agents for bank assistance, route planning or ticket reservation. These approaches have to be modified in the context of an ambient intelligence environment, where the interaction is addressed to a heterogeneous set of physical devices. Another differential factor for these interfaces is established by its idiosyncrasy. They are highly dynamic spaces whose configurations may change over time: devices can be added or removed; people can get in and out of the environment, or bring new mobile devices that have to be integrated into the environment. The interaction interface should be aware of these changes, automatically adapting to the specific characteristics of each environment.

Some research has been carried out in the field of home interfaces, but it has been mainly focussed on specific pc tasks (Tetzlaff et al., 1995) instead of highly integrated environments. However, the design assumptions adopted for a personal computer have found to be unsuitable for more dynamic environments (Mateas et al., 1996).

There are several efforts in the design and development of dialogue interfaces for these environments. The DHomme project creates dialogues for ambient intelligence environments, employing a combination of generic dialogue interface components and ontological domain knowledge (Milward & Beveridge, 2004). It presents networks of objects where each device carries the linguistic and dialogue management information, developing plug and play networks of objects and speech components (Rayner et al., 2001). These ideas are related to our spoken interface, as it can be seen later. Also related to intelligent environments, Quesada et al. centred on the dialogue management in a home machine environment (Quesada et al., 2001). Nevertheless, they employ an agent-based architecture and ontology description languages for independent domains

(Pérez et al., 2006), while we focus on a specific language for ambient intelligence description and interaction. Other important research focus is the use of context in the dialogue interfaces. Spoken language interaction requires dialogue models as well as domain and conceptual knowledge (Dahlbäck & Jönsson, 1997). Sharing our idea of context-adaptive approach, Porzel and Gurevych increase the conversational abilities of the dialogue interfaces by supplying factors relevant to context dependent analysis (Porzel & Gurevych, 2002). On the other hand, the BirdQuest system combines dialogue interaction with information extraction to build a shared domain ontology (Flycht-Eriksson & Jönsson, 2003).

The SmartKom project goes one step further by supporting multimodal interaction with multiple applications, ranging from consumer electronics control to mobile services (Reithinger et al., 2003). Following the multimodal interface approach, the Embassi project allows to add and remove modality analyzers dynamically (Elting et al., 2003). They focus on multimodal data fusion, which is not part of the research developed in this work.

3. OUR TEST BED: A PROTOTYPE OF AMBIENT INTELLIGENCE ENVIRONMENT

Different and highly heterogeneous technologies may be found inside an ambient intelligence environment, from hardware devices, such as sensors, switches, appliances, web cams, etc. to software, such as voice recognizers, multimedia streaming servers, mail agents, etc. On the one hand, all of these elements have to be seamlessly integrated and controlled using the same user interface. For instance, people have to be able to start a broadcasting music server as easily as to turn off the lights. On the other hand, the interaction has to be kept as flexible as possible. It should be based on multiple and distinct modalities, such as GUIs,

Figure 1. Snapshot of the developed environment

voice, touch, and so forth, so that their preferences and capabilities can be considered.

Bearing in mind these conditions, we have developed a working prototype based on a real environment. It includes an ontology, which provides a mechanism to represent the environment and communicate its state, and two different plug and play user interfaces (a graphical and a spoken dialogue interface), which interact with and control the elements of an ambient intelligence environment. These interfaces are automatically created and managed with the information extracted from the ontology. This environment consists of a laboratory, furnished as a living room, with several devices.

There are two kinds of devices: control and multimedia. Control devices are lighting controls, a door opening mechanism, a presence detector, smart-cards, etc. Multimedia devices, such as speakers, microphones, a TV set and an IP video-camera are accessible through a backbone IP. Control devices are connected to a KNX network and a gateway joins the two networks. The access to the physical layer is harmonized through a SMNP (Simple Management Network Protocol) layer. The interaction with the interfaces produces physical changes in the environment. A

key aspect was to try to avoid the use of simulated mechanisms so that we could verify how our ideas behaved in a more realistic setting. Figure 1 shows a picture of the ambient intelligence environment employed as a test bed.

4. ENVIRONMENT REPRESENTATION

The environment representation is written in a set of XML documents. The process of description of the environment, its components and their properties in XML documents is out of the scope of this paper. Further information about this issue can be found at (Montoro et al., 2006). At start-up, the information from these XML documents is read and the following elements automatically built:

- A blackboard (Engelmore & Mogan, 1988) which, among other things, works as an integration layer between the physical world and the spoken dialogue interface.
- A Spanish spoken dialogue interface which, employing the blackboard, works as an interaction layer between the environment and its occupants.

Figure 2. Schema of the high-level architecture of the platform

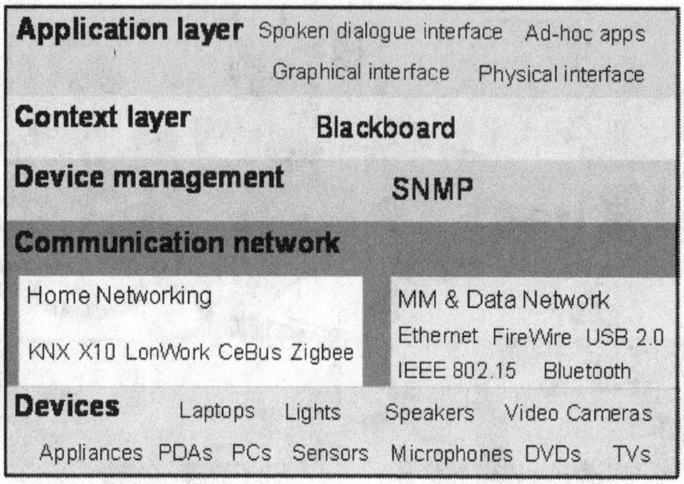

The blackboard holds a representation of multiple characteristics of the environment. These include its distribution (buildings and rooms), the entities it holds, their location, their state, the possible relationships between them and the flows of information. The nature of the entities can range from a physical device (a light, an appliance, etc.) to an abstract concept (the number of people in a room, the list of people allowed to get in it, etc.). The blackboard is used as a proxy information and context server. Applications and interfaces can ask the blackboard to obtain information about the state of any entity or to change it. Entities (e.g. lights or appliances) can be added or removed from the blackboard in run-time. Applications and user interfaces do not interact directly with the physical world or between them, but they only have access to the blackboard layer. This way, the blackboard layer isolates the applications from the real world. The details of the physical world entities are hidden from the clients (Salber & Abowd, 1998), making it easier and more standard to develop context aware modules and interfaces.

A schema of the different layers that compose the environment can be seen in Figure 2.

Entities from the blackboard are associated to a type of entity. All the entities of the same type inherit the same general properties. This means that if we define a new entity, its properties will come attached to it. As a result, as long as that type of entity is already defined, to write the XML environment representation only requires to define the entities presented on the environment and their type.

If a new device with new functionalities appears in scene, a new type of entity with its available properties will have to be created. The same way, to change the composition of the world, it is only necessary to modify the entities present in the XML environment representation, adding or removing the entities corresponding to the new devices.

Some of these general properties associated to the type of entity are employed to create the spoken dialogue interface and to represent linguistic information. This information is composed of a verb part (VP), describing the actions that can be taken with the entity; an object part (OP), specifying the name that it receives; a modifier part (MP), depicting the kind of object entity; a location part (LP), denoting where it is in the environment; and an indirect object part (IOP), indicating the receptor of the action. One entity has associated several sets of parts, corresponding to all the possible ways to interact with the entity. A single part can be formed by one or more words, allowing the use of synonyms.

Additionally, entities inherit the name of their associated grammar and the action method that has to be called after its linguistic information is completed. Action methods vary for each type of entity and execute all the possible actions that can be requested by an occupant (for instance to turn on, turn off, dim up and dim down the light in an entity of type *dimmable_light*). This linguistic information is transformed into specific grammars and a spoken dialogue interface.

5. DIALOGUE REPRESENTATION

This environment information is employed to automatically create a spoken dialogue interface. This interface is based on the environment representation stored on the blackboard and it dynamically adapts to the specific characteristics of the environment. A detailed explanation about the XML definition process for the spoken interface can be found in Montoro et al. (2004).

As it was said above, the spoken dialogue interface is composed of a set of grammars and a spoken dialogue structure. Grammars support the recognition process by specifying the possible sentences that can be uttered, limiting the number of inputs expected by the recognizer (Dahlbäck & Jönsson, 1992). This way, occupants will be allowed to carry on dialogues related to the current configuration of the environment. A grammar is created for each type of entity: grammars are based on a grammar template associated to the type of entity. In the interface creation process, the entities only have to fill in their corresponding grammar template with their set of linguistic parts (VP, OP, etc., see above).

The dialogue structure is based on a linguistic tree. Before creating the dialogue interface, the tree only has an empty root node. Every set of linguistic parts is transformed in a tree path, with a node for each part. Nodes are attached to parent nodes, which represent previous parts of the same set. Nodes store the word corresponding to that part and the name of its entity. Parts with more than one word (synonyms) will be transformed into different nodes and following parts of the same set will hang from every synonym node.

Words are analyzed by a morphological parser (Carmona et al., 1998) in order to get their number and gender. Repeated words are analyzed only the first time, and this information is stored for later use in the generation process. As an example, let us suppose that the entity *light_1* has the following set of linguistic parts: "VP turn_on switch_on OP light LP ceiling above", where the first two words correspond to the verb part, the third one to the object part and the last two words to the location part. "Turn on" and "switch on" are synonyms, the same as "ceiling" and "above". Starting from an empty tree, it would be created the linguistic tree shown in Figure 3.

Another set of linguistic parts may have a word at the same level as a previous set. In this case, a new node for that part will not be created. That node will be reused and, if necessary, the name of the entity to which it belongs will be appended. Let us suppose, for instance, that the entity *light_1* has the following two sets of linguistic parts: "VP turn_off OP light LP ceiling above" and "VP turn_off OP fluorescent", which correspond with three possible ways of interacting with it. In this case, the word "turn off" is at the same level in both sets of parts, so that only one "turn off" node is created. A "light" and a "fluorescent" node will be attached to it. If now, we have a new entity called *radio_1*, with this set of linguistic parts: "VP turn_off OP radio", it is only necessary to append the name of the entity *radio_1* to the "turn off" node. Next, the "radio" node is added as its child, at the same level as the "light" and "fluorescent" nodes. Starting from an empty tree, it would be created the linguistic tree shown in Figure 4

This automatic process is followed for all the sets of linguistic parts of all the entities presented

Figure 3. Partial linguistic tree

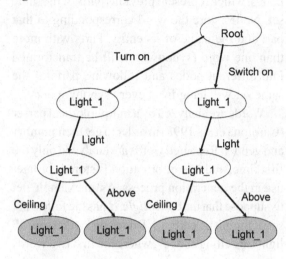

Figure 4. Linguistic tree for light_1 and radio_1 entities

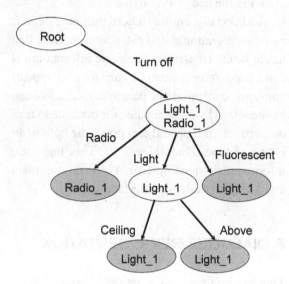

in the intelligent environment. Once the grammars and the linguistic tree are completed, it is obtained an adapted spoken dialogue interface that supports a wide set of natural language sentences to interact with the current intelligent environment.

Linguistic representation is associated to the entities of the environment. When these appear or disappear (new elements are introduced or removed from the environment) the spoken dialogue interface automatically changes and adapts to the new configuration (see previous section).

6. INTERPRETATION AND GENERATION

When the dialogue interface is created, people may carry on conversations with the environment. Dialogues follow a mixed initiative approach (Walker et al., 1998), where it is assumed that they know what they can say given the current interaction context. They will only be guided by the interface if it is necessary and either the interface or the person can take the initiative.

The dialogue interface is managed by a dialogue manager, which is in charge of receiving the utterance from the speech recognizer, interpreting it and generating a result (a spoken answer or an action). An overview of the interface architecture is shown in Figure 5, and a detailed explanation of each module is presented in Section 6.1 and Section 6.2.

This dialogue manager is based upon a simple but effective structure. This simplicity makes it possible to easily adapt to different environments or new ambient intelligence projects and automate the procedures of creation and interaction.

Initially, the interface is asleep and does not recognize any utterance. If someone wants to initiate a conversation she has to wake it up by uttering the word *Odyssey* (the name given to the spoken interaction interface). At that point, following the ideas of (Searle, 1969), the interface considers that the goal of the utterances is to complete an action. If she does not say anything in the next seven seconds (or seven seconds after the last dialogue interaction) the interface returns to the sleeping mode.

Figure 5. Architecture of the interpretation and generation modules

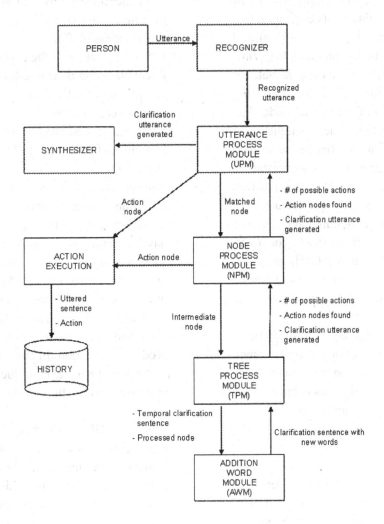

6.1. Interpretation

When the interface receives an interaction utterance from the recognizer it sends it to the Utterance Process Module (UPM). The UPM checks for matches between the utterance and the children of the linguistic tree root (verb part nodes). If there is a match, the UPM goes down the tree to the matching node and checks for new matches with its children. This process continues until the UPM reaches an action node (the sentence was fully interpreted and the interface may execute an action) or until there are no more matches (the interface needs clarification).

Executing an Action

If the UPM reaches an action node, it sends the information of the node to the Node Process Module (NPM). The NPM gets the word related to the first node of the followed tree path (which corresponds with the verb part, i.e., the action that has been requested). Then, the NPM orders the execution of the verb part by the action method associated to the action node. This execution usually implies a physical change in the environment, although it may also involve a dialogue response. For instance, given the linguistic tree in Figure 4, let us suppose that the inhabitant utters: *Please, could you turn off the ceiling light?* The UPM receives the sentence, obtains its corresponding semantic tags (*turn on*, *light* and *ceiling*) and checks for matches with the linguistic tree. *Turn off* matches with the "turn off" node, *light* matches with the child of the "turn off" node, and *ceiling* matches with the child of the "light" node. The "ceiling" node is an action node. Then the NPM takes the control and checks that the demanded action is *turn off*. As this node is associated to the *light_1* entity, it executes the *light_1* action method, considering that the requested action is *turn off*. Therefore, this action method can have two effects: it can turn off the *light_1* or it can inform that the *light_1* is already off. In any case, the UPM considers that the action was completed and goes back to its initial state, waiting for other utterances.

The interface does not need to produce a positive oral feedback when an action is executed, since there is physical correspondence in the environment that can be perceived by its occupants (in the example, the *light_1* is turned off).

Clarification

If after an utterance, the UPM does not reach an action node, some clarification is needed. The NPM receives the information of the last reached node from the UPM and, again, gets the verb part (the requested action) but does not execute any action. Now, the UPM sends the information of the node to the Tree Process Module (TPM). The TPM visits all the children of this node, constructing a sentence to request more information (see Section 6.2). This sentence is based on the visited nodes, always considering the physical context represented on the blackboard.

The TPM is based on a recursive depth-first tree search. Its procedure is (several examples can be found later in this section):

- It visits the first child of the node and checks if the requested action is different

from the current physical state of any of the entities associated to it. This information is extracted from the blackboard. If so, it stores the name of the entities with a different state and their tree level. Besides, it gets the word related to the node to build the answer sentence.

- After that, it recursively continues with the first child of this node, following the same steps.

- The recursive process with the first child of a node is repeated until the TPM reaches an action node, or until the node does not have any entity with a different state. If the TPM reaches an action node, and it has an entity with a different state to the requested one, it increments by one the number of actions that can be offered in the answer sentence and stores the name of the entity that produces the action. In any case, it goes up to the parent node to continue the recursive tree inspection with the following child of the node.

- When the TPM visits a node which is not a first child (a second or a following one), it makes sure that its entities were not already processed in other nodes of the same level. This makes possible that synonyms can be represented in the tree, but only one of them is considered in the interpretation and generation processes.

- This algorithm is repeated until the TPM has inspected all the child nodes and their subsequent children.

This tree search only considers those nodes with entities with a different state to the requested one and only processes the first synonym. The TPM only has to follow the paths to the action nodes that can be processed for the current state of the environment, avoiding all the others. Once the TPM has visited all the appropriate nodes, it has a full answer sentence (later explained in Section 6.2) and the number of actions that can be offered. The UPM receives this information and, depending on the number of possible actions, it behaves as follows:

- If the number of actions is equal to zero, the UPM responds that there is not any element in the environment that, in its current state, can perform the requested action.

- If the number of actions is equal to one, the UPM directly executes the action method of the entity associated to that action. With this, the number of turns is reduced and the recognizer is assisted by employing the current physical context as one of the possible sources of information that improves the interpretation and understanding (Ward & Novick, 1995).

- If the number of possible actions is two or three, the UPM utters the answer sentence built during the TPM tree search. This sentence presents the two or three possible entities that can perform the requested action, guiding the person through the dialogue (Yankelovich, 1996).

- If the number of actions is over three, the UPM does not offer all the possible options. It utters a more schematic clarification question for the general request. Therefore, the interface does not employ a sentence with too many options, which may be difficult to remember and tedious to hear, but it still guides the person (Marx & Schmandt, 1996).

As we have seen, the interpretation varies depending on the current context of the environment. The same utterance may lead to different interpretations in different contexts. For dissimilar contexts, the UPM can execute an action or consider that the inhabitant wants to interact with some entity of the environment.

As an example, let us suppose two different cases for the environment represented in Figure

4. They both share the same scenario, where the *light_1* and *radio_1* are both on:

1.   In the first case, the inhabitant utters: *Turn off the light*, so that the UPM stops at the "light" node. Next, the NPM assumes that the requested action is *turn off* and the TPM starts the clarification process. First, it goes down to the "ceiling" node and checks that the state of *light_1* (on) is different from the requested one (*turn off*), so it processes this node. Next, it adds the entity *light_1* to the list of visited entities under the "light" node, appends the word *ceiling* to the answer sentence and, given that it is an action node, increments the number of actions to offer. After that, it goes to inspect the "above" node. There it checks if its entities are already in the list of visited entities (i.e., if this is a synonym node of a previously processed one). As the "above" node has the entity *light_1*, which is in the list of visited entities under the "light" node, it does not process it. This concludes the tree search. The TPM returns the answer sentence, the number of offered actions and the list of action entities to the UPM. This verifies that there is only one possible action and executes it, i.e., it turns off the ceiling light.

2.   In the second case the inhabitant utters Turn off, so that the UPM stops at the "turn off" node. Again, after the NPM checks that the requested action is turn off, the TPM starts with the clarification procedure. First it checks that the state of radio_1 is different from the requested one and that it is an action node. The TPM adds the entity radio_1 to the list of visited entities under the "turn off" node, appends the word radio to the answer sentence and increments the number of actions to offer. Next it goes to the "light" node. Once there, it works as explained in the previous case. This appends the word ceiling to the answer sentence and incre-

ments again the number of actions to offer. Finally it goes to "fluorescent" node. This node contains the entity light_1, which is in the list of visited entities under the "turn off" node (i.e., it is a synonym), so it is not considered. The UPM receives the answer sentence and the number actions to offer. As the number of actions to offer is two, it utters the answer sentence: *Do you want to turn off the radio or the ceiling light?* Notice that, as we have explained above, multiple synonyms are omitted in this clarification answer (it only refers to the ceiling light and not to the fluorescent).

These very same utterances may produce different interpretations in a different context. Let us suppose a scenario where the *radio_1* is on and the *light_1* is off. If the inhabitant repeats the two previous sentences:

1. For the sentence *Turn off the light*, now the UPM will inform that all the lights are off.
2. For the sentence *Turn off*, now the UPM will turn off the *radio_1* because it is the only action entity with a different state to the requested one.

Another possible situation is produced when there is more than one entity of the same type in the environment (e.g. two or more lights). In this case, for the utterance *Turn off the light* there can be three possible situations:

1. If all the lights are off, the UPM will inform about that respect.
2. If only one light is on, the UPM will turn off that light.
3. If more than one light is on, the UPM will utter a clarification question. This clarification sentence will refer only to those lights that are on, omitting the lights that are already off.

As it has been illustrated in these examples, the interpretation varies depending on the entities of the environment and their current state. New entities can appear or disappear (e.g., a new light can be added to the environment), entities can change their state (e.g., from on to off) or there can be multiple entities of the same type. The dialogue interface adapts to these situations, automatically altering its structure and behaviour.

Finally, after the interface utters a clarification sentence, the UPM interpretation process suffers a modification for the following interactions. As usually, it checks for matches with the linguistic tree nodes, starting from the root. Nevertheless, after uttering a clarification sentence it also checks for matches starting from the node where it stopped in the previous interaction. From both tree searches, the UPM selects either the node at a lower level or the one that corresponds with an action node. With this, the UPM allows either to continue with a previous interaction (after a uttering a clarification sentence) or initiate a new dialogue (leaving behind the clarification dialogue).

As it can be seen, clarification answers are important to assist people in the dialogue process. They are especially useful when there are multiple elements of the same type, to assist novice people who do not know how to address to an element or to help them to learn to engage new entity functionalities.

Error Recovery

The recognition, interpretation and clarification processes may lead in some cases to misrecognitions and misinterpretations. Additionally, people may not provide enough information to process an utterance. To recover from these problems, the interface counts on some specific features.

As we have seen above, after a clarification answer the UPM permits either to continue with a previous dialogue path or to initiate a new one. This was designed to allow to recover from misinterpretations of the interface. If the clarification answer provided by the interface does not correspond with one of the occupant goals, she can start a new dialogue from the beginning, instead of continuing with an erroneous dialogue path.

As an additional feature, the UPM does not only check the root of the linguistic tree and the node where it stopped in the previous interaction (see above). If there is not any match for these two nodes, it will also check their children for matches. With this, the interface may either recover from speech recognizer misrecognitions or accurately interpret sentences where only part of the information was provided. For instance, if for the scenario represented in Figure 4 the recognizer returns the sentence *The ceiling light*, the UPM will not get any match for the root node. Then it will check the children of the root node, i.e., the children of the "turn off" node, so it will get a match for the "light" node and for its child, the "ceiling" node. Therefore, it has recovered from recognition noise and, thanks to the use of the contextual information of the environment; it can correctly interpret (Nagao & Rekimoto, 1995) that the original utterance was *Turn off the ceiling light*. In this case, the "turn off" node is automatically selected because the current physical state of the light is on. The selected node will vary depending on the physical contextual information extracted from the blackboard.

Anaphora Resolution

The spoken dialogue interface supports simple resolution of pronominal anaphora to refer to the last mentioned entity. This is the most common case for anaphora resolution that can be found in the interaction with an ambient intelligence environment. To allow the use of anaphora, the linguistic tree automatically holds anaphora resolution nodes, one for each verb. These nodes are composed of a verb and a pronoun. Besides, after the UPM reaches an action node and executes its corresponding action, it stores the followed tree path. When the UPM goes to an anaphora

resolution node (a person has employed a pronoun to refer to an entity) it goes to the tree node corresponding to that verb. Once there, it goes down through the stored tree path until it reaches an action node and executes its associated action. Let us suppose that someone utters: *Could you turn on the radio?* The UPM reaches the "radio" action node, turns the radio on and stores the full tree path of this action. Then she utters: *Please, turn it down*. The UPM then reaches the "turn it down" anaphora resolution node, so it jumps to the "turn down" node. Once there, it follows the stored path, i.e., it goes down until the "radio" node. As this is an action node, it turns the radio down.

6.2. Generation

As we have seen above, the generation process is carried out at the same time as the clarification process. The answer sentence is formed by words extracted from the nodes with entities that have a different state to the requested one.

Initially, the answer sentence is empty. Before the clarification process, it is filled with the question sentence *Do you want to* and the words presented in the tree path that goes from the root node to the node where the UPM stopped. Words are added to the answer sentence by an Addition Word Module (AWM). The AWM gets the number and gender of the word and appends its right form to the answer sentence, preceded by the appropriate article (in Spanish, nouns, adjectives and articles have number and gender). For instance, if in Figure 4 the UPM stops at the "turn off" node, the answer sentence will get its initial form by *Do you want to turn off*. After that, the TPM appends the other appropriate words that it gets during the clarification process. Words are added as it was explained in the clarification section. Additionally, if a previous word of the same level was already added, before attaching the new word it appends the word *or*, in order to show alternatives. Furthermore, in Spanish it is necessary to append the *from* preposition before the modifier and location parts and *to* before the indirect object part. Following with the previous example, the TPM uses the AWM to append *the radio*. Next, since the "light" node is at the same level as the "radio" node, it appends *or* and *the light*. After that, as *ceiling* is a location word, it appends *from* followed by *the ceiling*. The final answer sentence is (omitting some words, for a better translation to English): *Do you want to turn off the radio or the ceiling light?*

As it can be seen, the generation process also employs and adapts to the current context of the environment, obtaining more suitable sentences for the given situation.

Additionally, the interface does not only generate answer sentences but also lightweight audio signs (Mynatt et al., 1997). These audio signs are environmental sounds that try to provide information in a less intrusive way. They avoid disturbing sentences if they are not necessary. Currently, environmental sounds are employed in two situations:

1. An audio sign (similar to a yawn) is produced when the recognizer returns to the sleeping mode. If this happened because the interaction with the environment was finished, it is not necessary to distract the occupant with this information. If not, she is still paying attention to the conversation, and an audio sign is enough to let her know about the new recognition mode.

2. A different audio sign (similar to an interjection) is used when the UPM does not get any match at all. This sign is repeated in the next unsuccessful interpretation and only after a third consecutive failure, the interface informs about the problem and requires the occupant to change the sentence. This sign was introduced after checking with subjects that, in a few cases, the recognizer produced substitution or insertion errors, i.e., it provided a different sentence to the uttered one or it interpreted noise (not an utterance)

as a sentence (Schmandt & Negroponte, 1994). In the first case, it was verified that it is faster and more efficient to reproduce an audio sign than utter a whole sentence. In the second case, a recognizer error does not unnecessarily distract the occupant.

7. EXAMPLES OF INTERACTION

In the implemented ambient intelligence environment (see Section 3), we have defined a spoken dialogue interface that allows to interact with its components (see Section 6). In this section we show a transcription of a real dialogue carried out in this environment. This interaction is based on some of the components of the environment: two lamps, both with a dimmable light and a reading light, the main fluorescent lights (i.e., five different lights) and a radio tuner. The speech recognizer results are shown between braces and comments to the interaction in italics.

1. Person (P): Odyssey {Odyssey}
2. Interface (I): Yes?
3. P: Can you turn on the light? {turn on light}

The number of possible lights to turn on is five; the interface shortens the generated answer

4. I: Which light would you like to turn on?

The person does not provide any answer for seven seconds. The interface assists her offering all the possible actions

5. I: You can turn on the fluorescent light, the reading light on the left or on the right and the ambient light on the left or on the right
6. P: The light on the left, please {light left}

The interface jumps one node in the tree and needs clarification between two possible lights

7. I: Do you prefer to turn on the reading light on the left or the ambient light on the left?
8. P: The ambient light

The interface turns on the ambient light on the left

9. P: I want to turn on the ceiling light {turn on ceiling}

The recognizer only returned part of the uttered information. The interface checks that there is only one entity in the ceiling that can be turned on, so it recovers from the mistake and turns on the ceiling light (fluorescent)

10. P: Can you turn on the light?

She repeats the sentence of Point 3. In this occasion, there are only three possible entities that can fulfill the requested action, so the answer differs and the interface offers the possible actions

11. I: Do you prefer the reading light on the left or the ambient light on the left or on the right?
12. P: The light on the left, please {light left}

She repeats the sentence of Point 6. In this case, there is only one light on the left that is turned off. The interface does not need more information and directly turns on the reading light on the left

13. P: Turn it off {turn it off}

She employs an anaphora, so the requested action is applied to the last entity. The interface turns off the reading light on the left.

14. P: Could you switch on the radio? {switch on radio}

The interface needs information about the radio station, so it utters a proper sentence

15. I: Which radio station do you prefer?
16. P: M80, please {M80}

The interface turns on the radio with M80 station

17. P: I would like you to turn up the volume of the radio {turn up}

The recognizer only returned turn up. Currently, there are two entities that can perform that action, so the interface tries to clarify which is the right one

18. I: Do you prefer the volume of the radio or the ambient light on the left?
19. P: The radio

She does not specify all the requested information (volume), but with the previous information the interface correctly interprets the sentence and turns up the volume of the radio

20. P: Louder, please

The interface repeats the last action, so it turns up the volume of the radio again

21. P: Switch it off {switch if off}

The interface resolves the anaphora and turns off the radio

22. P: I want you to turn off the ambient light on the left {light ambient left}

The recognizer does not return the requested action (verb). The interface checks what actions can be performed with that entity and responds offering them

23. I: Do you prefer to turn off, turn up or turn down the ambient light on the left?
24. P: I prefer to turn it off {turn it off}

The interface turns off the ambient light on the left

25.   P: I would like you to switch off the light {switch off light}

Since there is only one light on, the interface does not need clarification like in previous cases. It directly turns off the fluorescent light

The answers and actions performed by the interface are automatically produced, considering the entities of the environment. If the environment had a different configuration the spoken dialogue interface would automatically adapt to the new environment, modifying its behaviour. If for the previous case, the lamps did not have the dimmable lights (i.e., the environment only had three different lights), the same requests would produce different responds or reactions. For this situation, the dialogue would be:

1.   P: Odyssey {Odyssey}
2.   I: Yes?
3.   P: May you turn on the light? {turn on light}

The number of possible lights to turn on is three. The interface offers all the possible lights that can be turned on

4.   I: Do you prefer to turn on the fluorescent light, the reading light on the left or the reading light on the right?
5.   P: The light on the left, please {light left}

The interface jumps one node in the tree. Since now there is only one light on the left, it interprets that she is referring to the reading light on the left and turns it on

In this example, the same utterances lead to different answers in Point 4 and Point 5. Besides, after Point 5 the interface can execute an action instead of requiring clarification, like in the previous example.

The variations in the behaviour of the spoken dialogue interface depend on the current context and configuration of the environment. This is based on the entities defined in the environment and their associated linguistic information (see Section 4 and Section 5).

8. EVALUATION

The environment is open for public use, what allows us to examine its functionality. The interface logs the sentences received by the recognizer, the number of turns, the time required to complete a task, the entities that were object of spoken interaction and its responses. The examples employed in the previous sections were very simple to facilitate the comprehension of the interface performance. Nevertheless, the tested dialogue interface is based on the environment presented in Section 3, where inhabitants can find five different lights, a door opening mechanism, an FM tuner, a TV set, etc., and supports multiple interactions. Every test shares a common idea. It is done by subjects in the ambient intelligent environment. Spoken interactions produce real changes in the environment, which can be perceived by its inhabitants. Interface answers are based on the current physical state of the entities of the environment.

The metrics of a spoken dialogue interface can be classified in objective and subjective. The first category implies the recognition and comprehension levels, the number of turns, the amount of necessary corrections, etc. This category tries to determine the task success and the dialogue costs (Walker et al., 1997). The later tries to obtain an opinion on issues such as usability, effectiveness, overall satisfaction, etc.

8.1. Evaluation Model

To evaluate the interface we built an evaluation model where subjects had to carry on 23 different tasks related to some entities of the environment.

Interactions were based on the five lights of the environment, the electronic door lock, a radio tuner with 14 different radio stations and simulated air conditioning (that informed about its activation and the current temperature of the environment) and phone call (that simulated a ring tone as it was making a phone call) systems. Each subject performed the tasks individually. To do so, they received a small map (corresponding with the real environment where they were) with a number in each one of the lights of environment (see Figure 6). Numbers 1 and 3 represent two reading lights. Numbers 2 and 4 correspond with two dimmable lights. And number 5 represents the fluorescent light. This map was employed to avoid informing them about how to refer to the physical entities in the oral interaction.

Moreover, each subject received the form shown in Figure 7, with the 23 tasks they had to perform. This template employed general terms to refer to the entities. These tasks were chosen to obtain information about how different people refer to the same elements, if they employ anaphora, if they use words out of context, how much information they provide in each spoken interaction, if they need clarification from the interface, etc. For each performed action the evaluator recorded the uttered sentences, the recognizer outputs, the sentences uttered by the dialogue manager and the performed action. After concluding the interaction with the environment, each subject had to fill in a form where they expressed their grade of satisfaction and opinion about the interaction with the interface (see Figure 8). Questions 1 to 6 and 9 were graded from 1 (very unsatisfactory) to 5 (very satisfactory), while questions 6 and 7 allowed to write open answers.

8.2. Evaluation Results

Evaluation was performed with 37 individual subjects. A small group of these worked in the area of new technologies, while most of them did not have any special relationship with it. Subjects belonged practically equally to both genders and were distributed in a wide range of ages. Most of the subjects that performed the study did not have any previous relationship with the authors. They were not familiar with the employment of spoken dialogue interfaces. The speech recognizer was not previously trained and subjects performed these actions by the first and last time in their interaction with the environment. None of them received any verbal example of how to interact with the interface. Each subject had to perform every one of the 23 tasks shown in Figure 7, guided by the sketching represented in Figure 6. They obtained an immediate result of their interactions because their utterances produced physical changes in the environment. Once they finished the interactions they filled in the form shown in Figure 8. With all the collected data a list of objective and subjective evaluation parameters was built.

Objective Evaluation Parameters

The 37 subjects performed the 23 proposed tasks. There were only two situations where a subject could not perform a specific task and had to continue with the others. From the collected data, the following exhaustive list of evaluation parameters was extracted:

- Parameter #1. Number of successfully completed tasks in the whole session.
- Parameter #2. Number of uttered sentences necessary to complete the session.
- Parameter #3. Number of uttered sentences that included an anaphora.
- Parameter #4. Number of uttered sentences that implied especial words like more, less, louder etc.
- Parameter #5. Number of uttered sentences where the recognizer was unable to return any value. This could be produced because the subject employed a sentence that was out of the context of the dialogue

Figure 6. Environment map employed for evaluation

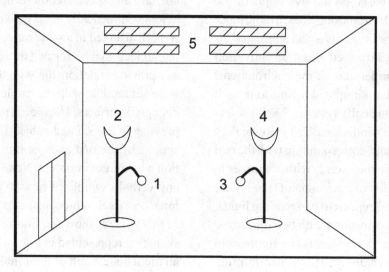

Figure 7. Template with the 23 tasks

```
1 .... Activate 5
2 .... Activate 1
3 .... Deactivate 1
4 .... Activate 4
5 .... + 4
6 .... + 4
7 .... - 4
8 .... Deactivate 4
9 .... Activate 3
10 ... Activate radio
11 ... Activate other station
12 ... Activate 2
13 ... + Radio
14 ... + 2
15 ... Activate door
16 ... Deactivate radio
17 ... Activate air conditioning
18 ... Air conditioning
19 ... Deactivate 2
20 ... Deactivate air conditioning
21 ... Deactivate 3
22 ... Call Javier
23 ... Deactivate 5
```

interface or, more frequently, due to a recognition error.

- Parameter #6. After parameter #5, number of times where the subject repeats the same sentence.
- Parameter #7. After parameter #5, number of modified sentences respecting the origi-

nal one. It can be seen that the sum of #6 and #7 must be equal to #5.

- Parameter #8. Number of sentences where the recognizer only obtained part of the uttered sentence.
- Parameter #9. For parameter #8, in how many sentences the interface could respond with a satisfactory clarification answer.

Figure 8. User questionnaire

```
1. Do you find useful to employ spoken dialogues to interact with
   the environment?
2. Would you use this system to interact with your environments?
3. Do you think that the system understood your requests?
4. Do you consider that the system dialogue was agile?
5. Did you understand the answers provided by the system?
6. Do you think that the spoken dialogue interaction is more useful
   than conventional interaction modes?
7. When do you think it can be more useful?
8. What would you add, remove or modify to improve the system?
9. Was your interaction with the system satisfactory?
```

Table 1. Performed tasks and uttered sentences

Performed tasks	Uttered sentences	Uttered sentences by task
834	1743	2

- Parameter #10. For parameter #8, in how many sentences the interface could not respond with a clarification answer.
- Parameter #11. For parameter #8, in how many sentences the interface could interpret the requested action and directly execute it. It can be seen that the sum of #9, #10, and #11 must be equal to #8.
- Parameter #12. Number of sentences where the recognizer returned the full uttered sentence but the subject did not provide all the requested information to perform an action.
- Parameter #13. For parameter #12, in how many sentences the interface could respond with a satisfactory clarification answer.
- Parameter #14. For parameter #12, in how many cases the interface could interpret the requested action and directly execute it. It can be seen that the sum of #13 and #14 must be equal to #12.
- Parameter #15. Number of sentences where the recognizer returned a word that was not uttered by the subject.
- Parameter #16. For parameter #15, in how many cases this led to provide an erroneous clarification answer or execute an incorrect task.

The values of each of these 16 parameters for the 37 subjects are represented in Table A of Appendix section.

This information allowed us to obtain some information about the functionality and performance of the interface.

For the number of tasks and uttered sentences, see Table 1.

Subjects performed 834 tasks and uttered 1743 sentences. This means that, in average, they needed 2 sentences per task. A common example for this situation is the sequence:

- Person: "Turn on the light"
- Interface: "Which light would you like to turn on?"
- Person: "The reading light on the left"

This can be a reasonable number of utterances per task, considering that the experiment was carried out with novice subjects who did not know how to address to the devices in the environment. Although we do not provide here the exact figures

Table 2. Sentences where the speech recognizer worked erroneously

Sentences where the recognizer did not return any value	Sentences where the recognizer returned less information	Sentences where the recognizer returned an erroneous value
467	216	31
27%	12%	2%

Table 3. Behaviour with sentences where the recognizer only returned part of the uttered information

Sentences where the interface answered with an appropriate clarification question	Sentences where the interface could directly execute an action	Total number of sentences partially or totally interpreted	Sentences where the interface could not provide any kind of interpretation
117	66	183	33
54%	31%	85%	15%

of the evolution, the number of turns decreases once people know how to address to each element of the environment (see related information below in Table 5). This value can also be improved by decreasing the number of sentences where the recognizer is not able to return any value (see Table 2), what produces a new turn.

For recognition errors:

According to the figures in Table 2, in 27% of the uttered sentences the recognizer did not return any value. In an additional 14% of the sentences, the recognizer returned less or erroneous information. These low rates in the recognition results are mainly produced by the use of a general purpose untrained recognizer. This engine was selected in order to test the performance of the interface in adverse conditions. However, this error rate is excessive. These values would have to be improved to achieve a truly satisfactory performance of the interface. For the behaviour of the interface with the sentences where the recognizer only returned part of the uttered information see Table 3 (the 12% of total sentences, see Table 2).

For this circumstance, in 85% of the situations the interface could make a right interpretation of the uttered sentence. Moreover, in 31% of the cases, the interface could directly execute an action although it did not have all the information.

These figures show how the proper use of the physical context allows to decrease the number of turns and recover from recognition errors or lack of information in the utterances.

For sentences where the recognizer returned information not provided by the subject see Table 4 (2% of total, see Table 2).

Half of these situations led to an erroneous interpretation, i.e., to execute an erroneous action or answer with an unexpected sentence. This means that 1% of total sentences were misunderstood. In the other half of the situations, the interpretation was not affected. The correct use of the context made possible to know that the received sentence did not was not appropriate for the current situation of the environment and it could be discarded. For sentences where the recognizer returned all the information uttered by the subject see Table 1 (1029 sentences or 59% of total, see Table 1 and Table 2).

This implies that, in most of the cases (81%), subjects provided in the same sentence all the necessary information to execute an action. This number was lower for the first interactions and increased when subjects learnt how to address to the entities of the environment. This increase is also due to the employment of interface assistance and clarification answers, which guided them in

Table 4. *Behaviour with sentences where the recognizer returned wrong information*

Sentences that led to an erroneous interpretation	Sentences where the interpretation was not affected
16	15
51%	49%

Table 5. *Sentences correctly recognised*

Sentences where subjects provided part of the information necessary to execute an action	Sentences where subjects provided all the requested information
198	831
19%	81%

the following interactions. For sentences where the recognizer returned all the information uttered by the subject, but this only provided part of the requested information see Table 6 (198 in total, see Table 5).

Once more, the possibility of recovering in case of misinformation and directly executing the associated action (42% of the situations) is granted by the employment of the contextual information of the real world represented in the blackboard. This helps again to decrease the number of turns and obtain a more efficient dialogue. For sentences where the interface only received part of the information (414 in total, see Table 7), including those where the recognizer returned all the uttered information (198, see Table 5) and those with recognition errors (216, see Table 3).

In 92% of the sentences that only had part of the information, it was possible to make a partial or full interpretation. Just in 8% of these situations, the received sentence led to a misinterpretation. This was always produced when the recognizer returned erroneous information (see Table 3).

And for sentences that employed anaphora or special words, like *more*, *less*, *louder*, etc. see Table 8.

Subjects could employ anaphora and special words in 6 different actions respectively. This means that they have been used them in 16% of the possible situations. This indicates that their presence in the dialogue is necessary although they do not represent a high percentage of the possible interactions.

Table 6. *Behaviour with fully recognised sentences where subjects only provided part of the information*

Sentences that produced a clarification answer	Sentences that directly performed the associated action
115	83
58%	42%

From these results, it is possible to detect two specific problems. Firstly, the difficulty of the interface to recover from insertion errors (the recognizer interprets noise as a valid input). This problem is minimized by the fact that these sentences only correspond to 2% of total (see Table 2 and Table 4). Secondly, the high rate of rejection (recognizer cannot produce an output) and substitution (recognizer output differs from input) errors produced by the recognizer. Nevertheless, for the later case, the interface can satisfactorily recover and produce a partial or full interpretation in 85% of the situations (see Table 3). It is remarkable that, independently of the received utterances or the possible recognition errors, 92% of the sentences were correctly interpreted (see Table 8), what means a correct performance of the interpretation process.

Finally, we can point out that in between 36% (see Table 7) and 42% (see Table 6) of the situations, the interface could make a complete interpretation of the sentence, even though it only contained part of the information. This allowed to save turns and time, thanks to the use of the

Table 7. Behaviour with sentences where subjects only provided part of the information

Sentences that led to an appropriate clarification answer (Partial interpretation)	Sentences that led to an appropriate execution of an action (Full interpretation)	Total number of appropriate partial or full interpretations	Sentences that did not lead to an appropriate interpretation
232	149	381	33
56%	36%	92%	8%

Table 8. Use of anaphora and special words

Anaphora	Special words
36	35
16%	16%

physical contextual information provided by the blackboard.

Subjective Evaluation Parameters

These parameters were obtained from the answers provided by each subject (punctuating from 1 -very unsatisfactory- to 5 -very satisfactory-) and according to the questions shown in Figure 8. Full results are shown in Table B of Appendix section.

These answers were anonymous and subjects were motivated to be as sincere and critical as possible in their evaluation. From these answers, it is possible to obtain the average value for each question (measured from 1 to 5, see Table 9).

In general terms, subjects were satisfied with the interaction interface, with a punctuation of 4.47 over 5. These are high satisfaction results, although the number of sentences per task (see Table 1) and recognition errors (see Table 2) are still elevated. Nevertheless, the number of erroneous interpretations is very low and the interface performance is satisfactory once it received a sentence (see Table 7). This can also indicate the predisposition of people to employ a spoken interface to interact with the environment. In any case, lower recognition errors could lead to better satisfaction results. The lowest score is obtained

in the agility of the interface (3.75 over 5). Since the behaviour of the interface is satisfactory for the received sentences, the cause can be found again in the recognizer errors. This score is also expected to increase with better recognition results. For question #7, subjects identified four main topics where this kind of interfaces can be of special utility (see Table 10).

Although the tests were not carried out with people with special necessities, half of the subjects point out this group as one of the main targets for spoken interfaces in ambient intelligence. Other 28% considered that they are suitable for comfort, what could again show their acceptation to introduce them in their everyday environments. For the question #8, subjects required to improve the voice recognition rate (20% of them), more information about the dialogue state (20%), a bigger adaptation to each person (15%), a wider available vocabulary (15%), or the employment of gesture recognition (5%).

9. CONCLUSION AND FUTURE WORK

In this paper, we have presented a spoken dialogue interface that adapts to ambient intelligence environments. Adaptation occurs at the interface creation and interaction processes. In both cases, the interface and its behaviour vary depending on the environment and its state. Dialogues are automatically created and they allow to interact with the environment and control its devices by means of spoken language interaction.

Table 9. Average punctuation for each question

	Q. 1	Q. 2	Q. 3	Q. 4	Q. 5	Q. 6	Q. 9
Average	4.58	4.36	3.97	3.75	4.55	4.05	4.47

Dialogues are dynamic since their composition change and automatically adapt to the current configuration of the environment. If a new device or element appear or disappear, it is only necessary to modify the XML representation of the environment (see Section 4) to obtain a new dialogue configuration that automatically adapts to the present configuration of the environment.

Since dialogues are created for general purpose and they provide standard mechanisms of communication with the blackboard layer, they could be reusable for any other ambient intelligence environment project. The new environment would only need an accessible representation of its entities, their properties and their state. The dialogue interface would only have to change the protocol to access to this information, to adapt it to this new environment. The rest of the modules would remain as explained (see Section 6). The paper focuses on the interpretation and generation processes and it just briefly explains how the plug and play dialogues for any given environment are built, which is described in Montoro et al. (2004) in more detail. To evaluate this research an ambient intelligence environment has been built. This environment consists of a laboratory furnished as a living room, provided with a range of devices. There are two kinds of devices: control and multimedia. Control devices are lighting controls, a door opening mechanism, a presence detector, smart-cards, etc. Multimedia devices are speakers, microphones, a TV set, an IP video-camera. The interface has been tested with real subjects in order to obtain an accurate measure of its performance and their satisfaction. Results show an appropriate response of the spoken interface in different situations and a satisfactory

level of acceptation. In the future we still have to add new capabilities to the interpretation and generation processes. Current dialogues allow managing the entities of the environment but not asking about their state. Some modifications have to be done in order to allow people to make such questions. The interface must be provided with a new question part and a new questioning tree, very similar to the explained linguistic tree. Only a few characteristics of the interpretation and generation modules have to undergo some changes to support this new tree.

Currently, the interface only performs one action per turn. For instance, if someone requests two different actions in the same utterance, only the first one is considered. Some changes must be done in the UPM to allow to carry on simultaneous actions. The use of multimodal approaches can benefit the interface. A new face recognition module can help to identify who is in the environment. This information can be used by the spoken dialogue interface to improve their functionality. Following with this idea, the synchronization of speech and hand gestures can be helpful for the interaction (Bourguet and Ando, 1998). For this, a new gesture recognition module should be built. Other possible modal interaction can be produced by showing the information on a screen, besides uttering a request. Then, the environment inhabitant could answer either by speaking or clicking on the selected choice. Finally, the interface can be improved by adding a virtual agent that provides a visual support to the speech interaction. People in the environment could address to the virtual agent and engage in a more human-like interaction. A new study with subjects will be developed in soon to obtain information about

Table 10. Situations where the spoken interface can be especially useful

Remote interaction	People with special necessities	Comfort	Working environment
5	19	10	2
14%	53%	28%	5%

the possible improvements in the interaction with this virtual agent.

ACKNOWLEDGMENT

This paper has been funded by the Spanish Ministry of Science and Education, project number TIN2007-64718.

REFERENCES

Adler, A., & Davis, R. (2004). Speech and Sketching for Multimodal Design. In *Proceedings of the 9th International Conference on Intelligent User Interfaces* (pp. 214-216).

Bourguet, M., & Ando, A. (1998, April 18-23). Synchronization of speech and hand gestures during multimodal human-computer interaction. In *Proceedings of CHI'98,* Los Angeles (pp. 241-242).

Brumitt, B., & Cadiz, J. J. (2001.) *Let There Be Light! Comparing Interfaces for Homes of the Future.* Paper presented at the 2001 IFIP TC.13 Conference on Human Computer Interaction (Interact 2001).

Carmona, J., Atserias, J., Cervell, S., Márquez, L., Martí, M. A., Padró, L., et al. (1998). *An Environment for Morphosyntactic Processing of Unrestricted Spanish Text.* Paper presented at LREC'98, Granada, Spain.

Clark, H. H., & Brennan, S. E. (1991). Grounding in communication. In Levine, J., Resnick, L. B., & Behrand, S. D. (Eds.), *Shared Cognition: Thinking as Social Practice* (pp. 127–149). Washington, DC: APA Books. doi:10.1037/10096-006

Dahlbäck, N., & Jönsson, A. (1992). *An empirically based computationally tractable dialogue model.* Paper presented at COGSCI'92.

Dahlbäck, N., & Jönsson, A. (1997). *Integrating Domain Specific Focusing in Dialogue Models.* Paper presented at EuroSpeech-97, Rhodes, Greece.

Das, S., & Cook, D. J. (2004). Smart Home Environments: A Paradigm Based on Learning and Prediction. In *Wireless Mobile and Sensor Networks.* New York: Wiley.

Elting, C., Rapp, S., Möhler, G., & Strube, M. (2003). *Architecture and Implementation of Multimodal Plug and Play.* Paper presented at the 5th International Conference on Multimodal Interfaces, Vancouver, British Columbia, Canada.

Engelmore, R., & Mogan, T. (1988). *Blackboard Systems.* Reading, MA: Addison-Wesley.

Flycht-Eriksson, A., & Jönsson, A. (2003). *Some empirical findings on dialogue management and domain ontologies in dialogue systems - Implications from an evaluation of BirdQuest.* Paper presented at the Workshop on Discourse and Dialogue, Sapporo, Japan.

Karat, C., Halverson, C., Horn, D., & Karat, J. (1999, May 15-20). Patterns of entry and correction in large vocabulary continuous speech recognition systems. In *Proceedings of CHI'99,* Pittsburgh, PA (pp. 568-575).

Marx, M., & Schmandt, C. (1996, April 13-18). MailCall: Message presentation and navigation in a nonvisual environment. In *Proceedings of CHI'96,* Vancouver, British Columbia, Canada (pp. 165-172).

Mateas, M., Salvador, T., Scholtz, J., & Sorensen, D. (1996). Engineering Ethnography in the Home. In *CHI 96 Conference Companion* (pp. 283-284).

Milward, D., & Beveridge, M. A. (2004, July 19-21). *Ontologies and the Structure of Dialogue.* Paper presented at CATALOG, 8th Workshop on the Semantics and Pragmatics of Dialogue, Barcelona, Spain.

Montoro, G., Haya, P. A., & Alamán, X. (2004). *Context adaptive interaction with an automatically created spoken interface for intelligent environments.* Paper presented at INTELLCOMM 04, Bangkok, Thailand.

Montoro, G., Haya, P. A., Alamán, X., López-Cózar, R., & Callejas, Z. (2006). A proposal for an XML definition of a dynamic spoken interface for ambient intelligence. In *Proceedings of the International Conference on Intelligent Computing (ICIC 06),* Kunming, China (pp. 711-716).

Mozer, M. C. (2005). Lessons from an adaptive house. In Cook, D., & Das, R. (Eds.), *Smart environments: Technologies, protocols, and applications* (pp. 273–294). Hoboken, NJ: J. Wiley & Sons. doi:10.1002/047168659X.ch12

Munguia Tapia, E., Intille, S. S., & Larson, K. (2004). *Activity recognition in the home using simple and ubiquitous sensors.* Paper presented at Pervasvie 2004, Vienna, Austria.

Mynatt, E. D., Back, M., Want, R., & Frederick, R. (1997). Audio Aura: Light-weight audio augmented reality. In *Proceedings of ACM UIST'97,* Banff, Alberta, Canada (pp. 211-212).

Nagao, K., & Rekimoto, J. (1995). Ubiquitous talker: Spoken language interaction with real world objects. In *Proceedings of IJCAI-95* (Vol. 2, pp. 1284-1290).

Pérez, G., Amores, G., Manchón, P., Gómez, F., & González, J. (2006). Integrating OWL Ontologies with a Dialogue Manager. *Procesamiento del Lenguaje Natural, 37,* 153–160.

Pérez, G., Gabriel de Amores, J., & Manchón, P. A. (2006). Multimodal Architecture for Home Control by Disabled Users. In *Proceedings of the IEEE/Acl 2006 Workshop on Spoken Language Technology,* New York (pp. 134-137). Washington, DC: IEEE Computer Society.

Porzel, R., & Gurevych, I. (2002). *Towards Context-adaptive Utterance Interpretation.* Paper presented at the 3rd SIGDial Workshop on Discourse and Dialogue, Philadelphia.

Quesada, J. F., García, F., Sena, E., Bernal, J. A., & Amores, J. G. (2001). Dialogue Management in a Home Machine Environment: Linguistic Components over an Agent Architecture. *Procesamiento del Lenguaje Natural, 27,* 89–96.

Rayner, M., Lewin, I., Gorrell, G., & Boye, J. (2001, September). *Plug and Play Speech Understanding.* Paper presented at the 2nd SIGdial Workshop on Discourse and Dialogue.

Reithinger, N., Alexandersson, J., Becker, T., Blocher, A., Engel, R., Löeckelt, M., et al. (2003). *SmartKom - Adaptive and Flexible Multimodal Access to Multiple Applications.* Paper presented at the 5th International Conference on Multimodal Interfaces, Vancouver, British Columbia, Canada.

Salber, D., & Abowd, G. D. (1998). *The design and use of a generic context server.* Paper presented at Perceptual User Interfaces Conference (PUI'98).

Schmandt, C., & Negroponte, N. (1994). *Voice communication with computers: conversational systems.* New York: Van Nostrand Reinhold.

Searle, J. (1969). *Speech Acts.* London: Cambridge University Press.

Tetzlaff, L., Kim, M., & Schloss, R. J. (1995). Home Health Care Support. In *CHI 95 Conference Companion.*

Wahlster, W. (Ed.). (2006). *SMARTKOM: Foundations of Multimodal Dialogue Systems, Cognitive Technologies Series.* Berlin, Germany: Springer. doi:10.1007/3-540-36678-4

Walker, M. A., Fromer, J., Di Fabbrizio, G., Mestel, C., & Hindle, D. (1998, April 18-23). What can I say? Evaluating a spoken language interface to email. In *Proceedings of CHI'98,* Los Angeles (pp. 582-589).

Walker, M. A., Litman, D. J., Kamm, C. A., & Abella, A. (1997). *PARADISE: A framework for evaluating spoken dialogue agents.* Paper presented at the Thirty-Fifth Annual Meeting of the Association for Computational Linguistics.

Ward, K., & Novick, D. G. (1995, May 7-11). Integrating multiple cues for spoken language understanding. In *Proceedings of CHI'95,* Denver, CO.

Weiser, M. (1991). The computer of the 21st century. *Scientific American, 265*(3), 66–75. doi:10.1038/scientificamerican0991-94

Yankelovich, N. (1996). How do users know what to say? *Interactions (New York, N.Y.), 3*(6).. doi:10.1145/242485.242500

APPENDIX (TABLE 11 AND 12)

Table 11. Objective evaluation parameters for each subject

	#1	#2	#3	#4	#5	#6	#7	#8	#9	#10	#11	#12	#13	#14	#15	#16
#1	23	37	5	1	3	3	0	4	2	1	1	4	2	2	1	1
#2	23	38	3	0	5	3	2	7	3	0	4	1	1	0	1	0
#3	21	37	0	3	3	3	0	6	2	2	2	4	2	2	0	0
#4	16	50	0	1	18	12	6	5	2	1	2	3	2	1	0	0
#5	23	43	0	0	12	12	0	4	3	0	1	3	3	0	1	0
#6	23	47	2	3	11	3	8	8	4	3	1	5	3	2	0	0
#7	20	35	0	0	4	0	4	6	5	0	1	3	3	0	1	0
#8	23	36	0	0	7	7	0	8	3	2	3	1	1	0	2	0
#9	22	64	1	0	26	24	2	4	2	1	1	6	4	1	6	5
#10	23	44	2	3	12	8	4	4	0	1	3	2	1	1	1	1
#11	23	48	4	2	14	7	7	4	1	0	3	8	3	5	1	0
#12	23	52	0	0	8	3	5	10	6	2	2	8	4	4	1	1
#13	22	45	0	1	14	8	6	2	1	0	1	2	2	0	1	0
#14	23	52	1	3	15	3	12	3	3	0	0	6	4	2	1	0
#15	23	53	1	3	19	7	12	9	6	2	1	4	2	2	2	1
#16	23	69	0	3	33	10	23	8	4	3	1	4	2	2	1	0
#17	23	50	0	0	15	9	6	3	1	1	1	11	5	7	1	0
#18	23	33	0	0	3	2	1	5	2	0	3	6	3	3	0	0
#19	22	54	0	0	13	7	6	7	6	1	0	12	7	5	0	0
#20	23	56	0	0	20	13	7	9	4	1	4	2	1	1	0	0
#21	23	58	3	2	26	17	9	2	1	0	1	8	5	3	0	0
#22	22	39	0	0	7	2	5	4	2	0	2	7	4	3	0	0
#23	23	62	0	1	14	2	12	10	8	0	2	9	5	4	2	2
#24	23	40	1	0	8	4	4	4	4	0	0	7	2	5	1	1
#25	23	52	0	0	21	20	1	9	5	2	2	3	2	1	0	0
#26	23	51	2	0	15	8	7	8	7	0	1	5	2	3	1	1
#27	22	38	1	0	7	5	2	2	2	0	0	7	3	4	0	0
#28	23	40	0	0	9	2	7	5	3	0	2	3	3	0	0	0
#29	23	46	0	0	10	7	3	4	3	0	1	10	5	5	0	0
#30	23	37	0	0	3	2	1	10	4	2	4	4	2	2	0	0
#31	23	55	0	3	15	11	4	3	1	2	0	7	6	1	1	1
#32	23	63	3	1	19	17	2	4	2	0	2	14	9	5	2	2
#33	23	53	0	0	18	10	8	14	5	3	6	4	2	2	0	0
#34	23	42	0	0	11	5	6	6	4	0	2	0	0	0	0	0
#35	23	36	2	1	3	3	0	2	1	0	1	9	6	3	1	0
#36	23	56	0	3	23	20	3	9	3	3	3	3	1	2	0	0
#37	23	32	5	1	3	2	1	4	2	0	2	3	3	0	2	0

Table 12. Answers of the subjects to the subjective evaluation

Question 1	Question 2	Question 3	Question 4	Question 5	Question 6	Question 9
5	4	4	4	4	5	4
4	4	4	3	5	4	4
5	5	4	3	4	4	4
5	5	3	4	5	5	5
5	3	4	4	5	4	4
5	5	2	2	4	2	4
5	5	4	5	5	5	5
5	5	5	3	5	3	5
5	3	4	4	3	5	4
4	5	4	4	4	4	5
5	4	4	4	5	4	5
5	4	4	4	4	5	5
4	4	4	3	5	5	4
4	4	4	3	5	4	5
5	5	4	4	5	5	5
4	4	3	3	3	4	3
4	4	4	4	4	3	4
3	4	4	2	4	2	4
5	5	5	4	5	4	5
5	4	4	4	5	3	4
5	5	4	3	5	5	5
5	5	4	4	5	4	4
5	4	4	3	4	4	4
5	5	4	4	4	4	5
4	4	4	4	5	3	4
4	5	4	4	4	5	4
3	4	4	3	4	2	4
5	5	4	4	4	4	5
5	4	3	4	5	5	5
4	4	5	5	5	4	5
4	5	4	4	5	4	4
5	4	3	4	4	5	5
5	4	4	4	5	3	4
5	4	5	4	5	4	5
4	5	4	5	5	5	5
5	4	5	5	5	5	5

This work was previously published in International Journal of Ambient Computing and Intelligence, Volume 2, Issue 1, edited by Kevin Curran, pp. 24-51, copyright 2010 by IGI Publishing (an imprint of IGI Global).

Chapter 4
Spatio–Temporal Footprints

Hans W. Guesgen
Massey University, New Zealand

Stephen Marsland
Massey University, New Zealand

ABSTRACT

The recognition of human behaviour from sensor observations is an important area of research in smart homes and ambient intelligence. In this paper, we introduce the idea of spatio-temporal footprints, which are local patterns in space and time that should be similar across repeated occurrences of the same behaviour. We discuss the spatial and temporal mapping requirements of these footprints, together with how they may be used.

INTRODUCTION

A common task that an ambient intelligence system could be required to perform is recognising human behaviour from observations in the environment; this can be useful for a variety of applications from monitoring the activities of elderly patients to identifying appropriate lighting and heating conditions (Cook, 2006; Mozer, 2005). The observations on which such recognition is based can range from direct observations made by video cameras to indirect observations detected by sensors. Although video cameras give a more complete picture, and hence might lend

themselves more easily to recognising behaviours (with a consequent increase in the amount of computational processing required), it is often behaviour recognition based on sensors that is the preferred option, since the latter is less obtrusive and therefore more easily accepted in applications such as smart homes.

There is a significant body of research on behaviour recognition based on sensor data, which ranges from logic-based approaches to probabilistic machine learning approaches (Augusto & Nugent, 2004; Chua et al., 2009; Duong et al., 2005; Gopalratnam & Cook, 2004; Rivera-Illingworth et al., 2007; Tapia et al., 2004). Although the reported successes are promising, it has become clear that all approaches fall short of being perfect. Due to

DOI: 10.4018/978-1-4666-0038-6.ch004

Copyright © 2012, IGI Global. Copying or distributing in print or electronic forms without written permission of IGI Global is prohibited.

the limited information that is in the sensor data, noise, and the inherently complexity of human behaviours, it is often impossible to determine the correct behaviour from the sensor data alone, in particular if behaviours are overlapping or are being executed by more than one person.

Several researchers have realised that additional information can be useful to boost the behaviour recognition process (Aztiria et al., 2008; Jakkula & Cook, 2008; Tavenard et al., 2007). In this article, we focus on how spatio-temporal information, enriched with context information, can be used for this purpose. When a particular activity occurs, like preparing breakfast, it leaves a 'footprint' in space-time, i.e., a particular pattern of sensor observations in some set of locations over some period of time. The activity starts at some specific time and in some specific location, goes on for a specific duration in some specific area, and terminates at a specific time at some specific location. Since footprints differ from behaviour to behaviour—but often relatively little between different instances of the same behaviour—we can use these to inform the behaviour recognition process: if something is happening at 07:00 in the kitchen, it is more likely to be preparing breakfast than taking a shower. We can also use them to detect abnormal behaviour: if the inhabitant of the smart home uses the shower at 03:00 (when usually this is not a footprint that is seen), then this can be interpreted as abnormal.

Figure 1 shows an example of a possible set of footprints over three days, with a linear time axis that repeats each day, and a single space axis that could identify rooms, or similar (this is discussed in more detail in the next section). It can be seen that some behaviours repeat more-or-less identically over the three days, while others only occur once. The challenge with such representation of behaviour as footprints is to identify and recognise the various behaviours that are represented.

The rest of this article investigates the role of spatio-temporal footprints in more detail. We start with a discussion of what space-time means in the context of smart homes, arguing that there is more than one space-time (or more precisely, representation of space-time). We then look at how behaviours leave footprints in space-time and explore invariants in these footprints, with the goal of classifying different forms of invariants. Finally we will look into how the footprints are distributed in space-time and what influences this distribution.

SPACE-TIME

When reasoning about time, we usually associate a time axis with the data. The time axis might use a calendar as reference system and absolute dates/times to refer to points on the axis. Or it might use some artificial start point as zero time, such as the time when the smart home became operational, and some counter to advance time along the time axis. In the latter case, we would not be able to refer back to times before the birth of the smart home, while the first case would provide an infinite extension of time into both the past and the future.

As we will see later when discussing footprint invariants, it may sometimes be advantageous to view the time axis as a circular reoccurrence of time points. For example, if we are only interested in when behaviours occur during the day, then we might want to abstract from years, months, and days, which would leave us with references to times of the day. At the end of the day, we would 'warp' time and start at the beginning of the time axis again.

Independently of whether we use linear or circular time, we still have to decide whether we view time as continuous or discrete. For example, when referring to 13:00, do we really mean this exact point on a continuous time axis? If this is the case, then a behaviour that occurs one millisecond after this time point would not match 13:00, unless we allow for 'fuzzy' matches. On the other hand, if we view it as a discrete time

Figure 1. An example of space-time with footprints

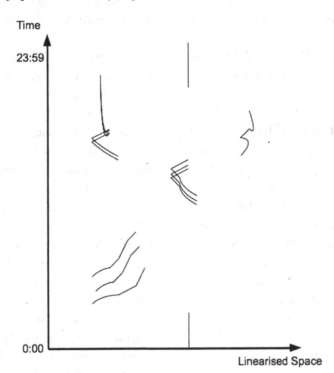

stamp, surrounded by, say, 12:55 and 13:05, then it would make sense to associate the behaviour with 13:00 rather than 12:55 or 13:05. This can be thought of as temporal 'resolution'.

Similar considerations can be made when referring to space. Although space is more complex than time (partially because we can move freely in space, but not in time), it has many similarities to time. In the simplest case, it has the same dimensionality, for example if we can move only along a predefined trajectory (Mukerjee & Joe, 1990). The trajectory can be viewed as continuous, in which case we would associate the distance from the origin with locations on the spatial axis, or it can be discrete, in which case we need a way to associate distances with reference points on the spatial axis.

As with time, we can envision different representations of space. Not only can we extend the dimensionality of space to two or three, we can also move away from a canonical Euclidean space to a more abstract space. For example, we can use the rooms of the smart home to define space points, or the areas covered by the sensors of the smart home. Given some knowledge of the physical locations of sensors, the house can infer that when sensor events occur, the house inhabitant must be in the physical vicinity of that sensor (obviously, there are exceptions to this for certain sensors such as thermometers, and for remote-controlled or time-controlled devices). The spatial pattern could then be some mapping between sensor locations, which could be based on the underlying physical layout of the house, but does not have to be.

The importance of this is that different resolutions can make recognition of particular footprints easier or more difficult. As the resolution becomes finer, footprints that appear to be exactly aligned start to separate, meaning that identifying them as examples of the same behaviour can require a clustering algorithm. Breakfast might not occur exactly at 08:00 each day, but it is likely that it happens at times that we associate with morning. Or reading a book might always occur in the lounge, but sometimes while sitting on the sofa and sometimes while lying back in an easy chair.

FOOTPRINT IDENTIFICATION

Each activity leaves a footprint in space-time (see Figure 1). If it is possible to determine mappings between footprints for the different instances of the same behaviour occurring in the smart home, then we can use that information to improve the behaviour recognition process. This section discusses what type of mappings we might usefully want to identify. There are effectively three different things that we might want to detect (where the first two are positive—examples of the same pattern—while the final one is negative):

- The same (or very similar) pattern occurring at the same time and place
- The same (or very similar) pattern occurring at different times and/or places
- Different patterns occurring at the same time and place as another

As an example of the first of these, consider the case that breakfast always takes place in the kitchen at 08:00. Then the mapping between this footprint on different days is simply the identity, as it leaves the same footprint in space-time each time it occurs. Of course, this assumes that we have chosen a suitable representation for space-time (e.g., one that only looks at the time of the day in a discrete way and uses the rooms of the smart home as spatial entities). It is unlikely that we observe this invariant very often, as it would require very rigid patterns of behaviour and a relatively abstract form of space-time.

The next type of transformation is that where we match patterns despite shifts in space-time.

Here we can distinguish among three different types of shift:

- Shifts on the time axis only
- Shifts on the space axes
- Shifts on all axes

For example, the afternoon tea break might occur at different times but always in the lounge (time-only shift), while the afternoon nap might occur always at the same time but either in the bedroom or in the lounge (space-only). An example of a (coupled) shift in space-time would be breakfast at the weekend: while breakfast during the week happens at 08:00 in the kitchen, it might be shifted to 10:00 in the dining room on Saturday and Sunday.

The particular footprint that identifies a behaviour caused by some set of sensors being activated in time. While we want some robustness to minor variation in the footprint, we need to be careful that just because two footprints occur in the same place and time, they are not necessarily the same event. To continue the breakfast analogy, a person working at home could go into the kitchen at 10:00 to make a cup of tea. This is not an example of them having a second breakfast (the weekend one), but a different behaviour that happens to occur at the same time and place.

There is one example of footprint change that we might need to be particularly careful about, which is the deformation of footprints in space-time. This again might be restricted to particular axes such as time, or might include all axes. We start the discussion of this by restricting ourselves to the time axis. The projection of a footprint onto the time axis is a time interval, consisting of a start point and an end point. We can restrict the deformation of the time interval to one of its boundaries, either the start or the end point, but not both. An example would be breakfast that always starts at 08:00 but might last between 10 and 20 minutes, or doing the dishes after dinner might start at any time, but always finishes in time to be ready for the soap opera on TV at 18:00. If we do not restrict ourselves to one of the boundaries, we obtain a deformation which (more or less) keeps the centre of the interval invariant. For example, taking a shower might always occur at around 20:00, starting about 10 minutes before that time and ending about 10 minutes after that time.

This same effect can be seen for space. In this case, we have to consider boundaries of regions in (usually) multi-dimensional space rather than start and end points of time intervals, which means that instead of considering two classes of deformation (one boundary vs. two boundaries), we have to consider an infinite number of classes. One way to achieve this is by determining the percentage of the boundary that stays the same and associating the behaviours with a finite set of classes that are given by a range of percentages. For example, we might want to distinguish just between those deformations that change more than 50% of the boundary and those that keep at least 50% of the boundary invariant.

It should be noted that our discussion of footprint invariants is closely related to the discussion around neighbourhood graphs in (Freksa, 1992), where Freksa introduces three forms of neighbourhood graphs for Allen's temporal logic (Allen, 1983). The graphs are based on shifts and two forms of deformations of time interval, in a way closely related to the one outlined above. Similar discussions can be found around the region connection calculus, which is used for reasoning about spatial relations (Randell et al., 1992).

Thus, we are lead to consider two related methods of footprint identification: identifying the same footprint occurring in different places in space-time, and distinguishing between different footprints that occur at the same place in space-time.

FOOTPRINT PROBABILITY DISTRIBUTIONS

The examples of the previous sections indicate that footprints are not necessarily distributed evenly in space-time. A straightforward way to find the distribution of footprints is to empirically approximate for each behaviour the probability of a footprint occurring at a particular location (or within a particular cluster) in space-time. This does not require any extra knowledge about the behaviour or about particular regions in space-time, but it does require enough data to approximate the probabilities within reasonable error margins.

As an alternative to this approach, we can analyse the regions occupied by a particular behaviour in space-time in order to find the distributions of the corresponding footprints. Breakfast on weekends as opposed to weekdays is an example for that, as illustrated previously. Obviously, the footprints are not distributed evenly over the two clusters, but have a higher density in the weekday breakfast cluster than in the weekend breakfast cluster. We know that there are five weekdays per week, but only two weekend days (for the average working person). Assuming that the breakfast behaviour occurs exactly once per day, we conclude that the probability of a breakfast footprint being in the weekend cluster of breakfast footprints is 2/7, whereas the probability of it being in the weekday one is 5/7. Taking this approach a step further, we can then compute conditional probabilities, which give us further insides into where a footprint is located in space-time. For example, if we know that a behaviour occurred on a weekday, then the conditional probability of it being in the weekday cluster is 1 (and 0 for the weekend cluster).

In general, this leads to an approach where context information is taken into consideration when behaviours are related to space-time footprints. In the example above, the context is of a spatio-temporal nature, but this does not have to be the case, as it can make sense to utilise other types of context information as well, such as:

- **Linked behaviours.** If a person has already had breakfast then they are unlikely to be having a second one, and if they have just had a shower they are unlikely to be having a bath. This kind of data can help to separate out the different footprints that might be recognised at the current time.
- **Environmental information.** If it is cold outside and not all rooms of the home are heated properly, then the footprints of certain behaviours might shift in space-time along the spatial axes. Rather than taking a meal in the dining room, the inhabitant might choose to have it in the lounge where there is a fireplace.
- **Personal information.** If the inhabitant is sick, he or she might choose to go to bed earlier than usual. This most likely has an effect on the footprints of events happening towards the end of the day, which would shift along the temporal axis.
- **Socio-economic information.** If there is a recession, the inhabitant might choose to save costs and therefore might decide to reduce the duration of hot showers. As a consequence, the footprint of that behaviour would be deformed.

Although in principle there is no limit to how much context information we use to get a better understanding of the relationship between behaviours and their space-time footprints, it is not practical to use context information excessively. Each bit of information requires us to explicitly model the correlation between the information and its impact on the behaviour–footprint relation, which requires a significant amount of world knowledge. In other words, we trade off the need for sufficient training data against the need for explicit modelling.

CONCLUSION

We have presented a representation of behaviours as patterns of activity in space-time, where each behaviour is represented as a trajectory of sensor events over some relatively short time window. It is hoped that by representing the behaviours in this way, individual behaviours will be more clearly recognised despite translation in space, time, or both. Additionally, it may give a useful pictorial representation of events that enables a carer to analyse the actions of a person and identify abnormal events once the smart home has raised an alarm.

Some of the challenges of recognising and using such footprints are caused by the natural variability between different instances of the same behaviour. We have discussed this in the context of things taking slightly more or less time, and the location changing, but it is also the case for different orderings of the actions within a behaviour. The extent to which this is a problem will have to be examined once we are able to use real data to examine the footprint pattern.

REFERENCES

Allen, J. (1983). Maintaining knowledge about temporal intervals. *Communications of the ACM, 26*, 832–843. doi:.doi:10.1145/182.358434

Augusto, J., & Nugent, C. (2004). The use of temporal reasoning and management of complex events in smart homes. In *Proceedings of ECAI-04,* Valencia, Spain (pp. 778-782).

Aztiria, A., Augusto, J., Izaguirre, A., & Cook, D. (2008). Learning accurate temporal relations from user actions in intelligent environments. In *Proc. 3rd Symposium of Ubiquitous Computing and Ambient Intelligence.*

Chua, S.-L., Marsland, S., & Guesgen, H. (2009). Spatio-temporal and context reasoning in smart homes. In *Proceedings of the COSIT-09 Workshop on Spatial and Temporal Reasoning for Ambient Intelligence Systems*, Aber Wrac'h, France (pp. 9-20).

Cook, D. (2006). Health monitoring and assistance to support aging in place. *Journal of Universal Computer Science, 12*(1), 15–29.

Duong, T., Bui, H., Phung, D., & Venkatesh, S. (2005). Activity recognition and abnormality detection with the switching hidden semi-Markov model. In. *Proceedings of, CVPR-05*, 838–845.

Freksa, C. (1992). Temporal reasoning based on semi-intervals. *Artificial Intelligence, 54*, 199–227. doi:10.1016/0004-3702(92)90090-K

Gopalratnam, K., & Cook, D. (2004). Active LeZi: An incremental parsing algorithm for sequential prediction. *International Journal of Artificial Intelligence Tools, 14*(1-2), 917–930. doi:10.1142/S0218213004001892

Jakkula, V., & Cook, D. (2008). Anomaly detection using temporal data mining in a smart home environment. *Methods of Information in Medicine, 47*(1), 70–75.

Mozer, M. (2005). Lessons from an adaptive house. In Cook, D., & Das, R. (Eds.), *Smart environments: Technologies, protocols, and applications* (pp. 273–294).

Mukerjee, A., & Joe, G. (1990). A qualitative model for space. *In Proceedings of AAAI-90*, Boston (pp. 721-727).

Randell, D., Cui, Z., & Cohn, A. (1992). A spatial logic based on regions and connection. *In Proceedings of KR-92*, Cambridge, MA (pp. 165-176).

Rivera-Illingworth, F., Callaghan, V., & Hagras, H. (2007). Detection of normal and novel behaviours in ubiquitous domestic environments. *The Computer Journal*.

Tapia, E., Intille, S., & Larson, K. (2004). Activity recognition in the home using simple and ubiquitous sensors. In *Proceedings of PERVASIVE-04*, Vienna, Austria (pp. 158-175).

Tavenard, R., Salah, A., & Pauwels, E. (2007). Searching for temporal patterns in ami sensor data. In *Proceedings of Am, I2007*, 53–62.

This work was previously published in International Journal of Ambient Computing and Intelligence, Volume 2, Issue 1, edited by Kevin Curran, pp. 52-58, copyright 2010 by IGI Publishing (an imprint of IGI Global).

Chapter 5

iCampus:
A Connected Campus in the Ambient Event Calculus

Stefano Bromuri
Royal Holloway University of London, UK

Visara Urovi
Royal Holloway University of London, UK

Kostas Stathis
Royal Holloway University of London, UK

ABSTRACT

iCampus is a prototype multi-agent system whose goal is to provide the ambient intelligence required to connect people in a university campus and make that campus inclusive and accessible. Software agents called guides run on mobile phones to help students with information about people, places, and events, thus providing people real-time, location-based advice that makes them more aware of what is going on in the campus. The work outlines how to specify iCampus in the Ambient Event Calculus and implement it using the agent environment GOLEM to deploy guide agents over a campus network. The work is illustrated by showing how iCampus improves the mobility of blind or partially sighted students within a campus, which has been the main motivation behind the work.

1. INTRODUCTION

John is a visually impaired university student in his 1st year. Although his university is small, the university's campus has 72 areas between buildings and park areas in which John has to learn to find his way. During term time, teaching takes place in different buildings and, many times, John has to move quickly from a building to another in order to find his way to the classroom. Once he finds the classroom, he may have to wait outside the class until the previous lecture has finished and once the class is empty, enter the room and find out where to sit.

Many tasks can be complicated for John and the practice so far has been to assign to him a helper,

DOI: 10.4018/978-1-4666-0038-6.ch005

Copyright © 2012, IGI Global. Copying or distributing in print or electronic forms without written permission of IGI Global is prohibited.

typically another student. However helpers are not constantly present, therefore John relies mostly on his memory and on people nearby. Due to the fact that he has only partial information about his surroundings he is faced with problems such as how to find a new building or a classroom, especially if the map and the information board in the entrance of the building are not accessible. He is also facing problems such as how to find where his best friend is standing in the class, including deciding when to enter the class and where to sit.

We study how to use Ambient Intelligence (Sadri & Stathis, 2008) to help people like John. For this purpose we are experimenting with *iCampus*, an ambient intelligence system where John downloads a guide, a software agent that works proactively to help the student with its everyday activities within the campus. His activities typically involve discovering the current location of friends, places, and events within the campus, not necessarily only teaching. As a result of using *iCampus*, John is able to find the location of lectures, people who are nearby but he cannot see, building entrances and other information that can help him within the campus.

iCampus assumes a mobile phone with GPS and bluetooth capabilities based on a campus map. In the case of John the mobile is equipped with an additional screen reader library, which reads to him the information that is visualised on the screen of the phone. When John is outdoors, the *iCampus* uses the GPS service to provide him information about the outdoor environment, while indoors the campus contains access points that provide indoor information using the bluetooth services of his mobile device.

In the remainder of the paper we first discuss the *iCampus* concept and how a user can interact with the application, then we show how we have organised the interaction of guide agents in the GOLEM platform, where we also outline our current implementation. We conclude with an evaluation of the application and our plans for future work.

2. THE CONCEPT OF *ICAMPUS*

iCampus maps the physical environment of a campus to an electronic environment with people's avatars, guide agents, places, events, and objects (Stathis et al., 2005). The kind of information offered on demand by *iCampus* agents include discovery of people e.g. a friend, identification of the location of places and objects within them e.g. a building or a board in a room, and happening of events e.g. whether a lecture has started or not. *iCampus* also supports requests that provide functionalities such as path finding, alerts for the user and personalisation operations which allows the user to specialise the application with his/her own profile (Mamdani et al., 1999).

"Who is around" queries allow the user to see other people that are nearby. Locality is based on the location of the user and the specified radius for the area of interest. Users can see each other if they make available their position to others. Figure 1 shows how John searches his friend Visara. John can locate Visara because she has published her location as visible. Similarly, "What is around" queries examine the current place of the user including objects such as electronic boards, projectors, or sub-places such as rooms, corridors, and lecture theatres. Once people, places, or objects have been discovered, "Where is" queries find the exact location of a person, place, or object. Once an object/user is localised, *iCampus* provides any additional information that is associated to it. As shown below, for brevity of interaction "Who is around" and "What is around" can be combined to one query.

Additional features of *iCampus*, include: "Guide me to", which provides information about how to move from the current location to a destination one, "Alert me about", which allows a user to register about events of interest in the campus, and "my *iCampus*", which allows a user to personalise the system according to a user's needs. An example combining all these features includes John who uses "Alert me about" inau-

Figure 1. Screen shots of a mobile phone running iCampus. The first (leftmost) shows how a user runs a "Who & what is around" query, the second shows the results, and the third and fourth the names of people and buildings respectively.

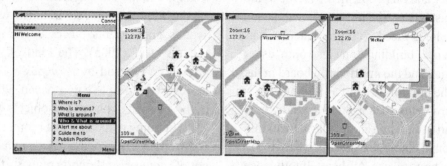

gural lectures and listens to only the accessible routes using "Guide me to" because he has specified on "my *iCampus*" that he is partially sighted.

Figure 2 shows how John requests "Guide me to" that will allow John to be guided to a location of interest. The path returned consists of a set of important reference points, which are read to John in order to guide him to the desired location.

Other items in the menu of *iCampus* allow the user to state his coordinates in the campus by

selecting "Publish Position" and disconnect from the system, if required, by selecting "Disconnect".

3 *ICAMPUS* IN THE AMBIENT EVENT CALCULUS

We represent the physical environment of a campus with a distributed agent environment represented in the Ambient Event Calculus (AEC) (Bromuri & Stathis, 2009). This framework provides a formalism that allows us to perform distributed queries

Figure 2. Screen shots of the "Guide me to query".

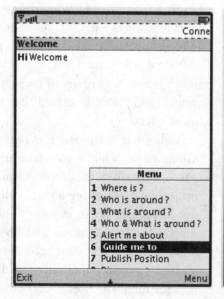

on the distributed agent environment and allows a developer to specify users or software agent interactions over a distributed network. The AEC assumes a number of system entities as follows.

- **Containers:** These entities represent a portion of the distributed agent environment running on a particular host computer, which in *iCampus* represent places in the map. They also mediate the interactions between entities running or better contained in it, such as users, agents, and other objects, whose interactions are specified in terms of events (Bromuri & Stathis, 2009). We organise the campus as a distributed tree of containers, where every container represents a key place in the campus. Outdoors, the users connect to the computers where containers are running by using their own mobile devices. When users are indoors, they are considered to be components in sub-places represented by sub-containers. For example consider a classroom (a sub-place) contained in the first floor (a sub-container) of a building in the campus (a container).

- **Avatars and Agents**: In *iCampus* we make use of software agents (Stathis & Toni, 2004) to make the ambient intelligent. Users connect their mobiles to a container by means of an avatar that forms part of the campus electronic environment. The interface enables the user to query the system using the operations as it was shown in the previous section. In *iCampus* we require three types of agents to support the user: (a) *avatars* that are allow users to have presence in the virtual environment, (b) *guides* that are the personal agents specific to a user and (c) *location agents* that can answer queries regarding the information held in a container.

- **Objects**: passive reactive entities representing resources available to agents and

avatars in a topology of containers. In the particular case of *iCampus*, objects represent external resources with a virtual presence like a projector or databases available to agents to proactively alert avatars and other agents about their personal schedule in outdoor and indoor environments. Moreover, in indoor environments objects can represent bluetooth connections to a particular host where a container is deployed.

We have used the Ambient Event Calculus to specify a platform for distributed agent environments called GOLEM (Bromuri & Stathis, 2007). GOLEM supports the deployment of containers, agents, avatars, and objects over a network. In particular, GOLEM enables inter-agent communication via message passing and interaction of agents with objects as well as agent mobility. We have used the deployment functionality of GOLEM to implement the required agent interactions in *iCampus*. Figure 3 shows the deployment of four containers representing places of buildings and rooms in the *iCampus* system.

In particular, GOLEM supports the hierarchical deployment of containers organised in a distributed topology. This topology represents all the physical locations of host computers where containers are needed to capture campus interactions. Given such a topology, queries in GOLEM are specified in the logic-based language supported by the AEC. We have tested our implementation on a specific campus network utilising host computers that run containers for one building and a GPS enabled Samsung Omnia HD8910 for which we developed a J2ME client for the user to connect to GOLEM. Using this implementation, to locate the position of someone that is currently connected to the network we use a query of the form shown in Box 1.

Such queries make use of the primitive predicates of the AEC such as neighbouring_at/9, which allows the developer to specify queries

Figure 3. GOLEM containers topology in iCampus

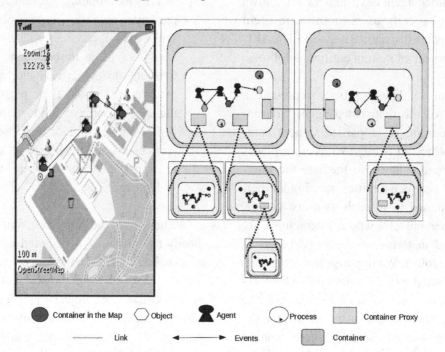

from one container to neighbouring containers in order to discover the position Pos (longitude and latitude) of an avatar identified by a Name and a Surname. A detailed description of the AEC functionality is outside the scope of this paper; the interested reader is referred to Bromuri and Stathis (2009).

4 CONCLUSION AND FUTURE WORK

iCampus is a prototype multi-agent system providing the ambient intelligence required for an inclusive and accessible campus. In this short presentation we have presented the main concept behind *iCampus* and illustrated how it can be used to help partially sighted students with information about buildings, objects, and people, by giving them real time location-based advice, and thus making them more aware of what is going on in the campus. We have also specified part of the current status of the *iCampus* in the Ambient Event Calculus, the platform GOLEM, and the combination of GOLEM with the GPS technologies and mobile phones.

Previous attempts to combine GPS technologies with mobile phones has been proposed by the Loadstone and WayFinder projects. Loadstone

Box 1.

```
whereis(Name, Surname, Radius, place, Pos, T) ←
neighbour_instance_of(C, Path, Path*, Radius, Id, avatar, T),
neighbouring_at(C, Path, Path*, Radius, Id, avatar, name, Name, T),
neighbouring_at(C, Path, Path*, Radius, Id, avatar, name, Surname, T),
neighbouring_at(C, Path, Path*, Radius, Id, avatar, position, Pos, T).
```

(2009) uses a GPS bluetooth receiver to guide users through geographical locations. Where no GPS is available, the user can monitor cellular phone sites for knowing roughly his or her position. WayFinder Access (2009) on the other hand is based on map systems and updated databases to provide information for pedestrians and vehicular navigation about locations of interest and proximity information. Other systems, like Hub et al. (2004), Ra et al. (2004), and Ros and Blasch (2000) focus on enhancing the perception range of the visually impaired users in the immediate surroundings, using wearable interfaces, or improving the capabilities of the cane by means of tactile or sound information according to the obstacles in the environment.

We focus on a high-level representation of a virtual environment, where the user is guided indoors/outdoors as in Loadstone with the additional feature of personalisation through intelligent agents that adapt responses according to the user's needs. Moreover, our system is distributed and updating does not involve the modification of a centralised database as in WayFinder. Our approach is orthogonal to Hub et al. (2004), Ran et al. (2004), and Ros and Blasch (2000) that are easily integrated in our system.

Future work involves extending our guide agents to plan paths using the techniques described in Stathis and Toni (2004), enable agents to set up alerts for users, and consider the architecture that would allow GOLEM containers to be deployed in mobile devices.

ACKNOWLEDGMENT

We wish to thank Samsung UK for letting us have their latest mobile phone software for Samsung Omnia HD8910 where we carried out our experimentation. Without their help, the work reported here would not have been possible.

REFERENCES

Bromuri, S., & Stathis, K. (2007). Situating Cognitive Agents in GOLEM. In *Engineering Environment-Mediated Multi-Agent Systems* (LNCS 5049, pp. 115-134).

Bromuri, S., & Stathis, K. (2009). Distributed Agent Environments in the Ambient Event Calculus. In *DEBS '09: Proceedings of the 3rd International Conference on Distributed Event-Based Systems* (pp. 1-12). New York: ACM Publishing.

Hub, A., Diepstraten, J., & Ertl, T. (2004). Design and development of an indoor navigation and object identification system for the blind. In *Assets '04: Proceedings of the 6th International ACM SIGACCESS Conference on Computers and Accessibility* (pp. 147-152). New York: ACM Publishing.

Loadstone. (2009). *Loadstone Project*. Retrieved October, 28, 2009, from http://www.loadstone-gps.com/

Mamdani, A., Pitt, J., & Stathis, K. (1999). Connected Communities from the standpoint of Multi-agent Systems. *New Generation Computing*, *17*(4), 381–393. .doi:10.1007/BF03037244

Ran, L., Helal, S., & Moore, S. (2004). Drishti: An Integrated Indoor/Outdoor Blind Navigation System and Service. In *PERCOM '04: Proceedings of the Second IEEE International Conference on Pervasive Computing and Communications* (pp. 23). Washington, DC: IEEE Computer Society.

Ross, D. A., & Blasch, B. B. (2000). Wearable interfaces for orientation and wayfinding. In *Assets '00: Proceedings of the Fourth International ACM Conference on Assistive Technologies* (pp. 193-200). New York: ACM Publishing.

Sadri, F., & Stathis, K. (2008). Ambient Intelligence . In Rabunal Dopico, J. R., Dorado, J., & Pazos, A. (Eds.), *Encyclopaedia of Artificial Intelligence*. Hershey, PA: Information Science Reference. doi:10.4018/978-1-59904-849-9.ch013

Stathis, K., Spence, R., Bruijn, O. D., & Purcell, P. (2005). Ambient Intelligence: Agents and Interaction in Connected Communities . In Purcell, P. (Ed.), *The Networked Neighbourhood*. Springer.

Stathis, K., & Toni, F. (2004). Ambient Intelligence using KGP Agents. In *Proceedings of the 2nd European Symposium for Ambient Intelligence*, Eindhoven, The Netherlands (pp. 351-362). Berlin, Germany: Springer-Verlang.

WayFinder. (2009). *Wayfinder access*. Retrieved October 28, 2009, from http://www.wayfinder.com

ENDNOTE

[1] In the logic-based representation of GOLEM the number following the backslash "/" after a predicate name indicates the number of parameters required for the predicate.

This work was previously published in International Journal of Ambient Computing and Intelligence, Volume 2, Issue 1, edited by Kevin Curran, pp. 59-65, copyright 2010 by IGI Publishing (an imprint of IGI Global).

Chapter 6
How Intelligent are Ambient Intelligence Systems?

María J. Santofimia
University of Castilla-La Mancha, Spain

Francisco Moya
University of Castilla-La Mancha, Spain

Félix J. Villanueva
University of Castilla-La Mancha, Spain

David Villa
University of Castilla-La Mancha, Spain

Juan C. López
University of Castilla-La Mancha, Spain

ABSTRACT

Since the appearance of the Ambient Intelligence paradigm, as an evolution of the Ubiquitous Computing, a great deal of the research efforts in this field have been mainly aimed at anticipating user actions and needs, out of a prefixed set. However, Ambient Intelligence is not just constrained to user behaviour pattern matching, but to wisely supervise the whole environment, satisfying those unforeseen requirements or needs, by means of rational decisions. This work points at the lack of commonsense reasoning, as the main reason underlying the existance of these idiots savant systems, capable of accomplishing very specific and complex tasks, but incapable of making decisions out of the prefixed behavioral patterns. This work advocates for the integration of the commonsense reasoning and understanding capabilities as the key elements in bridging the gap between idiot savant systems and real Ambient Intelligence systems.

1. INTRODUCTION

The Ubiquitous Computing concept was first defined by Mark Weiser (1995) as a new computing era where electronic devices merge into the background, becoming invisible, in such a way that people could make use of those devices in an unconsciously way, focusing just on their needs and not in the interaction.

One decade later, the IST Advisory Group first stated the concept of Ambient Intelligence (Ducatel et al., 2001), which builds on the Ubiquitous Computing paradigm where people are

DOI: 10.4018/978-1-4666-0038-6.ch006

Copyright © 2012, IGI Global. Copying or distributing in print or electronic forms without written permission of IGI Global is prohibited.

surrounded by all kind of intelligent intuitive devices, capable of recognizing and responding to their changing needs. In these contexts, people perceive the surrounding as a service provider that satisfies their needs or inquiries in a seamless, unobtrusive, and invisible way. Therefore, these contexts have to be supported on a service-oriented architecture capable of dealing with the device heterogeneity and service dynamism, exhibited in these contexts. Nevertheless, the state of the art in Ambient Intelligence, demonstrates that these are well addressed issues, by any of the flavored service-oriented architectures, in the form of an OSGi framework, such in the case of the AMIGO project (2009), web services such as in the Hydra project (2009), middleware technology as in the approach proposed in Villanueva et al. (2009), or a Multi-Agent System such as in the CHIL project (2009). However, there are some other aspects of the Ambient Intelligence that have not been so effectively addressed as the previous ones. Aspects such as the ambiguity, uncertainty, or incompleteness of the context information, prevent Ambient Intelligence systems from being fully context-driven. In the words of Lenat et al. (1990), bottlenecks arise when systems attempt to respond to unexpected situations. This happens to be the most common situations found in Ambient Intelligence contexts. How people react to these unexpected situations provides an idea about the direction where efforts are to be addressed. Generally, when facing novel situations we tend to establish some similarities with past experiences, or resort to the general knowledge about how things work (so-called commonsense), or even look for advice in books, for instance. In any case, Lenat et al. (1990), believe that only Ambient Intelligence systems will be flexible enough to support the scenarios envisioned in Ducatel et al. (2001) when commonsense reasoning starts being considered an structural part of such systems. Automating commonsense reasoning is a task that requires an expressive enough language, a knowledge base where to store such a large

amount of knowledge, and a set of mechanisms capable of manipulating this knowledge, so as to infer new information. Regarding the knowledge base, Cyc (Lenat, 1995) and WordNet (Fellbaum, 1998) are by far the most evolved and sucessful approaches. However, Cyc is the most complete, in terms of the amount of comprising facts, the representation language used –CycL–, and the mechanisms provided to infer and reason upon the stated knowledge, based on planning, deduction, and rules. Essentially, Ambient Intelligence challenges demand a high level of autonomy and self-sufficiency, and this work analyzes how an approach based on Cyc could bridge the gap that prevent Ambient Intelligence systems from being intelligent. Therefore, the remainder of this article is committed to this justification. Section 2 revises the state of the art of Ambient Intelligence systems, so as to identify the main shortcomings, and how these can be overcome by adopting a commonsense approach. Section 3 analyzes the benefits of an approach based on Cyc. Finally, last section outlines the conclusions that can be derived from this work.

2. AN ONTOLOGY FOR AMBIENT INTELLIGENCE

The previous section pointed out commonsense reasoning as a means to support systems capability to react to unexpected situations. However, before getting into the details about how these tasks are performed, we set the basis for the knowledge representation task, prior to tackling the reasoning one. This knowledge engineering task (Brachman et al., 2004) can be summarized so as to identify the relevant entities, their properties and their relationships one to each other, or in other words, providing an ontology for the application domain.

The importance of providing an ontology for Ambient Intelligence is twofold. On the one hand, it unifies the vocabulary used to describe the domain knowledge, by stating the type of objects that

Figure 1. An ontology for ambient intelligence

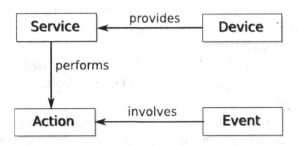

play an important role in the domain, their properties and relationships. Moreover, interoperability among the different architectural elements of an Ambient Intelligence system draws on this unified vocabulary. On the other hand, providing an ontology allows that information modelled by means of this ontology can be automatically plugged into large bodies of knowledge, and therefore logically related (Taylor et al., 2007). As will be explained later, this is one of the many strengths of Cyc, the possibility of plugging ontologies into the knowledge base in an automatic fashion.

The work found in the literature related to ontologies for Ambient Intelligence, commonly assign a key role to the user concept. In Preuveneers et al. (2004) the ontology proposed clearly focuses on the role played by the user. This approach is founded on Dey et al. (2001) where only context information that affects users is being considered. An extensive survey can be found at Chen et al. (2005). Based on these, we believe that although being important, the user concept should not be part of the ontology. Basically, users tend to be either the agents of the actions that take place in the contexts, or the sink of the services provides by the Ambient Intelligence system. Moreover, due to the eminently service-oriented character of Ambient Intelligence systems, it is sensible to advocate for an ontology where the focus is on the service concept.

Based on these premises, Figure 1 depicts the proposed ontology for an Ambient Intelligence domain. The *device* concept represent the devices

deployed in the domain. These devices provide a set of *services*, represented by the concept *service*. Furthermore, each service perform *actions*, represented by the concept *action*. Finally, the *events* taking place in the context are represented by the concept *event*. Although quite simple, this ontology suffices to reason about the actions that need to be performed in response to the events taking place in the context.

3. AUTOMATIC SERVICE COMPOSITION

One of the main challenges that have to be faced by ambient systems is how to provide the right services that meet the requirements emerging in the context. So far, this work has pointed out that an approach based on commonsense reasoning could provide these systems with the flexibility and dynamism required to support these sort of decisions. However, little has yet being said about how to capture the results of the reasoning task into services or actions to be performed, apart from the interoperability support provided by the ontology. Since the services provided by the ambient system comprise the basic available tools to implement the solution, supporting service composition seems to be the best approach to answer to these context or user requirements and needs.

This solution has been addressed by means of a wide range of technologies, refer to Urbieta et al. (2008) for an extensive survey of dynamic service composition approaches for Ambient Systems. However, the most popular and widely implemented approach is the Web Services technology. Nevertheless, independently of the selected approach, there are some commonalities regarding the information required to support the composition task. The service description provides information for the service identification, while the binding information refers to the requirements for the composition process, such as protocol-dependant details. For example, web services uses WSDL (Christensen et al., 2001) (Web Services Description Language) for describing the service, exposing the messages that can be exchanged with the service, as well as the binding information that contains the protocol specific details. The composition process starts by locating the services that offer a required functionality, by matching the service descriptions. For example, webservices can be discovered using UDDI (Newcomer, 2002) (Universal Description, Discovery and Integration). Once the appropriate services are identified, and the binding requirements are fullfilled, services can be bound.

Despite being considered automatic or dynamic, the approaches provided to date require some higher level entity addressing the requirements of the services taking part in the composition. Furthermore, only basic services are considered, ignoring the possibility of performing some modifications over the available services that provide extra functionalities. Therefore, it is more correct to refer to these approaches as service binding or combination, rather than composition.

Requirements for automatic service composition (Meyer and Kuropka, 2006) lead us to conclude that only by an appropriate middleware architecture can services be automatically composed. Therefore, the work in Santofimia et al. (2008) claims for an approach based on the combination of a Distributed Object-Based Service architecture (Villanueva et al., 2009) and a Multi-Agent System approach to support service composition. Adopting this solution seems to ef-fectively meet the requirements to implement the services that respond to the user and context needs.

4. CYC FOR AMBIENT INTELLIGENCE

It is evident that exhibiting an autonomous and self-suffcient behavior needs to be founded on the knowledge about how things work, and eventually, in the capability of making decisions based on that knowledge. In this regard, the dramatic advances achieved by Cyc uphold it as the most promising approach to provide Ambient Systems with the *intelligence* and flexibility required when dealing with unforeseen scenarios.

This section goes through those aspects of the Cyc system that make it the most appropriate choice. To start with, one of these aspects refers to how events are handled in Cyc. If events are the basic elements that describe how contexts evolve, it is obvious that an appropriate theory is required in order to efficiently represent that knowledge.

Cyc implements a Davidsonian (Davidson, 2006) interpretation of events and actions. In the knowledge base, events are asserted as individuals about which facts can be stated, so as to specify the moment in time when the event took place, the location, or the performer agent, for instance.

Theories of actions and events have been closely related to those of planning, so as to talk about *action planning*, supported on theoretical frameworks, as the one proposed in Hommel et al. (2001). Moreover, goals play an essential role in achieving the autonomy and self-sufficiency, so many times referred here. On the basis of these goals, the system behavior is determined by those actions that work towards the achievement of these goals. How these actions are selected is the responsibility of the planner, based on the information held in the knowledge base.

The planning problem has been traditionally stated in terms of a description of the world, or initial state, the goal to be achieved and the possible actions that can be performed at that initial state. Needless to say, the action descriptions are specified in terms of prerequisites that are to be satisfied so as to perform the action, and the effects of executing the action. The Cyc planner is an extended version of the SHOP (Nau et al., 1999) system, that has been optimized to reason about actions and events.

It has to be remarked that both, events and planning, are the most appealing features in advocating for an approach based on Cyc. Combining these features with the proposed ontology and the middleware framework for Ambient Systems, it is possible to compose a plan, as a set of actions performed by services, that lead the system to satisfy, achieve, or maintain any of the goals that the Ambient System is committed to.

5. CONCLUSION

As an step towards real intelligent systems, this work advocates for an approach based on commonsense reasoning to drive the system behavior in response to the events taking place in the context. However, the commonsense reasoning capability cannot be considered, on its own, as the silver bullet for Ambient Systems, since without an extensive knowledge base that gathers the knowledge about the everyday life, reasoning capabilities can be of a little help.

The Cyc knowledge base seems to overcome this drawback, providing a large knowledge base, with roughly 3.5 millions of assertions, at the moment of writing this article. Along with such as an extensive amount of knowledge, it also provides an exceptional way of managing the events that take place in Ambient Intelligence contexts, that, combined with an event-optimized planner, envisions the Cyc system as the backbone of the Ambient Systems that are to come.

Finally, the main contribution of this work is not only constrained to advocate the integration of Cyc, but it also proposes an ontology for modeling Ambient Systems and a middleware architecture,

intended to support the service composition, considered an essential requirement to exhibiting an autonomous and intelligent behavior.

ACKNOWLEDGMENT

This work has been funded by the Spanish Ministry of Industry under project CENIT Hesperia.

REFERENCES

AMIGO. (2009). *The Amigo Project*. Retrieved October 27, 2009, from http://www.hitech-projects.com/euprojects/amigo

Brachman, R., & Levesque, H. (2004). *Knowledge Representation and Reasoning (The Morgan Kaufmann Series in Artificial Intelligence)*. San Francisco: Morgan Kaufmann.

Chen, H., Finin, T., & Joshi, A. (2005). The SOUPA ontology for pervasive computing. In *Ontologies for Agents: Theory and Experiences* (pp. 233-258). Basel, Switzerland: Birkhäuser Basel.

CHIL. (2009). *The CHIL project*. Retrieved October 27, 2009, from http://chil.server.de

Christensen, E., Curbera, F., Meredith, G., & Weerawarana, S. (2001). Web service definition language (wsdl). Retrieved from http://www.w3.org/TR/wsdl

Davidson, D. (2006). *The Essential Davidson*. New York: Oxford University Press.

Dey, A. K., Abowd, G. D., & Salber, D. A. (2001). A conceptual framework and a toolkit for supporting the rapid prototyping of context-aware applications. *Human-Computer Interaction, 16*(2), 97–166..doi:10.1207/S15327051HCI16234_02

Ducatel, K., Bogdanowicz, M., Scapolo, F., Leijten, J., & Burgelman, J. C. (2001). *Scenarios for ambient intelligence in 2010*. Brussels, Belgium: ISTAG.

Fellbaum, C. (1998). *WordNet: An Electronic Lexical Database (Language, Speech, and Communication)*. Cambridge, MA: MIT Press.

Hommel, B., Musseler, J., Aschersleben, G., & Prinz, W. (2001). The theory of event coding (TEC): A framework for perception and action planning. *The Behavioral and Brain Sciences*, *24*, 849–878. doi:10.1017/S0140525X01000103

Hydra. (2009). The Hydra project. Retrieved October 27, 2009, from http://www.hydramiddleware.eu

Lenat, D. B. (1995). CYC: A large-scale investment in knowledge infrastructure. *Communications of the ACM*, *38*(11), 33–38.. doi:10.1145/219717.219745

Lenat, D. B., Guha, R. V., Pittman, K., Pratt, D., & Shepherd, M. (1990). CYC: Toward programs with common sense. *Communications of the ACM*, *33*(8), 30–49. doi:10.1145/79173.79176

Meyer, H., & Kuropka, D. (2006). Requirements for automated service composition. In *Proceedings of the Business Process Management Workshops* (pp. 447-458).

Nau, D., Cao, Y., Lotem, A., & Muftoz-Avila, H. (1999). Shop: Simple hierarchical ordered planner. In *IJCAI'99: Proceedings of the 16th International Joint Conference on Artificial Intelligence* (pp. 968-973). San Francisco: Morgan Kaufmann.

Newcomer, E. (2002). *Understanding Web Services: XML, WSDL, SOAP and UDDI*. Reading, MA: Addison-Wesley.

Preuveneers, D., Van den Bergh, J., Wagelaar, D., Georges, A., Rigole, P., Tim Clerckx, T., et al. (2004). Towards an Extensible Context Ontology for Ambient Intelligence. In *Ambient Intelligence* (LNCS 3295, pp. 148-159).

Santofimia, M. J., Moya, F., Villanueva, F. J., Villa, D., & Lopez, J. C. (2008). Integration of intelligent agents supporting automatic service composition in ambient intelligence. In *Proceedings of the IEEE/WIC/ACM International Conference on Web Intelligence and Intelligent Agent Technology* (Vol. 2, pp. 504-507).

Taylor, M. E., Matuszek, C., Klimt, B., & Witbrock, M. J. (2007). Autonomous classification of knowledge into an ontology. In *Proceedings of the FLAIRS Conference* (pp. 140-145).

Urbieta, A., Barrutieta, G., Parra, J., & Uribarren, A. (2008). A survey of dynamic service composition approaches for ambient systems. In *SOMITAS '08: Proceedings of the 2008 Ambi-Sys workshop on Software Organisation and MonIToring of Ambient Systems*, Brussels, Belgium (pp. 1-8). ICST (Institute for Computer Sciences, Social-Informatics and Telecommunications Engineering).

Villanueva, F. J., Moya, F., Rincon, F., Santofimia, M. J., Villa, D., & Barba, J. (2009). Towards a unified middleware for ubiquitous and pervasive computing. *International Journal of Ambient Computing and Intelligence*, *1*(1), 53–63. doi:10.4018/jaci.2009010105

Villanueva, F. J., Villa, D., Santofimia, M. J., Moya, F., & Lopez, J. C. (2009). *A framework for advanced home service design and management*. Paper presented at the International Conference on Consumer Electronics.

Weiser, M. (1995). The computer for the 21st century. In *Human-computer interaction: Toward the year 2000* (pp. 933–940). San Francisco: Morgan Kaufmann.

This work was previously published in International Journal of Ambient Computing and Intelligence, Volume 2, Issue 1, edited by Kevin Curran, pp. 66-72, copyright 2010 by IGI Publishing (an imprint of IGI Global).

Chapter 7
Interaction *Per Se*:
Understanding "The Ambience of Interaction" as Manifested and Situated in Everyday & Ubiquitous IT-Use

Mikael Wiberg
Umeå University, Sweden

ABSTRACT

Interaction is a core concept in the fields of Ubiquitous computing, Ambient systems design, and generally in the fields of HCI and Interaction Design. Despite this, a lack of knowledge about the fundamental character of interaction still exists. Researchers have explored interaction from the viewpoints of user-centered design and design of graphical user interfaces, where interaction stands for the link between technology and humans or denotes the use aspect. A framework is proposed for exploring interaction as a design space in itself between a human and the technology. It is proposed that this framework for interaction as a design space for Interaction Design, in which the very form of the in-between, the interaction, be explicitly targeted. It is an opportunity to go beyond user and usability studies to seek answers to fundamental questions concerning the form and character of interaction as implemented in today's interactive systems. Moreover, this framework is an opportunity to expand and explain a new design space for Interaction Design. The proposed framework, anchored in two exemplifying cases, illustrates the character and the form of interaction as it situates itself in online, ubiquitous and everyday IT use.

INTRODUCTION

The ambience of interaction as the seamless flow of turn-takings between people and computational materials highly integrated in our everyday lives is a fundamental and crucial aspect for any practical design and use of interactive systems. As new digital technologies are rapidly blending themselves into our everyday lives to the extent that they are becoming inseparable, ambient and ubiquitous we need a fundamental grounded understanding of this ambient character of interaction per se as it situate itself as an everyday activity.

From a scholarly viewpoint, the notion of interaction *per se* is a core concept in the fields of Ubiquitous computing, Ambient systems design, and generally in the fields of human-computer

DOI: 10.4018/978-1-4666-0038-6.ch007

Copyright © 2012, IGI Global. Copying or distributing in print or electronic forms without written permission of IGI Global is prohibited.

interaction (HCI) and Interaction Design, as it is about the interplay between humans and the digital technology designed to support us. For over 15 years there has been an explicit focus on design for interaction, from the publication of "Designing Interaction" (ed. by Carroll, 1991) to the publication of "Designing interactions" (Moggridge, 2006). Beyond that, the focus on interaction has been central since the birth of Human Computer Interaction as an academic field of research and as a profession.

With this focus on interaction we have, as a community, invented and developed a number of methods and approaches to interaction. We have developed approaches for Interactive Systems Design that are technology-centered, including approaches for requirement analyses (e.g., Mylopoulos et al., 1999; Kawaguchi, 2003), interface design (e.g., Miller, 1997; Souza et al., 2000; Oliveira & Rocha, 2005; Blackwell, 2006; Ruthven, 2008), design guidelines (e.g., Häkkilä & Mäntyjärvi, 2006) and UI principles (e.g., Beier & Vaughan, 2003). There has also been a long tradition of research into usability studies (e.g., Gould & Lewis, 1985; Nielsen & Molich, 1990; Jeffries et al., 1991; Sauro & Kindlund, 2005; Hollingsed &. Novick, 2007; Frøkjær & Hornbæk, 2008; Pilgrim, 2008) and methods for evaluating user performance (e.g., Card et al., 1980; Kolehmainen et al., 2008) and UI efficiency (e.g., Amant et al., 2003).

From another point of view, we have developed methods for analysis that are human-centered approaches to HCI and Interaction Design including user-centered design (e.g., Vredenburg et al., 2002; Mao et al., 2005; Keinonen, 2008), participatory design (e.g., Muller & Kuhn, 1993; Shapiro, 2005), and design ethnography (e.g., Huges et al., 1992; Hughes et al., 1995; Simonsen & Kensing, 1997). In line with this focus, analysis instruments and techniques including task analysis (e.g., Pinelle et al., 2003) and techniques for designing interaction technologies as a scaffold for human activities and computer supported collaboration, have been

developed. Recently we have seen how human modeling techniques, including e.g., Persona descriptions (Chang et al., 2008; McGinn, 2008) are growing in popularity as a way of presenting an image of the user as the focus for the design. Given a clear focus on Interaction Design with the human as focus, we have seen the growing interest in user experience design (McClelland, 2005; Forlizzi & Battarbee, 2004).

Working as a bridge between user-centered and technology-oriented studies of interaction technology design, the field of design-oriented research (e.g., Dahlbom & Mathiassen, 1997; Fallman, 2003; Zimmerman et al., 2007) has filled an important role. It has advanced our knowledge of how to work with prototypes in interaction research, how to move from empirical user studies to design and how ethnographic observations can lead to, or work as, a method for identifying implications for design. The latter approach has recently been criticized by Dourish (2006, 2007).

From a review of these methods and approaches to HCI and Interaction design, we can see that these approaches address either the technology or the human side of HCI and sometimes both. However, while doing so, these approaches still fail to explicitly address the "in between" aspects of human-computer interaction, i.e. to explicitly focus on interaction *per se* as a form element in which Interaction Design becomes the form making of the interaction itself, as a temporal element, and how a specific interaction form should be understood, implemented and communicated to its potential users. This paper explores that specific issue.

In more detail, this paper proposes a new way of approaching interaction, as a form element in itself based on an identified need for understanding the essence of Interaction per se, i.e., what the design space interaction *per se* constitutes. There are a number of advantages in explicitly focusing on the design space between the user and the technology: 1) Concentrating on interaction *per se* as a new design space that can be identified, carved out and worked through is an interesting opportunity for innovation both in terms of the development of new interaction models and modalities, as well as new ways of approaching existing technologies and human capabilities. 2) It is an opportunity to rethink and question the meeting point between humans and technology. and, 3) The focus of Interaction Design changes from mostly graphical design towards the design of interaction behaviors as an aspect of the temporal form (Mazé, 2007) of interaction *per se*.

While one way of pointing out this need for further explorations of interaction *per se* is to identify this space "in between" as a missing aspect of current approaches to HCI and Interaction Design, we also see a possibility of reaching this same conclusion based on another argument which is that we need to shift perspective from a first-person perspective on HCI to a third-person perspective, i.e., while we have a large body of research that has explored users' understanding of complex (or simple) user interfaces and ways of capturing users' interests, motivations, and emotions while interacting with any digital material, we still have few studies aimed at questioning the interaction situation. Despite several contextual approaches to HCI which adds to our understanding of in which context the interaction occurs or take place. we have a limited number of studies that is looking at questions like, *"What does it look like when user x is trying to solve task y?"* Alternatively, *"Should the user really engage in this interaction in the first place?"* As acknowledged in earlier research more and more people interact with computers in public places, where users do not want to interact *per se*, instead, the computer is only a way to complete their tasks.

There are several good examples of how questioning the fundamental understanding of the core interaction model has led to new areas of innovation within the field of HCI, including inventions of new interaction models, interaction modalities and even whole application domains; e.g., VR, Embodied interaction and Social navi-

gation. Virtual Reality or VR set a new direction for HCI as an important step towards simulated computer worlds. Embodied opened up an interesting theoretical orientation within HCI while also being concrete enough to serve as a guide for, e.g., design of gesture-based user interfaces and more recently has influenced the design and implementation of multi-touch displays. Finally, the concept of "Social navigation" has worked as a model for how we might interact and navigate together with, or informed by, others on the web, and has already proven its success in a multitude of commercial implementations of web sites, typically e-commerce web sites including on-line bookstores, and other retail firms.

However, there remains a lack of good models for advancing interaction innovations in a *systematic* and *intentional* manner. As a field of research, we sure know how to conduct user studies, and we have a good understanding of enabling digital technologies. However, our theories on interaction *per se* are either too broad to serve as a practical guide for design, or to narrow, in those instances where an interaction theory is synonymous with a defined concept that guides or inspires the design.

If the focus in the area of interaction research is not primarily about the design and implementation of new digital products and services, the discovery of Interaction Design should focus on new knowledge of novel and accurate methods, techniques, and approaches to HCI, to reach new knowledge on how to design for interaction, then we also need a development in our field on what we mean when talking about interaction (as also highlighted by Dubberly, 2009), and good models capable of describing interaction as a unique object of study, and allow for detailed studies and analysis of interaction *per se*.

Interaction is here viewed as the events taking place in the intersection between *digital technologies enrolled and embedded in everyday life*, and *the human activities enrolled in everyday digital technologies*. This intersection is ephemeral, dynamic and temporal, in constant flux, and an emergent property of humans and technologies engaged in human-machine interplay typically labeled "interaction".

To address this dynamic intersection a theory of interaction *per se*, i.e., a framework of concepts and a description of the relations between concepts that can help us to identify, describe and analyze any particular interaction as it surfaces in everyday life. Such a theory about the basic qualities of interaction should also highlight and describe the *internal mechanisms* of interaction, as well as how these mechanisms might work in relation to the elements of importance as outlined in the framework. A good theory of interaction in the context of HCI should not only be descriptive, but should be able to serve as a framework for predictions (Whitaker et al., 2000), at the same time as it is concrete enough to be applicable in practice, to function as a useful guide and to inform design decisions about interaction *per se* as a design space itself. Interaction Design is inherently dual natured, being both an area of research as well as a profession executed on a daily basis for the design and development of digital products and services.

To address this challenge a theorizing process around interaction as a design space is sketched out. This design space is a multi-dimensional space which covers, and in every unique design situation answers, basic questions concerning: 1) The necessity of any particular interaction *per se*, 2) the modes of interaction, 3) the form of interaction, 4) the underlying basic model for interaction, 5) the mechanisms for interaction, and finally 6) the behavior of the interaction.

From these listed dimensions, we are therefore interested in questions that arise about interaction concerning:

1. **Necessity of interaction:** Is it necessary for the user to engage in the interaction in the first place? (meaningfulness)

2. **Modes of interaction:** Through which means is the user expected to engage in the interaction? (resources for input/output)

3. **Form of interaction:** When engaging in the interaction, what does it look like from a functional as well as from an aesthetical point of view? (appearance)

4. **Basic model of interaction:** What is the basic turn-taking model assumed between the human and the computer? (actions & information flows)

5. **Mechanisms for interaction:** What is the user expected to do, and what is the computer expected to handle? (responsibilities)

6. **Behavior of the interaction:** How does the interaction as a temporal form unfold over time? (dynamic aspects of interaction)

In order to carefully approach and study this design space, and to be able to answer these questions for any particular study of interaction, or even use this as a framework for Interaction Design we need to address this through *the sketching of a model of interaction*. This model of interaction about the inner intersection of human-computer interaction is based on the fundamental assumption that interaction *per se* cannot be separated from either the everyday settings in which it emerges, nor from its enabling technologies.

A good understanding of interaction *per se* requires us to leave the narrow focus on a snapshot in time, i.e., when a user operates a certain application on a computer. Instead, the analysis starts with a basic understanding of how interaction as a phenomenon happens, and how interaction is in fact embedded in our everyday lives. It is part of our online activities, sometimes labeled "mediated activities" (activity theory), which highlights the fact that digital technologies are so embedded in our everyday lives that we do not even need to specify IT as being part of one such concept. In the analysis, therefore, the focus is on interaction from the perspectives of:

1. Interaction as technology embedded in everyday life
2. Interaction as everyday life embedded in technology

With the understanding of interaction as the interaction between these two viewpoints, the interest is not only on the *internal mechanisms*, but also on the interaction outcomes, or the *external qualities* of interaction *per se*. Of course this means that the two different interaction models might produce the same outcome or result, but the manner in which it is produced, and the way it is perceived (both by the user and by an observant) while being produced can be altogether different.

In this article, an examination of current research on understanding interaction in the contexts of HCI and Interaction Design was carried out. The understanding of interaction in the context of technology embedded in everyday life and of interaction in the context of everyday life embedded in technology is described. After presenting these two main aspects of interaction as being related to our everyday activities as well as being related to the mediating technologies, a sketch of the design space of interaction as a framework of concepts for analyzing interaction is suggested. A model of interaction *per se* as a form element in itself, situated in between humans and supporting technologies, as the inner intersection of human-computer interaction is presented. With this outline of the dimensions of the framework, it is possible to illustrate how it can be used to analyze two different interactive systems in terms of interaction and to show that the dimensions of the interaction framework can point at some specific characteristics of these technologies. Moreover, the way their unique designs demand a unique kind of interaction to show the "temporal form" of the interaction can also be illustrated. The presented framework can be applied in interaction research for both analytical purposes and for systematically building a knowledge base about interaction as a design space, thus showing its potential as a concrete tool for professional Interaction Design projects. A discussion of this approach and the main conclusions from this project will follow.

The description of an agenda for future interaction research, given this framework in place will include the following: 1) the systematic identification of new dimensions, aspects and interaction design variables (including both internal mechanisms and external qualities) of interaction per se, 2) the struggle towards the discovery of new knowledge on interaction per se as a dynamic and temporal form element for design, and 3) the search for a better understanding of how a particular interactive solution might scale in relation to a wide range of identified perspectives.

RELATED RESEARCH: MODELING INTERACTION *PER SE*

Before initiating the exploration of interaction as the inner intersection of human-computer interaction, a review of current interaction models in HCI was conducted in order to understand how the current body of research in the field of Human-Computer Interaction defines, addresses, frames and models interaction.

Most recently Dubberly et al. (2009) raised three fundamental and basic questions:

1. "Do we agree on the meaning of the term "interaction"?
2. "Has the subject been fully explored?"
3. "Is the definition settled?"

In their view, the answer is "NO!" to all three of these questions. They then describe the current frameworks developed to address interaction starting off with the work by Davis (2008), and Buchanan (1998) the latter through contrasting earlier design frames (a focus on form, and more recently on meaning and context) with another design frame, i.e., a focus on interaction. In doing so, Dubberly et al. (2009) points out that Bu-

Figure 1. Basic model of human-computer interaction

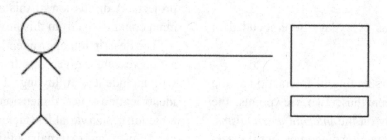

chanan (1998) frames interaction as being about the *relationship* between people and the objects designed for them and they continue to argue that interaction is a key aspect of function.

If then moving backwards in time we can see that throughout the years there has been a wide range of models developed to describe and analyze human-computer interaction, ranging from models of the basic components of human-computer interaction (e.g., Benyon et al., 2004), to more advanced frameworks and theories on the complex interplay between humans and technologies.

The most basic models typically describe HCI as including three elements; humans, computers and the interaction between them, in models like those that are outlined in Figure 1, or in models that describe this as a loop between the user and the computer via input/output flows (e.g., Heim, 2007).

However, in reviewing this genre of HCI models from a graphical perspective it becomes obvious that most of the focus has been on humans and computers with very little focus on modeling the interaction *per se* (in these models, interaction is typically represented only as a thin line in between the human and the computer). This is also the case when reviewing the amount of academic literature published in the area of HCI, i.e. most literature on HCI is concerned with human factors or understanding humans interacting with computers, or about design of computer support to scaffold human activity.

According to Dubberly et al. (2009), these canonical models of human-computer interaction are structured along a basic archetypal structure – the feedback loop. In their description of this basic structure, they describe how information flows from a system through a person and back to the system again. It is argued that the driver of this loop is a person with a goal, and that he/she acts to achieve it (provides input to the system), measures the effect of the actions taken (interprets output from the system), and compares the results with the goal. The outcome of this comparison then directs the next action taken by that person. Dubberly et al. then describes Norman's "Gulf of execution – Gulf of evaluation" interaction model (Norman, 2002), as well as Norman's "Seven stages of action" model (Norman, 2002) then outlines three important additional questions in relation to these simple feedback-loop models of interaction: -*"What is the nature of the dynamic system?"*," *What is the nature of the human?"*, *"Do different types of dynamic systems enable different types of interaction?"* While these questions might be focal given the traditional interaction model paradigm which focus on the human, or the dynamic technology, a shift towards a focus on interaction *per se* could lead to other models of interaction, and thus also raise other questions about interaction *per se*, i.e., questions more closely related to the character and dimensions of interaction rather than questions about system properties or human factors. As pinpointed by Dubberly et al., we still lack a good, shared understanding of what is meant when we talk about interaction. This is the issue being addressed in this paper.

After reviewing the current literature on models of interaction there are several examples of input-output models for HCI (see Marchionini & Sibert, 1991; Boehner, 2005; Barnard et al., 2000) this includes the human processor model (Card, et al., 1983), models describing standards for designing good consistent interaction, including the WIMP-standard and other GUI standards (e.g., Dam, 1997), as well as a number of other models describing different specific interaction modalities and interaction paradigms (e.g., Jacob, 2006; Ishii & Ullmer, 1997; Jacob et al., 1999; Abowd & Mynatt, 2000; Bellotti et al., 2002). Several recent models of users in relation to advances in the field of HCI including models of human perception in relation to HCI (e.g., Kweon et al., 2008; Dalsgaard & Hansen, 2008) can be found.

To summarize, there have been several good models developed that address and describe different ways of designing and evaluating computer support for interaction, several developed to describe and analyze human needs, behaviors, motivations, activities and goals for engaging in interaction with computers, and models that can describe how humans might gain from interaction with computers in solving various tasks.

There have been neither very few attempts to address the basic dimensions and aspects of interaction *per se* nor how it could be modeled. Interaction *per se* could be a both a valuable addition to the current body of research on interaction as well as for the profession of Interaction Design. The exceptions to this include the theorizing of interaction in relation to systems (Bernard et al., 2000), the research and design driven approach to HCI (Zimmerman et al. 2007), and the need for new approaches to HCI including the identified need to integrate theory with HCI design work (Sutcliffe, 2000). In widening the scope of this literature review we can find good models for informing design based upon analysis of basic and frequent human activities including e.g. the

task-artifact model (Carroll & Rosson, 1992), task analysis (e.g., Pinelle et al., 2003), and the reference task model (Whittaker et al., 2000). It also takes into account the models developed in related areas of research, including relevant CSCW literature. The literature review also shows a number of workplace interaction models (e.g., Suchman, 1995; Whittaker et al., 1997), computer supported group collaboration models (e.g., Ellis et al., 1991; Whittaker, 1996; Hindmarsh et al., 2000), coordination models (e.g., Dourish & Bellotti, 1992; Neale et al., 2004) and models describing other social aspects related to HCI. HCI social models include distributed cognition (e.g., Hollan et al., 2000) and situatedness of human activities (Suchman, 1987). However, while these models have proven very valuable in understanding and describing computers in social contexts, they do not address nor model the dimensions of interaction *per se*.

This literature review could be expanded towards the direction of additional interaction concepts. In order to address certain specific kinds of interactions, the following terms were coined: *"embodied"* interaction (e.g., Klemmer et al., 2006), *"tangible"* interaction (e.g., Homecker & Buur, 2006) *"social"* interaction, and *"seamless"* interaction (e.g., Wiberg 2001) as well as a wide set of models of *"mobile"* interactions (e.g., Hinckley et al., 2000). However, while these models more specifically address various types of interaction and in doing so help to categorize different kinds of interaction, they fail to address interaction *per se*. In fact, the adding of another word before the word "interaction" in order to be more specific can be interpreted as a further sign of the lack of good ways to describe interaction *per se*.

The addition of a descriptive moves the focus away from the concept of interaction towards that descriptive. In adding a word like "embodied", "mobile" or "social," the focus changes to the descriptive word rather on that added word, or the two words together, but avoids addressing how those added words change or add to our understanding of interaction *per se*. These additional words can help us learn more about a certain "use" context, or particular user need important for design, that should, however, not be confused with attempts made to formulate more detailed models about interaction *per se*.

From another perspective, the field of HCI has witnessed several valuable attempts to build theories of interaction through design. These include "Proof of concept" approaches (e.g., Toney et al., 2003) and the "Artifact as theory nexus" approach formulated around the idea that artifacts can manifest interaction theories through their design (Carroll & Kellogg, 1989) and that special characters of a certain interaction model can be explored through the design of a prototype (Lim et al., 2008).

The lack of a shared fundamental understanding of interaction *per se*, has led to dramatic effects on our ability to discover new knowledge in the field of HCI systematically. Why is it that we have so effectively avoided addressing interaction *per se*? One interpretation is that we have been standing too close to the subject, thus failed to see it. In other words, we have typically had a first person perspective on interaction in the interaction research that has been undertaken. In taking departure from the individual and his/her goals and activities and how technology helps or fails to support him or her in carrying out these tasks a more objective stance is suggested.

To tackle this issue, this paper proposes a third person perspective on interaction so that we can look at interaction from the outside, i.e., interaction as understood and perceived by an observer of the person interacting with some digital technology. Thus we are able to look at interaction as a phenomenon "in the world" which can be studied and observed, including how people engage in interaction with digital devices in their everyday lives, and how parts of our everyday lives becomes part of online digitalized interaction.

EVERY DAY IT-USE: INTERACTION AS TECHNOLOGY EMBEDDED IN EVERY DAY LIFE

This section identifies interaction *per se* as an everyday phenomenon and how we frequently involve digital technologies in our everyday lives, thus making this phenomenon surface and having impact from how it changes and form professional work settings to the reshaping of our everyday lives.

If starting out with a contextualization of interaction as an ingredient, or element of our everyday lives, we can easily see how we constantly adopt new technologies, e.g., notebook computers, net-books, mobile phones, PDAs, etc, and how frequently we use these technologies, along with the wide range of specific applications that sits on these devices. Through this perspective, we can clearly see that interaction with computers is not a detached activity, separate from the rest of our lives, and instead is highly entwined with everything else in which we are constantly involved. To illustrate this we can use a simple user-centered model as outlined in Figure 2, which illustrates how we incorporate these technologies into the sphere of our everyday activities.

This inclusion of interaction technologies raises a number of questions about the ways in which we interact with digital technologies on a general level. In this research, the questions that have arisen have been categorized in terms of functionality, frequency, offload and access, and composition as follows:

Functionality: Interaction as interplay to solve a specific task, i.e., "What task is to be solved through active engagement with digital technologies?"

Frequency: How seldom or often does the interaction happen? Is it repetitive or a unique occasion?

Offload and Access: Does the technology serve as a cognitive help, to offload the user? Is

Figure 2. Incorporation of interactions in our everyday lives

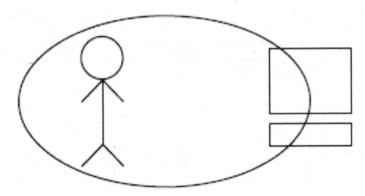

the technology a storage support to offload our memory and to make retrieval easier? Does it serve as a computational support to offload our cognitive capabilities, or does it provide access to data? The question is not about having these things implemented, rather it is about what the interplay looks like and how it is implemented in any digital technology.

Composition: Which digital tools and services are used, and how these tools are assembled, combined or interlinked internally either for one specific purpose, or as part of an overall composition? (e.g., the way in which the iPhone is used today is a good example of how people build their own composition of services on an open technical platform). Expanding this category also covers questions like, "What is the set-up of technologies that people use in their everyday lives?"

The nature of these questions can be further summarized in Table 1, as they relate to each category identified.

In addressing questions, related to *functionality* and *frequency* of interaction, as well as interaction from the viewpoints of how interaction with computers might *offload* the user or allow *access* to digital material while considering the complete *composition* of different digital tech-

nologies embedded in our everyday lives we see are able to see that the nature of these questions is distinct. Questions regarding *functionality* refer to the purpose of the interaction *per se; frequency* must always be related to a specific context in order to know if it is high or low, i.e., there is a need for a reference point. *Offload and access* is about the interplay between the user and the computational resources available. The idea is to focus on *composition* leaving the simple loop model of interaction, and instead focusing on the entire interactional palette that a typical user constantly keeps running across with multiple digital devices and enabling technologies.

UBIQUITOUS IT-USE: INTERACTION AS EVERYDAY LIFE EMBEDDED IN TECHNOLOGY

In examining how we, humans, are constantly present, mirrored, and in many other ways active in the digital world, to the extent of ubiquitous IT-use, we can identify interaction through the existence of online communities, virtual worlds, social networking services, and even through the frequent use of email as an online tool for social interaction.

Online interaction should not be forgotten in any modeling of interaction *per se* on the contrary,

Table 1. Dimensions of interaction as technology in everyday life

	Dimensions	Aspects	Nature of questions raised
1	**Functionality**	What a certain application can do for its user	Interactional purpose
2	**Frequency**	How often the application/digital device is used In which situations a specific application is used	Interaction contextualized
3	**Offload & Access**	- Offload to the environment (compare Norman) - Access resources - Read/write aspects	Interactional resources interplay
4	**Composition**	The combination of different technologies, OSs, applications, services, digital devices, networks, etc.	From self-contained interaction to an interactional palette

as pinpointed by Hollan (2000), the complex networked world of online interaction should be a focal aspect of our understanding of interaction.

For human-computer interaction to advance in the new millennium we need to understand the emerging dynamic of interaction in which the focus task is no longer confined to the desktop but reaches into a complex networked world of information and computer-mediated interactions (Hollan et al., 2000, p. 192).

A simple technology-centered model illustrates how parts of us are frequently involved in online interaction, and how we are represented frequently and actively in this complex, networked, and digital world (Figure 3).

The inclusion of humans in the networked world of interactions raises questions about the various interactions that we engage in when participating and using these online worlds. The number of different questions raised can also be cataloged into 4 broad categories: *representation, services, connections* and *sessions* as follows:

Representation: How is the human represented in online services? (Including the whole range of solutions from the creation of simple, straightforward user accounts, to the design of complete online avatars.)

Services: Which services are available to the user as represented in the online world? How does the user benefit from employing these services? What is expected, in terms of interactional engagement, from the use of these services?

Connections: What are the established paths given a certain service? Moreover, how can the user configure or reconfigure the paths for different purposes? (Again including the whole range of connection configurations from basic online accounts to the set-up of buddy lists, social networks, etc.).

Sessions: How does the user initiate, join or engage in sessions of interaction? How does the user keep an overview of ongoing and active sessions? How are these sessions related to the three aspects above?

The nature of these questions is further summarized in Table 2 as they relate to each category identified.

When looking at these categories from a general perspective, it is easy to see how various online services, communities, virtual worlds, and social networking services could be analyzed via these questions. In essence, questions related to representation concern images of the user, or the user's actions, i.e., the visible signs of the interaction performed by a user, as represented in an

Figure 3. Inclusion of humans in the complex networked world of information and computer-mediated interactions

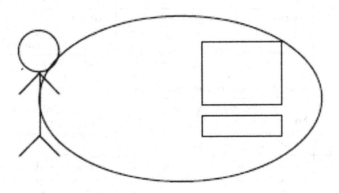

online space. The nature of the questions related to services deals with the tools available for interaction. The nature of questions about connections captures the paths that the interaction might take across the services and finally, questions concerning ongoing sessions are in fact questions about interaction as it is carried out via the connections and services available.

THE DESIGN SPACE OF INTERACTION

In the exploration of interaction as a design space S. Heim's book "The Resonance Interface: HCI foundations for interaction design, was inspiring. The title communicates an interesting aspect of interactive technologies, i.e., interaction is in a

sense like resonance; it grows out of the interplay between our technologies and us. Resonance is a good metaphor for understanding Interaction as an emergent property with its own structure, form and appearance. Resonance surfaces as a temporal and ephemeral body between a musical instrument and the human ear in a similar way as interaction grows out of the interplay between the technology used and perceived by the human using the technology. Clearly, there is a temporal dimension in both resonance and interaction, both are only possible to observe as they happen, meaning that they are highly situational, temporal and volatile. At the same time, knowing about the preconditions for interaction allows them to be studied in detail before and after the interaction.

In the same way as *resonance* constitutes an interesting object of study in any music related

Table. 2. Dimensions of interaction as everyday life embedded in technology

	Dimensions	Aspects	Nature of questions raised
1	Representation	How the user is re-presented in the online world	Presentation or representation of the user
2	Services	Ensembles of resources for computational activities	Interactional tools
3	Connections	Established paths across the networked world	Interactional paths
4	Sessions	The number and types of various ongoing sessions	Interaction in action

Table 3. Dimensions of interaction as technology embedded in everyday life (see section 3)

	Dimensions	**Aspects**	**Interaction Design Variables**
1	**Functionality**	What a certain application can do for its user	- Affordance - Agency - Design of application behavior
2	**Frequency**	How often the application/digital device is used In which situations the application is used	- Scale (design for frequent or non-frequent use) - Repetitions - Guidance (help)
3	**Offload & Access**	- Offload to the environment (compare Norman) - Access resources - Read/write aspects	- Computational support - Storage support - Information representations
4	**Composition**	The combination of different technologies, OSs, applications, services, digital devices, networks, etc.	- Borders & Interfaces, e.g. inter-application interfaces, (APIs), copy/paste/insert/export, import, user accounts, settings, etc. - Interoperability - Formats - Synchronization & data transfer

area of research, it can be argued that so too does *interaction per se* constitute a similar unique object of study in the area of HCI. More specifically, this paper takes a close look at the preconditions for interaction, i.e., the stable and "designable" aspects of interaction including the dimensions, aspects and design variables that form the design space of interaction.

Working from the two aspects of interaction as *1) technology embedded in everyday life* and, *2) everyday life embedded in technology* a model of the design space of interaction has been sketched out. The basis for this design space was outlined in sections 3 and 4 through the categorization of various questions that have been raised about interaction as well as the nature of those questions. In the following tables, possible design variables of each dimension have been added to further sketch out this design space. The intention is not to construct a complete model of the design variables of interaction. Nor is the aim for a complete identification of all the dimensions of interaction. Instead, the dimensions, aspects and variables outlined in Table 3 should serve the overall purpose of bring forth the perspective of interaction as the inner intersection of human-computer interaction.

These two dimensions of interaction (i.e., interaction as technology embedded in everyday life as summarized in Table 1, and interaction as everyday life embedded in technology, as summarized in Table 2) form the basis for our exploration of interaction as the inner intersection of human-computer interaction. Having said this it is argued that in the intersection of these two dimensions we should be able to extract a number of variables, that taken together, constitutes a design space from the viewpoint of Interaction Design, and a conceptual contribution to the way we might model and understand interaction per se.

Specifically, examining these two tables in more detail we can see from Table 3 how the dimension of *functionality* can be further elaborated through the design variables of *affordance* (Norman, 2002), *agency* (Suchman, 2006) and application *behavior* (e.g., Dirgahayu, 2008). Interaction *frequency* can be further addressed through the design variables of *scale, repetitions* and *guidance*. Furthermore, *offload & access* can be explored in design via the variables of *computational support, storage and information retrieval solutions* and *information representations* including the entire range from icon design to simulator environments;

Table 4. Dimensions of Interaction as everyday life embedded in technology (see section 4)

	Dimensions	Aspects	Interaction Design Variables
1	**Representation**	How the user is represented in the online world (representations of the user)	- Gestalt & authentification - Media - Network (might be represented through its peers)
2	**Services**	Ensembles of resources for computational activities	- Compounds - Configurations
3	**Connections**	- Established paths across the networked world	- Accounts - Security - Spatiality
4	**Sessions**	The number and types of various ongoing sessions	- Access - Overview - Switches - Borders - Temporality

from simple tangible tags to complex intelligent systems. Finally, *composition* can be explored in the design space through the design variables of *borders & interfaces* (e.g., APIs), *interoperability* issues, *formats*, and ways of dealing with *synchronization & data transfer* across devices, services and networks.

In a similar way, Table 4 points at a set of design variables. The dimension of *representation* as an important aspect of online interaction might be explored through the design variables of *gestalt & authentification*, choice of *media* or *network model* (ranging from technical peer-to-peer solutions to social networking models) for the representation of the user. The interactive *service* design can be explored through the design dimensions of *compounds* design, i.e., to establish the necessary conditions for a certain digital service, and then design the range of *configurations* available for the user. Further, *connections* could be explored through the design variables of set-up and form of *user accounts*, implementation of *security* in relation to interaction, including everything from login routines to backbone network virus scanning. In addition, the dimension of *sessions* as a way of modeling interaction might be explored through the design dimensions of session *access* design (e.g., session management design), session *overview* solutions and ways of dealing with

session *switches* and design of *borders* between ongoing sessions.

While we find good support in the literature for these design variables, it is also possible to see many practical examples of how these dimensions surface in practice. If taking a step back from this theoretical approach and looking instead at interaction in everyday life and everyday life as interaction we can take a third person view. When taking this third person perspective and looking at the complete interactional situation, rather than as a de-contextualized event, discover that in our everyday lives we do in fact live with this design space and frequently also accept common design failures as exemplified in the following section (i.e., section 5.1). We become accustomed to new ways of interacting as they surface in the interaction landscape (see section 5.2).

Interaction in Everyday Life

In our everyday lives we constantly live with design failures (Petroski, 1994), which we tend to accept, at least when it comes to computers perhaps it is just un-reflected behavior or alternatively, because we have not treated interaction *per se* as a design space that could be as carefully designed as any other consumer product. It might, for example, be interesting to know the total amount of minutes/week that people in any big city just sit and wait for their computer to wake up from hibernate mode, or even worse, if it needs to boot? Another example is that it usually takes any person that is about to show a slideshow presentation a couple of minutes just to get an ordinary projector to work with their computer (instead of spending that time talking to those present). As formulated by Mazé (2007) interactions occupy time. Furthermore, nowadays people seem to just accept the fact that their computers crash or that their wireless keyboard loses its connection. Many people would never even try to pair a Bluetooth headset with their mobile phone, or upload their camera pictures to an online photo service. From the perspective of Interaction Design this has very little to do with the particular design of a button or a specific menu layout. Instead, it could be argued that people accept these things because the entire experience of the interaction is outrageous while at the same time, there is no language to address what is wrong or how it could be repaired or improved upon. On the other hand, when people are presented with new ways of interacting with digital technologies that solve such basic problems they adopt such solutions quickly.

Everyday Life as Interaction

The forms for how we interact with and via the online digital world are constantly changing. New services are constantly developed and the legions of users move from one social online space to the next following the changing trends. How we present ourselves in these online worlds is also under constant development, from simple user profiles to the complex design of online avatars. In this emergent interaction landscape people learn to navigate, jump between services, combine services in *mesh-ups* (Plewe, 2008), or attach information streams (e.g., RSS- or media streams) to themselves as they move along. They figure out how to *scrabble* between services, *chirp*

on Twitter (Krishnamurthy et al., 2008) or *scrap* personal notes (Bernstein et al., 2007) and *life-hack* new paths across the interaction landscape, sometimes guided via some D.I.Y community. Additionally, people develop their ways of presenting themselves to others on the net, and some even develop their own set of online personalities. Through these online personalities, they comment upon the world around them, and new phenomena emerge out of these movements, e.g., the rise of the "blogosphere" (Agarwal & Liu, 2008).

The Form of Interaction *Per Se*: Situated and Manifested in Between Man and Machine

The tables above, together with the practical examples from section 5.1 and 5.2 illustrate that interaction touches upon a wide set of dimensions possible to address from a design perspective. As such, it clearly sets the scene for Interaction Design. Nevertheless, given these insights, what does interaction look like when carried out? Interaction Design is sometimes described as being about the design of a temporal form (Mazé, 2007), but in which situations is this form present, and what does the interaction *per se* look like in these situations?

In this paper, an alternative way of looking at human-computer interaction is presented in order to address these questions. This is presented as an intersection-oriented perspective on HCI through a Venn diagram approach to the modeling of interaction, as illustrated in Figure 4, thus moving away from the modeling of interaction as a thin line between a user and a computer.

In this venn-diagram model of human-computer-interaction we can see how interaction might be modeled as a design space situated in between the user and the technology, thus constituting the inner intersection of this diagram in Figure 4. In more detail, this model can be explained as follows: In human-computer interaction, we have humans (1) interacting with digital technologies

Figure 4. Interaction as the Inner Intersection of Human-Computer Interaction

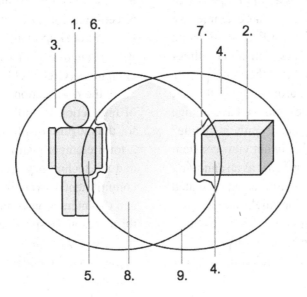

(2). From the wide range of digital technologies available, nowadays we incorporate some technologies into our lives (3) and create a composition of these technologies that works for us in our everyday life (see section 3). From the viewpoint of digital technologies, we also embed parts of our everyday lives in the digital world (4), as described in section 4 above. The part of us that is represented in the digital world (5) is sometimes described generally through e.g., Persona descriptions, or manifested as a representation of the individual in the form of anything from a simple user account (username and password) to a full-blown avatar (6). Similarly, the technologies that we incorporate into our everyday lives are typically configured, integrated, and covered with some kind of user interface (sometimes graphical, but in other cases more physical, ranging from simple buttons to tangible user interfaces.) (7). But from the perspective proposed in this paper this also includes how the technology presents itself to the user. Given this description, we can now identify an interesting intersection between area 3 and 4 in this model, i.e., between the ways users incorporate digital technologies into their everyday world, and the ways in which humans

engage themselves in interaction in the networked world. Therefore, if we also subtract 6 and 7 from this intersection we can see a new design space emerging with its own form and content, i.e. the design space of the inner intersection of human-computer interaction (8).

This identified design space (8) can be explored through the dimensions listed in Tables 3 and 4. At the same time an interesting design challenge might be to explore the border issues of this design space (9) in relation to people, available technologies, representations of us as users of these technologies, and the interfaces we create to scaffold interaction with any digital material. These border issues might include the *appearance* of the interaction as it is performed in any public space (e.g., what does it look like when a person is calling someone via voice-dial and then takes the call via a Bluetooth headset?) Another issue might concern *scale*. That is, for any particular solution for interaction that works for a small-scale implementation, a limited number of users, a limited number of information items, or similar, will the solution scale up when running the same configuration with thousands of users and thousands of information items? Will the solution work when scaling up the frequency of use at the individual level? As an example, we can take the "new WiFi identified" alert on an iPhone. This solution works well for the times when a user walks around and there might only be a few WiFi networks around. Nevertheless, what if the trend continues and we have a huge number of WiFi networks constantly available? Then the user would probably not view constant WiFi alerts as a feature, but rather as an annoying system message. Finally, a third concept related to the borders of interaction might be *strength*, serving as a concept that could denote whether or not a particular manifestation of interaction is in line with established social, cultural, ethical or natural conventions.

Having sketched out this design space as the inner intersection of human-computer interaction one might ask about the main reasons to claim this space. From our perspective, we argue that Interaction Design is about this inner space for two reasons. First, this space appears because of the mutual inclusion and adoption of (1) digital technologies into our everyday lives, and (2) how we include parts of our everyday lives in the digital world. This is a long-term, contextual perspective on interaction its importance, and its development. The second reason is more momentous and deals with the *mutual interactional commitment* in which people engage. In any situation in which we are to interact with digital technology, we commit ourselves to the interaction model and we expect the technology to do likewise. This engagement is about the building of a relationship with the digital technologies. We trust them to work in a certain way, and we count on being able to use the technologies in a certain way given a set-up of specific interaction models.

From a more philosophical viewpoint engagement and interactional commitment is about building relationships (See Buchanan's work from 1998), and these relationships are built over time. Having this said we should also consider the power that comes into play when designing interaction

as a relationship to technology. As formulated by Greenfield (2006) *we engage ourselves in interaction*, or more importantly *the powerful informatics we are engaging* through our interactions with computers (Greenfield, 2006, p. 11).

In the next section this developed framework of interaction is applied on two different cases for the purpose of illustrating: (1) interaction as a form element manifested in between the user and the technology, (2) interaction as a mutual commitment between the user and the technology, and (3) interaction as an observable form from a third person perspective. This is shown through two basic workshop sessions, and through the application of the identified dimensions, aspects and design variables of interaction *per se* as outlined above.

TWO CASES EXPLAINED WITH THE FRAMEWORK

In the Hollywood movie, "Minority Report" the actor, Tom Cruise, is using a transparent wall-size multi-touch display, and he literary has all the information readily available as he is seamlessly interacting with the information in any way he wants. This is a good example of interaction in action, and it is a good example of the necessary *mutual interactional commitment* this scenario requires from both the user and the technology to make this interaction occur and more impressively work.

This research explored the use of two different software applications (MidoMi and Ocarina, i.e., two different iPhone 3G applications) for illustrating this mutual commitment that constitutes interaction *per se*. The assumptions made about the level of human engagement expected, and the role of the technology in making the inner intersection of interaction work has been specifically studied as a way of exploring the dimensions of interaction as identified and outlined in sections 3 and 4. For this study, we arranged a workshop with 10 interaction designers, and we looked at the specific use sessions, observed and interviewed the users, and looked at the whole situation from the third person perspective.

Two criteria were kept in mind for the selection of the two software applications. First, to study mobile interaction since this is an interaction modality that in many cases needs to work in public places (which addresses the third person perspective) and, second, as a means of breaking away from the traditional desktop mode of interaction for software applications.

Case 1: The MidoMi iPhone 3G Application

The MidoMi application (Figure) is a music search application for the iPhone 3G. In this application, the user is asked to sing for 10 seconds into the iPhone microphone. After that, the application uses speech recognition to translate the song into an online query to an online music database. The database then returns a list of search results related to the request, the user can then click through the list and listen to a few seconds from each song. Simultaneously the application sends another request to two additional online resources, the iTunes database and the YouTube database to check if the songs found can be bought from iTunes, and if there is a related music video to watch on www. youtube.com. As such, the Midomi application collects several different Internet resources and makes use of them in the creation of one new service for its user. In this way, the application saves the user both work and time in comparison to the user going through each step separately.

It was clear that this application addressed the issue of mutual commitment between the user and the technology. If the user is expected to sing aloud into the microphone of the phone then the user must be able to trust that the technology will recognize this as a query to the music database behind this software. Further, it is interesting to note that mention was made that the relationship

Figure 5. The Midomi application running on an iPhone 3G

between the user and the system was *unbalanced* in favor of the user. The application seamlessly handled the internet connection, the speech recognition, online search in several databases, etc. and then delivered all the information back to the user in a structured way. Although the mutual commitment was somewhat unbalanced the whole interaction was interpreted as relying on a very basic interaction cycle of *"singing → searching → selecting and playing song → Sing again"*, almost like *"sing, listen, sing, listen, sing…"* or like a simple dialogue with the system. From this perspective, there was little effort expected from the user in comparison with the huge payback in terms of collected information.

In relating the outcome of this study to the concepts identified in section 3 we can see that, in relation to the statements made during this workshop, the concept of *functionality* was expressed from statements that Midomi functioned as an agent in terms of how it supports the user, based on simple requests (through the act of singing). In terms of *frequency* of use, it supports the less frequent user and music listener (who only may remember a few words or the tune) by not expecting the user to know the name of the artist or the title of the song (which is something a frequent user might know). In terms of *offload and access,* the Midomi application supports automated access to several Internet resources (including music databases, iTunes store and YouTube) through one simple interface. Finally the *composition* was addressed through comments about how these normally separated Internet services were "nicely integrated" into one application.

On observation, it was particularly noticeable how the technology enhanced the user's experience by providing the correct song in playable format based on a simple humming of the song by the user. Moreover, to see this elegant interplay between the user and the technology was quite amazing in terms of how smooth the whole interaction cycle worked. Thus, the third person perspective allows for the study of the form of interaction, i.e. the observable interplay between the user and the technology ("the inner intersection of HCI" see Figure 4, no. 8).

This case study exemplified the dimensions identified in Section 3, *"interaction as technology embedded in everyday life."* The third person perspective applied here allowed us to see aspects of the form of interaction *per se.*

In Case 2, the dimensions identified in Section 4, *"interaction as everyday life embedded in technology,"* are illustrated in terms of how playing this digital instrument locally is in fact transformed into a real-time performance over the internet for a global audience.

Case 2: The Ocarina iPhone 3G Application

Ocarina, designed by Smule is a software application, actually a digital instrument, which runs on the iPhone 3G. The developers of the Ocarina integrated three of the resources available on the phone: the microphone, the multi-touch screen and the wireless Internet connection running over 3G or WLAN. Through a clever integration of these resources, a new and novel instrument was designed that completely changed the phone into a musical instrument.

To play on the Ocarina the user holds the "flute" with two hands like any traditional flute, and then blows into the microphone (see the yellow arrow

indication for this in Figure 6, left) while fingering chords on the multi-touch screen. As the chords are played the tunes are available on the internet for others to access, via their own Ocarina software, as a real-time internet-based browser interface that connects to Ocarina players around the world (see Figure 6 for an example screenshot).

This unique integration of different resources into a coherent whole changes the mobile phone into an "internet flute." However, the change is not about the device itself, but rather the way we interpret the *interactional form* associated with it. With this new form, the device communicates a new *functional behavior*, and a new way of presenting itself to its user. At the same time, we can see how this device now demands a different *commitment* from its user to complete the interaction.

From our workshop study, it was clear that this application addressed the issue of a mutual commitment between the user and the technology. It is an application that clearly re-purposes the technology from a mobile phone to an "Internet flute," thus also altering the form of interaction between the user and the technology, i.e., the inner intersection of the HCI cycle. In terms of the interactional commitment and the form of the inner intersection, it was a shared opinion in the workshop that this software application clearly has borrowed part of its interaction model from a traditional flute, i.e., to press buttons on the device while blowing into it. The repurposed technology not only altered the use, it also added digital dimensions. While the music played locally, it was also being broadcast over the Internet in real-time. Thus, the user is part of the technology via a digital representation on the internet in the "online flute community" that has formed around these users.

In this workshop the mutual interactional commitment and the interactional form was also clear. In this cycle, the user is expected to blow into the microphone and play on the buttons on the multi-touch screen just like playing on an ordinary flute. The user commits to change his/her input

Figure 6. The Ocarina application running on an iPhone 3G

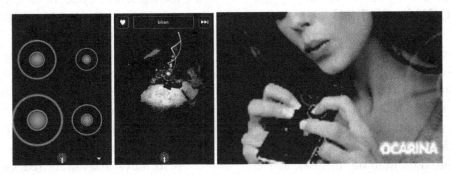

method (from talking into the microphone (the phone mode) to blowing (the Ocarina Internet flute mode of interaction) fulfilling his/her part of the commitment. From the technology side the mutual commitment is fulfilled. The technology supports the user's playing as follows: automatically establishes the internet connection, broadcasts the music played, collects and represents information about other persons playing, etc. There are several processes running in the background that are important for the experience of the interaction. When this interaction cycle is complete and this mutual commitment is in place and working seamlessly then the form of the interaction *per se* is so clear and obvious that it has been recognized as also being "magical" and "addictive":

Ocarina is one of the most magical programs I've ever seen for the iPhone, and probably for any computer – David Pogue, NY Times.

Smule's addictive Ocarina turns the iPhone into the ancient flute-like instrument – Ed Biag, USA Today.

From our perspective, the "magical" or "addictive" thing about the experience is not the technology, but the way the inner intersection is configured, i.e., the way in which the interaction *per se* has been carefully designed.

In relating the outcome of this study to the concepts identified in section 4 we could see

that, in relation to the statements made during this workshop, the concept of *representation* was expressed through statements about Ocarina as bring local playing to the online community of Ocarina players. In terms of *services*, it was clear that Ocarina is a good example of a compound of hardware and software resources that taken together present itself to its user as a complete package, i.e., as an online musical instrument. Given a simple installation the preconfigured *connections* also worked as a structure for putting the resources together, and finally, the usage of the information about ongoing Ocarina playing (*sessions*) and their whereabouts added a location-based community service to this software which scaffolds a social awareness service among the players, and across their geographical distances.

In this second study, we also applied the third person perspective. In doing so it was possible to view the complete interaction cycle from the outside, i.e., via a perspective on the interaction as understood and perceived by an observer of the person interacting with the digital technology. Here, we particularly noticed how seamlessly the user picked up the new interaction modality with the iPhone, even when performed in a public space. Again, the third person perspective allowed us to study the form of interaction, i.e., the observable interplay between the user and the technology ("the inner intersection of HCI").

APPLYING THE INTERACTION FRAMEWORK IN DESIGN

Any good theory should not only be capable of *describing*, and *analyzing* a particular phenomenon, but must also functions as a tool for making *predictions* (Whittaker et al., 2000). In the area of HCI, we typically work with predictions through the design of novel interactive systems. We implement ideas from our theories, and intentionally design for an expected use, i.e. we try to be theoretically informed when making prototyped statements about predicted IT use. From an Interaction Design perspective, we might call this intentional interaction design, i.e., Interaction Design aimed at an expected (or predicted) kind of interaction. When considering how the proposed framework could be used in a practical Interaction Design project, we need to deliberate on to what extent the framework could help us in making explicit and specific statements about the form of interaction we're about to design. In reviewing current implementations of interactive systems and "intentional Interaction Design choices," we might pose questions similar to; "Was it deliberately decided to design computers in such a manner that the user should sit and wait for several minutes for it to boot?" i.e., was it part of the interaction form proposed when designing the boot part of the interaction? Alternatively, was booting the computer not considered part of the user experience?

In applying the framework as presented to real Interaction Design projects, it is proposed that we do so through a concept-driven Interaction Design process in which the form of the interaction *per se,* as the inner intersection of HCI, is carefully *designed,* conceptually *described* and *defined* so as to arrive at a clear-cut innovative Interaction Design. Should we work with this inner intersection in mind I believe that we could break away from the "taken for granted" models of software design and from the traditional assumptions about what interaction modalities need to be applied to close the interaction cycle. In the end, it is about an innovative process aimed at either:

1. Designing something new, e.g., a new interaction technology that could potentially change an existing situation into a future desired situation.
2. Redesigning an existing solution, in which the main challenge given this perspective is to move away from redesigning some particular interface elements (e.g., buttons) and instead questioning the interactional situation *per se,* i.e. to question even the idea of buttons as the solution.

There is some potential for the proposed framework when doing evaluations of computer software. Here, the suggestion is to leave the current focus on either technology aspects or user experiences, but carefully review how the mutual commitment to close the inner intersection of the interaction cycle is manifesting. This perspective puts an equal emphasis on the people and the technologies involved while engaged in the entire interactional situation. For such a combined design and evaluation method, it is suggested that it be structured as follows: (1) *Build a scenario* of how the mutual commitment is expected to work for a given technology and a target user. (2) *Evaluate* if the scenario is plausible. (3) *Test the system,* prototype or application with real people. (4) *Draw conclusions,* not about technology issues nor about users' individual experiences of a particular technology, but instead about the interaction *per se,* i.e., report on neither the user behaviors, nor usability issues in the user interface, but instead formulate conclusions in relation to the dimensions of interaction *per se* as presented in this paper.

DISCUSSION

A proposed a model of interaction *per se* as referring to the situated and manifested temporal form in between man and machine has been presented. The goal was aimed at striking a balance between technology-centered studies of interaction technologies and the current trend towards the study of user experiences. Here, our focus is on the entire interaction cycle, i.e., the form of the interaction *per se*, and how it manifests as a temporal form at the intersection between users and digital technologies. In this paper, we have set out to study this form and describe the elements, dimensions and variables of this socio-technical design space.

Through the modeling of this design space situated in between humans and their technologies, we have specifically looked at how these two entities are coming together and have described this as a mutual commitment between the user and the technology and have illustrated this through the study of two software applications. One might now wonder if these two applications were just two fun illustrations of new technologies, or if there was any deeper meaning behind these two studies. In our research, these two software applications serve as good examples that clearly illustrate that we can completely redefine the whole interactional situation based on how we understand and work with this unique and dynamic material that we typically refer to as digital technology.

From our perspective, we view our proposed framework as a manifestation that represents a five dimensional shift for HCI and Interaction Design:

1. From *function-driven Interaction Design to purpose-driven Interaction Design,*
2. From a *first person perspective* on Interaction Design to the inclusion of a third *person perspective* on Interaction Design,
3. From a focus on *fixing problems* in the existing world (within paradigm design) to a focus more oriented towards *fundamental solutions* for future preferred situations (including new paradigm explorations),
4. From interaction as an *input-output loop* to a focus on the *outcome of interaction*, i.e. a focus on what grows out of the interaction,

i.e., the "effect" and appearance of interaction *per se,*

5. From *"implications for design"* to the generation of *interaction theories* as to better describe, analyze and predict the dynamic form of interaction *per se.*

In this view, to interact is about engaging in interplay with the digital material, i.e., it is about "becoming interaction." This may constitute a phenomenological turn for HCI where people and technologies are becoming inseparable and in which interaction *per se* is becoming an important focus of attention through the creation of a relationship with the digital as we engage ourselves in the interaction. Here, it is every person's responsibility to choose whether to engage in a certain kind of interaction as it emerges in the interplay between people and interaction technologies. While Suchman (2006, p. 267) argues that *"intra-action"* "underscores the sense in which subjects and objects *emerges* through their encounters with each other", we argue that *"interaction per se"* underscores that the inner intersection of HCI as a dynamic and temporal form element *emerges* out of the interplay between subjects and objects as they mutually engage and effect each other.

CONCLUSION

In this paper, we have identified and explored interaction *per se* as the situated and manifested temporal form in between man and machine. Through this exploration we have sketched out a theoretical framework for addressing interaction *per se* as a unique object of study, and have identified important basic aspects and dimensions to consider when conducting interaction research, and when doing Interaction Design. In our exploration of interaction *per se* we have specifically taken into account the perspectives of *Everyday IT-use,* i.e., "interaction as technology embedded in everyday life", and *Ubiquitous IT-use,* i.e., "interaction as everyday life embedded in technology" for the purpose of framing interaction.

This work has been positioned in relation to previous research on models for understanding and analyzing human-computer interaction. The need for models capable of addressing interaction *per se* as a form element that can be explored at the same level of details as previous research focused on human aspects or computer support for meaningful, playful or effective interaction has been illustrated. Through a workshop study of two software applications, we have illustrated how the proposed framework can be used to analyze current interaction support from the viewpoint of interaction as the focal object of study. In addition, we have discussed the implications of our findings for interaction research in general, and how the framework could be useful as a tool in professional Interaction Design projects. The results from our studies of interaction *per se* suggest that the proposed framework can be a valuable guiding tool for interaction research and Interaction Design projects.

As for specific implications for interaction research, we have found it important to expand the focus, and develop theories about interaction *per se*. Furthermore, it is usually argued that people and technologies are intertwined into one object of study as claimed by the socio-technical approach. However, here we have introduced the design space and temporal form of interaction *per se*, as a third, manifested, situated, and intertwined component and we would like to highlight the importance of studying this temporal form that manifests itself in between users and technologies as an equally important object of study.

Given the proposed framework, it is expected that future interaction research will be able to more systematically:

1. Identify new *dimensions, aspects* and interaction design *variables* (both Internal and external dimensions) of interaction *per se*,

2. Create further knowledge about interaction *per se* as a temporal and dynamic *form element* for design,

3. Strive for a better understanding of how this view on interaction can *scale* from a level of analysis on individuals and their activities (how people engage themselves in interaction with and through digital material) to the analysis of interaction on the level of social groups (social interaction with digital technology as a resource), organizational levels (including the re-questioning of computer-aided routines), and ultimately on the level of the interaction society (including studies of e.g., the construction of interaction cultures, norms, values and beliefs, i.e., what we expect that computational materials can do for our society.

In the end, one such truly grounded theorizing process around interaction per se, that specifically highlight this intertwined, or highly ambient character of ubiquitous and everyday IT-use, i.e., *the ambience of interaction* is expected to be crucial for any understanding of design and use of systems designed to blend itself into our everyday physical, social and computational world.

REFERENCES

Abowd, G., & Mynatt, E. (2000). Charting past, present, and future research in ubiquitous computing. *Transactions on Computer-Human Interaction (TOCHI), 7*(1).

Agarwal, N., & Liu, H. (2008). Blogosphere: research issues, tools, and applications. *SIGKDD Explorations Newsletter, 10*(1).

Amant, R., Dinardo, M., & Buckner, N. (2003). Balancing efficiency and interpretability in an interactive statistical assistant. In *Proceedings of the 8th international conference on Intelligent user interfaces (IUI '03)*. New York: ACM Press.

Barnard, P., May, J., Duke, D., & Duce, D. (2000). Systems, interactions, and macrotheory. *Transactions on Computer-Human Interaction (TOCHI), 7*(2).

Beier, B., & Vaughan, M. (2003). The bull's-eye: a framework for web application user interface design guidelines. In *Proceedings of the SIGCHI conference on Human factors in computing systems (CHI '03)*. New York: ACM Press.

Bellotti, V., Back, M., Edwards, W. K., Grinter, R., Henderson, A., & Lopes, C. (2002). Making sense of sensing systems: five questions for designers and researchers. In *Proceedings of the SIGCHI conference on Human factors in computing systems: Changing our world, changing ourselves (CHI '02)*. New York: ACM Press.

Benyon, D. (2004). *Designing Interactive Systems*. Reading, MA: Addison-Wesley.

Bernstein, M., Kleek, M., Schraefel, M., & Karger, D. (2007). Management of personal information scraps. In *Proceedings of the extended abstracts on Human factors in computing systems (CHI '07)*. New York: ACM Press.

Blackwell, A. (2006). The reification of metaphor as a design tool. *Transactions on Computer-Human Interaction (TOCHI), 13*(4).

Boehner, K., DePaula, R., Dourish, P., & Sengers, P. (2005). Affect: from information to interaction. In *Proceedings of the 4th decennial conference on Critical computing: between sense and sensibility (CC '05)*. New York: ACM Press.

Buchanan, R. (1998). Branzi's Dilemma: Design in contemporary culture. *Design Issues, 14*(1).. doi:10.2307/1511825

Card, S. K., Moran, T., & Newell, A. (1980). The keystroke-level model for user performance time with interactive systems. *Communications of the ACM, 23*(7)..doi:10.1145/358886.358895

Card, S. K., Moran, T. P., & Newall, A. (1983). *The psychology of human-computer interaction*. Mahwah, NJ: Lawrence Erlbaum Associates.

Carroll, J. M. (Ed.). (1991). *Designing interaction: psychology at the human-computer interface*. New York: Cambridge University Press.

Carroll, J. M., & Kellogg, W. A. (1989). Artifact as theory-nexus: hermeneutics meets theory-based design. In, *Proceedings of the SIGCHI conference on Human factors in computing systems: Wings for the mind (CHI '89)* (Vol. 20).

Carroll, J. M., & Rosson, M. B. (1992). Getting around the task-artifact cycle: how to make claims and design by scenario. [TOIS]. *ACM Transactions on Information Systems, 10*(2).. doi:10.1145/146802.146834

Chang, Y., Lim, Y., & Stolterman, E. (2008). Personas: from theory to practices. In *Proceedings of the 5th Nordic conference on Human-computer interaction: building bridges (NordiCHI '08)*. New York: ACM Press.

Dahlbom, B., & Mathiassen, L. (1997). The future of our profession. *Communications of the ACM, 40*(6)..doi:10.1145/255656.255706

Dalsgaard, P., & Hansen, L. (2008). Performing perception—staging aesthetics of interaction. *Transactions on Computer-Human Interaction (TOCHI), 15*(3).

Dam, A. (1997). Post-WIMP user interfaces. *Communications of the ACM, 40*(2).

Davis, M. (2008). Toto, I've Got a Feeling We're Not in Kansas Anymore.... *Interaction, 15*(5).. doi:10.1145/1390085.1390091

Dirgahayu, T., Quartel, D., & Sinderen, M. (2008). Designing interaction behaviour in service-oriented enterprise application integration. In *Proceedings of the 2008 ACM symposium on Applied computing (SAC '08)*. New York: ACM Press.

Dourish, P. (2007). Responsibilities and implications: further thoughts on ethnography and design. In *Proceedings of the 2007 conference on Designing for User eXperiences (DUX '07)*. New York: ACM Press

Dourish, P. (2006). Implications for design. In *Proceedings of the SIGCHI conference on Human Factors in computing systems (CHI '06)*. New York: ACM Press.

Dourish, P., & Bellotti, V. (1992). Awareness and coordination in shared workspaces. In *Proceedings of the 1992 ACM conference on Computer-supported cooperative work (CSCW '92)*.

Dubberly, H., Pangaro, P., & Haque, U. (2009). What is interaction? are there different types? *interactions, 16*(1).

Ellis, C., Gibbs, S., & Rein, G. (1991). Groupware: some issues and experiences. *Communications of the ACM, 34*(1)..doi:10.1145/99977.99987

Fallman, D. (2003). Design-oriented human-computer interaction. In *Proceedings of the SIGCHI conference on Human factors in computing systems (CHI '03)*. New York: ACM Press.

Forlizzi, J., & Battarbee, K. (2004). Understanding experience in interactive systems. In *Proceedings of the 5th conference on Designing interactive systems: processes, practices, methods, and techniques (DIS '04)*. New York: ACM Press.

Frøkjær, E., & Hornbæk, K. (2008). Metaphors of human thinking for usability inspection and design. *Transactions on Computer-Human Interaction (TOCHI), 14*(4).

Gould, J., & Lewis, C. (1985). Designing for usability: key principles and what designers think. *Communications of the ACM, 28*(3). doi:10.1145/3166.3170

Greenfield, A. (2006). *Everyware: The dawning age of ubiquitous computing*. Berkeley, CA: Peachpit Press.

Häkkilä, J., & Mäntyjärvi, J. (2006). Developing design guidelines for context-aware mobile applications. In *Proceedings of the 3rd international conference on Mobile technology, applications & systems (Mobility '06)*. New York: ACM Press.

Heim, S. (2007). *The Resonant Interface – HCI Foundations for interaction design*. Reading, MA: Addison-Wesley.

Hinckley, K., Pierce, J., Sinclair, M., & Horvitz, E. (2000). Sensing techniques for mobile interaction. In *Proceedings of the 13th annual ACM symposium on User interface software and technology (UIST '00)*. New York: ACM Press.

Hindmarsh, J., Fraser, M., Heath, C., Benford, S., & Greenhalgh, C. (2000). Object-focused interaction in collaborative virtual environments. *Transactions on Computer-Human Interaction (TOCHI), 7*(4).

Hollan, J., Hutchins, E., & Kirsh, D. (2000). Distributed cognition: toward a new foundation for human-computer interaction research. *Transactions on Computer-Human Interaction (TOCHI), 7*(2).

Hollingsed, T., & Novick, D. (2007). Usability inspection methods after 15 years of research and practice. In *Proceedings of the 25th annual ACM international conference on Design of communication (SIGDOC '07)*. New York: ACM Press.

Hornecker, E., & Buur, J. (2006). Getting a grip on tangible interaction: a framework on physical space and social interaction. In *Proceedings of the SIGCHI conference on Human Factors in computing systems (CHI '06)*. New York: ACM Press.

Hughes, J., King, V., Rodden, T., & Andersen, H. (1995). The role of ethnography in interactive systems design. *Interaction, 2*(2).. doi:10.1145/205350.205358

Hughes, J., Randall, D., & Shapiro, D. (1992). Faltering from ethnography to design. In *Proceedings of the 1992 ACM conference on Computer-supported cooperative work (CSCW '92)*. New York: ACM Press.

Ishii, H., & Ullmer, B. (1997). Tangible bits: towards seamless interfaces between people, bits and atoms. In *Proceedings of the SIGCHI conference on Human factors in computing systems (CHI '97)*. New York: ACM Press.

Jacob, R. (2006). What is the next generation of human-computer interaction? In *Proceedings of the extended abstracts on Human factors in computing systems (CHI '06)*. New York: ACM Press.

Jacob, R., Deligiannidis, L., & Morrison, S. (1999). A software model and specification language for non-WIMP user interfaces. *Transactions on Computer-Human Interaction (TOCHI), 6*(1).

Jeffries, R., Miller, J., Wharton, C., & Uyeda, K. (1991). User interface evaluation in the real world: a comparison of four techniques. In *Proceedings of the SIGCHI conference on Human factors in computing systems (CHI '91)*. New York: ACM Press

Kawaguchi, A. (2003). Capturing and analyzing requirement: in case of software and applying to hardware. In *Proceedings of the 2003 conference on Asia South Pacific design automation (ASP-DAC)*. New York: ACM Press.

Keinonen, T. (2008). User-centered design and fundamental need. In *Proceedings of the 5th Nordic conference on Human-computer interaction: building bridges (NordiCHI '08)*. New York: ACM Press.

Klemmer, S., Hartmann, B., & Takayama, L. (2006). How bodies matter: five themes for interaction design. In *Proceedings of the 6th conference on Designing Interactive systems (DIS '06)*. New York: ACM Press.

Kolehmainen, K., Hongisto, M., & Kanstrén, T. (2008). Optimizing dynamic performance scaling for user interface performance. In *Proceedings of the International Conference on Mobile Technology, Applications, and Systems (Mobility '08)*.

Krishnamurthy, B., Gill, P., & Arlitt, M. (2008). A few chirps about twitter. In *Proceedings of the first workshop on Online social networks (WOSP '08)*. New York: ACM Press.

Kweon, S., Cho, E., & Kim, E. (2008). Interactivity dimension: media, contents, and user perception. In *Proceedings of the 3rd international conference on Digital Interactive Media in Entertainment and Arts (DIMEA '08)*. New York: ACM Press.

Lim, Y-K., Stolterman, E., & Tenenberg, J. (2008). The anatomy of prototypes: Prototypes as filters, prototypes as manifestations of design ideas. *Transactions on Computer-Human Interaction (TOCHI), 15*(2).

Mao, J.-Y., Vredenburg, K., Smith, P., & Carey, T. (2005). The state of user-centered design practice. *Communications of the ACM, 48*(3).. doi:10.1145/1047671.1047677

Marchionini, G., & Sibert, J. (1991). An agenda for human-computer interaction: science and engineering serving human needs. *SIGCHI Bulletin, 23*(4).

Mazé, R. (2007). *Occupying time: design, technology and the form of interaction*. Stockholm, Sweden: Axl Books.

McClelland, I. (2005). 'User experience' design a new form of design practice takes shape. In *Proceedings of CHI '05 extended abstracts on Human factors in computing systems*. New York: ACM Press.

Miller, C. (1997). Computational approaches to interface design: what works, what doesn't, what should and what might. In *Proceedings of the 2nd international conference on Intelligent user interfaces (IUI '97)*. New York: ACM Press.

Muller, M., & Kuhn, S. (1993). Participatory design. *Communications of the ACM, 36*(6).. doi:10.1145/153571.255960

Mylopoulos, J., Chung, L., & Yu, E. (1999). From object-oriented to goal-oriented requirements analysis. *Communications of the ACM, 42*(1). doi:10.1145/291469.293165

Nielsen, J., & Molich, R. (1990). Heuristic evaluation of user interfaces. In *Proceedings of the SIGCHI conference on Human factors in computing systems (CHI '90)*. New York: ACM Press.

Norman, D. A. (2002). *The Design of Everyday Things*. New York: Basic Books.

Oliveira, R., & Rocha, H. (2005). Towards an approach for multi-device interface design. In *Proceedings of the 11th Brazilian Symposium on Multimedia and the web (WebMedia '05)*. New York: ACM Press.

Petroski, H. (1994). *The Evolution of Useful Things: How Everyday Artifacts-From Forks and Pins to Paper Clips and Zippers-Came to be as They are*. New York: Vintage Books.

Pilgrim, C. (2008). Improving the usability of web 2.0 applications. In *Proceedings of the nineteenth ACM conference on Hypertext and hypermedia (HT '08)*. New York: ACM Press.

Pinelle, D., Gutwin, C., & Greenberg, S. (2003). Task analysis for groupware usability evaluation: Modeling shared-workspace tasks with the mechanics of collaboration. *Transactions on Computer-Human Interaction (TOCHI), 10*(4).

Plewe, D. (2008). Transactional arts: interaction as transaction. In *Proceeding of the 16th ACM international conference on Multimedia (MM '08)*. New York: ACM Press.

Ruthven, I. (2008). The context of the interface. In *Proceedings of the second international symposium on Information interaction in context (IIiX '08)*. New York: ACM Press.

Sauro, J., & Kindlund, E. (2005). A method to standardize usability metrics into a single score. In *Proceedings of the SIGCHI conference on Human factors in computing systems (CHI '05)*. New York: ACM Press.

Shapiro, D. (2005). Participatory design: the will to succeed. In *Proceedings of the 4th decennial conference on Critical computing: between sense and sensibility*. New York: ACM Press.

Simonsen, J., & Kensing, F. (1997). Using ethnography in contextual design. *Communications of the ACM, 40*(7)..doi:10.1145/256175.256190

Souza, C., Prates, R., Barbosa, S., & Edmonds, E. (2000). Semiotic approaches to user interface design. In *CHI '00 extended abstracts on Human factors in computing systems*. New York: ACM Press. doi:10.1145/633292.633513

Suchman, L. (1987). *Plans and Situated Actions: The Problem of Human-Machine Communication (Learning in Doing: Social, Cognitive and Computational Perspectives)*. New York: Cambridge University Press.

Suchman, L. (1995). Making work visible. *Communications of the ACM, 38*(9).. doi:10.1145/223248.223263

Suchman, L. (2006). *Human-Machine Reconfigurations*. Cambridge, UK: Cambridge University Press.

Sutcliffe, A. (2000). On the effective use and reuse of HCI knowledge. *Transactions on Computer-Human Interaction (TOCHI), 7*(2).

Toney, A., Mulley, B., Thomas, B., & Piekarski, W. (2003). Social weight: designing to minimize the social consequences arising from technology use by the mobile professional. *Personal and Ubiquitous Computing, 7*(5)..doi:10.1007/s00779-003-0245-8

Vredenburg, K., Mao, J.-Y., Smith, P., & Carey, T. (2002). A survey of user-centered design practice. In *Proceedings of the SIGCHI conference on Human factors in computing systems: Changing our world, changing ourselves (CHI '02)*. New York: ACM Press.

Whittaker, S. (1996). Talking to strangers: an evaluation of the factors affecting electronic collaboration. In *Proceedings of the 1996 ACM conference on Computer supported cooperative work (CSCW '96)*. New York: ACM Press.

Whittaker, S., Swanson, J., Kucan, J., & Sidner, C. (1997). TeleNotes: managing lightweight interactions in the desktop. *Transactions on Computer-Human Interaction (TOCHI), 4*(2).

Whittaker, S., Terveen, L., & Nardi, B. (2000). Let's stop pushing the envelope and start addressing it: a reference task agenda for HCI. *Human-Computer Interaction, 15*, 75–106..doi:10.1207/S15327051HCI1523_2

Wiberg, M. (2001). RoamWare: an integrated architecture for seamless interaction in between mobile meetings. In *Proceedings of the 2001 International ACM SIGGROUP Conference on Supporting Group Work (GROUP '01)*. New York: ACM Press.

Zimmerman, J., Forlizzi, J., & Evenson, S. (2007). Research through design as a method for interaction design research in HCI. In *Proceedings of the SIGCHI conference on Human factors in computing systems (CHI '07)*. New York: ACM Press.

This work was previously published in International Journal of Ambient Computing and Intelligence, Volume 2, Issue 2, edited by Kevin Curran, pp. 1-26, copyright 2010 by IGI Publishing (an imprint of IGI Global).

Chapter 8
Auditory Augmentation

Till Bovermann
CITEC, Bielefeld University, Germany

René Tünnermann
CITEC, Bielefeld University, Germany

Thomas Hermann
CITEC, Bielefeld University, Germany

ABSTRACT

With auditory augmentation, the authors describe building blocks supporting the design of data representation tools, which unobtrusively alter the auditory characteristics of structure-borne sounds. The system enriches the structure-borne sound of objects with a sonification of (near) real time data streams. The object's auditory gestalt is shaped by data-driven parameters, creating a subtle display for ambient data streams. Auditory augmentation can be easily overlaid to existing sounds, and does not change prominent auditory features of the augmented objects like the sound's timing or its level. In a peripheral monitoring situation, the data stay out of the users' attention, which thereby remains free to focus on a primary task. However, any characteristic sound change will catch the users' attention. This article describes the principles of auditory augmentation, gives an introduction to the Reim Software Toolbox, and presents the first observations made in a preliminary long-term user study.

INTRODUCTION

The world around us is full of artificially gathered data. Upon that data we draw conclusions and make decisions, which possibly influence the future of our society. The difficulty hereby is not the data acquisition – we already have plenty – but our ability to process it (Goldhaber, 1997). Arising from this circumstance, at least two demands for '

data preparation can be identified: first, it should gain an appropriate amount of its user's attention depending on both the data domains' nature and the users' needs (Goldhaber, 2006), and second, it should utilise appropriate representations that truly integrate data and algorithmic functionality into the human life-world. Our awareness of being-in-the-world (Heidegger, 1927) is often caused by the intensiveness of multi-sensory stimuli. The experience of walking through a cavern, feeling a fresh breeze that contrasts with the pure solid

DOI: 10.4018/978-1-4666-0038-6.ch008

Copyright © 2012, IGI Global. Copying or distributing in print or electronic forms without written permission of IGI Global is prohibited.

rock under the feet, hearing echoes of footsteps and water drops serves as a good example for this: All the simultaneous impressions make us aware of our body and its integration into the cavern. The lack of a single sense or only a misleading impression would change the holistic interpretation of the scene. In traditional computer-related work, however, many of our senses such as hearing, taste or smell are underused. Historically developed paradigms such as the prominent Graphical User Interface (GUI) are not able to fully embed the user into the information to be mediated. Possible explanations for their nevertheless widespread use should be searched more in their (historically developed) technical feasibility (Sutherland, 1963), rather than in usability and user-oriented simplicity.

For about the past ten years, though, there has been a shift towards multimodal and tangible representations of computer-based processes and abstract data, which try to close the gap between the users' reality and the abstract environment of data and algorithms. This takes us closer to data representations that benefit from the various aspects of the human's being-in-the-world by incorporating other modalities than vision and general-purpose pointing devices. However, a key prerequisite for an effective and ergonomic interface to digitally stored data is that the interface designer takes care of the common interplay between the human and his environment and integrates the resulting interface into this complex interrelationship.

We argue that haptic feedback, feature-rich control, and the use of many modalities are essential to sufficiently mediate complex information from computers to humans. Tools to achieve this are for example tangible interfaces and auditory displays. While tangible user interfaces (TUI) provide rich and at the same time direct control over digitally stored data (Brave, Ishii, & Dahley, 1998), sound and therefore Auditory Displays (AD) are widely recognised as very direct and flexible in their dynamic allocation of user attention and information conveyance (Bovermann,

Hermann, & Ritter, 2006). Tangible auditory interfaces (TAI), a superset of both AD and TUI, has been introduced as paradigm by the authors (Bovermann 2010). They provide valuable guidelines for tangible auditory interface design. We believe that this combination can, after Rohrhuber (Rohrhuber, 2008), help to unfold the true potential of ergonomic user interfaces (Bovermann, Groten, de Campo, & Eckel, 2007). TAIs offer an information-rich interface that allows users to select, interpret and manipulate presented data such that they particularly profit from their naturally excellent pattern recognition abilities.

One paradigm that evolved from the research in TAI is auditory augmentation. It draws on peoples' knowledge about everyday objects, whether they are simple like stones or more specialised and integrated into our daily work respectively into technology-driven systems as computer interfaces like for instance keyboards or computer mice. To add a data representation to such objects, rather than manipulating their intentional usage, we introduce auditory augmentation as a paradigm to vary the objects' sonic characteristics such that their original sonic response appears as augmented by an artificial sound that encodes information about external data. All this manipulation does not affect the sound's original purpose. The sonic reaction to an excitation of such an enhanced object then does not only reflect its physical structure, but also features the attached data. In other words, the structure-borne sound is artificially altered to render an additional information layer of data-inherent features.

We implemented an auditory augmentation system (Figure 1) called the *Reim* toolbox.[1] It features a lightweight and modular concept that is intended to help users in creating and manipulating custom data-driven auditory augmentations of objects they have ready at hand. Reim is currently available as a library for the SuperCollider language.

In the next sections, we will give a detailed overview of data as we understand it in relation

Figure 1. General model of Reim-based auditory augmentations

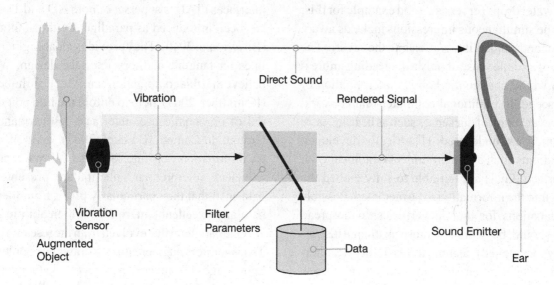

to auditory augmentation followed by an overview of the related work and research fields. This is followed by a detailed introduction to the auditory augmentation paradigm and its implementation in the Reim toolbox. Various application scenarios are demonstrated with interaction examples, and first insights are reported from a qualitative user study in which we observed people in an unobtrusive data monitoring environment that incorporates an auditory augmentation setup.

DATA: THE NON-MATERIALISTIC MATERIAL

Due to their usage in digital environments, data (e.g., audio, video or text files) are widely viewed as a material such as wood or stone. This implies both a certain materialistic characteristic and a way to treat it that is based on our common experience with reality. This circumstance has its origin in our often subconscious understanding of data. Already the phrases data handling, data processing, or data mining implicate that data is widely recognised

as a basic, materialistic resource. The used words originate in crafting or other physical work.

Data, though, is immaterial and disembodied. Its physical shape, the modality it is represented in, does by no means determine or affect its content; even more, data is pure content. There is for example absolutely no difference in a digital recording of Strawinsky's *Sacre du Printemps* whether it is represented as a series of magnetic forces on a rotating plate (i.e., a hard-drive), as states of electronic NAND-gates on computer chips (as it is the representation e.g., in computer memory), or as a series of high- and low-voltages in a copper-cable.

Neglecting this fact, data mining and data analysis, however, suggest its users to handle data as material. They process, analyse, and shape it like other work fields process, analyse and shape material like ore, stone, or wood. Nevertheless, the nature of data being a "non-materialistic material" has some inherent features, marking it different to material in the common sense. One of these features is that a data set is not bound to one phenotype. Its formal information content does not change depending on its actual representation: A change of modality does to no extent change the data itself. The subject matter of a book contains no other information than the same text represented as bits and bytes on a hard disk. A change of representation does, however, change the way people perceive a data set, since we derive our understanding of data from its actual representation. This circumstance makes it essential to look at the influence on the representation on the human perception and interpretation when dealing with data exploration and monitoring tasks.

Technically, however, data is independent of its representation type; nevertheless it has to be represented in some way. If this representation is well-suited for an algorithmic processing by computers, it is – most of the time – not in a form that supports human perception or structure recognition. The reason for this is not that the machine-oriented representation is too complex to understand. Moreover the pure physical representation (binary values coded as voltages in semiconductors or magnetic forces on hard drives) is completely inappropriate to be sensed or decoded by the human without appropriate tools.

RELATED RESEARCH FIELDS AND APPLICATIONS

Tangible Interfaces

The young research field of tangible interfaces (TI) picks up the concept of physically interfacing users and computers – a circumstance that was not present in the more traditional GUI-based designs (Ullmer & Ishii, 2000). To achieve this, the community around TI introduced physical objects to the virtual world of the digital, fully aware of all their interaction qualities, but also of their limitations caused by their embedding in the physical world. Tangible interfaces exploit real-world objects for the manipulation of digitally stored data, or – from a different point of view – enhance physical objects with data representations (either measured or rendered from artificial algorithms). This on first sight straightforward idea turned out to be a powerful approach to the conscious development of complex yet natural interfaces.

The used physical objects strongly affect the user experience of a tangible interface. Their inherent natural features of which users already have a prototypical concept are valuable for the designer and make it easy to develop interfaces that are naturally capable of collaborative and multi-handed usage (Fitzmaurice, Ishii, & Buxton, 1995). Even further, the usage of tangible objects implicitly incorporates a non-exclusive application such that the system designer does not have to explicitly implement it (Patten & Ishii, 2007).

Auditory Displays

Not only have research and perception of input technologies changed over the last century, but also the research in display technology has developed by discovering also non-visual modalities. The former focus on primarily visual displays has broadened to cover auditory (Kramer, 1994) and haptic cues (Brave & Dahley, 1997; Massie & Salisbury, 1994) . Particularly auditory displays (AD) have seen a strong uplift, since they connect to our human's excellent abilities to perceive auditory structures even in noisy signals. Furthermore, in our auditory perception, we are sensitive to different patterns than those that are pronounced in visual display techniques. Sound rendering provide a way to display a reasonable amount of complexity. Therefore they are suitable to display high-dimensional data. The benefit of sound, compared to other non-visual modalities, is that it can be synthesized in a reasonable quality and spatial resolution.

The human perception of sound differs strongly from visual perception. Humans developed different structure detection and analysis techniques for sound stimuli than those that are used in the visual domain. For instance, timing aspects like rhythm, a spectral signal decomposition and the native support of time-based structures are unique to auditory perception. The combination of visual and auditory displays, however, makes it possible to get a more complete interpretation of the represented data. Thus, the provision of the same data by more than one modality makes it possible to extend the usage of human capabilities in order to reveal the data's structure. Auditory displays also natively support collaborative work (Hermann & Hunt, 2005), and allow for subconscious and ambient data representations (Hermann, Bovermann, Riedenklau, & Ritter, 2007; Kilander & Lonnqvist, 2002).

Tangible Auditory Interfaces

While both auditory display, as well as tangible interface research are highly promising as individual research fields, a combination of their techniques and experiences introduces valuable cross-links and synergies beneficial for both. We therefore propose the term tangible auditory interface (TAI) for systems that combine tangible interfaces with auditory displays to mediate information back and forth between abstract data space and user-perceivable reality (Bovermann 2010). The two parts form an integral system for the representation of abstract objects like data or algorithms as physical and graspable artefacts with inherent sonic feedback. The tangible part hereby provides the means for the manipulation of data, algorithms, or their parameterisation, whereas the auditory part serves as the primary medium to display data- and interaction-driven information to the user.

Key features of TAIs are their interfacing richness, directness, capabilities as a multi-person device for ambient augmentation, and their values in ergonomics. The latter is due to the fact that the interplay of sound and tangibility suggests a nature-inspired interface gestalt that can be directly derived from nature. In this regard, audio is a common affiliate to physical objects; most of them already make sound, e.g. when touched or knocked against each other. Furthermore, auditory displays profit from a direct control interface (Hermann & Hunt, 2005). Especially an auditory display that is designed for direct interaction with data profits from a close interaction loop between user and data representation as it can be provided easily by a tangible interface.

Reality-Based Interaction

Reality-based Interaction (RBI) is a framework introduced by Jacob et al. that aims to unify emerging human computer interaction styles such as virtual, mixed and augmented reality, tangible interaction, ubiquitous and pervasive computing (Jacob, Girouard, Hirshfield, Horn, Shaer, Solovey, & Zigelbaum, 2008). Their key statement for unifying these approaches into one field is that all of them – intentionally or unintentionally – utilise at least one of the four principles of RBI that are *Naïve Physics, Body Awareness and Skills, Environment Awareness and Skills*, respectively *Social Awareness and Skills*.

As the authors state, these principles – i.e., to base interaction techniques on pre-existing real-world knowledge and skills – can help to reduce the overall mental effort that is required to operate a system because users already possess the needed skills by their being-in-the-world. They claim that this reduction of mental effort may speed up learning, improves performance, and encourages improvisation and exploration, since users do not need to learn interface-specific skills. Designing data monitoring systems according to RBI therefore implies the use of multi-modality in both directions, to and from the user.

RBI forces to think both problem and user centred, rather than tool oriented. As an example, let us consider RBI's answer to the question of what is the typical reality-based approach to handle sounds. Natural sonic events are always connected to objects (re)acting with their environment. A loud bang, for example, always has a cause, be it an explosion or a slamming door. Auditory Displays on the other side grant digital information a physical voice. There is no natural pendant for them, apart from an internal physical model that is completely rendered in the virtual (like it is the case in Model-Based Sonification (Hermann & Ritter, 1999)). Here is where the benefit of RBI comes into play: To be human-understandable and therefore closely linked to RBI themes, not only the sonic outcome of a physical model should be perceivable by the user. Moreover, RBI claims that the overall performance of the system will increase when an interface is part of the user's direct environment, be it integrated either via VR, AR or any other related interfacing technology.

Another feature of RBI is the explicit utilisation of tradeoffs regarding the above-described principles in order to sharpen the designer's awareness in interface design. These tradeoffs are usually caused by the implementation of desired qualities of the system that cannot be implemented without automated algorithmic systems. They further state that each tradeoff in an RBI-based system should be explicitly made. Tradeoffs, however, are not only optional for RBI-related system design, moreover they deserve a central place: An application that makes use of dynamic/algorithmic data processing (e.g., that has to use a computer) and is designed after the RBI framework has to have parts that result from these tradeoffs. Otherwise, the system could be built better –at least in terms of RBI – without the use of computers (i.e., exclusively in reality). The tradeoff in the design of auditory augmentations, for example, is caused by the need to control the system's sonic appearance by means of externally acquired (i.e., otherwise unconnected) data.

We integrated the tradeoff according to the guideline we derived from the RBI framework: Try to develop the desired application strictly according to the RBI principles, which especially means to avoid the mentioned tradeoffs. When desired features, such as the integration of additional, dynamically changing data, cannot be integrated without breaking these rules, the designer has to

introduce tradeoffs. Each compromise has to be accompanied by an explicit discussion of reasons and possible benefits. This approach results in an application that can be located in the Venn diagram exemplified in Figure 2. The following sections review several relevant auditory and tangible interfaces.

Audio-Haptic Ball

The audio-haptic ball senses physical interactions such as accelerations and applied pressure, allowing to make use of these interactions as excitations of a Sonification Model (Hermann & Ritter, 1999) resulting in an auditory and dynamic data representation (Hermann, Krause, & Ritter, 2002). By this, the user can experience the model-based sonification as plausible result to interactions such as shaking, rotating or squeezing the ball. Since the auditory output directly corresponds to the users' interaction with the ball, mediated via the sonification model, interaction can be used to explore and interpret data structures. The formal software development process for the audio-haptic ball interface used for Model-Based Sonification can be described as

1. designing a dynamic model, which often borrows from physical principles,
2. parameterizing the model with given data,
3. interacting with the ball (i.e. shake it, etc.),
4. sound is continuously rendered according to the dynamic model.

This approach especially requires the re-implementation of basic natural functionality, namely the dynamics of objects in a 3D space. Although this approach makes it literally possible to shake and squeeze data sets of higher dimensionality, it remains difficult to explain and understand what happens in such a space, and how the modelled n-dimensional object can be embedded into 3D reality so that it can be excited with the audio-haptic ball.

Figure 2. Venn diagram of RBI and its related research areas (left) and the (hypothetical) location of an RBI-based application

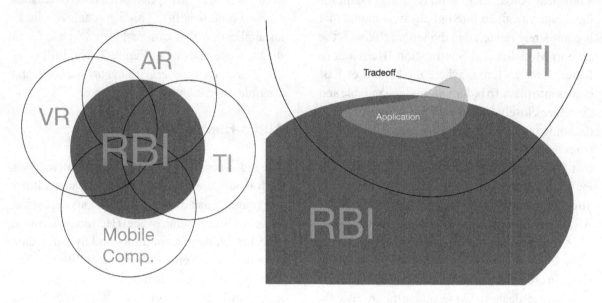

Pebblebox

The *Pebblebox* is another audio-haptic interface for the control of a granular synthesiser which extracts information like onset, amplitude or duration of grain-like sounds captured from physically interacting pebbles in a box (O'Modhrain & Essl, 2004) . These high-level features derived from the colliding stones are used to trigger granular sounds of e.g., water drops or wood cracking to simulate rain or fire sounds. The performance of the *Pebblebox* massively relies on the fact that the captured signal has to be a superposition of transient sound events. A change of the sound source such as it is implemented in the Scrubber, another closely related interface also developed by the authors of the *Pebblebox* (Essl & O'Modhrain, 2004), has to extract a completely different feature set from the input signal. It is designed in assuming incoming scrubbing sounds in order to synthesise artificial scrubbing sounds.

Auditory augmentation, however, does not rely on such assumptions: it directly uses the object's sound as the input signal of an audio filter, which is parameterized by given data. The resulting sound

is then directly played back to the user. The idea to involve data of the users' interest into the sound filtering process is essential for our approach to auditory augmentation.

AUDITORY AUGMENTATION AND THE REIM TOOLBOX

One of the human's natural qualifications is his ability to literally get a grip of almost every physical object easily. Technically speaking, a human is able to understand the basic features and often also the inner structure of an object by physically exploring it with his various senses and actuators (i.e., ears, nose, skin and eyes, and arms, hands, legs, fingers, etc.). We propose that dealing with data should be as easy as discovering e.g., the current fill-level of a box with sweets. We propose this both for everyday scenarios involving information such as temperature, humidity, stock exchange quotation, etc., but also for technology-oriented measurements like CPU load or network load. Taking this attempt literally motivates a more direct representation of data than it is state of the art. The augmentation of action feedback on everyday objects with appropriate data representations.

The paradigm of auditory augmentation is aimed to help interface designers to represent digitally stored data as auditory features of physical objects. It can be formally described as the process of artificially inducing auditory perceivable characteristics to existing physical objects. The structure-borne sound gestalt hereby is altered according to externally acquired data. However, this process does not change the natural interaction sound's presence or timing. An auditory augmentation system can be used to alter the sonic characteristics of arbitrary objects. Each object can therefore provide a different impression of the data, unveiling a different set of possible structural information of the represented data. Note that, although powerful and built for non-linear analysis and exploration, this paradigm is neither intended nor appropriate to systematically search for specific structure in data, or even to observe exact class labels for a data set. Moreover, it shifts the task of observing structures in possibly unknown data into a naturally perceivable form, where the human ability to find and understand structural information can be utilised.

As shown in Figure 1, an auditory augmentation system consists of the following parts: An audio-transducer (Vibration Sensor) captures structure-borne vibrations of arbitrary objects, which are fed into a parameterised audio filter (Filter). Its parameters are controlled according to externally acquired data such as the temperature or stock exchange quotations (Data). The filtered signal then is transformed into an audible sound (Sound Emitter), being a superposition of the originating vibration and the data under investigation. The resulting augmentation has negligible latency, and smoothly overlays with the original sound (Direct Sound). The overall auditory character of the complete setup depends on the input's audio characteristic, the filter, the data state, and the sound rendering including possible distortion by the loudspeaker. Note that the resulting sound mixes with the real sound of the interaction.

We introduce the Reim toolbox as an implementation for the auditory augmentation paradigm. Its lightweight and modular concept intends to help people familiar with a basic sound synthesis knowledge in the creation and customisation of such data-driven object augmentations. Systems, build according to Reim, draw on peoples' knowledge about every-day objects, whether they are as simple as pebbles, or more specialised and integrated into daily, technology-driven systems like keyboards or other computer interfaces.

Usage Scenarios

To show the potential of auditory augmentation as a tool for data exploration and monitoring, this section presents examples on how an everyday usage of such a setup might look like. It especially focuses on an ergonomic interaction design, drawing from familiar manipulation skills.

Let us consider two data sets that share the same characteristics in distribution and local density. There are no obvious differences in their structure. A user wants to investigate if there are other, possibly non-linear structural differences between the data sets. By linking each data set to a Reim augmentation, he investigates into this direction. Around him, the user collected surfaces of various characteristics: one of granite, one made of wooden, etc. He attaches the transducers of the Reim system to small glass objects and scrubs them over the surfaces. Each combination of surface, glass object/data set and scrubbing technique results in a characteristic sound. Exploring these combinations for differences between the sounds of each object enables the user to find structural differences between the data sets. When he found interesting reactions, he captures and analyses the source vibrations (i.e., the sounds that appear when scrubbing the objects on the surfaces without the data-inherited overlay) for further analysis, because these sounds offer information on the non-linear structures in the data sets under exploration. It can be seen as a classifying discriminant. Instead of using only rigid bodies, it is also possible to attach the transducers to drinking glasses filled with grainy material of different sizes and shapes. The user then sequentially loads the data sets to the glass/tool aggregates and shakes them. This way he can test which of the glasses emit a characteristic sound augmentation that can be used to differentiate between the data sets. Both scenarios become more powerful by Reims feature to record and playback input sounds with different data sets. Also the feature to change the synthesis process as well as the range of the parameter mapping increases the flexibility of the system.

In another scenario, dealing with unobtrusive data monitoring, a person wants to keep track of a slowly changing data stream such as the weather situation around his working place. In order to acquire this information without being disturbed by a constantly sounding auditory display, or having to actively observe e.g. a webpage, he acquires the data automatically from weather sensors and feeds them to his auditory augmentation setup. After this, he attaches the connected transducer to a computer input interface that he is using regularly (e.g., the keyboard, or the mouse), resulting in an auditory augmentation of the artefact's structure-borne sound with the weather data. Every time the attached sensor values change, the auditory character of the augmented device changes, giving the user a hint on the current weather conditions.

Adding auditory augmentation to structure-borne sounds means to insert a thin layer between people's action and an object's auditory re-action. The proposed auditory augmentation can be easily overlaid to existing sounds, and does not change prominent auditory features of the augmented objects like the sound's timing or its volume. In a peripheral monitoring situation, the data gets out of the way for the user if he is not actively concentrating on it. A characteristic change, however, tends to grab the user's attention.

Level of Abstraction

Reim supports two different abstraction levels: The first level incorporates mostly direct and physical manipulation with direct sonic feedback, whereas the second abstracts from these natural manipulation patterns.

In the first, the user's experience of an augmented object does not differ from handling non-augmented objects, apart from the fact that the object-emitted sounds are also data-driven. Due to his being-in-the-world, the user feels familiar with the objects manipulation feedback. He gets a feel for the process by gaining experience of the data-material compound's reaction over time. Non-linear complexity of material properties and their reactions to e.g., pressure and speed of action can be used intuitively, i.e., without additional cognitive effort. Data easily becomes integrated into everyday life.

The second level allows gaining assessment and increasing repeatability in the explorative process of Reim. It enables the user to capture the vibration of a physical excitation that then can be used to either repeat the data-representation process with the exact same prerequisites or to sonify other data items with it. This demand requires to capture the transducer's input and use it for the representation of several data sets as well as the addition of recording capabilities to the system such that the data's representation can be easily captured and replayed to others. Related to this are the offering of pre-recorded standard excitation sources, or the provision of a standard set of objects to add data-driven auditory augmentations. This abstraction, or, in terms of RBI, tradeoff allows to programmatically explore and compare data, while still utilizing the sound characteristics of the augmented object.

Implementation

According to the general model of auditory augmentations (cf., Figure 1), a setup of such a system requires the following hardware: a vibration sensor capable of audio signals (e.g., a dynamic microphone like the AKG C411, or a piezo-based pickup system like the Shadow SH SB1), a computer with an audio interface to capture the sensed signal and to apply the filter model to the signal, and a sound emitter (i.e., either loudspeakers or headphones) for signal playback.

We implemented the Reim toolbox to help with the administration of the data as well as with the filter design. The toolbox makes it easy to apply data based parameters to signal filter chains and to implement, collect, store, and share presets for the synthesis process. Both data processing and sound rendering are realised in the *SuperCollider* language (McCartney, 2002), and are available for free upon request.

APPLICATIONS

Auditory augmentation can be used in various usage scenarios. This section describes systems utilising the Reim toolbox for the two, in terms of their usage very different, scenarios of data exploration and unobtrusive monitoring that we described above. All introduced applications are demonstrated in videos on the corresponding website.[2]

Exploration

Schüttelreim[3] is an approach to implement the mentioned use case of active data exploration and comparison. In this setup, the transducers are statically attached to box-shaped objects, which should contain a grainy material such as several buttons or marbles. As shown in the video example, shaking the box results in an audible reaction that reflects the physical structure as well as the data-inherent parameters. This is realised with the attached transducer that captures the rattling of the box' content and feeds it into a filter. Loudspeakers near the exploration area then play

back the augmentation in real-time. When the data attached to the *Schüttelreim* object is substituted by another one, this substantially changes the resulting sound depending on the variation in the attached data item. Since people are trained to listen to manipulation-caused sounds, able to precisely control their handling, *Schüttelreim* allows to turn data into highly controllable sonic data objects. We claim that, by extensive use, people will learn to shake and manipulate the boxes in such ways that they can perceive certain aspects of the data, which possibly leads to a valid differentiation and classification of the structural information of the attached data.

A different example application incorporating auditory augmentation is *Paarreim*. In contrast to *Schüttelreim*, *Paarreim*'s interaction design is not based on the manipulation of self-contained sounding objects. Furthermore, it is focused on the physical interaction between objects and surfaces. It features several independent objects, each attached to one data set. These rigid objects with little natural resonance can be scrubbed over various surfaces that are made of different materials, each with a characteristic haptic texture. It results in substantially different excitations of the data depending on the interplay between their gestalt and the texture, which in turn change the sound of the auditory augmentation. The user gets detailed insights into the data structures and can learn to use specific material combinations that help him classify data into groups according to their sonic reaction. Having more than one object at hand allows for a comparison of the sounds, and therefore the data items. The actual auditory augmentation is realised by loudspeakers near the exploration area, which play back the sound synthesis. The setup of such a system is shown in Figure 3 and in the corresponding video on the website.

Figure 3. A Paarreim exploration session

Unobtrusive Monitoring

Object manipulations result in structure-borne sounds that inherently transport information about the incorporated objects and the accompanying physical reaction. It is packed in a very dense form, yet is it easy to understand.

Wetterreim[4] utilises this feature for a dedicated scenario: the day-to-day work on a computer as it is common at almost any office workplace. As the source for the auditory augmentation, we chose the keyboard, one of the main interfaces for the daily work with computers. Typing on it results in a characteristic sound that is shaped by the design of the keyboard and its interplay with the writer's fingers. A contact microphone captured the keyboard's structure-borne sound, on which we based a Sonification of weather-indicating measurements. When filtering the captured sound by data-driven filter parameters, an audio stream is created, which is close to the characteristics of the original but additionally features character-istics of the integrated data. The filter output is superimposed to the original sound such that it is perceived as one coherent auditory gestalt. The developed filter parameterisation for the weather data allows people to perceive a drop in pressure or an approaching cloud front as a change in the object's auditory characteristic. An example for the use of *Wetterreim* is given in the correspond-ing video on the website.

WETTERREIM CASE STUDY

To gather feedback on the implemented auditory augmentation system, we conducted a qualitative user study. We asked three people to integrate *Wetterreim* into their day-to-day work for a period of four or more days. After this period, we collected their statements in an unstructured interview. During the setup, the audio transducer was attached to the participant's commonly used keyboard (as shown in Figure 4). Its signal was fed into an external computer that was exclusively used for data acquisition and sound rendering. The data that were augmented to the participant's keyboard were acquired from the nearest publicly available weather station. Its update rate varied between every half an hour and every hour. We used the filter setup shown in Figure 5. The weather conditions during the study are shown in Table 1. In an initial setup session, filter ranges were adapted for each participant in order to reflect their individual preferences and the sonic character of their keyboard. Overall, our observations based on the unstructured interviews unveiled the fol-lowing aspects:

Sound Design

Participant 2 found the used ringing sound to be natural and pleasant. However, Participant 1 reported that the augmented sound irritated her in the beginning. Participant 1, Participant 2 and

Figure 4. The hardware setup used by Participant 1. The transducer was attached to the external video adapter of her laptop. This made it easy for (dis-)assembly, since she only used Wetterreim at her workplace, but carried her laptop with her

Figure 5. Schematic of the sound synthesis used in the case study

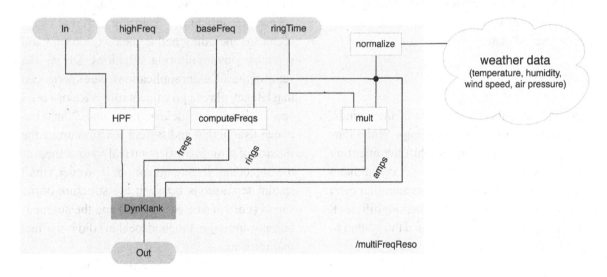

Table 1. The weather conditions for each participant during the Wetterreim study.

User	# of Days	Weather Conditions
Participant 1	**4 days**	**Contrary weather, changes between 35°C, sunny and 20°C with thunderstorm and sometimes heavy rain in the evening.**
Participant 2	10 days	Constant over the time, no rain, around 20°C.
Participant 3	8 days	20°C – 25°C, rainy and sunny.

Participant 3 stated that they missed the sound when it was absent by accident.

Localization

Participant 2 found it astounding that the sound seemed to originate from the keyboard although the loudspeaker was at a completely different position.

Data-to-Sound Mapping

The differences in the rendered sound according to the data were considered by Participant 1 and Participant 2 to be reasonably distinguishable, even without direct comparison.

Exploration

All participants reported that they also used the setup playfully; Participant 2 and Participant 3 stated to actively trigger it by purpose to hear the system's actual state.

Attention

Regarding the subconsciousness of the sounds, participants reported mixed feelings. While Participant 1 found it difficult to shift her attention away from the sound, Participant 3 stated that a change in feedback was rising his attention even when he was concentrating on something different. However, no participant mentioned the system to be bothersome.

Sound Level

The adjustment of the augmentation's volume was experienced by all users to be difficult. Especially Participant 1 reported to usually type relatively weak, making it difficult to properly adjust the amplitude of the augmentation.

In general, the application – unobtrusive monitoring of near real-time data – worked out

for the participants. We especially found out that users perceived the auditory augmentation and the original sound as a single natural sound, they were not bothered by the Sonification, and they had difficulties adjusting the volume of the auditory augmentation. For a future setup, we plan to investigate into this issue.

CONCLUSION

In this article, we introduced auditory augmentation as a paradigm to represent data as an artificially induced overlay to the common structure-borne sounds of an arbitrary object. With Reim, we presented a toolbox for the design and implementation of such tangible auditory interfaces. It utilises everyday objects and their interrelations to transform abstract data into physically manipulable and auditorily perceivable artefacts. The toolbox has been demonstrated at hand of several design studies featuring different usage scenarios including active data exploration and subconscious monitoring situations. During the setup of the different applications, we experienced that latency plays a prominent role in Reim-based applications. Long delays (more than 20ms) between user action and system reaction broke the illusion of sonic identification and compactness of the object and its augmentation. However, small spatial separations between the structure-borne sound (i.e. transducer location) and the augmentation source (i.e. the loudspeaker) did not affect that illusion.

Because of Reim's simple technical assembly, the participants in the qualitative user study were able to understand the setup without any problems. Additionally, it turned out that the Reim system is well applicable for a long-term case study. During such a study on *Wetterreim*, subjects used an auditory augmentation of weather data in their usual working environment. Local measurements of weather-related data have been augmented to the structure-borne sounds of their computer keyboard. Participants reported that the augmentation worked well, though it turned out that the particular data domain was not of much use. However, the augmentation was perceived as part of the augmented object, a fact that indicates that auditory augmentations can well merge into the everyday soundscape. Participants were also able to differentiate between several weather situations.

Many participants stated that they were not able to separate source sounds from data-driven sounds. Although this is an essential effect regarding the acceptance of the system, it uncovers an inherent issue of Reim-based applications: the sound of the data object combination is perceived as an entity; users are not able to split it into its components to separate the data communicating part from the structure-borne sound. Long-term usage of a Reim-based system, though, should overcome this effect. People will adapt to the auditory specifics of the used objects and develop implicit knowledge on how to separate the physically induced sounds from the data-dependent sounds. This effect is supported by the fact that the physical part of the sound bases in a static set of parameters, reflecting the same object characteristics in all excitations. Changes in the sound therefore always originate in a change of the data-driven augmentation. These observations and considerations suggest that auditory augmentation is a promising approach for tangible auditory interfaces, both for data exploration and subconscious monitoring.

ACKNOWLEDGMENT

This work was partly funded by the CRC673-Alignment in Communication and the Excellence Initiative of the German Research Foundation.

REFERENCES

Bovermann, T. (2010). *Tangible Auditory Interfaces: Combining Auditory Displays and Tangible Interfaces*. PhD thesis, Faculty of Technology, Bielefeld University, Germany.

Bovermann, T., Groten, J., de Campo, A., & Eckel, G. (2007). Juggling Sounds. In *Proceedings of the 2nd International Workshop on Interactive Sonification*, York, UK.

Bovermann, T., Hermann, T., & Ritter, H. (2006). Tangible Data Scanning Sonification Model. In *Proceedings of the International Conference on Auditory Display* (ICAD 2006), London, UK (pp. 77-82).

Brave, S., & Dahley, A. (1997). inTouch: a medium for haptic interpersonal communication. In *Proceedings of the Conference on Human Factors in Computing Systems* (pp. 363-364).

Brave, S., Ishii, H., & Dahley, A. (1998). Tangible interfaces for remote collaboration and communication. In *Proceedings of the 1998 ACM Conference on Computer Supported Cooperative Work* (pp. 169-178).

Essl, G., & O'Modhrain, S. (2004). Scrubber: an interface for friction-induced sounds. In *Proceedings of the 2005 Conference on New Interfaces for Musical Expression* (NIME '05), Singapore, Singapore (pp. 70-75).

Fitzmaurice, G. W., Ishii, H., & Buxton, W. (1995). Bricks: Laying the Foundations for Graspable User Interfaces. In *Proceedings of CHI 1995* (pp. 442-449).

Goldhaber, M. H. (1997). The Attention and the Net. *First Monday*, *2*(4).

Goldhaber, M. H. (2006). How (Not) to Study the Attention Economy: A Review of The Economics of Attention: Style and Substance in the Age of Information. *First Monday*, *11*(11).

Heidegger, M. (1927). Sein und Zeit. Halle A. D. S: Niemeyer.

Hermann, H., & Hunt, A. (Eds.). (2005). *IEEE Multimedia, Special Issue Interactive Sonification*. Washington, DC: IEEE.

Hermann, T., Bovermann, T., Riedenklau, E., & Ritter, H. (2007). Tangible Computing for Interactive Sonification of Multivariate Data. In *Proceedings of the 2nd Interactive Sonification Workshop*.

Hermann, T., Krause, J., & Ritter, H. (2002). Real-Time Control of Sonification Models with an Audio-Haptic Interface. In *Proceedings of the International Conference on Auditory Display 2002* (pp. 82-86).

Hermann, T., & Ritter, H. (1999). Listen to your Data: Model-Based Sonification for Data Analysis. In *Proceedings of the Advances in Intelligent Computing and Multimedia Systems*, Baden-Baden, Germany (pp. 189–194).

Jacob, R. J. K., Girouard, A., Hirshfield, L. M., Horn, M. S., Shaer, O., Solovey, E. T., & Zigelbaum, J. (2008). *Reality-based interaction: a framework for post-WIMP interfaces*.

Kilander, F., & Lönnqvist, P. (2002). A Whisper in the Woods: An Ambient Soundscape for Peripheral Awareness of Remote Processes. In *Proceedings of the International Conference on Auditory Display 2002*.

Kramer, G. (Ed.). (1994). *Auditory Display*. Reading, MA: Addison-Wesley.

Massie, T. H., & Salisbury, J. K. (1994). The PHANTOM Haptic Interface: A Device for Probing Virtual Objects. In *Proceedings of the ASME Winter Annual Meeting, Symposium on Haptic Interfaces for Virtual Environment and Teleoperator Systems*.

McCartney, J. (2002). Rethinking the computer music language: SuperCollider. *Computer Music Journal*, *26*(4), 61–68. .doi:10.1162/014892602320991383

O'Modhrain, S., & Essl, G. (2004). PebbleBox and CrumbleBag: tactile interfaces for granular synthesis. In *Proceedings of the 2004 Conference on New Interfaces for Musical Expression* (NIME '04), Singapore, Singapore (pp. 74-79).

Patten, J., & Ishii, H. (2007). Mechanical constraints as computational constraints in tabletop tangible interfaces. In *Proceedings of the SIGCHI Conference on Human Factors in Computing Systems* (pp. 809-818).

Rohrhuber, J. (2008). Implications of Unfolding. In *Paradoxes of Interactivity* (pp.175-189).

Sutherland, I. E. (1963). *Sketchpad, a man-machine graphical communication system*. Unpublished doctoral dissertation, Massachusetts Institute of Technology, Cambridge, MA.

Ullmer, B., & Ishii, H. (2000). Emerging Frameworks For Tangible User Interfaces. *IBM Systems Journal*, *39*(3-4), 915–931. .doi:10.1147/sj.393.0915

ENDNOTES

[1] The name of the implemented system is motivated by a german saying *sich einen Reim machen auf*, which can be translated best as put two and two together.

[2] Auditory Augmentation Demonstration Media: http://www.techfak.uni-bielefeld.de/ags/ami/publications/BTH2010-AA/

[3] *Schütteln* is German for *to shake*.

[4] *Wetter* is German for *weather*.

This work was previously published in International Journal of Ambient Computing and Intelligence, Volume 2, Issue 1, edited by Kevin Curran, pp. 27-41, copyright 2010 by IGI Publishing (an imprint of IGI Global).

Chapter 9
Collecting Datasets from Ambient Intelligence Environments

Piero Zappi
University of California San Diego, USA

Clemens Lombriser
ETH Zürich, Switzerland

Luca Benini
University of Bologna, Italy

Gerhard Tröster
ETH Zürich, Switzerland

ABSTRACT

This paper describes a methodology and lessons learned from collecting datasets in Ambient Intelligence Environments. The authors present considerations on how to setup an experiment and discuss decisions taken at different planning steps, ranging from the selection of human activities over sensor choices to issues of the recording software. The experiment design and execution is illustrated through a dataset involving 150 recording sessions with 28 sensors worn on the subject body and embedded into tools and the environment. The paper also describes a number of unforeseen problems that affected the experiment and useful considerations that help other researchers recording their own ambient intelligence datasets.

INTRODUCTION

Ambient Intelligence (AmI) describes a paradigm where smart, electronic environments are sensitive and responsive to the presence of people and their activities (Ramos et al., 2008). AmI systems use

sensors invisibly embedded into objects of daily use and environments of everyday life. People moving in such settings engage many computational devices and systems simultaneously even if they are not aware of their presence (Jaimes & Sebe, 2007). The pervasive sensing enables context-aware computing by providing software that is able to adapt to aspects of the situations

DOI: 10.4018/978-1-4666-0038-6.ch009

Copyright © 2012, IGI Global. Copying or distributing in print or electronic forms without written permission of IGI Global is prohibited.

in which it operates (Li et al., 2009). A major challenge is the detection of human factors in context information, which can be grouped in three categories (Schmidt et al., 1999): information about the user (habits, emotional state, etc.), his/her social environment (social interaction, group dynamics, etc.), and his/her tasks (spontaneous activity, general goals, etc.).

This work focuses on the recognition of human activities, which allows for activity-based computing (Davies et al., 2008), and is seen here as a sense and classify problem. Common approaches can be divided into those relying on video tracking systems (Mitra et al., 2007) and others relying on multimodal sensor networks that include body-worn sensors, smart sensors and sensors embedded in furniture (Ward et al., 2006; Jeong et al., 2008; Amft, 2007). In this paper, we focus on the second group. In such settings, data is collected from a large number of sensors and is fused using machine learning algorithms to recognize people activity. Typical algorithms include decision tree classifiers, Bayesian networks, linear discriminant classifiers, neural networks, Hidden Markov Models, voting techniques and many others (Duda et al., 2000). These algorithms belong to the class of *supervised classifiers* which learn by example. In a *training phase*, they require a large set of sample instances of all classes. From these instances, they optimize their model parameters to reflect the classes. The recognition performance can then be tested using a *validation set*, a second set of class instances, which have not been seen used in training. Complex classification algorithms or complicated signal patterns often require large datasets for reliable training and testing.

Establishing large datasets from AmI environments is costly and time-consuming, but crucial for the research community (Ponce et al., 2006). Besides deploying and maintaining sensors, data needs to be collected over weeks, months, or even years. All data needs to be annotated by humans, such that activities of interest are marked in the sensor streams. Aware of these limits, many researchers share the datasets they have obtained from their instrumented environments (Intille, 2009; BoxLab, 2009). The objective is to accelerate the creation of novel applications in the fields of human-computer interaction, healthcare and ubiquitous computing. But what are the specific problems encountered when collecting datasets? What should researchers be aware of when they plan experiments? We present the methodology and we have learned from recording various complex datasets of everyday activities. For every step we present, we describe how we have solved it during a joint project of the University of Bologna and ETH Zürich. The experiment consists of 28 sensors implementing 5 sensing modalities and recording 64 atomic activities within 8 scenarios of everyday life. The dataset is freely available for research purposes[1]. The article is organized as follows; the next section presents an overview of freely available datasets. We then describe our methodology and the individual steps we have followed to produce our dataset. The article concludes with a number of lessons learned.

RELATED WORK

The UCI Machine Learning Repository (Asuncion & Newman, 2007) is a well-known database for machine learning. Created in 1987, it includes at date of writing 187 datasets for machine learning algorithms. Among others, it also contains datasets related to natural human computer interaction. The Semeion Handwritten Digit dataset includes 1593 handwritten digits from 80 persons. The CMU Face Image dataset includes 640 black and white face images of people taken with varying poses, expressions, and size. The Parkinson dataset is composed of biomedical voice measurements from 31 people, 23 with Parkinson's disease.

Such a database does not yet exist for activity recognition. However several instrumented home are developing activity recognition datasets. Some examples are the Smart Medical Home Research

Laboratory (University of Rochester, 2001), the PlaceLab (Intille, 2006), the AwareHome (Georgia Institute of Technology, 2000), or the SmartHome (Duke University, 2003).

The PlaceLab Intensive Activity 1 and 2 (PLIA1, PLIA2) (Munguia et al., 2006) and PlaceLab Couple 1 (PLCouple1) (Logan et al., 2007) are three freely available datasets collected within the MIT PlaceLab database. PLIA1 and 2 include four hours of continuous household activities (cooking, cleaning up etc.) each performed by a single person, while PLCouple 1 are the recording of normal lifetime activity performed by a couple living in the Place Lab for 2.5 months. Activities have been monitored by over 100 sensors including contact, humidity, electrical current flow, temperature, and water flow sensors. In the PLCouple 1 dataset the male tester was wearing an RFID reader able to detect over 400 objects that were tagged, while in the PLIA 2 dataset the user was wearing 5 accelerometers. All activities are captured in audio and video. Following the idea that people activities can be inferred by looking only at objects used, two single-person apartments have been filled with around 80 reed switch sensors each for a period of two weeks (Tapia et al., 2004). The sensors were installed in households and furniture such as drawers, refrigerators and containers to record opening-closing events (activation deactivation events) as the subjects carried out everyday activities.

The CASAS Smart Home project is a multidisciplinary research project at Washington State University to create an intelligent home environment. A three bedroom, one bathroom, one kitchen and one living/dining room apartment has been filled with an array of motion sensors together with temperature, water flow and contact switch sensors. 19 datasets are available at time of writing (Washington State University, 2009). The datasets include a single execution of normal everyday activities performed by multiple persons as well as a recording of people living and working in the smart home for extended period of time. The

Wearable Action Recognition Database (WARD) is a benchmark database for human action recognition using a wearable motion sensor network (Yang et al., 2009). Activities performed by 20 subjects (7 female and 13 male) aging from 19 to 75 years old are recorded using 5 sensor boards embedding a three axis accelerometer and a dual axis gyroscope placed on user wrists, ankles and on waist. 13 activities like standing, jogging, lying and cycling are performed by each subject.

The Grand Challenge project at Carnegie Mellon University Quality of Life Technology centre (CMU QoLT) aims at collecting large datasets of daily activities and to make it freely available on the web (Carnegie Mellon University Quality of Life Technology centre, 2008). At the time of writing, a dataset recording four subjects while cooking different recipes is available. Testers were monitored using cameras, microphones, body worn accelerometers and a motion capture Vicon system. Current datasets present limitations restricting their usefulness in developing novel activity recognition techniques. Some datasets (PLIA1, PLIA2 and WARD) provide only limited numbers of repetitions of each activity, which are not enough to train and validate machine learning algorithms. Furthermore, most datasets focus on a single sensing modality, e.g., just smart objects, body worn sensors, or environmental sensors. More general approaches leverage the benefits of all three modalities. Finally, annotations are not always available (e.g., in PLCouple1 only the data of one of the two subjects is labelled). These deficiencies motivated our effort in building an ambient intelligence dataset including sensors of multiple modalities: smart objects, environmental sensors, and body worn sensors. Since there is a lack of literature describing in detail how datasets should be created, we want to discuss a methodology that guides researchers in creating their own new datasets and describe how we have followed it for our own dataset.

Figure 1. Decision chain for setting up an activity recognition experiment

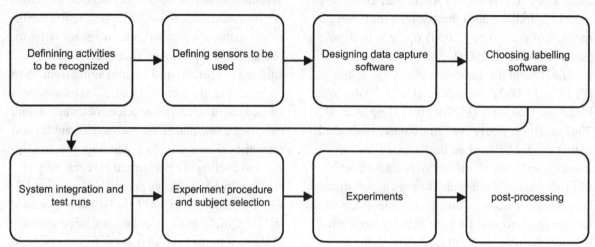

METHODOLOGY TO COLLECT DATASETS

Collecting a high-quality dataset is a complex task that needs to be carefully planned. We present here a methodology on how to approach an experiment and discuss decisions that should be taken at the different steps of the planning (see

Defining the Activities

The context-recognition literature identifies different classes of activities, which may be distinguished by the time granularity they describe. Fine-grained activities have a short duration of up to a few seconds and include individual hand gestures, tool manipulations, or single steps of a longer work process. Recognizing fine-grained activities allows an exact reconstruction of what the subject has been doing in a period of time. Other datasets describe more abstract and long-term activities, such as eating lunch, doing sports, or watching TV. Coarse-grained activities are typically used to collect statistical data of the subject's life over a period of weeks or months.

Activity granularity largely effects the requirements on experiment duration, sensor lifetime, and the number and diversity of possible activities

within the dataset. Additional constraints result from defining the location of the experiment. Possible choices include subject moving within a confined space like a single room or apartment or subject allowed to freely move about in the world. This decision will affect possible sensors locations. In most cases, a real life implementation does not model all possible activities of a human. Only certain activities of interest are defined within a dataset. Everything else is considered to be the "NULL" class – any unforeseen activity by the user of no immediate interest to the system. To evaluate the realistic performance of an activity recognition system, NULL class activities need to be included within a dataset. In an open ended dataset recording, there will be a natural amount of such unknown activities. In a constraint recording session however, such activities should be added in order to provide more real world performance ideas. The outcome of this step in the methodology should be a list defining all activities of interest.

In our project we defined two levels of activity abstractions: *atomic activities*, representing individual hand gestures, such as grasping an object or using it, and *composite activities*, which are more abstract and are defined through a sequence of atomic activities – such as "drinking water" is a

Table 1. Settings, sessions, composite activities and number of atomic activities $|A_s|$ defined

Setting	Session	Composite Activities	$|A_s|$
Kitchen	Preparing Dinner	Heat water, add soup, cook soup, slice bread, use computer, prepare table, eat, clean up dishes	44
	Relaxing	Select a book, read, return book	12
	Working	Use computer, drink water, select book, read, write, return book	21
Assembling furniture	Assembling a shelf	Get tools, mount middle shelf, mount upper shelf, mount lower shelf, return tools	14
	Attaching a crossbar	Get tools, mount crossbar, hammer a nail, return tools	12
Distractions		Scratch head, use phone, tie shoes, cough	

composite activity defined by "picking up a glass", "dipping a glass", and "placing down a glass."

To obtain a sufficient number of atomic and composite activities, we have chosen three different settings: assembling a shelf, cooking a meal in the kitchen, and learning in the study. Within those we have defined composite activities peculiar to each of the scenarios – reading a book for the study, or heating water from the kitchen. We have then further refined the atomic activities to be recorded, which defined the individual hand gestures to complete the composite activity. Table 1 lists the activities selected for the recording.

To produce meaningful results, a sufficient diversity of activities on both levels is needed. We have defined 78 atomic activities and 18 composite activities.

Choosing Sensors

Often used sensor modalities include cameras monitoring the environment, 3-axis acceleration sensors worn by the subject or placed on objects, RFID sensors to identify objects, and ultrasound or wireless signal strength for determining the locations. Further modalities that focus on specific context information are: temperature sensors, (reed) switches, microphones, Pyroelectric Infra-Red (PIR) and Force Sensitive Resistors (FSR) for touch. The subject's health parameters or cognitive state can be inferred from the galvanic skin

response (GSR), the electrocardiogram (ECG), blood pressure and oxygen levels, breathing sensors, electrooculography (EOG), or electroencephalography (EEG).

Sensor placement is crucial to the recording quality. It is also important to embed sensors into the experiment in a way that does not interfere with the subject's natural way of performing the activities. For example, an acceleration sensor can determine human gait: if a person walks, periodic peaks can be detected in the signal when the subject places down its foot. The human body however dampens the amplitude of the peaks with every joint to protect the brain. The higher the accelerometer is thus placed on the body, the smaller the amplitude and the signal to noise ratio gets. Placing the sensor at the foot has the best sensing quality, but the size and weight of the sensor and its battery may bother the subject.

The information content a sensor provides has to be considered as well. If a single sensor should be used to detect many different activities, they might be difficult to distinguish from each other. Adding additional redundant sensors may help distinguish activities which look very similar from the point of view of a sensor. An accelerometer on a wrist may for instance have difficulties in distinguishing the motion of picking up something versus placing it down again. Adding an additional sensor on the item being picked up may simplify the recognition task considerably.

Figure 2. Selection of sensors used in the experiment. Acceleration sensors track body and object movements, while light sensors detect open cupboards and drawers

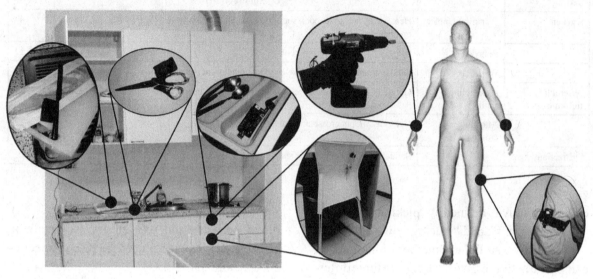

It is always advisable to use video capture. Even if it may not be used for the activity recognition algorithms, videos document the experiments and allow determining what has happened when sensor signals look strange.

The outcome of the sensor selection step should be a list of sensors defining their position and orientation (Figure 2). This list is especially important for complex settings where many sensor nodes are involved to ensure uniformity over multiple recordings.

In our project we choose to embed sensing devices both on the body to recognize gestures, and on various tools and other objects used when performing the activities. Table 3 lists the sensor locations and modalities used throughout the experiment.

Activities were recorded by body-worn sensors featuring 3-axis accelerometers at both wrists and on the left leg right above the knee and bend sensors monitoring the extension of the fingers of the right hand. Further accelerometers were placed on 12 objects and tools the subjects interacted with and on a shelf leg, a shelf board, and a chair. An additional 8 light sensors were placed in

drawers and cupboards to monitor whether they have been opened by the test subject. Work on the computer was sensed by recording the number of key presses and mouse movements. A PIR motion sensor recorded when the subject entered and left the room after each recording. Finally, a camera filmed the room during the experiment.

Most sensors had to distinguish 3-5 activities, with the exception of the right and dominant hand of the subject, which was to be involved in the recognition of 35 activities.

Testing Sensor Data Collection

Nothing is more frustrating than investing a lot of time into experiments and then having to conclude that much of the data is missing, corrupt, or in another way unusable. Ensuring that data collection is working from individual sensors as well using all sensors at the same time is therefore crucial. Especially when using high sampling rates and wireless communication, it must be carefully tested whether enough bandwidth is available and sensors do not interfere with another sensors communication. Tests should run with all sen-

Table 2. Packet error rate as a function of the number of nodes streaming on the wireless channel

	6 nodes	4 nodes	3 nodes
Node 1	0.001	---	---
Node 2	0.454	---	0.006
Node 3	0.527	0	---
Node 4	0	0.295	0
Node 5	0	0.001	0
Node 6	0.002	0.691	---

sors active and ideally for the same time as the experiment duration.

The recording system should check the integrity of the data streams as well as the signal quality during the whole experiment. In case of sensor failure, the experimenter can react to the situation and decide whether to interrupt the experiment to take appropriate measures. Synchronization is a further issue to consider: the clocks of small microcontrollers shift by significant amounts of time, especially during long-term recordings. Data collection systems therefore require a strategy to include timing information in the recorded data or to synchronize the clocks during the experiments. A possibility is to use synchronization activities at the start and end of a recording. Such activities must be easily detectable by all sensing modalities and allow data synchronization in the post-processing (Bannach, 2009). Last but not least, the amount of data storage needed for an experiment needs to be estimated and a strategy for backing up data after each recording as well after a complete recording session needs to be found. It is advisable to keep multiple redundant copies for security. The outcome of this task is a framework for collecting data from all sensors. It should also provide an exact procedure for starting and stopping an experiment and how to store data. Test runs provide a good estimate of how much data will be generated, such that the necessary data storage can be organized before experiments start.

For our experiment we used acceleration sensors sampling at 50 Hz. Literature suggests around 30 Hz as a good compromise between the expected recognition performance and generated data volume (Lombriser, 2007). The light sensors were sampled at 20 Hz. Data from sensors has been collected through different media by a single laptop PC to ensure data synchronization. The PIR sensor readings were gathered using a serial cable, data from the right wrist and the bend sensors were sent using a Bluetooth radio, all other sensor nodes are based on Tmote platforms and use the TinyOS wireless stack based on IEEE 802.15.4.

The IEEE 802.15.4 wireless protocol allows communication over 16 channels equally spaced in the 2.45 GHz ISM band. Thus, different networks can coexist in the same physical space by communicating on different channels. To evaluate how many nodes can coexist on the same channel we tested several network made up of a varying number of nodes. Each node samples its accelerometer and sends a message containing 10 samples each. Messages are retried three times if not acknowledged by the sink. Table 2 presents the packet loss as a function of the number of nodes streaming on the same channel. As can be seen from this table, up to 3 nodes can reliably stream data sampled at 50 Hz on the same channel. These values compare to literature values (Shnayder, 2005). In our experiment we decided to share a channel between 2 sensors and consequently used one sink node dedicated to each channel.

During the tests, we experienced nodes failures or communication loss which reduced the quality of the acquired streams. Messages losses vary from 0% up to 38.0% (PIR sensor) with an average of 8.7% (see Table 2). Higher packet losses are due to sensor that failed at the beginning of an experiment and whose failure was not recognized until the end of the test, while lower data losses are mainly due to temporary occlusion due to movements of the user or to interference between sensors streaming on the same channel. The high data loss on the PIR sensor is not a real loss of packets, but it is simply due to the fact that this sensor was not available during all experiments.

For the experiments, we have developed a sensor health indicator for the experimenter. During the experiment, it continuously checks whether a packet has been received within the last 5 seconds. In case of failure, the tool highlights corresponding label with a red box (see Figure 3). Therefore, an experimenter is alerted when a sensor runs out of energy and fails and he can decide on whether or not to continue the experiment or to take appropriate measures such as replacing a battery and reconnecting a sensor while the experiment continues.

Online Labeling Software

Sensor signals must be annotated to indicate when activities have happened. Those annotations can be added after the recording, but it is recommended to do this online during the experiment. Online labeling may not have the same accuracy as post-labeled data, but it can be corrected in a post-processing step, which is greatly simpli-

fied by approximate marks at the beginning and end of an activity. Thus, the labeling should be detailed enough as to make the post-processing step more efficient.

Depending on the experiment, labeling can be done by the subjects themselves (e.g., alerted by a phone signal, a user annotates his/her current activity on the phone itself), or by the experimenters following the experiment and recording what is happening. In the latter case the supervisors need to be fast enough to annotate the activities with the correct label without too many mistakes. For certain activities automatic labeling is also an option. For example a door opening activity might be automatically labeled through a contact sensor. The order in which activities are executed often is not relevant. However knowing the sequence of activities eases the on line labeling and the correction of labels in the post processing phase. Thus, it reduces the time and, consequently, the cost to create the dataset. The outcome of this step should be a strategy and tool for labeling the activities during the experiment, including the decision of which activities should be labeled how

Table 3. Sensor locations per modality and the wireless transmission error rate

CATEGORY	POSITION	MESSAGE LOSS (%)	CATEGORY	POSITION	MESSAGE LOSS (%)
Infrastructure	PIR	38.0	Furniture	Shelf board	3.4
	Computer	0.0	(light)	Chair	4.3
Tools (acceleration)	Hammer	0.9		Food cupboard	2.0
	Screw Driver	2.1		Dish cupboard	2.1
	Scissors	0.0		Cutlery drawer	2.6
	Knife	10.9		Garbage	0.6
	Book 1	12.7		Pot drawer	1.8
	Book 2	9.8		Shelf leg	5.9
	Phone	13.8		Tool Drawer	0.1
	Stirring spoon	3.7		Desk drawer	2.6
	Drill	0.6	Body worn (acceleration)	Glove	0.5
	Wrench Small	23.7		Wrist	0.6
	Wrench Big	15.3		Left leg	10.2
	Pen	0.7	Average		8.7

Figure 3. Labeling software used in our experiment - a) list of activities to be performed b) button to start/stop activity label, c) sensor health indicator (green – sensor active; yellow – sensor not used; red – sensor broken)

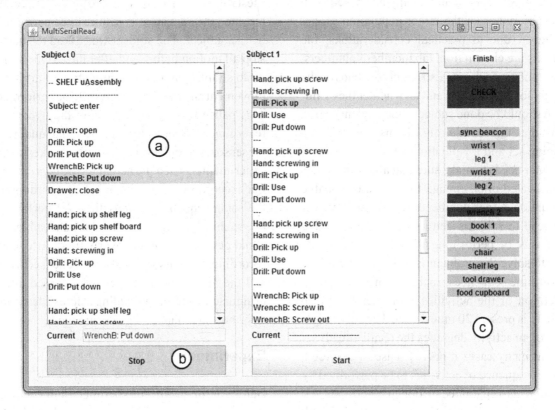

and what is left to a post-processing phase. Figure 3 shows our online labeling tool. It displays the current activities that are labeled for the different subject taking part in the experiment and shows on the right side the health of the sensor values.

In our experiments we followed a fixed sequence of activities to ease supervisor work when switching between activities. This affected also the design of our labeling software where activities are listed in the exact order they should happen and successive occurrences result in label repetition in the list. For example, let us consider the scenario of "build a shelf". In this scenario four screws should be fixed on the shelf. The screenshot of the labeling software during this phase is presented in Figure 3. As can be seen, the list of actions with the single screw is repeated four times (only the last three are shown) rather than a single time. The

motivation is that the supervisor always sees next action following the current one and should not scroll up or down to find next activity. Furthermore, if an activity should be repeated a number of times it is easier to remember how many times it has been already performed. Another important aspect of our labeling software appearance is that activities are grouped according to relative macro activities (i.e., a visual separator is placed between a cluster of activities). This is helpful for the supervisor in order to realize when he/she has to change the composite activity.

Experiment Procedure and Subject Selection

Depending on the goal of the dataset, the sequence of activities may or may not be predetermined. In places such as the PlaceLab, normal living behavior should be recorded, thus no restrictions are to be taken. Subjects should ideally be chosen such that they represent the target population group. However, due to practical considerations, the subjects are chosen from lab member volunteers. The number of subjects also largely depends on the budget for paying them and on whether the evaluation should be done subject-independent or not. Since machine learning algorithms require both a training set and a validation set, the experiment designer needs to make sure that all the activities are repeated often enough to make a reasonable evaluation. A high number of repetitions however can lead to subjects getting tired and changing their way of performing their activity. A good way to solve the problem is to include activities in multiple sequences, such as to have a natural repetition of the activities. Consider that if an activity is present 20 times in the dataset, a single miss of an activity degrades the recall already by 5%. In many cases it makes sense to enforce a certain sequence of activities to be performed by the subject to guarantee sufficient repetitions. Alternatively, if no fixed activity sequence is wished, the experiment duration needs to be prolonged to ensure enough repetitions.

For our dataset we were interested in getting a large number of activities from the same subject. We therefore settled on 2 male subjects, but a higher number of recording sessions. As we wanted to be able to distinguish the classes of interest from all other possible happenings, we included a "distractions" dataset that includes a number of activities that were not considered in the proposed scenarios, but rather should only increase the variability of the sensor data contained and show the classifier robustness. These activities can be randomly inserted into the training and validation sets. The experiment procedure was as follows: the new subject would come in and receive an explanation of the purpose of the experiment and the sequence of composite and atomic activities to

be performed in the recording session coming up. Then the sensors were mounted and turned on and a test run was performed, where the experimenter repeated the next atomic gesture to be performed by the subject. The subject was asked to shortly stop all motion before and after the atomic activity to simplify a later discrimination of arbitrary movement and the actual activity to be performed. This pause was also kept during the upcoming recordings. After the dry run, the signal quality of the sensors was quickly and visually checked by the experimenter. Then the actual recordings started. Each recording session included 20 recordings of the same sequence of activities. We performed one such recording session per day and subject to avoid getting the subject overly tired. After each recording, the sensor signals were checked again and the all sensor data files were copied into a designated directory including a notes file stating any abnormal happenings during the recording.

Experiment

Before starting with the experiment, subjects need to give their approval for the data collected to be used after the experiment. The data needs to be anonymized as far as possible, specially the one collected with cameras and microphones, and the duration of the data storage may have to be negotiated as well. After having instructed the subject on the experimental procedure, some experiments may require conducting a test run, which is not recorded, before the actual performance of the experiment. During the recording, the incoming sensor data should be monitored for its quality and completeness. When sensors fail, a decision on whether the recording session can continue or needs to be aborted needs to be taken. The basis to this is how important the sensor is for the recording, and whether it could be quickly fixed to continue the test.

After every recording session, all generated data should be checked for its completeness, and a backup should be done. Then, it should be verified that the remaining data storage on the recording devices has enough space for the next recording. It is good practice to not overwrite any recording files, in particular in case of an accidental restart of the recording software. During the whole time of the experimentation, an experiment log should be kept, which holds notes on any unforeseen events that will happen during the recording sessions. It will be a valuable resource additional to video or sound recordings which will enable people that work on the data to reconstruct those occasions when they inspect the sensor data. Our experiment included 150 recording sessions performed during two weeks. The two subjects were taken in turn to complete the same scenarios, iterating between experimenter labeling and supervising the experiment, then as subject. For the experiments we used checklists produced during the previous steps. Of special importance were the sensor placement and orientation as well as the activity sequence lists. Those ensured an efficient preparation and coherent sensor recording. Redundant sensors and batteries for replacement of failing sensors were also available. It ensured that we could continue with further recordings after some sensors had problems.

Post-Processing

Post processing includes additional checks on data integrity, data reconstruction for temporary sensor failures, a clean organization of the recorded data, writing software to load the data into different analysis tools, and finally producing a permanent backup of all collected raw data and associated scripts. One of the most time consuming task is post-recording label treatment. As humans are producing the labels during the experiment, there might be some inaccuracies some missed or wrongly labeled activities or inaccurate label boundaries. This requires to go through the dif-

ferent labels and to correct them, which may require a multiple of the recording time. During the planning of the experiment, enough time needs to be included for this processing step. In the PLCouple datasets from PlaceLab, for example, only labels for one of the two inhabitants of the flat are available as the budget ran out before the activities of the second person could be labeled (Logan et al., 2007). The result of this final step should be a dataset that is well documented and easily usable by a wide range of people. A website should be created to provide to other researcher an overview of the dataset and an easy mean to distribute it.

For our dataset, we hand-corrected the labels entered by the experimenter at runtime. The goal was to create a common ground truth to be used for training recognition algorithms. We had to insert missing labels and correct wrong ones. As the experimenters were sometimes too early or late in entering the label boundaries, we discussed on a few examples the patterns of the signal we would use as start and end for each activity to be labeled. Since most of the work was done during the experiments, in the post processing phase we should adjust labels beginning and end, add missing labels and remove mistaken ones. This activity required an overall work of 14 days full time. Even if this was a time consuming activity it is much less than the time it would have taken to label the activity just by looking at the video or at sensor reading. We evaluated that the accuracy of the experimenters in labeling the activity is 96.75%, with a precision of 97.83% and a recall of 98.87%. It is interesting to note that even the "gold reference" labeling performed by the human brain is not perfect. Most errors came from mixing up two different activities or setting the label too late. This is the value to be beaten by the recognition algorithms in order to be better than a human.

LESSONS LEARNED

The previous section has outlined in detail the methodology we followed to build our dataset. Each step has been discussed and several considerations have been presented to motivate our choices. However, there will always be unforeseen problems that affect the experiments. We report on important ones.

Define Sensor Orientations Unambiguously

A misunderstanding between the experimenters led to the case that the acceleration sensor on the leg of the subject was mounted upside down during some recordings. The problem was only detected when we analyzed the models generated by the machine learning algorithms. We then had to find the affected datasets by visual inspection and included a special preprocessing step for 3D rotation and calibration for those sets. A detailed description of how sensors should be placed on subject body and on tools is essential when recordings are made by multiple subjects and experimenters or over multiple days. As an alternative, pictures can be taken to capture the room where tests take place and how sensors are oriented. The ideal solution would be an automatic orientation check at the beginning of each recording session.

Restrict Number of Different Devices to a Minimum

Data acquisition software may work differently on different computers. Therefore, before starting the experiment session, the software should be tested on the computer that will be used during the tests. In the first experiments we lost data of some sensors because we used a different model of the serial to USB converter, which sporadically introduced own status information into the data stream. After having detected the problem,

we could filter this data out by a special preprocessing step within the data recording. A second problem that we encountered was that we had used different versions of firmware on some sensors. The newer version introduced a timestamp of 16 bit instead of only 8 bits into the data stream. The subsequent data was then shifted by 1 byte which was not detected by the sensor health checks, but introduced an unrecoverable data loss when the data was rounded before it was written into the logfile. This could be averted by adding more checks to the data protocol, or by reducing the number of different stream formats used by the sensors.

A Picture is Worth a Thousand Words

Taking pictures and videos of the experiment and its environment during the recording is essential to understanding signal patterns in the post-processing step or for algorithm training. Furthermore, it helps researchers using the dataset to better understand how activities were performed when they receive the dataset. Figure 4 shows an example of 6 instances of the wrist acceleration signals for picking up a book from a bookshelf. It is already difficult to spot those varying patterns within the signal. If something unexpected happens during the recording, e.g., the book falls on the floor and is being picked up; such events are extremely difficult to understand from pure acceleration signals. The videos proved extremely useful in finding and correcting missing or wrong labels in the post-processing step. Experiment notes described abnormal events, but are not suited to explain the signals in detail.

When using a dataset created by others, even an accurate description of the activities and the environment where they take place is not as useful as videos or pictures. This information can be used to choose how to preprocess sensor data or to build a model that describes the user and his/

Figure 4. Example 3-axis acceleration sensor signals from the subject wrist while picking up a book from a bookshelf. Six instances of the activity are shown. Finding such instances without online marks or video correlation is difficult and error prone.

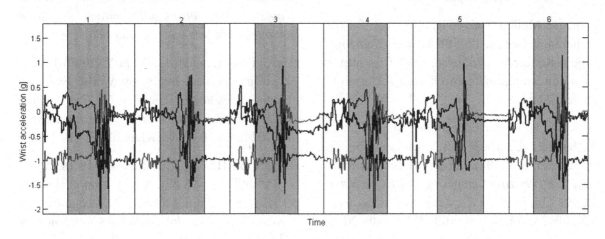

her environment. Furthermore, if other experiments should be carried on to validate an approach, videos are an excellent help to assure correct reproduction of the setting.

CONCLUSION

AmI environments are able to sense their context and interact with people living within them. Among the other, human activities are an important factor affecting context, thus the ability to recognize them plays a central role for AmI systems. Research into activity recognition algorithms requires the availability of datasets on which new techniques can be trained and tested. Deploying and collecting data from sensors in everyday settings however is a costly and time-consuming task. Therefore, researchers are sharing large datasets of data collected from smart spaces. Through this article, we have identified experiment design decisions and created a methodology for recording datasets from AmI environments. Our lessons learned show that even small details may jeopardize the quality of the datasets. We hope this information will be useful to researchers developing similar datasets.

REFERENCES

Amft, O., Lombriser, C., Stiefmeier, T., & Tröster, G. (2007) Recognition of user activity sequences using distributed event detection. In *Proceedings of the European Conference on Smart Sensing and Context (EuroSSC)* (pp. 126-141). Berlin: Springer.

Asuncion, A., & Newman, D. (n.d.). *UCI Machine Learning Repository*. Retrieved October 20, 2009, from http://www.ics.uci.edu/~mlearn / MLRepository.html

Baldauf, M., Dustdar, S., & Rosenberg, F. (2007). A survey on context-aware systems. *International Journal of Ad Hoc Ubiquitous Computing, 2*(4), 263–277..doi:10.1504/IJAHUC.2007.014070

Bannach, D., Amft, O., & Lukowicz, P. (2009). Automatic Event-Based Synchronization of Multimodal Data Streams from Wearable and Ambient Sensors. In *Proceedings of the European Conference on Smart Sensing and Context (EuroSSC)* (pp 135-148).

BoxLab. (2009). *Making Home Activity Datasets a Shared Resource*. Retrieved November 11, 2009, from http://boxlab.wikispaces.com/

Carnegie Mellon University Quality of Life Technology Centre. (2008). *Grand Challenge project*. Retrieved October 26, 2009, from http://www.cmu.edu/qolt/Research /projects/grand-challenge.html

Cook, D., Schmitter-Edgecombe, M., Crandall, A., Sanders, C., Davies, B., Siewiorek, N., & Sukthankar, R. (2008). Activity-Based Computing. *IEEE Pervasive Computing / IEEE Computer Society* [and]. *IEEE Communications Society,* 7(2), 20–21. doi:.doi:10.1109/MPRV.2008.26

Duda, R. O., Hart, P. E., & Stork, D. G. (2000). *Pattern classification*. New York: John Wiley & Sons.

Duke University. (2003). *Duke Smart Home Program*. Retrieved October 23, 2009, from http://www.smarthome.duke.edu/home/

Georgia Institute of Technology. (2000). *Aware Home Research Initiative*. Retrieved October 23, 2009, from http://awarehome.imtc.gatech.edu/

Intille, S. S. (2009). *Developing Shared Home Behavior Datasets to Advance HCI and Ubiquitous Computing Research*. Retrieved November 11, 2009, from http://web.mit.edu/datasets/Home.html

Intille, S. S., Larson, K., Munguia Tapia, E., Beaudin, J., Kaushik, P., Nawyn, J., & Rockinson, R. (2006). Using a live-in laboratory for ubiquitous computing research. *Pervasive computing*, 349-365.

Jaimes, A., & Sebe, N. (2007). Multimodal human-computer interaction: A survey. *Computer Vision and Image Understanding. Special Issue on Vision for Human-Computer Interaction*, 108(1-2), 116–134.

Jeong, K., Won, J., & Bae, C. (2008). User activity recognition and logging in distributed Intelligent Gadgets. In *Proceedings of the IEEE International Conference on Multisensor Fusion and Integration for Intelligent Systems* (pp. 683-686).

Li, X., Feng, L., Zhou, L., & Shi, Y. (2009). Learning in an Ambient Intelligent World: Enabling Technologies and Practices. *IEEE Transactions on Knowledge and Data Engineering, 21*(6), 910–924..doi:10.1109/TKDE.2008.143

Logan, B., Healey, J., Philipose, M., Tapia, M. E., & Intille, S. (2007). A long-term evaluation of sensing modalities for activity recognition. In *Proceedings of the International Conference on Ubiquitous Computing* (pp. 483-500). Berlin: Springer.

Lombriser, C., Bharatula, N. B., Roggen, D., & Tröster, G. (2007). On-Body Activity Recognition in a Dynamic Sensor Network. In *Proceedings of the Second International Conference on Body Area Networks (BodyNets)* (No. 17).

Mitra, S., & Acharya, T. (2007). Gesture Recognition: A Survey. *IEEE Transactions on Systems, Man and Cybernetics. Part C, Applications and Reviews, 37*(3), 311–324..doi:10.1109/TSMCC.2007.893280

Munguia, E. T., Intille, S. S., Lopez, L., & Larson, K. (2006). The design of a portable kit of wireless sensors for naturalistic data collection. In [Berlin: Springer.]. *Proceedings of the PERVASIVE, 2006*, 117–134.

Ponce, J., Berg, T., Everingham, M., Forsyth, D., Hebert, M., Lazebnik, S., et al. (2006). Dataset issues in object recognition. In *Proceedings of Toward Category-Level Object Recognition* (pp. 29-48).

Ramos, C., Augusto, J. C., & Shapiro, D. (2008). Ambient Intelligence - the Next Step for Artificial Intelligence. *IEEE Intelligent Systems, 23*(2), 15–18..doi:10.1109/MIS.2008.19

Schmidt, A., Beigl, M., & Gellersen, H. W. (1999). There is more to context than location. *Computers & Graphics, 23*(6), 893–901..doi:10.1016/S0097-8493(99)00120-X

Shnayder, V., Chen, B., Lorincz, K., Fulford-Jones, T. R. F., & Welsh, M. (2005). *Sensor networks for medical care* (Tech. Rep. No. 08-05). Cambridge, MA: Harvard University.

Tapia, E. M., Intille, S. S., & Larson, K. (2004). Activity recognition in the home setting using simple and ubiquitous sensors. In *Proceedings of PERVASIVE, 2004,* 158–175. doi:10.1007/978-3-540-24646-6_10

University of Rochester. (2001). *Smart Medical Home*. Retrieved October 23, 2009, from http://www.futurehealth.rochester.edu /smart_home/

Ward, J. A., Lukowicz, P., Troster, G., & Starner, T. E. (2006). Activity Recognition of Assembly Tasks Using Body-Worn Microphones and Accelerometers. *IEEE Transactions on Pattern Analysis and Machine Intelligence, 28*(10), 1553–1567. PubMed doi:10.1109/TPAMI.2006.197

Washington State University. (2009). *CASAS Smart Home Project*. Retrieved October 26, 2009, from http://ailab.wsu.edu/casas/

Yang, A., Jarafi, R., Sastry, S., & Bajcsy, R. (2009). Distributed Recognition of Human Actions Using Wearable Motion Sensor Networks. *Journal of Ambient Intelligence and Smart Environments*.

ENDNOTE

[1]   http://www.wearable.ethz.ch/research/groups/sensor_nets/dataset
http://www-micrel.deis.unibo.it/~wsn/AmI-dataset.html

This work was previously published in International Journal of Ambient Computing and Intelligence, Volume 2, Issue 2, edited by Kevin Curran, pp. 42-56, copyright 2010 by IGI Publishing (an imprint of IGI Global).

Chapter 10
Ambient Interface Design (AID) for the Ergonomically Challenged

Rosaleen Hegarty
University of Ulster, UK

Tom Lunney
University of Ulster, UK

Kevin Curran
University of Ulster, UK

Maurice Mulvenna
University of Ulster, UK

ABSTRACT

Mobile devices offer convenient communication capabilities and have the potential to create intermediary support for ergonomically challenged users. With the global proliferation of increasing longevity, assisting the elderly and those living with impediments through human engineering and computing technology is pivotal to biotechnological attainment. To remain independently empowered, seamless integrations through efficient affable interfaces are required to provide sedulous location-independent and appliance-sensitive media viewing for the user. The Ambient Interface Design (AID) system assists with finding personal preferences and provides a synchronisation framework, coordinating connectivity across various environmentally distributed devices via sensor data mapping. Cooperative interface communication coupled with context awareness will be abstracted to a representation that facilitates optimisation and customisation to these displays. To overcome personal challenges in the efficient selection and acquisition of online information, AID mediates between the needs of the user and the constraints of the technology to provide a singular customised encapsulation of 'ability preference and device' for each authenticated member. A particular emphasis is the application of a human-centered design ethos.

DOI: 10.4018/978-1-4666-0038-6.ch010

Copyright © 2012, IGI Global. Copying or distributing in print or electronic forms without written permission of IGI Global is prohibited.

INTRODUCTION

Ambient Intelligence (AmI) seeks to provide seamless integration of technologies to support a ubiquitous yet pervasive transparent framework for the implementation of electronic assistive environments. These 'smart', utilitarian electronic spaces are perceptive and responsive to the presence of an individual or individuals within a context domain (Aarts, 2005). Home, work and educational environments built on the ambient intelligence paradigm will offer flexible functionality through ubiquitous embedded computing facilitated by means of wireless communication and robust ad hoc networks. Smart behaviour associated with the technology is its ability to detect events, triggered by user actions within a designated milieu and to respond in an intelligent acceptable way to provide duteous 'virtual services' for that user. AmI utilises multi-disciplinary approaches to enhance greater human technology communication through distributed intelligence, data and information communication and amongst other disciplines it incorporates social science, psychology, ethics and law (Remagnino & Foresti, 2005). Moving the user to the foreground has acute legal and ethical implications that should be reflected in the design theory (Remagnino & Foresti, 2005). Personalisation of the user provides for adaptive and anticipatory utility within the ergonomics of the system.

The objective of this study concentrates on user ergonomics through the development of a system that incorporates multiple display devices in the development of an Ambient Interface Design (AID) for the ergonomically challenged. The purpose of which is for user convenience in multiple settings in overcoming challenges met by those wishing to remain independent and living with disability through aging; hence a comfortable and productive environment is created.

Through the use of wireless network technologies advanced mobile communication will be enabled with sensor components such as Radio Frequency Identification (RFID) readings to activate AID in a new context. AID will sanction the 'firing up' of Internet sessions on a selected device tailored to a user's ability and preference, and continue with the seamless coalescence and switching to other appliances whilst perpetuating a constant session browsing experience for the user.

This is achieved by caching the mobile web session and associated objects and relaying them to another possibly central repository, to facilitate viewing to commence as a new 'continued' session on a different platform. Personal Computers (PCs), Flat screens, smart mobile phones, and Personal Digital Assistants (PDAs) are proposed for this implementation encompassing sensor technology in ambient space supported by wireless networks over distributed locations.

Thus the new session is permitted by utilising user audience preference or by identifying user movement from within an edifice and incorporating the information held in a database on each individual user regarding ability and preference. The 'continued' session will display the terminating screen of the previous device as the launch screen for the new contrivance - hence permitting persistent successive viewing for the user enabling Internet mobility with successful ergonomics.

Motivation for AID

Ambient Intelligence (AmI) summons an imperative paradigmatic shift in social networking and computing systems. The human centered approach characterises a new direction in computing technology to *"augment consciousness"* (de Man, 2003) and accommodate human-machine co-operation (van Loenen, 2003). The emphasis is on efficient user affable and immersive interfaces with distributed virtual services that surround; empowering the user with control (Ducatel, Bogdanowicz, Scapolo, Leijten, & Burgelman, 2001; Cassens & Kofod-Petersen, 2007).

By embedding computational intelligence into the network and relocating the user to the foreground, this permutation will occur (Aarts, 2005). Supporting the users' presence with anticipated intuitive perceptive interactions, the modification will be apparent; thus the user becomes the focus, and no longer the technology.

AmI is a *"novel anthropomorphic human-machine model of interaction"* creating synergies between the user and the environment (Remagnino & Foresti, 2005). The vision for AmI is to permeate society operating omnipresently, non-intrusively and transparently. It is in the application of ascribing human characteristics such as sensory perception and cognitive behavioural interaction correlating to events, responses and user profiling in the machine model to physical or hidden measures such as embedded devices and wireless networks that the essence of ambient intelligence is encapsulated to provide user proficiency (Ishii, 2008) and enhanced human technology accomodation.

As a consequence of our mobile online international information infrastructure, modern society citizenship is becoming that of 'dual personality' combining both the digital and physical citizen in tomorrow's world (Ishii & Ullmer, 1997). The Internet has radically infiltrated society, influencing information exchange and consummation. It's depth of features extends to, interactive blog content with the shift change from traditional broadcast to YouTube video and tagged repositories such as Flickr and Facebook (Lopez-de-Ipina, Vazquez, & Abaitua, 2007).

Web Organisations such as Google, Yahoo, AOL and Microsoft are offering diverse functionality in the form of media-news, images, maps and advertisements. Internet technology has the potential to abet social exclusion and provide social interaction for society. Evidence of this phenomenon is most apparent amongst our youth culture (Lopez-de-Ipina, Vazquez, & Abaitua, 2007), as most forms of social interaction are extended via text, Bibo, Flickr, and Facebook amongst others. This implies optimisation of information exchange in the future and not restricted to 'youth culture'.

Despite current practices of Internet access such as the keyboard and mouse combination; it is generally accepted that these interactions fall short of natural communication and has the potential to exclude enfeebled citizens. Thus by introducing sensor activity in the environment and possibly on the user, interactions with technology has the potential to become more natural and intuitive in nature. The constant focus is on "pervasive and not invasive" for user convenience (Punie, 2003).

The Focus Group for AID

Technological advancement is an active area of research today with particular emphasis on members living with disability and cognitive dysfunction in a population aging society (Jorge, 2001; Dong, Keates, & Clarkson, 2002; Tham, 1998). In maintaining autonomy and social independence for these individuals whilst improving self-efficacy, individualism becomes a key element in the design process (Newell, 2008; Warschauer, 2004; Stanford Encyclopedia of Philosophy, 2009). This group's requirements are heterogeneous (Hawthorn, 2000); therefore enabling the provision of equality in overcoming some disability and without discrimination on ethnicity, background or technical illiteracy makes this a multi-faceted task at a user sensitive design stage.

By providing for minority groups such as those living with disability often in a serendipitous manner leads to better functionality for all. Evidence of this is demonstrated by the text predication systems used in mobile phones. Text predication was originally developed for those with physical disabilities unable to use the standard QWERTY keyboard, and this led to adaptive and predictive interfaces found today on all handheld text messaging telecommunication devices (Newell, 2008). These and similar challenges have stretched the design process to explore novel methods in overcoming the question of using personal interface real estate in an optimum way.

INTERFACE DESIGN

Too often interfaces were designed with the presumption that they will be the tools of able bodied users with high level cognitive and perceptual capabilities (Gajos, 2008). Interfaces should be adaptable to meet the needs and reflect the context of respective users over multiple mobile and stationary heterogeneous devices, which is the objective of this research in creating successful ergonomics in ambient space. These heterogeneous devices include PDAs, PCs, Smart phones, Flat screens and Laptops facilitating the mobility and flexibility that is the underlying premise of Information and Communication Technology (ICT).

The intention is to adapt applications and interfaces to user preferences and in so doing increase efficiency and ease of use when moving between each to complete a task such as an online reservation. This sense of fluidity promotes achievement and reduces stress in permitting the user to fulfil a task with increased flexibility without a requirement to re-authenticate as all information is cached and retrieved from the last available page to the new display device. Individual requirements suggests a prerequisite for 'Personalised Interfaces', mediating between the needs of the user and the technology hence overcoming individual capabilities, preferences and tasks to enhance satisfaction, speed, and performance (Gajos, Weld, & Wobbrock, 2008).

Ambient Intelligent Interfaces

Ambient Intelligence has indeed brought a new perspective to the psychology of Human Computer Interaction. The technology is no longer the focus; rather the user becomes central through a physical and digital co-existence (Remagnino & Foresti, 2005). Carbonell reflects on ambient interface interactions as having to be reconfigured for throughput to output terminals of varying media and screen dimensions (Carbonell, 2006). Implementation of these constraints gives rise to 'interface plasticity' and 'adaptive multimodality' (Calvary, Thevenin, & Coutaz, 2003). However maintaining simplicity whilst asserting notions of 'calm' remains the consummation in these phenomena and a reflection of the technology we seek in providing ergonomics.

This anthropomorphic model of distributed cognition between media and man has co-existed and evolved from cave paintings embodying spiritual expression and social interaction through to today's smart technology; with implications for increased social convergent media – creating synergies between the user and the environment (Lugmayr, Risse, Stockleben, Kaario, & Laurila, 2008). It is an observation that mobile devices despite their technological image are in fact socially driven communication tools utilising the Web (Lugmayr, Risse, Stockleben, Kaario, & Laurila, 2008).

DESIGN PRINCIPLES

The intention of this research is to provide a synchronisation framework that will provide coordinated connectivity across various environmentally distributed devices via sensor data mapping and tracking to provide location-independent and application-responsive screening for the personalised user experience. This ergonomic system may be placed within a user's home or social care establishment. The AID system's main function is the autonomous realisation of a user's presence via Radio Frequency IDentification-RFID supported readings with the aim of delivering contextual personal user preference interfaces permitting implicit and explicit interaction within a dynamic system.

Based on the Supple toolkit (Gajos, 2008; Gajos, Weld, & Wobbrock, 2008) application, which implements 'decision-theoretic optimization' in automatically generating user interfaces; we will implement a Grails web based Java framework that will utilise a database for authentication,

Figure 1. High-level architecture of AID system components

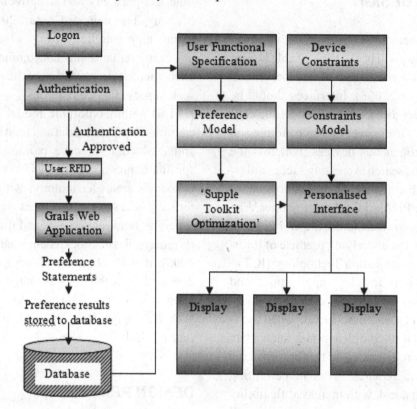

preference elicitation, and interface optimisation and customisation. This information will be used to optimise user preferences at run time over all currently connected device displays. The AID system (Figure 1) will take as input the preference elicitation information along with the associated device constraints and customise the interface accordingly.

Contextualised content viewing is required for the automated provision of services based on the users profile and preference. Adaptability to a user's situation is enabled by context awareness, *"Context is any information that can be used to characterise a situation of an entity"* (Schmidt, 2005). This entity can be a person, place or computational device, alternatively has real existence and can change dynamically. Schmidt et al., say *"context can give meaning to something else* (Schmidt, 2005). The sources available to contextual information in this research include sensors

in mobile devices, RFID tags, network servers and application servers among others. Generally context will refer to the identification of users, tasks and their objectives and exploited and adapted by the system.

This communication will permit a many to many (n:n) exchange via shared distributed devices utilised in smart architectural space enabling the creation of surround and fluid protean displays, as illustrated in Figure 2.

A one too many (1:n) configuration is substantiated when a user's tag reading whilst dynamically adapting to user requirements through reconfiguration, 'trust,' 'security' and 'safety' standards must also be adhered to, and integrated into the system design. The core of the application architecture is to provide natural interactions and abstraction of the underlying technical communication infrastructure; hiding complexity, whilst enhancing experience and confidence. Successful

Figure 2. 1:n Interface integration across heterogeneous devices

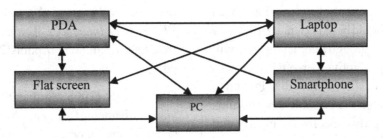

ubiquity however, requires transparency integrated into the ecology of one's environment facilitated through peripheral interfacing.

The key components of AID work to ensure continuity of service between multiple parts and include a sensor network, web server, session server, and user session (to store user history, cookies, current web page state and bookmarks amongst other user facilities) to different displays. The server side can act as a coordinator to manage the data, and facilitate screen resizing before exporting to a newly activated device. The client side component will have the necessary functionality to manage session synchronisation as a feature. The server must also maintain a user's personal profile and orchestrate this profile to heterogeneous devices within dynamic environments. In addition the server will also be responsible for carrying out routine authentication and authorisation and provide session state and mobility handling within the system.

Communication within the AID system will be server controlled, with clients communicating through the server (Figure 3). There will be instances where a single client to server communication will occur as in authentication, and device discovery within the network and indeed server to client communication. A client to server to client instance whereby the client can cause the server to affect another client, and also a client to client where data can transfer from one client to another directed by the server.

CONCLUSION

Technologically integrated spaces will change our perception of information and our behavioural interactions associated with its provision. The main aim in this proposed system is to deliver contextual user preferences without the need for direct user manipulation in overcoming age or disability related issues in providing for ergo-

Figure 3. (a) Clients (devices) communicate with the server and vice versa, (b) client to server to client instance and (c) client to client directed by the server

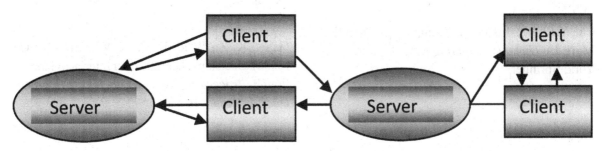

nomics. In recognising individual capabilities and needs an enhancement of satisfaction, speed and performance should be experienced. Ubiquity and seamless access through Internet services will assist in providing adaptive personal interfaces in mixed mode modality and media. Proactive collaboration between the possible devices aims to capture and simplify tasks for the elderly and those with disability in a sensitive, secure and intuitive environment endorsing efficient support in tailoring to the user requirements.

This will help to ensure seamless continuity between components providing usability and maximum user convenience. AID will as a prerequisite for 'Personalised Interfaces', aim to mediate between the needs of the user and the technology to help reduce personal challenges and provide a customised user experience for the efficient selection and acquisition of online information customised to preference, ability and chosen device.

In so doing a mobile persistent browsing experience will be filtered to the user as they roam un-tethered keeping data and communications ubiquitous. Citizens on the move are becoming networks on the move as individuals carrying devices are integrated into a framework of networks supporting a dynamic experience (EISTP, 2004; Filipe & Mamede, 2005).

REFERENCES

Aarts, E. (2005). Foreword. In Cai, Y., & Abascal, J. (Eds.), *Ambient Intelligence in Everyday Life - State of the Art Survey* (p. vii). New York: Springer.

Cai, Y. (2007). Instinctive Computing. In Pantic, M. (Ed.), *Human Computing (LNAI 4451)*. New York: Springer.

Calvary, G., Thevenin, D., & Coutaz, J. (2003). *A Reference Framework for the Development of Plastic User Interfaces*. Retrieved June 20, 2008, from http://iihm.imag.fr/publs/2003/MuiBook03.pdf

Carbonell, N. (2006). Ambient Multimodality: towards Advancing Computer Accessibility and Assisted Living. *International Journal on Universal Access in the Information Society (UAIS)*, 18-26.

Cassens, J., & Kofod-Petersen, A. (2007). *Explanations and Case-Based Reasoning in Ambient Intelligent Systems*. Retrieved November 26, 2007, from http://ceur-ws.org

de Man, H. (2003). Foreword. In T. Basten, M. Geilen, & H. de Groot (Eds.), *Ambient Intelligence: Impact on Embedded System Design* (p. vii). New York: Kluwer.

Dong, H., Keates, S., & Clarkson, P. J. (2002). Accommodating older users' functional capabilities. In Brewster, S., & Zajicek, M. (Eds.), *HCI BCS London* (pp. 10–11).

Ducatel, K., Bogdanowicz, M., Scapolo, F., Leijten, J., & Burgelman, J. C. (2001). *ISTAG Scenarios for Ambient Intelligence in 2010*. Tech. Rep.

Filipe, P., & Mamede, N. (2005). *Towards Ubiquitous Task Management*. Retrieved January 14, 2008, from http://www.inesc-id.pt/ficheiros/publicacoes/2166.pdf

Gajos, K. Z. (2008). *Automatically Generating User Interfaces*. Unpublished doctoral dissertation, University of Washington, Seattle, WA. Retrieved July 30, 2009, from http://www.cs.washington.edu/ai/puirg/papers/kgajos-dissertation.pdf

Gajos, K. Z., Weld, D. S., & Wobbrock, J. O. (2008). Decision-Theoretic User Interface Generation. In *Proceedings of AAAI'08, NECTAR paper track*, Chicago, IL.

Hawthorn, D. (2000). Possible implications of aging for interface designers. *Interacting with Computers, 12,* 507–528..doi:10.1016/S0953-5438(99)00021-1

Ishii, H. (2008). Tangible User Interfaces, MIT Media Laboratory. In Sears, A., & Jacko, J. A. (Eds.), *The human-Computer Interaction Handbook, Fundamentals, Evolving Technologies and Emerging Applications.* New York: CRC Press.

Ishii, H., & Ullmer, B. (1997). Tangible bits: Towards seamless interfaces between people, bits and atoms. In *Proceedings of CHI'97* (pp. 234-241).

Jorge, J. (2001). Adaptive Tools for the Elderly. *New Devices to cope with Age-Induced Cognitive Disabilities.*

Lopez-de-Ipina, D., Vazquez, J. I., & Abaitua, J. (2007). *A Web 2.0 Platform to Enable Context-Aware Mobile Mash-ups.* Retrieved November 3, 2008, from http://paginaspersonales.deusto.es/dipina /publications/SentientGraffitiAml07.pdf

Lugmayr, A., Risse, T., Stockleben, B., Kaario, J., & Laurila, K. (2008). *Semantic Ambient Media Expereinces SAME 2008 (NAMU Series).* Retrieved October 28, 2008, from Newell, A..F. (2008). Commentary on Computers and People with Disabilities: Accessible Computing – Past Trends and Future Suggestions. *Transactions on Accessible Computing, 1*(2), 9.1-9.7.

Punie, Y. (2003). A Social and Technological View of Ambient Intelligence in Everyday Life: What Bends the Trend? In Proceedings of the *The European Media and Technology in Everyday Life Network, 2000-2003.* Retrieved November 27, 2007, from www.lse.ac.uk/collections/EMTEL/reports /punie_2003_emtel.pdf

Remagnino, P., & Foresti, G. L. (2005). Ambient Intelligence: A New Multidisciplinary Paradigm. *Transactions on Systems, Man and Cybernetics – Part A. Systems and Humans, 35*(1), 1–6.

Remagnino, P., & Foresti, G. L. (2005). Ambient Intelligence: A New Multidisciplinary Paradigm. *IEEE Transactions on Systems, Man, and Cybernetics. Part A, Systems and Humans, 35*(1), 1–6.. doi:10.1109/TSMCA.2004.838456

Schmidt, A. (2005). Interactive Context-Aware Systems Interacting with Ambient Intelligence. In Riva, G., Vatalaro, F., Davide, F., & Alcaniz, M. (Eds.), *Ambient Intelligence, The Evolution of Technology, Communication and Cognition, Towards the Future of Human-Computer Interaction* (p. 164). Amsterdam: IOS Press.

Stanford Encyclopedia of Philosophy. (2009). *Computer Information Ethics.* Retrieved September 10, 2009, from http://plato.stanford.edu/entries/ethics-computer

Tham, Ng. A. (1998). *Equality service accessible for all citizens, in particular elderly and disabled: TIDE.*

van Loenen, E. J. (2003). On the role of Graspable Objects in the Ambient Intelligence Paradigm. In *Proceedings of the Media Interaction Group,* Philips Research Labs, Eindhoven, The Netherlands. Retrieved May 21, 2008, from http://www.minatec.com/grenoble-soc/proceedings03/ Pdf/Van%20Loenen.pdf

Warschauer, M. (2004). *Technology and Social Inclusion* (pp. 5-10). Cambridge, MA: MIT press. Retrieved from http://www./3s.de/web/upload/documents /1/SAME0820-lugmayr.pdf

This work was previously published in International Journal of Ambient Computing and Intelligence, Volume 2, Issue 2, edited by Kevin Curran, pp. 57-64, copyright 2010 by IGI Publishing (an imprint of IGI Global).

Chapter 11
Adapting Technical Theatre Principles and Practices to Immersive Computing and Mixed Reality Environments

Tim Boucher
Consultant, USA

To envision the future of technology, we would do well to first look to the past. The past provides a vocabulary of possibilities which can be rearranged and supplemented with fresh ideas and technology to craft not just new opportunities, but a new language of experience. If the future consists of virtual, augmented or mixed reality events in pervasive, ambient or ubiquitous computing spaces, much inspiration and practical guidance may be gained through the examination of principles and practices associated with contemporary and traditional live performance.

Though my professional background is in web programming, development, and design, I've spent the last two years apprenticing to the stage, with an eye towards technologies which will eventually revolutionize live events. Working in technical theatre as an assistant stage manager, carpenter, electrician, stagehand and bit part ac-

tor, I've learned firsthand traditional stagecraft techniques and lore (practical wisdom transmitted on the job in the form of story-telling) going back – in their essence – countless generations. Though the milieu of the theatre is flexible enough to accommodate a tremendous variety of special events and performances, within the West and within the United States in particular, a consistent methodology and process has developed whereby a show concept is taken from a written script through to a finalized performance. The person who typifies and oversees this process within the business of the theatre, perhaps most completely, is the stage manager.

If a staged dramatic event, such as a play, were compared to a computer program, the playwright would be the programmer. The playwright determines the basic parameters of the event: what happens when and where (setting), how it happens (dialogue and dramatic action), and who it happens to (the cast of characters, or

DOI: 10.4018/978-1-4666-0038-6.ch011

Copyright © 2012, IGI Global. Copying or distributing in print or electronic forms without written permission of IGI Global is prohibited.

dramatis personae). The playwright, in a sense, outputs a script as his source code. The artistic director, meanwhile, interprets this source code according to his or her artistic vision. The director communicates this vision to designers and production staff, making critical decisions about how the performance *ought to go*. Though these roles may overlap or differ slightly from theatre to theatre, generally the production manager is then the person responsible for assembling the resources, materials and personnel to execute the vision of the artistic director within the context of a particular theatre. However, the stage manager – unseen and unknown by the audience - is the one person whose responsibilities mesh and interface directly with all components of the running of a particular theatrical performance, starting in the rehearsal process and continuing through the actual run of the show.

The stage manager is primarily responsibility for recording and enforcing in real-time the aesthetic choices of the artistic director. In a practical sense, this means that the stage manager sits in on the entire rehearsal process, and annotates the script according to the choices of the artistic director. That is, the stage manager literally marks up the "source code" of the script with information pertinent to *this particular instantiation* of the play. These important bits of information generally include: notes about actors' entrances and exits to and from the stage; blocking - or the motion paths taken by actors during a scene; props and costumes used on a scene-by-scene basis by each actor; and any set changes or scenery pieces to be moved by stagehands or running crew during live performance. Some of this information is indicated in a general way by the playwright who includes stage directions within the script, usually indicated by parentheses and italics (sometimes called "squigglies" in the business). But the stage manager's notations in these areas make explicit information often only sketched out or implied in the stage directions.

From this information collected, modified and finalized over the course of many weeks of rehearsals, the stage manager creates what is called a "prompt book" or, more inclusively, a "master book." Based on the script itself, the master book charts not only the above information, but also has embedded within it essential timing cues critical to the running of the live performance. These most commonly include light cues and sound or music cues transmitted to light board and sound board operators (though stage managers may sometimes control one of both of these boards themselves – along with other entertainment and show control technologies), along within timing cues transmitted by cue-lights or headset to actors and crew backstage to take specific actions at pre-determined times within the show. During live performance, this collection of practices performed by the stage manager, who is watching the show from a booth behind the audience, is known as "calling a show," and is in some ways analogous to what an orchestral conductor does during a symphony, except it may include not only musical elements, but technical and artistic elements as well. Thus, the master book - created and maintained by the stage manager - contains a detailed road-map governing how the source-code of the playwright's script is to be executed in real-time during the run of a show. As soon as a show reaches opening night, the stage manager becomes solely responsible for making certain that this road-map is followed - to the letter – whether the show lasts for just a few days, a period of weeks, or the course of several years.

The stage manager also acts as the hub of communications between the producers, the director of a performance, the actors and performers, technical staff and even house management staff assigned to audience hospitality services. In the United States, member stage managers are also responsible for making certain that a production strictly follows union rules, as dictated by Actors' Equity Association, the American union of stage actors and stage managers. The role of stage manager within the theatre, then, is that of a Renaissance man with experience and expertise in all aspects and stages of theatrical production, but also that of an detailed organizer and hands-on diplomat, mediating between and sensitive to the needs of a diverse group of people all working towards one goal: the creation of compelling entertainment for paying audiences.

The role of the stage manager is noteworthy within the context of pervasive computing and mixed reality environments, therefore, because it places human decision-making and expertise at the center of a complex web of artistic, technical and audience interactivity. Though today's theatre audiences are accustomed to passively consuming live media, mixed reality technology coupled with audience feedback and participation possibilities will undoubtedly unlock a new dimension in live performance: one in which the viewer will be squarely part of the action, making real-time aesthetic choices for themselves about the direction and substance of their entertainment experiences.

This work was previously published in International Journal of Ambient Computing and Intelligence, Volume 2, Issue 2, edited by Kevin Curran, pp. 65-67, copyright 2010 by IGI Publishing (an imprint of IGI Global).

Chapter 12
An Activity Monitoring Application for Windows Mobile Devices

Hayat Al Mushcab
University of Ulster, Northern Ireland

Kevin Curran
University of Ulster, Northern Ireland

Jonathan Doherty
University of Ulster, Northern Ireland

ABSTRACT

Obesity is rising at an alarming rate. A great challenge facing the health community is introducing population-wide approaches to weight management as existing health and medical provisions do not have the capacity to cope. Technology is fast becoming an important tool to combat this trend. The use of activity monitors is becoming more common in health care as a device to measure everyday activity levels of patients as activity is often linked to weight. This paper outlines a research project where Bluetooth technology can be used to connect a commercial wrist-worn activity monitor with a Windows Mobile device to allow the user to upload the activity data to a remote server.

INTRODUCTION

Obesity is a pan-European epidemic presenting a major barrier to the prevention of chronic non-communicable diseases. It is becoming an epidemic affecting the life of over a billion citizens globally (MRC, 2009; Hainer, Frelut, & Seidell, 2002; EMHF, n.d.). According to the World Health Organization (WHO), a majority of men are obese or pre-obese in most European countries except for Belgium, Denmark and Italy (IUFoST, 2007; Londahl, 2007). In the UK, two thirds of men and 50% of women are overweight. If current trends continue, the year 2010 will witness over three quarters of the British men being overweight (see, Obesity is also rapidly rising among children with estimates of 12 million children overweight, of which 2.9 - 4.4 million are clinically obese;

DOI: 10.4018/978-1-4666-0038-6.ch012

Copyright © 2012, IGI Global. Copying or distributing in print or electronic forms without written permission of IGI Global is prohibited.

Figure 1. Overweight and obesity in Adults. All figures are based on the IOTF criteria for defining overweight and obesity in children using age and gender-specific cut-offs equivalent to adult BMIs of >25 (overweight) and >30 (obesity) (The Oxford Health Alliance, 2010)

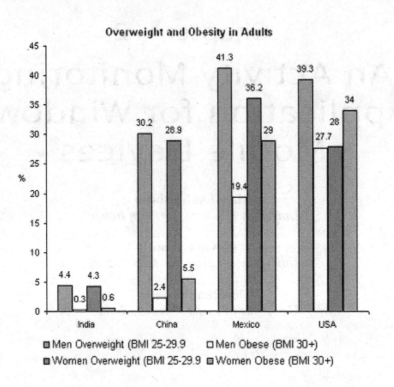

European Association for the Study of Obesity, 2004; Murphy, 2009). A great challenge facing the community is to introduce population-wide approaches to weight management as existing health and medical provisions do not have capacity to cope. Technology nowadays is being an essential tool to provide worldwide healthcare especially for those who are not able to visit their physicians or healthcare providers more often. The encouragement of taking preventative measures to the upward trend in chronic diseases is getting through and more people are self-managing their health. That makes an opportunity for companies to develop medical devices and services to empower individuals to manage their own healthcare (Murphy, 2009) (Figure 1).

Current common methodologies for measuring the activities of daily livings (ADL) such as direct observation, self-report questionnaires and diaries,

Doubly Labeled Water (DLW) - the measurement of energy expenditure- and heart monitoring can be inaccurate in measuring physical activities and are inconvenient for their time consumption. In addition they are unreliable since it could depend on the subject's memory and intrusive for the patient/ user (Steele, Holt, Ferris, Lakshminaryan, & Buchner, 2000; Firstbeat Technologies, 2007; Rowett Research Institute, n.d.).

Over the past few decades, the need for smart applications and devices that sense, classify and provide automated feedback related to the user's physical activities has relatively increased with the awareness level of the communities about health and physical fitness. However, such advanced technologies are still a challenge for the market to cohere because of the limitations that small monitoring devices could have such as the processing speeds, storage and display results. Nevertheless, companies are developing platforms for the sake of providing the next generation with medical devices to connect seamlessly to one another. This achieved by making these platforms act as enabling tools for the integration of devices with co-developed systems and through the promotion of the transmission of care beyond the hospital and doctor's office to the consumer's home. Such devices will offer services in many aspects including disease management and monitoring products that can measure and monitor different changes in the patient's vital signs like heart rate, blood pressure, blood oxygen levels, blood sugar levels and blood cholesterol levels. However, products monitoring vital signs monitoring products are mainly targeting patients with chronic diseases, elderly patients and overweight and obese people but can also be used for fitness training programs in general for users even with no medical life threatening conditions (The Future of Wireless Medical Devices, n.d.).

Evaluating clinical patients can be obtained by physical activity monitoring systems. This motion sensor technology is a great help for rehabilitation programs' quality improvements. Various devices are being used which differ with respect to technology, size and mode of expression of activity, all depending on the aim of the study or use of the system (Bracke, Puers, & Hoof, 2007; Metcalf, Voss, & Wilkin, 2002).

Nevertheless, technology progression within the past decade and the adaptive and programmable user interface have made inexpensive digital monitors and mobile technology advancement enable and support the creation of smart embedded applications. In addition, a plethora of such devices and applications ranging from a simple pedometer to a complex web-based tracking and coaching programs have surfaced for physical activity monitoring. Such improved devices with improved sensitivity, awareness and faster processing capabilities are more suitable for medical and research purposes (Steele, Holt, Ferris, Lakshminaryan, & Buchner, 2000; Ark &

Selker, 1999). However, proactivity and reactivity specification of the physical actions performed by the user are still required (Steele, Holt, Ferris, Lakshminaryan, & Buchner, 2000).

Here in this paper, we present a study of the physical activity systems and the Bluetooth technology with an embedded Windows mobile application developed to be connected and used for data upload to the web-based health monitoring system (MiLife) that is intended for round-the-clock use by a patient/ user. This windows mobile application connects with the MiLife system's wrest band - Personal Activity Monitor (PAM) - via Bluetooth wireless connection to transfer the data to the upload device then upload it to the system's server to be able to display one's progression and statistical results.

ACTIVITY MONITORING

In order to accomplish this project and develop the application it is essential to understand *What*, *Why* and *How*! *What* is exactly activity monitoring, *why* is it needed nowadays! and *how* is it possible to wirelessly access them! The Following study will explain *What* is activity monitoring, *why* they are becoming widely needed and commonly used, *how* it basically works and the different types of activity monitoring. Also, a complete research about Bluetooth technology, *why* it is applicable to connect it with the MiLife system and Windows Mobiles that are chosen for this project, *why* Bluetooth profiles and protocols needed for it and *how* the connection is actually established.

Obesity is defined as having excessive amount of body fat. It is more than cosmetic concern. It is a serious matter that increases a person's risk of having chronic non-communicable diseases and health problems such as: osteoarthritis, sleep apnea, asthma, high blood pressure, gallbladder disease, cholesterol, several forms of cancer, cardiovascular disease, stroke, type II diabetes, social stigmatization, depression and low self esteem (Bracke, Puers, & Hoof, 2007). There is also increased risk of dyslipdaemia, insulin resistance, breathlessness, gout and hyperuricaemia, reproductive hormone abnormalities, polycystic ovarian syndrome, impaired fertility and of course lower back pain. BMI (Body Mass Index) correlates with body fat in a person and can help predict the development of health problems related to excess weight (Weight-Control Information Network, 2003).

It is important to note that although BMI correlates with the amount of body fat, it does not directly measure it. That shows for example in athletes that may have a BMI that identifies them as overweight even though they do not have excess body fat. Weights that are greater than what is generally considered healthy to a given height are labeled as "Overweigh and Obesity". Overweight and obesity are determined in adults by using the BMI because of its correlation to the person's body fat. When the BMI is between 25 and 29.9, an adult individual is considered overweight and when the BMI is calculated as 30 or over, an adult is considered obese (Centers for Disease Control and Prevention, n.d.; University of Cambridge, 2007). Causes for obesity can be categorized into lifestyle, lack of physical activities or medical reasons (NHS, n.d.; Health and Fitness Institute.com, n.d.). Physical activity is measurable. It is defined as increased energy expenditure (EE) by any body movement produced by skeletal muscles. In other words, the energy expenditure is a consequence of the behavior (movement). To be able to define how physical activity mediates in health effect and to quantify the amount of physical activity it is essential to know its components like; intensity, frequency and duration, where the type of the activity is not required for the assessment yet it is still used for other health applications (e.g., Bone health) (McCarthy, 1960; Healthy People 2010 Operational Definition, n.d.).

Energy Estimation Measurements

There are four levels of physical activity intensity; low, light, moderate and vigorous. Each of these levels is defined certain energy expenditure results. These results are obtained by relating the total energy expenditure to resting energy expenditure. Metabolic Equivalents is a term used for the measure of a single activity and expressed as (MET = Total Energy Cost of an Activity / Resting Energy Expenditure "REE"), or by taking the Physical Activity Ratio (PAR = Total Energy Cost of an Activity / Basal Energy Expenditure "BEE"). Whereas the average intensity for a whole day is considered as the Physical Activity Level (PAL = Total Daily Energy Expenditure / Basal Energy Expenditure). Tables of intensity measures have been extensively compiled for adults and highly used for physical activity surveillance studies which identifies the threshold for each level of the physical activity as 3 METs is for the moderate level and for the vigorous physical activity it is at 6 METs. As these measure were originally developed for adults they were applied on children as well. However, the MET-value can be applied in children but with discarding walking and running from the activities performed by individuals because age can play a great role in increasing the MET-value since children spend more energy than adults which can be verified as that the decline in the REE and energy cost of locomotion (The ability to move from one place to another) by age is not at a proportional rate. Hence, MET may not be the best measure when it comes to age and size. Although when adjusting the resting energy expenditure REE and when adjusting the Stature (an approximate for body-size difference in number of steps taken) children will have similar energy cost for locomotion (walking and running) as adults and large part of this difference will disappear despite the age variance (Lal, 2008).

Another EE measurement method is the Heart Rate (HR), which is the most frequently indirect method used for three main reasons: 1. Heart

Table 1.

Food + Oxygen → ATP + Heat
↓cell work
Heat

Table 2.

Food + oxygen → heat + carbondioxide + water
Indirect Direct
calorimetry calorimetry

rate is easy to measure; 2. EE is easily obtained from HR data; and 3. HR-based EE-estimates are relatively accurate in steady exercise conditions. Nonetheless, with all its advantages, heart rate measurement method has its limitations. The inconsistencies in the heart rate and EE relationship is not taken into account when assuming a steady state condition. Individual laboratory is needed for best accuracy in relating HR level to the EE. Traditional method could assume a constant level of energy expenditure at low physical activity intensity which makes it inaccurate sometimes. Also non-metabolic (e.g., Mental or emotional stress) increase in HR could influence the EE results. And finally, prolonged physical activity could develop changes in body's metabolism which are not taken into account (Beattie, 2009).

To estimate the EE; it undergoes two stages: estimation of oxygen consumption (VO2) then deriving the EE based on information the VO2 estimation and the body's metabolism. The VO2 estimation method utilizes HR information and information on respiration rate where VO2 on/off-kinetics are derived from the time interval between two consecutive heart beats (R-R intervals) (Brandes & Rosenbaum, 2003).

Direct and Indirect Calorimetry and the Doubly Labeled Water (DLW) techniques are the most accurate methods for metabolism level measurement and they validate most other methods (Melanson & Freedson, 1994). Calorimetry is defined as the science of measuring the head eliminated or stored of chemical reaction or physical changes (Bao, 2003). The human body produces heat as a by-product to the metabolism process in the cell which can be represented as:

Hence, the rate of heat and the metabolic rate are directly proportional. The measuring of the heat produced is direct to the metabolic rate. That said, Calorie which is defined as the amount of heat required to raise the temperature of one gram of water by one degree Celsius, is the common unit to measure heat energy; and since it is a very small unit, EE and energy value of foods are measured with Kilocalorie. One Kcal is equal to 1000 Calories, whereas 1 Kcal is equal to 4.186 Kilojoules (KJ). This process of measuring the body's heat energy is called Direct Calorimetry. But when this method is not applicable for any medical or technical reason an Indirect Calorimetry method can be used which in order for it to measure the amount of heat produced in the body; it exploits the direct relationship between the amount of oxygen consumed and the heat produced in the body, so by measuring the oxygen consumption an estimation of the metabolic rate can be provided. A representation of the indirect calorimetry method is shown below where the type of nutrients plays a role in this method (Carbohydrate, Fat or Protein) and each should be calculated solely while actually the caloric expenditure during exercise is often estimated to be approximately 5 Kcal (21 KJ) per one litter of O_2 consumption:

Open-Circuit Spirometry is a technique that uses the computer technology that measures the oxygen consumption as the most common indirect calorimetry technique. A gas volume measuring device is used to measure the volume of air inhaled during the physical activity where after that the expired gas from the individual is channeled to a mixing chamber to be analyzed for O_2 and CO_2. The computer now will be able to calculate the

VO_2 (volume of O_2 consumed per one minute) and the VCO_2 which is the volume of CO_2 consumed after converting the fractions of O_2 and CO_2 by the analyzer. The results will be obtained at the end using this simple equation (Melanson & Freedson, 1994):

$$VO_2 = [\text{volume of oxygen inspired}] - [\text{volume of oxygen expired}]$$

A third biological approach to measuring the energy expenditure and considered the gold standard method is the Doubly Labelled Water (DLW). Activity level is directly proportioned to the energy expenditure estimates from the loss of isotopes. The individual drinks water with stable isotopes that contain Hydrogen and Oxygen elements $(2H_2O)$ and $(H_2{}^{18}O_2)$. This equilibrates with their body water in a few hours. Two different excretions developed from oxygen isotope are $(C^{18}O_2)$ and $(H_2{}^{18}O)$ and only one hydrogen isotope excretion $(2H_2O)$. The rate of CO_2 can be assessed from the difference of excretion in the saliva, urine or blood. Finally, to calculate the energy expenditure from the excretion difference in addition to the amount of oxygen consumed, Weir's algorithm is used (Brandes & Rosenbaum, 2003; Tryon, 2008).

However, indirect calorimetry and doubly labelled water techniques are not easy to use and very costly. They require laboratories, expensive analytical equipments (specially the ^{18}O) and skilled reliable technical staff. Another drawback for the DLW method is that it only assesses average EE over the 4 to 21 days of the analytical period and variation information is not obtainable within this period. Aside the fact that these two methods serve as criterion to other methods development, they are most feasibly to be used in epidemiological researches (Brandes & Rosenbaum, 2003; Tryon, 2008).

Monitoring Systems

When direct observation is not feasible for a case or a study of low frequent body movement a portable device is attached to the individual's body to record and measure his/her motions (Steele, Holt, Ferris, Lakshminaryan, & Buchner, 2000). Activity monitoring systems have progressed in the past few years, specifically 1990s, from a simple pedometer to a multi-sensor accelerometer. Storage of raw digitized movement data or average of data can be stored in selected epochs of time, usually 2, 15, 30, 60 or 120 seconds (Arvidsson, 2009; Beattie, 2009). They are usually used to measure calories burned and energy expenditure after some physical activities have been performed. Physical activity monitors are commonly small and easy-to-use by children and adults (Bio Trainer, n.d.).

A pedometer (Stepometer) is typically worn on the belt or waistband to calculate the distance that an individual has walked. It works by sensing the movement and counting the steps then converting them into distance. They perform this by determining the individual's stride length by detecting vertical acceleration of the hip during gait cycle. They are however limited in their discrimination of activities and posture (Bracke, Puers, & Hoof, 2007; Healthy People 2010 Operational Definition, n.d.; Arvidsson, 2009; Brandes & Rosenbaum, 2003). Many of them use a simple spring sensor that makes contact with ambulation by moving up and down. An electrical circuit closes with each step and the accumulated step count is displayed digitally on an LCD screen. A pedometers main problem is that they do not measure how hard (cannot differentiate between walking or running), how long or how often (Intensity, duration or frequency) a physical activity occurs. They also tend to underestimate the number of steps taken during higher intensity activities and consistent errors occur in say, a slow walking activity. On top of these limitations, pedometers do not have the ability to store or recall single-day values over a period of days; therefore it needs a daily written report before it resets itself. Finally, the most important limitation concerning pedometers is that they are incapable of measuring static movements, non-locomotor activities, upper body exercises or cycling (Bio Trainer, n.d.).

Nevertheless, advances in technology have made accelerometers a feasible option for physical activity assessment (Melanson & Freedson, 1994). To have a clear measurement of a movement which is less than 20Hz frequency, an activity monitoring system containing an accelerometer should be used. For a significant accuracy increase of frequency reading in an accelerometer device the system should filter the high frequent vibrations. To achieve this filtering purpose, a low pass characteristic sensor is used. Read-out electronics can be used to perform extra filtering to the frequency data (e.g., $\Sigma\Delta$ modulator and digital filtering techniques) (Bracke, Puers, & Hoof, 2007). An accelerometer could be placed on different parts of the user's body, by being embedded within wrist bands, bracelets, adhesive patches, or belts, to relay acceleration data using integrated transceivers. Software is necessary for acceleration data to be collected to recognize user activities and run real - time applications (Bao, 2003). Three types of common types are uniaxial, biaxial and triaxial accelerometers. The uniaxial monitor records the amount of physical activity performed by the individual between two predefined periods of time (Cardou & Angeles, 2007). A uniaxial monitor was the first accelerometer that was used for epidemiological purposes that indicated feasibility and productivity. It is the size for a wrist-watch and consists of cylinder with a mercury ball which connects with a mercury switch during body movement. Caltrac, ActiGraph, and the Biotrainer are examples of uniaxial monitoring systems (Arvidsson, 2009; Cardou & Angeles, 2007).

Two of the uniaxial accelerometers are equivalent to one biaxial accelerometer (Brandes & Rosenbaum, 2009) which can measure a full range of body movements from dedentary to intense physical activity. The biaxial accelerometer architecture is intended for microfabrication in single-crystal silicon, whereas millimeter-scale fabrications are intended to be by uniaxial and triaxial accelerometer (Cardou & Angeles, 2007). The difference between the uni- and triaxial accelerometers is that the latter accelerometer measures accelerations along three planes; vertical, anterior- posterior and mediolateral, while a uniaxial accelerometer measures the acceleration in a single plane when it is attached to the trunk or limbs. A Triaxial accelerometer then samples the signals from analog to digital usually (10 to 40 Hz) by signal conversion. Tritrac, RT3 and MiLife are examples of monitoring systems that contains a triaxial accelerometer.

BLUETOOTH

Bluetooth is an industry-standard protocol that enables a short-range wireless connectivity (Roche & Hanlon, 2009; msdn, n.d.). This technology is used for data transferring between different devices intended to replace the cables connecting portable and/or fixed devices such as phones, laptops, PCs, PDAs and any other handheld devices while maintaining high levels of security in a range of about15 meters and with data transfer rates of around 2 to 3 Mbps (Roche & Hanlon, 2009; msdn, n.d.; Bluetooth, n.d.). A Bluetooth connection allows electronic devices to communicate in a short-range wirelessly via piconets (a.k.a. ad hoc networks). Piconets are small computer networks that use Bluetooth protocols. Hence, as Bluetooth enabled devices enter and/or leave radio proximity hence piconets are dynamically and automatically established. Simultaneously each device can belong to several piconets in addition to its ability to connect and communicate with up to seven other devices within a single piconet. Innovation in Bluetooth solutions is enabled by a fundamental strength in

Figure 2. A profile containing another profile- direct or indirect dependencies (Bluetooth SIG, 2001a; Bluetooth SIG, 2001d)

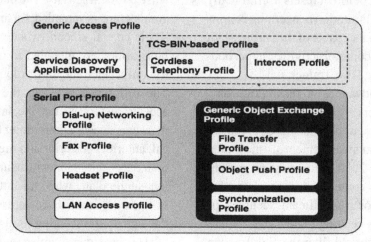

the Bluetooth technology which is the ability to simultaneously and homogeneously handle both data and voice transmissions; and this includes hands-free headset for voice calls, printing and fax order capabilities, synchronization between PDAs, laptops and Smartphones along with some mobile phones applications (Bluetooth, n.d.; Bennett, Clarke, Evans, Hopper, Jones, & Leask, n.d.).

Bluetooth profiles in devices are similar to Internet protocols in that they define general behaviors that allow Bluetooth enabled devices to communicate and therefore benefit from this wireless technology. A wide range of profiles defined by Bluetooth technology can describe different types of use cases. Developers are able to create and build application to work with, communicate and connect devices with each other by following the Bluetooth specifications guidance. Hence the variety of devices and advances in technology are growing and spreading widely, Bluetooth technology is being developed to cope to this digital evolution yet it is backwards compatible. Significantly, different products support different Bluetooth standards – versions 1.0, 1.1, 2.0 and 2.1. For example a mobile phone supporting a Bluetooth of version 2.0 has the ability to connect with a hands-free headset supporting Bluetooth

standard version 1.0. Each profile specification contains information at least on the following three topics: 1. Other profiles dependencies. 2. User Interface formats suggestions. 3. A profile doesn't use the whole Bluetooth protocols stack, however, each profile uses specific options and parameters at each layer to accomplish its task. Profile dependencies are considered when a profile implicitly or explicitly re-uses parts of another profile for example the Object Push Profile is dependent on another three profiles; the OBEX, Serial Port Profile and Generic Access profile, as Figure 2 illustrates (Roche & Hanlon, 2009; msdn, n.d.; Wikipedia, n.d.).

Bluetooth generic procedures that are related to other Bluetooth devices discovery when devices are 'Idle' which called 'Idle mode procedures' and the management aspect of linking and connecting these Bluetooth devices 'connecting mode procedures', in addition to procedures definitions to the use of different security level are all achieved by the *Generic Access Profile (GAP)*. In other simpler words, the description of lower layers usage (LMP* and Baseband) along with few other higher layers (L2CAP, RFCOMM and OBEX) of the Bluetooth protocol stack is made by the GAP (Bluetooth SIG, 2001a;

msdn, n.d.; Bluetooth SIG, 2001d; Sybase iAnywhere, 2009).

GAP includes the *Service Discovery Application Profile (SDAP)* which locates available ON Bluetooth devices in the surrounding area of an enabled Bluetooth device, then a user may select one or more of these available services and communicate/ connect with them. However, *Service Discovery Protocol (SDP)* is not directly involved in accessing services but it facilitates it by properly condition the local Bluetooth stack to access the desired service using the information retrieved via the SDP. Yet, the SDP is used to locate services in other Bluetooth enabled devices after being located via protocols and procedures defined by the service discovery profile by using a service discovery application on the device. Nevertheless, it is sometimes needed to enable another services such as RFCOMM or any other transport services or a particular usage profile (for example file transfer,, cordless telephony, LAN AP... etc) over the two devices as a result to the fact that SDAP is a specific- user- initiated application which makes this profile become in contrast to other profiles and consequently the service discovery interactions between two SDP entities in two different Bluetooth enabled devices. *TCS-BIN-Based Profile* - or it can also be referred to TCS Binary System is based on the Bluetooth Telephony Control protocol specifications and it will be used for cordless telephony profile. However, the Cordless telephony and Intercom profiles use the same protocol stack as shown in Figure 2. The TCS-BIN-Based profile defines two main roles in a Bluetooth connection: Gateway (GW) or Terminal (TL) where a topology of one GW and up to seven TLs are supported by the cordless telephony profile but on the other hand there are no specific roles defined for the intercom profile, it is totally symmetric (Bluetooth SIG, 2001a; msdn, n.d.; Bluetooth SIG, 2001b; Miller, 2001; Bluetooth SIG, 2001d; Sybase iAnywhere, 2009).

The foundation of the Bluetooth profile structure is the *Serial Port Profile (SPP)* that defines the procedures and protocols that are to be used by a Bluetooth-enabled device for RS232 (or similar) serial cable emulation. The SPP deals with legacy applications to communicate and connect wirelessly using Bluetooth as a cable replacement through a virtual serial port abstraction (which is operating system-dependent in itself). This profile carries four main profiles dependencies: Dial-Up Networking Profile, Fax Profile, Headset Profile, LAN Access profile and Generic Object Exchange Profile (Miller, 2001; Bluetooth SIG, 2001c).

Object Exchange (OBEX) is the Bluetooth adaptation to the infrared OBEX (IrOBEX). It is a transfer protocol that defines binary objects as well as a communication protocol that facilitates the exchange of those objects between two devices. OBEX and HTTP (Hypertext Transfer Protocol for the Internet) have a similar design and function that it is a client – server communication method that uses a reliable transport. In Transmissions HTTP is able to provide human- readable texts on a PC or a Laptop, but since OBEX is implemented in devices with limited sources, it is easier for it to parse by using "Headers" which are binary-formatted type-length-value triplets to exchange information about a request or an object. HTTP transactions are inherently stateless; generally a HTTP client opens a connection, makes a single request, receives its response, and either closes the connection or makes other unrelated requests. In OBEX, a single transport connection may bear many related operations. In fact, recent additions to the OBEX specification allow an abruptly closed transaction to be resumed with all state information intact (Bluetooth, n.d.; Bluetooth SIG, 2001a; msdn, n.d.; Bluetooth SIG, 2001b; Bluetooth SIG, 2001d; Sybase iAnywhere, 2009; Wikipedia, n.d.).

Bluetooth Technology on Windows Mobile OS

Windows mobile is a compact operating system combined with a suite of basic applications for mobile devices on the Microsoft Win32 Application Programming Interface (API). Increasingly, Windows Mobile phones are using Bluetooth technology more and more and most of Windows Mobile OS versions 6 and 6.1 have built-in Bluetooth capability - version 6.1 was used for implementing and installing the application. Bluetooth is supported by Microsoft for Windows XP with Service Pack 1 and later, Windows Embedded XP and on Windows embedded CE which operates a Windows Mobile device. Therefore, any Bluetooth application runs on Windows XP should appropriately run on Windows CE. Core services that are similar to those exposed by Transmission Control Protocol (the TCP part of TCP/IP protocol). Using common Windows Sockets programming techniques and specific Bluetooth extensions will enable the devices, applications and programmers to obtain Bluetooth connectivity and data transfers, like many networking protocols and services. Nevertheless, in order for an application to operate properly in a wireless environment, Bluetooth provides extensions such as Service/Device Discovery (SDP), notifications and also extensions that precede simple porting to similar technologies to Bluetooth such as IrDA. These extensions are used because of significant differences between a fixed, wired and a wireless ad-hoc network.

A MOBILE DEVICE ACTIVITY MONITORING APPLICATION

As previously mentioned, in a clinical setting there are benefits to face to face coaching and remote coaching. Both have been proven to be effective in behavioral change, but face to face can be time intensive and expensive, whereas remote coaching can be more affordable and consumes less time. The primary attributes of remote monitoring systems are to: (a) Record key information at the point of care, eliminating errors and duplication of effort and providing completeness of data (b)

Automate processes and information sharing (c). Provision for clinical decision support (d) Ensure secure acquisition and storage of patient data. (e). Provide reliable performance and (f) Assist patients in management of their own health from their own home.

The system chosen for this trial was Milife. MiLife[1] is an online, personalized coaching system along with a Bluetooth weighing scale, wrist band and Bluetooth adaptor. The wristband and weighing scales both communicate with a Bluetooth PC or MAC which is running the milife software. The wrist band needs to be 'paired' with the host pc every 10 days or less to ensure that all the activity data held on the wrist band can be uploaded onto the milife online system. The system also allows for the setting of targets with regards exercise and diet. Once the user has defined their diet and training plan, there is the option to receive reminders via email or SMS text to assure adherence to the plan is being followed. The entire system consisting of the hardware, software and online account cost £150 UK sterling.

The components of the MiLife system - also called Actors- are essentially linked and connected together to deliver optimized service to the user. Starting from the Personal Activity Monitor (PAM) that acquires data and retain it for certain amount of time to the PC where the data is transferred via Bluetooth then uploaded to the MiLife web server. However, the PAM was the main focus of this project (see Figure 3). The principle system elements are:

- **Accelerometer:** A LIS3LV02DQ triaxial accelerometer (3-axis) from STMicroelectronics. It acquires data on a firmware running on a Microchip PIC18LF2520 microcontroller (*PIC firmware*).
- **MMI:** Controlled by the PIC firmware. The Man-Machine Interface (MMI) consists of a LED and an MFB - a Light Emitting Diode and a Multi-Function Button.

Figure 3. Illustration of the main use cases of the MyLife system with all its actors - showing their involvement with the PAM firmware

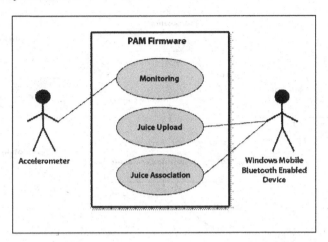

- **Power Management Circuit:** It identifies the PIC while its battery is charging and when it becomes fully charged.
- **PC:** A Bluetooth-enabled PC that runs the MiLife application software. Which is for this project will be substituted with a Windows Mobile Phone Version 6.1 that will adopt the application being developed.

The application is developed in c#.net on the .Net Compact Framework 2.0. It transfers the data that has been retained in the PAM to a Bluetooth-enabled Windows Mobile and then uploads it to the MiLife central server. The flow of work with the different state and events that the system goes through to reach the ultimate goal of allowing the user to explore his/her results online is shown in Figure 4 (Pearce, 2007).

Monitoring

After setting a valid time in the PAM, it will directly starts to monitor acceleration measured in three orthogonal directions X,Y and Z once every 100ms. The measurements after that will be passed to the PIC to be stored in a three 12-bit long, two's complement binary numbers form.

Earth's gravitational acceleration plays a scale factor - appointed as (λ) - linking these binary values given by the accelerometer datasheet. So an absolute acceleration of 340 per g is obtained if the PAM is not subjected to any acceleration other than gravity (Pearce, 2007).

Using (Equation 1) enables the PIC to calculate the magnitude of the PAM's acceleration from the three directions acceleration measurements. Dividing it by scale factor (λ), would give the 1g result expected.

Equation 1: Converting the three orthogonal acceleration measurements into an absolute acceleration value by the PIC

$$a_{abs} = \sqrt{X^2 + Y^2 + Z^2}$$

Using (Equation 2) in each epoch (an epoch is two minutes in time), the PAM sums all 1200 absolute acceleration values, as it is sampled once every 100ms. By that, a single 32-bit long value that is proportional to the average absolute acceleration is produced.

Equation 2: Summation of the absolute acceleration values over one epoch, where N=1200.

Figure 4. PAM state diagram illustrating state and events of the MiLife Windows Application

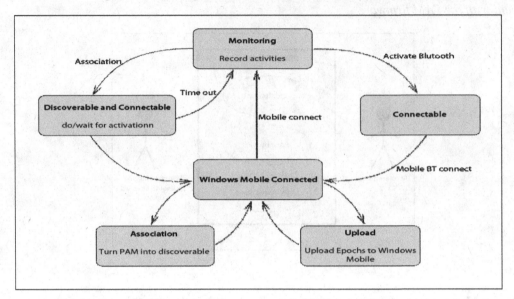

$$a_{abs\_sum} = \sum_{i=1}^{N} a_{abs(i)}$$

Afterwards, the PIC will convert the 32-bit epoch total into a single 8-bit binary value using a non-linear algorithm for the conversion. Progressively the epoch total value is compared to larger terms of the sequence specified by (Equation 3). The index of the term that is just larger than the epoch value is selected as the 8-bit representation.

Equation 3: The 32-bit epoch total is compressed into 8-bits for storage by using this sequence.

$$V_N = V_{N-1} + \left(\frac{V_{N-1}}{256} \right)$$

Using the PC software (GetStatus command), an overlapping data situation can be detected. That could happen if the PAM's flash memory was full and not yet uploaded; the old values are wrapped and overwritten with the new data (Pearce, 2007).

Discovering and Pairing Bluetooth Devices

Inquiry requests are sent from a device to discover other Bluetooth-enabled devices by using the inquiry scan channel of these devices even though when the requesting device can not know the exact characteristics of the inquiry scan channel because it has no prior knowledge of the devices that are to be discovered around it (msdn, n.d.; Bluetooth, n.d.; Wikipedia, n.d.; Bluetooth SIG, 2001d; Sybase iAnywhere, 2009).

Nevertheless, Windows maps the Bluetooth SDP onto the Windows Sockets onto the Windows Sockets namespace interfaces to facilitate the discovery of Bluetooth devices and services. The main functions that can be used for this mapping are the WSASetService, WSALookupServiceBegin, WSALookupServiceNext, and WSALookupServiceEnd functions in addition to the WSAQUERYSET structure. However, it is important for a person studying it or for a programmer to understand that SDP registration in separate from socket control. the WSASetService function is responsible to register a Bluetooth SDP record that corresponds to the server application that is prepared to accept client connection or when closing to deregister it (msdn, n.d.; Meghdadi & Arts, 2003).

Despite the small differences in specific user interfaces between one device and another that are implemented by manufacturers, there are still very basic steps that all devices go through in a first Bluetooth connection between two devices. Which is the *Pairing* process that should always be conducted in a secure environment. Steps have to be taken by both devices:

1. Turning the Bluetooth functionality on.
2. Make the devices visible for discovery.
3. Place both devices in the Connection Mode.
4. Enter the Passcode.
5. Delete or Disconnect trusted device.

These are typically how a user can pair two Bluetooth-enabled devices; however, the embedded functions used for the pairing process can be a bit more complicated but can be summarized as following:

The Windows Embedded CE device calls the SetBTDiscoverable function to put itself into Discoverable Mode. The Passcode or the PIN code will be passed to the SetBTDiscoverable function is the PIN code the user must enter to the device. After the user has dwTimeout milliseconds to enter the PIN code into the Bluetooth device using the device User Interface (UI). The PIN then must be associated with the Windows Mobile's 'Discoverable Name'. Before the SetBTDiscoverable function the Windows Mobile can obtain a handle to the BTPAIRAPI_DISCOVERY_ACTIVE event using the CreateEvent function. Then, after the SetBTDiscoverable is called, the Windows Mobile can use WaitForMulitpleObjects function to poll the event objects and finds out what happens afterwards, including whether Discoverable Mode was activated, whether pairing event occurred, and when Discoverable Mode became inactive

again (msdn, n.d.; Bluetooth, n.d.; Wikipedia, n.d.; Bluetooth SIG, 2001d; Sybase iAnywhere, 2009).

Juice Upload

Here we describe the uploading process of the data (Juice) to the PC. The application is responsible for storing and uploading the data to the Juice central server system of MiLife. After activating the Bluetooth Mode on the PAM by the user using the MMI actions (will be defined in the *Implementation* section) and the non-zero value user ID provided after the Juice Association (A onetime process where it defines the PAM with the PC application via Bluetooth and gives it the non-zero value user ID). The application now is able to create a Bluetooth connection to the PAM since it is Bluetooth connectable. Once the connection is established, the PAM will respond the upload data requests from the application for the epoch and scale readings (Scale is not included for the Windows Mobile application). The status of the epoch readings availability for uploading can be obtained by using the (GetStatus) message. However, the PAM will eventually treat the corresponding memory location (Flash memory) as *empty* as soon as the data sample has been completely uploaded and the application sends a 'disconnect' request message, then, a Bluetooth SPP disconnection will be initiated by the PAM (Pearce, 2007).

Data Upload to Server

Sequence of events take place when uploading data from the PAM to the Windows Mobile upload device. The following Sequence Diagram (Figure 5) illustrates these events which each will be explained afterwards along with the programming (c#.net) codes used to achieve each point.

By referring to the libraries that MiLife has provided to build up this application in addition to their recommended free online library "32feet" (In the Hand, n.d.) that has been used to build the

Figure 5. Sequence of events that takes place when the PAM uploads data

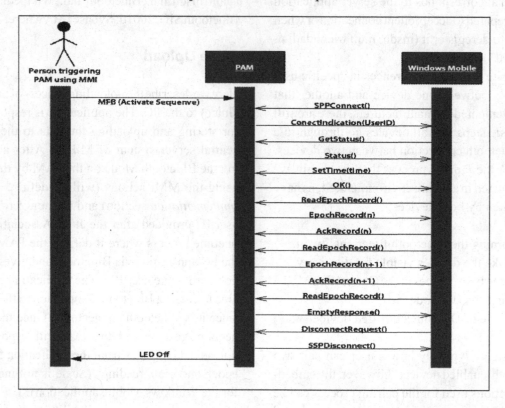

PC software for the MiLife system, these events took place sequentially (msdn, n.d.; Pearce, 2007; Khanna, 2005; Wigley & Foot, 2007):

- The MFB allows the PAM to enter the 'Bluetooth Active' Mode.
- The PIC will then attain a connectable mode.
- A SPP connection will be initiated by the windows mobile device to the PAM's incoming SPP service. When the connection is completed the PAM will send a ConnectIndication message including the stored UserID which will be received by the WM application.
- 'GetStatus' is the function used by the application to which the PAM responds with its current status giving the number of epochs available for upload.

- The PAM updates its clock value by using the 'SetTime' function issued by the WM application.
- The PAM then sends the epochs data record as response to the 'ReadEpochRecord' function that the WM application issues.
- The epoch record will be marked as read in the PAM after the WM application has dealt with the data record and issued an 'AckRecord' function.
- When the PAM have an empty response to the ReadEpochRecord request after a number of ReadEpochRecord/AckRecord sequence, that indicates that the PAM has no data remaining to upload.
- The WM application would not be able to an AckRecord function if the Bluetooth connection got lost (e.g., the user walks out of Bluetooth range during upload process) then the PAM will not be able to mark the

Figure 6. Prior to pairing

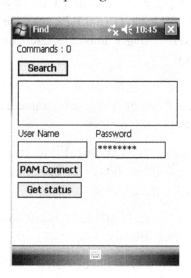

Figure 7. PAM's Bluetooth

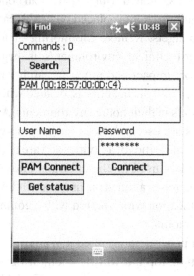

current upload record as 'Read'. However, the data will not be lost, the PAM will be able to upload the data from where the connection was lost next time the user attempts a connection.

- The WM application the issues a DisconnectRequest and the PAM disconnects the Bluetooth connection with the WM device.

- Finally, the PIC firmware puts the BT firmware in the PAM into 'Sleep Mode' once the link has disconnected.

Application Screenshots

What follows is an overview of different screenshots of the application running on a Windows Mobile CE operating system, version 6. Figure 6 shows the Windows Mobile application at its first page before discovering any Bluetooth Devices in its range.

Figure 7 illustrates discovering the PAM's Bluetooth. Here we can see that the "Connect" button appears to enable a connection between the PAM and the Windows Mobile device. Figure 8 shows the application prompting for the user's ID and Password to authorize data transfer from

Figure 8. Verification

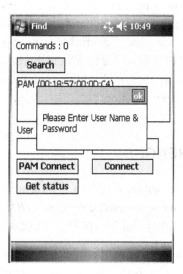

the PAM to the Windows Mobile application. After entering the user's ID, the application gets connected and the 'GetStatus' function would display the PAM's status and readings.

CONCLUSION

Obesity levels in populations are on the increase throughout the world. Due to the range of health problems associated with this medical condition, significant pressure is placed on health care provision budgets. Remote Monitoring of patients outside of clinical environments is beginning to have an impact and much research has been conducted into the benefits associated with keeping patients in their home environments. Activity monitors are useful devices for gauging various levels of intensities of activities and are becoming more widely used in clinical trials into obesity. This research examined the use of a windows mobile application which paired with a commercial activity monitor.

This paper demonstrated a Windows Mobile application for the MiLife monitoring system where the connection between the PAM and the Bluetooth-enabled WM device was crucial to implementing functionality on the windows mobile device. The application can be connected to the MiLife "Juice" central server to upload the collected data from the PAM and therefore allow the users to read their status and follow their scheduled progression.

REFERENCES

Ark, W., & Selker, T. (1999). A look at human interaction with pervasive computers. *IBM Systems Journal, 38*(4)..doi:10.1147/sj.384.0504

Arvidsson, D. (2009). *Physical activity and energy expenditure in clinical settings using multi-sensor activity monitors (Tech. Rep.)*. Gothenburg, Sweden: University of Gothenburg, Sahlgrenska Academy.

Bao, L. (2003). *Physical Activity Recognition from Acceleration Data under Semi-Naturalistic Conditions*. Cambridge, MA: MIT.

Beattie, J. (2009). Improving food quality and preventing disease. *Rowett Research Institute Newsletter, 10*(1), 1–3.

Bennett, F., Clarke, D., Evans, J. B., Hopper, A., Jones, A., & Leask, D. (n.d.). *Piconet, Embedded Mobile Networking*. Cambridge, UK: Cambridge University.

Bio Trainer. (n.d.). *Bio Trainer Clinical Studies*. Retrieved from http://www.biotrainerusa.com/clinical.asp

Bluetooth, S. I. G. (2001a). Generic Object Exchange Profile. *Bluetooth Specification 1.1* (Chapter 10, pp. 310-338).

Bluetooth, S. I. G. (2001b). *Technical Note, Bluetooth Tutorial*. Bluetooth.

Bluetooth, S. I. G. (2001c). Serial Port Profile. *Bluetooth Specification 1.1* (Chapter 5, pp. 172-196).

Bluetooth, S. I. G. (2001d). *Service Discovery Application profile. Bluetooth Specification 1.1* (Chapter 2, pp. 64-98).

Bluetooth. (n.d.). *Bluetooth Basics*. Retrieved from http://www.bluetooth.com/Bluetooth / Technology/ (2009)

Bracke, W., Puers, R., & Hoof, C. V. (2007). *Ultra Low Power Capacitive Sensor Interfaces*. New York: Springer.

Brandes, M., & Rosenbaum, D. (2003). Correlations between the step activity monitor and the DynaPort ADL-monitor. *Clinical Biomechanics (Bristol, Avon), 19*, 91–94. PubMed doi:10.1016/j.clinbiomech.2003.08.001

Cardou, P., & Angeles, J. (2007). Simplectic Architectures for True Multi-axial Accelerometers: A Novel Application of Parallel Robots. In *Proceedings of the IEEE International Conference on Robotics and Automation*, Italy.

Centers for Disease Control and Prevention. (n.d.). *Overweight and Obesity*. Retrieved from http://www.cdc.gov/obesity/defining.html

EMHF. (n.d.). Tackling Overweight and Obesity in Men in Europe. *European Men's Health Forum.*

European Association for the Study of Obesity. (2004). Retrieved from http://www.easo.org/working_groups_childhood_3.htm

Firstbeat Technologies. (2007). *An Energy Expenditure Estimation Method Based on Heart Rate Measurement.* Firstbeat Technologies Ltd.

Hainer, V., Frelut, M., & Seidell, J. (2002). *Obesity in Europe, The Case for Action.* International Obesity Taskforce & European Association for the Study of Obesity.

Health and Fitness Institute. com. (n.d.). *Medical Reasons for Obesity.* Retrieved from http://healthandfitnessinstitute.com/medical-reasons-for-obesity.htm

Healthy People 2010 Operational Definition. (n.d.). *Operational Definition: Objective* (pp. 22-2).

IUFoST. (2007). *Obesity.* International Union of Food Science and Technology.

Khanna, G. (2005). *Building Bluetooth Applications on the Windows CE 5.0 and Windows Mobile Platforms.* Microsoft.

Lal, R. (2008). *Measurement of Energy Expenditure.* School of Biological, Chemical and Environmental Sciences.

Löndahl, C. (2007). *Obesity - A Threat to a Public Health?* Swedish Council for Working Life and Social Research.

McCarthy, J. (1960). *Physical Activity. European Opinion Research Group EEIG* (pp. 183–186). Special Eurobarometer.

Meghdadi, T., & Arts, S. (2003, September). *Symbol Selects Socket Connection Solution Using Bluetooth® Wireless Technology for PPT 8800 Mobile Terminal.* Chicago: Frontline Supply Chain Week.

Melanson, J. R., & Freedson, P. (1994). Validity of the Computer Science and Applications, Inc. (CSA) activity monitor. *Journal of the American College of Sports Medicine.*

Metcalf, B. S., Voss, L. D., & Wilkin, T. J. (2002). Accelerometers identify inactive and potentially obese children (EarlyBird 3). *Archives of Disease in Childhood, 87,* 166–167. PubMed doi:10.1136/adc.87.2.166

Miller, M. (2001). *Discovering Bluetooth.* USA: SYBEX Inc.

MRC. (2009). Moderate obesity takes years off life expectancy, though not as many as smoking. *Medical Research Council Media Release.* msdn. (n.d.). *About Bluetooth.* Retrieved from http://msdn.microsoft.com/en-us/library/aa362761(VS.85).aspx msdn. (n.d.). *About Bluetooth.* Retrieved from http://www.palowireless.com/bluetooth/

Murphy, T. (2009, September 10). STOP Obesity Alliance Issues Recommendations to Ensure Health Reform Successfully Addresses Obesity Epidemic. *Medical News Today.* Retrieved from http://www.medicalnewstoday.com/articles/163443.php

NHS. (n.d.). *Obesity (Silver Spring, Md.).* Retrieved from http://www.nhs.uk/Conditions/Obesity /Pages/Introduction.aspx.

Pearce, S. (2007, July). *Juice PAM Firmware Functional Specification.* Cambridge Consultants.

Roche, J., & Hanlon, J. (2009, November 2). What is Bluetooth? *Cnet Australia.* Retrieved from http://www.cnet.com.au/what-is-bluetooth-240091501.htm?omnRef=NULL

Rowett Research Institute. (n.d.). Improving food quality and preventing disease. *Rowett Research Institute.*

Steele, B., Holt, L., Ferris, S., Lakshminaryan, S., & Buchner, D. M. (2000). Physical Activity in COPD Using a Triaxial Accelerometer. *Chest, 117*, 1359–1367. doi:10.1378/chest.117.5.1359

STMicroelectronics. (2001). *BluetoothTM Profiles Overview*. STMicroelectronics.

Sybase iAnywhere. (2009). *Bluetooth - A Technical Description of Blue SDK Profiles from Sybase iAnywhere*. Sybase.

The Future of Wireless Medical Devices. (n.d.). *Cambridge Consultants*.

(n.d.). *The Hand*. Retrieved from http://32feet.net/library/.

Tryon, W. W. (2008). Methods of Measuring Human Activity. *Journal of Behaviour Analysis in Health, Sports, Fitness and Medicine, 1*(2).

University of Cambridge. (2007, April). *Why are we so fat*? Retrieved from http://www.research-horizons.cam.ac.uk/ spotlight/why-are-we-so-fat-.aspx

Weight-Control Information Network. (2003). Medical Care for Obese Patients. *National Institutes of Health*, 3-5335.

Wigley, A., & Foot, D. (2007). *Microsoft Mobile Development Handbook*. Microsoft Press.

Wikipedia. (n.d.). *OBject EXchange*. Retrieved from http://en.wikipedia.org/wiki/OBEX

ENDNOTE

[1]   http://www.milife.com

This work was previously published in International Journal of Ambient Computing and Intelligence, Volume 2, Issue 3, edited by Kevin Curran, pp. 1-18, copyright 2010 by IGI Publishing (an imprint of IGI Global).

Chapter 13
Mobile Multimedia:
Reflecting on Dynamic Service Provision

Michael O'Grady
University College Dublin, Ireland

Gregory O'Hare
University College Dublin, Ireland

Rem Collier
University College Dublin, Ireland

ABSTRACT

Delivering multimedia services to roaming subscribers raises significant challenges for content providers. There are a number of reasons for this; however, the principal difficulties arise from the inherent differences between the nature of mobile computing usage, and that of its static counterpart. The harnessing of appropriate contextual elements pertaining to a mobile subscriber at any given time offers significant opportunities for enhancing and customising service delivery. Dynamic content provision is a case in point. The versatile nature of the mobile subscriber offers opportunities for the delivery of content that is most appropriate to the subscriber's prevailing context, and hence is most likely to be welcomed. To succeed in this endeavour requires an innate understanding of the technologies, the mobile usage paradigm and the application domain in question, such that conflicting demands may be reconciled to the subscriber's benefit. In this paper, multimedia-augmented service provision for mobile subscribers is considered in light of the availability of contextual information. In particular, context-aware pre-caching is advocated as a means of maximising the possibilities for delivering context-aware services to mobile subscribers in scenarios of dynamic contexts.

INTRODUCTION

Mobile computing has fundamentally challenged many aspects and tenets of what was perceived, and experienced, by most people in traditional computing scenarios. Though a radical paradigm shift in

DOI: 10.4018/978-1-4666-0038-6.ch013

itself, nevertheless, it was only over time that the nature of mobile computing began to crystallise. Indeed, it must be observed that this is an ongoing process. When the historical development of modern computing is considered, it can be seen why this is the case. If the 1960s are regarded as the beginning of the modern computing era, then conventional computing had been in existence

Copyright © 2012, IGI Global. Copying or distributing in print or electronic forms without written permission of IGI Global is prohibited.

almost 30 years before the use of computing in mobile scenarios became feasible. In this time, various techniques for engineering software solutions were developed and a consensus was growing about what constituted good practice principles. By introducing a mobile element into computing infrastructures, a further level of complexity was introduced into practically all elements of the software engineering lifecycle. In particular, data management and dissemination for mobile service delivery are interesting cases in point.

Data management for mobile users raises a number of difficulties. The ubiquitous issues of security and privacy are to the forefront of concerns for many. In particular, the issue of cache consistency, that is, ensuring that the data on the mobile device is consistent with that maintained on other devices, especially networked servers, is of particular importance. Data dissemination is dominated by the classic Push/Pull model, but its effectiveness is compromised by the inherent limitations of mobile computing. However, a more holistic view of data management and dissemination is emerging for mobile subscribers. In this view, the management and dissemination of data should be governed by prevailing contexts, particularly as these pertain to mobile subscribers.

Motivation

Consumers of electronic content are a diverse group. Thus meeting their needs and expectations can provide significant challenges for content providers. A brief look at the development of the internet is illuminating. Some organisations have a significant presence on the WWW, as they view this as a significant revenue generator. One critical objective is to increase the number of visitors to their site. This is true for the major international companies as well as for individuals who may maintain a blog for their own amusement. One technique that is being increasingly adopted is that of personalisation (Kobsa, Koenenmann, & Pohl, 2001). In essence, selective attributes of WWW site visitors are captured and used to filter, customise and prioritise the content presented to the visitor. Even though the nature of mobile computing usage differs significantly from its static counterpart, this principle can also be applied to great effect with mobile users, particularly when salient contextual elements unique to mobile subscribers are included. In addition, when mobile user behaviour is analysed, it can be seen that opportunities to deliver content pertinent to the prevailing context may arise. However, there are two key challenges that must be addressed if content providers are to take advantage of these opportunities.

- model of subscriber behaviour that enables correlation between their environment and their both their immediate and likely future behaviour must be constructed, such that potential contextual situations may be anticipated, and taken advantage of.
- Content must be pre-cached, either on the subscriber's host device or on a fixed network node such that it may be made available in that short period of time in which a select combination of contextual cues are valid.

As the mobile computing paradigm crystallized, the issue of mobile data management (Imielinski & Badrinath, 1994) became critically important. In particular, caching strategies in all their facets were widely investigated. A detailed description of these developments is beyond the scope of this discussion; however, the interested reader is referred to Barbará (1999) for a general discussion of some of the pertinent issues, and to Lee et al. (1999) for a discussion on semantic caching. From a historical perspective, it should be observed that much of this research took place in parallel with the WWW (Barish & Obraczke, 2000). More recent research considers the implications for caching in peer-to-peer (P2P) scenarios (Cao et al., 2007; Chow, Leong, & Chan, 2004).

Elements of context have been frequently harnessed implicitly for the refinement of caching strategies. Not surprisingly, location is the predominant element (Lee et al., 2002; Zheng, Xu, & Lee, 2002; Ren & Dunham, 2000). However, a number of researchers have considered the implications of their caching and pre-fetching algorithms from an energy and power perspective (Shen et al., 2005; Yin & Cao, 2004). Given the limited power resources of mobile devices, and the relatively power-intensive nature of wireless transmission, effectively harnessing these elements of context can contribute to system performance and longevity.

Data dissemination models tend to coalesce around the concepts of Pull and Push (Acharya, Franklin, & Zdonik, 1997), both in static and mobile usage scenarios. In each case, data that incorporates a dynamic component offers particular challenges (Bhide, Deolasee, & Katkar, 2002; Afonso & Silva, 2004). In addition, a range of ancillary but important issues arise. For example Lin and Lin (2004) consider the case for adopting intelligence in a Push model while Cheverst et al (Cheverst, Mitchell, & Davies, 2002) reflect on usability issues in context-aware mobile systems that adopt Push/Pull models.

CONTEXT-AWARE SERVICE DELIVERY

Given the dynamic and unpredictable nature of the average mobile subscriber's context, it can be seen that the content provider's task of preparing and delivering content such that it corresponds to the prevailing context is a complex endeavour, and one which careful planning is essential. In essence, this involves reconciling a number of conflicting objectives. Subscriber expectations must be met, the quality of their experience must be satisfactory and the service must be delivered in a timely manner. The cost must be acceptable to the subscriber while covering carrier costs and

any media royalties. All of these objectives must be fulfilled within the confines of a computationally limited device, and a wireless network with low data-rates and high latency while simultaneously operating with multimedia data that is resource and bandwidth intensive.

Technological Issues

Technological issues represent a critical constraint when designing mobile multimedia services, and a detailed understanding of these limitations is crucial. As an illustration of the issues involved, three facets are now considered - the device, an archetypical context sensor and wireless communications.

Device

With the exception of highly specialised niche domains, a service provider is almost invariably targeting a subpopulation that will be equipped with standard mobile phones. Such devices are characterised by limited computational resources in all their elements. This resource differential can come as a culture shock to some as subscribers who are used to operating on workstations may find the mobile experience unsatisfactory, and one in which they may need significant inducements if they are to adopt to successfully.

Working with multimedia is a computationally intensive process, and one which is compromised by the poor resources available on the mobile device. However, media capture and rendering are feasible, and for most services, these features are adequate. The small screen size is a major limitation; one quarter VGA - (320 x 240 pixels) being an upper limit and a resolution that most high-end phones now support. For smaller resolutions, the use of visual media elements may be unsuitable. It must be observed that part of the screen is usually accounted for by a standard banner at the top and a taskbar at the bottom, thereby limiting the amount of screen estate for a third party application. In principle, the programmer has access to the entire screen; however, in doing this, the perceived Look \& Feel (L\&F) of the device in question may be altered. For usability reasons, it is wise to ensure that the application both appears and functions in similar manner to other applications on the device.

Finally, the interaction modality must be considered. Most devices are equipped with a 5-way navigation pad, as well as an alphanumeric keyboard that conforms to the international standard (ITU-T, 2001). However, the use of intuitive multimodal interaction techniques such as eye-gaze, handwriting recognition and voice recognition for example, are not feasible on mobile devices, except in the simplest cases. Should it be possible to undertake the actual processing and interpretation on a fixed network node rather than on the device itself, then the options available increase; however, this is domain dependent.

Context Sensors

Having decided to use some element of the subscriber's context, or combination of contexts, a key decision involves how the necessary context can be harvested. In some cases, it may be possible to retrieve data from some existing infrastructure - a simple example might be harvesting the prevailing weather from a nearby weather station. Assuming that quality is acceptable, and that the cost overhead is not excessive, then this is a straightforward process. A more likely scenario is that an appropriate physical sensor, for example a location-sensor or an accelerometer, must be attached or embedded in the mobile device that the subscriber already possesses. In this case, the subscriber must be motivated to acquire such a sensor, or if the business model allows it, an appropriate sensor should be provided for free. From a device perspective, there are a number of considerations that must be taken into account. Assuming the sensor is integrated into the mobile device, the continuous monitoring and interpreting

of a subscriber's contextual state has implications for the power resource on the device, and as such must be quantified in some way. Secondly, the sensor must be monitored in software, and while this also has power implications, the memory consumed may have implications for service performance on the device. To clarify some of these issues, it is useful to consider one of the most useful aspects of a subscriber's context - location.

For the most part, techniques that enable the determination of subscribers' positions can be classified as either networked-based or satellite-based. Network-based techniques (Zhao, 2002) are inherently linked to cellular networks, and are heavily influenced by the topology of the network, which in turn is influenced by the nature of the local physical environment. The 3GPP has ratified three network-based techniques for 3G Universal Mobile Telephone Networks (UMTS) networks, and one that use satellite technologies, namely Assisted-GPS (3GPP, 2008). The three network-based techniques are: Cell-ID, Observed Time Difference of Arrival (OTDOA) and Uplink Time difference of Arrival (UTDOA).

A number of observations can be made about these techniques. Cell-ID gives a position which can only be accurate to within the radius of the cell. This may range from meters to kilometres. In any Public Land Mobile Network (PLMN) deployment, the cell size will not be uniform but will vary significantly between rural and urban areas. OTDOA and UTDOA are both dependent on signal measurement and, as such, need Line of Sight (LOS) conditions for an accurate reading. Crucially, they are both susceptible to fading and interference, thus the accuracy obtained may vary in a way that is difficult to quantify. Finally, all these techniques depend on the availability of network parameters, and as such, represent a service that the operator can provide but which the subscriber or service provider must pay for.

In the case of satellite technologies, the Global Positioning System (GPS) is currently the de facto standard. GPS receivers are commonly available and are increasingly being integrated with mobile devices. The accuracy of positions obtained with GPS varies but the error margin is usually of the order of 20 meters. As positions obtained with GPS are relatively accurate, and the service is free, it is an attractive solution for those service providers aspiring to deliver a services that utilises this aspect of a subscriber's context. If the application domain requires a more accurate position, the possibility of using a Satellite Based Augmentation System (SBAS) technology such as the European Ground Navigation Overlay Service (EGNOS) (Toran-Marti and Ventura-Traveset, 2004) or the Wide Area Augmentation System (WAAS) (Enge et al, 1996) may be considered. In essence, these are Differential GPS (DGPS) systems where the corrections to the GPS signal are broadcast from geostationary satellites. Most GPS receivers support this technology and position readings accurate to approximately 3 meters may be expected. A difficulty with this technology is that subscribers in urban environments and high latitudes may have difficulty accessing the signal due to the position and the scarcity of the broadcasting satellites. Recall that the GPS constellation includes over 24 satellites while EGNOS is only being broadcast from three. A solution to this, at least in the case of EGNOS, is SISNet \(Chen, Toran-Marti, & Ventura-Traveset, 2003), an initiative from the European Space Agency (ESA) and involves the transmission of the EGNOS signal (that is, DGPS corrections) over the internet. For mobile subscribers, there is a computational and cost overhead in using this service.

It is important to note that all the techniques described, with the exception of Cell-ID, work best outdoors and that their potential in indoors scenarios is limited. Indoor solutions require another suite of technologies, and at this time at least, there is no standardized solution for indoors. A number of techniques have been described in the literature (Hightower & Borriello, 2001), but of all these, the UBIsense system (Ubisense, 2010) is one that is receiving most attention.

From a deployment perspective, an increasing number of devices are being manufactured with GPS chips, and this trend will continue. Currently, the easiest way to integrate a GPS device is to acquire a Bluetooth enabled unit, as a significant number of mobile devices come with Bluetooth. The subscriber can host the device on their person such that the antenna is visible. As Bluetooth usually emulates a standard serial port, communicating with the device is not difficult. However, the device must be continuously monitored if the subscriber is to be tracked accurately. A dedicated thread is most intuitive way of managing the device. There is a memory overhead, possibly of the order of 512 bytes. This in itself is manageable but if the application itself is heavily multithreaded, for manipulating with other contextual elements for example, there may be performance issues.

GPS data conforms to the NMEA specifications (NMEA, 2008), and broadcasts from the GPS device are in the form of textual sentences, each labelled with a particular tag that distinguishes it and facilitates its parsing and subsequent interpretation. There are three tags of particular interest:

- \$GPGSA - This indicates the operating modes, the satellites used in the position calculation and various Dilution of Precision (DOP) values. By examining the "fix" (2D or 3D navigation), and the DOP values, the position calculation can be quantified.
- $GPGGA - This returns a latitude and longitude position as well as a position quality indicator, which can indicate whether this is a standard or differential GPS solution.
- $GPRMC - This indicates both position and bearing, thus giving a more complete state of the subscriber's spatial context.

In Table 1, an example of each type is presented, their size in bytes, and a cost indicator. While cost is not excessive, at least at first sight, it can be seen that data and cost overheads should be factored

Table 1. Cost of monitoring a subscriber over 1,2,4 and 8 hour intervals @ 1 cent per KB

NMEA	Size	1 Hour Size	1 Hour Cost	2 Hour Size	2 Hour Cost	4 Hour Size	4 Hour Cost	8 Hour Size	8 Hour Cost
Tag	(bytes)	(bytes)	(cent)	(bytes)	(cent)	(bytes)	(cent	bytes)	(cent)
$GPGSA	49	8820	86	176400	172	452800	345	705600	689
$GPGGA	64	115200	113	230400	225	460800	450	921600	900
$GPRMC	68	122400	120	244800	239	489600	478	979200	956
Total	181	325800	318	651600	636	1303200	1273	2606400	2545

into the design. However, if the position can be calculated on the device, then it is only necessary to transit the position (a tuple of longitude, latitude and bearing) at appropriate intervals, thus reducing the amount of data traffic and making a significant cost saving. On average, a standard position would require 16 bytes (including a DOP parameter) while it would require 181 bytes to consume the equivalent three NMEA sentences.

Wireless Networking

Service providers and subscribers are dependent on the network operator for transport of data, and as such are constricted by the characteristics of their networks. Usually, there are a number of network operators all vying for custom, and depending on the nature of the proposed service, one may offer a suitable package. However, it must be understood that network operators are innately conservative, and their first priority is to ensure that their networks are operational at all times. Thus, operators will not entertain extraordinary demands by service providers.

High latency and poor data rates have traditionally compromised the effectiveness of wireless data networks. In recent years, the situation has improved, and this trend will continue. However, depending on the geographic area where the service will be deployed, it is possible that the networks of a number of different operators may need to be availed of. This is not a problem in itself, but these networks may vary and it is

important their characteristics be understood, as it is necessary to ensure that the service will operate satisfactorily under variable networking conditions. As an example of this, 3G networks were deployed in an incremental basis - initially in urban areas and the selective rural areas, for example beside motorways. However, should the 3G base station be obscured, then the subscriber's phone would automatically connect to an older GPRS base station. For standard voice traffic, this is not a problem. For data traffic, such a change would have serious implications. In practice, a service provider must factor in the heterogeneous landscape that characterises wireless telecommunications.

In general a network operator will not guarantee wireless data rates. It depends on the number of subscribers using the network at any given instant. Not only that, but operators will not commit to a minimum data rate, thus worst case scenarios cannot be constructed. This is a potentially serious problem for service providers, as they cannot design a service with guaranteed Quality of Service (QoS) parameters. Indeed, this has led some researchers to question the validity of the QoS concept, at least from a subscriber perspective. A Quality of Experience (QoE) metric (Jain, 2004) has been suggested as a more effective alternative. Ultimately, it is envisaged that the incorporation of IP Multimedia Subsystem (IMS) (Poikselka et al., 2006) technologies will address the critical issue of QoS in broadband wireless networks.

Design

A mature understanding of the technical possibilities and limitations is an essential prerequisite for service design. Three essential models must be constructed - a context model, a media model and a delivery model.

Context Model

Acquiring elements of a subscriber's context introduces additional complexity into the design and delivery process. It beholds the service provider to ensure that the cost of this endeavour is fully understood and justified, and in this case, cost is not just limited to the financial realm. It must be ascertained that the selective contextual cues can be obtained easily and transparently, and with minimum disruption to the subscriber. In addition, it must be further ascertained that the contextual situation can be interpreted within the appropriate time constraints.

Consider the case of spatial context or location. To acquire this aspect of their context, the subscriber must be equipped with either a GPS sensor or the network operator must have a capability to determine it to a sufficient accuracy. To interpret spatial context in practice, it is essential that a model of the physical environment be obtained. A number of agencies, both governmental and commercial, can supply such models, usually in the form of Geographic Information System (GIS) data. Depending on the application, additional overlays can be obtained, for example a vector street map. A more likely scenario is that an application specific overlay must be developed. To determine the distance between the subscriber and some object of interest, a number of formulae can be adopted. The standard Euclidean distance can be calculated in the usual way. In practice, this assumes a straight path between the subscriber and the object in question. This may not be the case, and if a more accurate measurement is needed, it may be necessary to consider another technique,

possibly Manhattan distance, if the geographic area in question is in a city.

Finally, it can be useful to classify context elements according to their dynamicity. Some context may be almost semi-static in nature, for example, personal profile data. Such data may be stored on the network, rather than on the mobile device. Context that is sufficiently dynamic must be captured in situ; but its processing and interpretation may need to take place elsewhere. This process must be quantified.

Media Model

In a wireless multimedia service, individual media components will constitute a significant portion of any service payload. Given the poor data-rates that characterise wireless communications, it is essential that the trade-off between subscriber expectations and requirements, and selected media elements or formats be understood and justified. In some cases, high quality media will be required; in other cases, excessive quality will not increase subscriber satisfaction, and may have a detrimental effect on device performance.

A potential complication occurs when the respective abilities of mobile devices to render different media are considered. This capability differs between devices, and even between similar devices from the same manufacturers. In all cases, manufacturers will indicate which media formats their device supports. However, some caution must be exercised here. Frequently, a device will support a dedicated player for some media element. Such a player is usually optimised for the device in question, and constructed as a stand-alone application. However, third party service providers may not be able to access such applications, customise them or integrate them into their services. Rather, the application runtime environment supported by the device will usually support a suite of generic media players and codecs. It is beholden on service providers to identify those formats that are most appropriate for the domain in question,

Figure 1. A context-aware pull approach

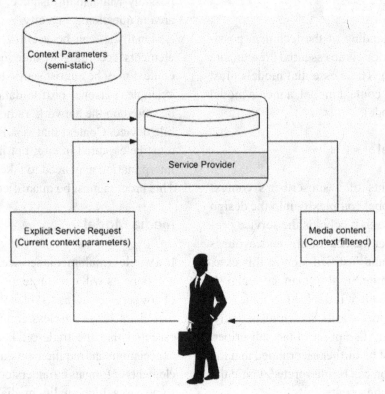

and which will perform on the widest variety of devices. One standard approach is to maintain a multimedia database that contains media elements stored in very high resolution formats. These are then converted on-the fly as needed.

Delivery Model

In essence, there are two classic models of data dissemination - Pull and Push. Both of these can be augmented be salient aspects of the subscriber's context, as per application domain requirements. There is a third model of particular relevance when considering dynamic data - Context-aware pre-caching. This could be implemented under the guise of a push or pull approach. For the purposes of this discussion, it will be considered separately as it is an apt solution in dynamic contextual scenarios.

In the case of Context-aware Pull (Figure 1), the service provider takes a relatively passive role, almost restricting them to the role of a content repository. Should the subscriber provide some contextual cues, or if the service provider has acquired some semi-static context elements, then there may be scope for adaptation and personalisation. Implementing a Pull approach is relatively straightforward and the onus is on the subscriber to initiate sessions. This limits the potential for the service provider to act in an opportunistic and proactive fashion in response to emerging context scenarios.

In a Context-aware Push scenario (Figure 2), the service provider is responsible for delivering the data on to the subscriber's device. Hence, every effort must be made to ensure that the data is relevant and timely. Contextual cues offer a means of achieving this, and their effective utilisation minimises the amount of redundant data

Figure 2. A context-aware push approach

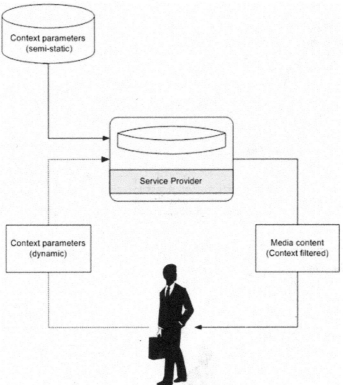

and increases user satisfaction. In the former case, there is a cost saving; in the later case, there is the possibility of additional revenue.

Finally, a context-aware pre-cache approach (Figure 3) may be considered. In this scenario, a certain contextual state may be envisaged as being likely to arise in the near future. When this state arises, a window of opportunity exists to provide a service to the subscriber. This window may be quite short in duration; hence every effort must be made to avail of it. Consider the mobile commerce domain. A mobile subscriber may be passing a shop, and only in this short time span while they are in the vicinity of the shop does an opportunity exist to deliver an advertisement to their mobile device, and hopefully motivate them to actually enter the shop. The delivery cycle can be shorted if this situation has been anticipated, and the advertisement prepared in advance. If there is a multimedia processing component, there

may be a considerable time saving. Though not quantifying this time saving, it may mean the difference between gaining a customer and failing to do so. The greater the multimedia component, the greater the need for acting in a proactive and anticipatory fashion. Pre-caching can occur either on the service provider's fixed networked node or on the subscriber's mobile device. In both cases, the service can still be modelled in either a push or pull fashion. By hosting the pre-cached data on the local device, the effects of issues like network latency are reduced though there may be a cost penalty. However, by making the pre-cache available locally, the service can be delivered instantly once the appropriate contextual state has been realised. In this way, the service can be delivered even in those situations where the duration of the appropriate contextual state is quite short. A practical illustration of these issues will now be presented in Section \ref{genie}.

Figure 3. A context-aware pre-cache approach

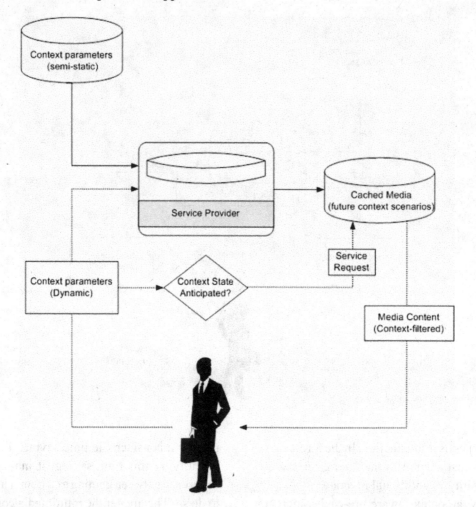

CONTEXT SENSITIVE CONTENT DELIVERY IN THE TOURIST DOMAIN

As a practical illustration of the issues discussed in the previous section, a brief description of an etourism application is now presented from a context and mobile multimedia perspective. The application in question - Gulliver's Genie (O'Grady, O'Hare, & Donaghy, 2007; O'Grady & O'Hare, 2004) has been an ongoing project for a number of years. It is extensively described in the literature and it has been the subject of user evaluations (O'Grady, O'Hare, & Sas, 2005). The overall objective of the Genie is to deliver multi-

media presentations to tourists on those attractions that they encounter while roaming.

In brief: the Genie is modelled and implemented using the intelligent agent paradigm. As the tourist roams, their prevailing spatial context is captured and interpreted on their device. Aspects of this are regularly passed to agents on a network node, which proceeds to identify and construct multimedia presentations, in anticipation of the tourist encountering an attraction while roaming. Given the likelihood of a context state arising, the presentation is actually downloaded and pre-cached on the device. Should the appropriate contextual state be triggered, this presentation will be rendered for the tourist immediately. More recently, the possibility of using the Synchronized Multimedia Integration Language (SMIL) (W3C, 2010) was validated.

Context and the Genie

Spatial context, personal profile and cultural interest profile are the three key elements of context harvested by the Genie.

Spatial context incorporates the tourist's geographical position and bearing. This is harvested from a normal GPS sensor attached to the device. Periodically, this is dispatched from the mobile device to a fixed network node. In this way, an approximate model of tourist behaviour can be maintained on the network node, and a more detailed model maintained on the device. Fundamental to the construction of this model is the availability of a geo-referenced model of the area. Using this as a basis, a model of the key tourist attractions can be constructed quite easily.

Personal profile includes those attributes of the tourist that are unique to their person. Age, nationality and spoken languages are three examples. These attributes change slowly over time, can be stored on a fixed networked node and enable the personalisation of the delivered service and constituent content.

Cultural interest profiles include a list of cultural interests particular to the tourist in question. This profile is overtly dynamic but not extremely so. Overtime, a preference for certain cultural interests will emerge. This will enable filtering and ranking of content. However, this does oblige the Genie to observe and interpret tourist interactions. Initially, the tourist fills in a questionnaire, which is used to seed their profiles. The personal profile remains relatively static; however, the interest profile can only be refined by explicitly observing tourist interaction. What is explicitly selected, and implicitly ignored, is observed by the Genie, and used to update the cultural interest model. There is a communications overhead here, but it is insignificant.

Figure 4. A presentation on the GPO in Dublin

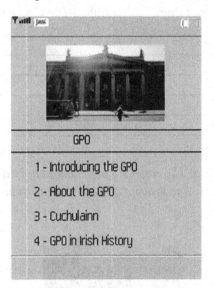

Media and the Genie

A Genie presentation consists of a number of Links which in turn are composed of individual media elements. Link, short for the term hyperlink, is a legacy term from when the Genie was modelled as a mobile WWW browsing application. This is no longer the case but the term endures. Each Link comprises a combination of either images and sounds, or a video sequence. Though rendering a video on a mobile device is indeed feasible, the option is not availed of in practice as their download time is excessive from a cost perspective. More importantly, it is questionable at least at this particular time juncture if the use of video would augment the subscriber experiences such that the cost/benefit ratio would be satisfactory.

A template of a simple Genie presentation may be seen in Table 2, and what the subscriber experiences may be seen in Figure 4. This presentation is for one of the most important buildings in Dublin - the General Post Office (GPO). The presentation is structured as follows:

The first Link, or Anchor Link, introduces the tourist to the tourist attraction (Figure 5). Its purpose is simply to allow the tourist orientate

Table 2. Structure and media composition of a Genie presentation concerning one of Dublin's most important tourist attractions - The General Post Office (GPO)

Link	Type	Title	Image	Audio	Video
1	Anchor	Introducing the GPO	✓	✓	X
2	Required	About the GPO	X	✓	X
3	Model - Folklore	Cuchulainn	✓	✓	X
4	Model - History	GPO in Irish History	X	✓	X

Figure 5. The Anchor Link is mandatory and introduces the attraction in question. The text beside the image is a transcript of what the tourist actually hears.

You are now approaching the General Post Office, or GPO, one the most famous landmarks in Dublin.

themselves and confirm that they are at the correct location. If interested, they can then select one of the other Links for further information.

The second Link is a required Link; hence, it is included in every presentation, regardless of context and personal profile (with the exception of language). Information contained in this presentation would be aimed at the broadest possible audience and, as such, would be general in nature. In this case, a brief overview of the attraction is presented (Figure 6).

The third Link is related to the tourist's Interest Model. In this case, the cultural interest is in the folklore domain. Hence, a presentation about the mythical Irish warrior Cuchulainn (translated - hound of Culainn) is presented as there is a famous sculpture of Cuchulainn in front of the GPO. In this case, a new image is depicted to bring the tourist's attention to the sculpture (Figure 7)

Likewise, the fourth Link is associated with a cultural interest - History. In this case, a brief history of the GPO is provided to tourists who

have expressed an interest in this topic (Figure 8).

Prioritizing and Filtering Multimedia Content

Once all the media content associated with a tourist attraction has been identified, the next stage is to filter that content according to the tourist's profiles. Recall that the only metadata or semantic tags associated with individual multimedia components is that of language; it is the Link itself that is semantically tagged from a profile perspective. Examples of Link attributes, and the values that they can adopt are illustrated in Figure 9. Various profile attributes can be catered for. For example, a very detailed link could be defined for Japanese adults who work in engineering with an interest in folklore. To digress slightly, it can be seen that the initial content aggregation and tagging stage is key, and that it is precisely at this stage that the service's unique and differentiating charac-

Figure 6. A required link is mandatory. In this case, it presents a brief overview of the GPO.

The GPO is one of the world's oldest postal headquarters. The original foundation stone was laid in 1814, and the building was completed 4 years later in 1818. The total cost was £50,000. As can be seen, the building is modelled on the Greek style, and is fronted by 6 ionic pillars. It is built of Wicklow granite, and Portland stone is used for the portico. Three statues can be seen on top of the building. These are Hibernia in the centre with Fidelity to her left and Mercury to her right.

Figure 7. A presentation for those with an interest in folklore, in this case prompted by the proximity of a sculpture of Cuchulainn

Within the GPO is a sculpture of the legendary Irish warrior - Cuchulainn. This is dedicated to those who died in the Easter rising. The text of the Proclamation of independence, and the names of the signatories, are inscribed on the base.

teristics can be realized. The person or people who undertake the initial tagging process must be extremely knowledgeable about the subject matter, and be capable of relating this to their audience. No technology can be expected to counteract the cumulative effect of poor media selection and inappropriate use of semantic tags.

Finally, it is necessary to prioritize the content. Only Links associated with a particular cultural interest are ranked in the order of the importance the tourist has attached to a particular cultural interest. This ranking is based on the tourist's interaction history. At this stage, a complete presentation is available for rendering. However, it may be necessary to refine it further in light of cost, for example. Some strategies for this will be outlined in Section \ref{finalselection}.

As the Genie is modelled and implemented using the intelligent agent paradigm, one agent is assigned the task of presentation preparation. This agent uses various commitment rules to fulfil its task. An illustration of these kinds of rules may be seen in Figure 10. However, it should be noted that the agent may be regarded as a wrapper for

Figure 8. The GPO has witnessed some of the most pivotal moments in Irish History, thus a presentation available for those with an expressed cultural interest in Irish history

The GPO is inextricably linked with the foundation of the Irish State. It was the headquarters of the Easter Rising which took place on Easter Monday 1916 which ultimately led to the formation of the independent Irish Republic. This garrison maintained a presence in the GPO for over a week before surrendering. However, only a shell of the original building remained standing. It would be another 13 years before the GPO reopened for business.

Figure 9. Semantic tagging of enabling personalization and content filtering

Attribute	Value
Tourist Attraction	General Post Office ¦ National Museum ¦ Dublin Castle ¦ ......
Media elements	Image & Audio ¦ Video
Link Type	Anchor ¦ Required ¦ Model
Link Category	Parent ¦ Child
Language	Irish ¦ English ¦ Italian ¦ French ¦ German ¦ ....
Ethnicity	Irish ¦ Japanese ¦ Canadian ¦ American ¦ African ¦ ....
Age Group	Child ¦ Teenager ¦ Adult ¦ ....
Occupation	Artist ¦ Architect ¦ Engineer ¦ ....
Cultural Interest	Art ¦ Architecture ¦ Folklore ¦ History ¦ Literature ¦ Religion ¦ ...

Figure 10. Sample commitment rules utilised by the agents for presentation assembly

Sample Commitement Rules for Content identification

//On identifying the nearest attraction, the presentation agent must be dynamically assembled
BELIEF(nearestExhibit(?tourist, ?attraction)) =>
COMMIT(Self,Now,BELIEF(true),request(agentID(PresentationAgent,?address),BuildPresentation
(?tourist, ?attraction)));

//Before a presentation can be assembled, the tourist's profile must be retreived
BELIEF(profileRequired(?tourist)) =>
COMMIT(Self,Now,BELIEF(true),request(agentID(ProfileAgent,?address),returnProfile (?tourist,
?attraction)));

//For each characteristic of the tourist's profile, corresponding content (links) must be identified, if
available.
BELIEF(profileAttribute(?tourist, ?attribute)) => COMMIT(Self,Now,BELIEF(true),
extractContent(?attribute));

//Once all the profile related content has been identified, it must be ranked.
BELIEF(presentionAvailable(?tourist) => COMMIT(Self,Now,BELIEF(true), rankContent(?tourist,
?history));

---

the technique employed. Thus an agent could be developed that incorporates other advanced techniques such as machine learning, Case Based Reasoning (CBR) and so on. Such an agent could be seamlessly slotted in to the existing architecture, provided it conformed to the appropriate agent profile or template, and complies with the current ontology.

Implications of Media Selection

As an illustration of the importance of media format selection, the effects of media selection are now explored.

For the sample Genie presentation just discussed, there are two image components. The image associated with the first presentation element is the default image for the second and fourth presentation elements. The third element has a distinct image due to the nature of the material being presented. The sizes of PNG, GIF and JPG formats for each image can be seen in Table 3 PNG produces the largest files while JPG produces the smallest. To put this difference into perspective, an additional 49KB would be transmitted if the PNG format had been selected. The implications of this are that under a basic GPRS connection, it would take 8 seconds longer to download the presentation. In the case of a 3G connection operating at 300 kbs, it would add just over 1 second to the download time.

In the case of audio, the effect is more pronounced as the files are invariably larger. The WAV format consumes the most KB while the most efficient is the AMR format. As can be seen from Table 4, the net difference is 540 KB for the entire presentation. This would mean an additional 88 seconds to the download time in the case of a GPRS connection or 15 seconds in the case of a 3G connection. Thus prudent selection of media formats can have a dramatic effect both on the cost and the timely delivery of data.

In terms of timeliness of the delivery of the multimedia presentation, it is instructive to reflect on the average walking speed of a normal person. Clearly, this will vary according to the nature of

Table 3. Implications of chosen image format on download times

Link	PNG	GIF	JPEG	DELTA	GPRS	3G
	(KB)	*(KB)*	*(KB)*	*(KB)*	*(sec)*	*(sec)*
1	34	19	6	28	5.7	1.5
2	-	-	-	-	-	-
3	38	19	17	21	4.3	1.1
4	-	-	-	-	-	-
Total	72	38	23	49	10	2.6

Table 4. Implications of chosen audio format on download times

Link	Wav	MP3	AMR	DELTA	GPRS	3G
	(KB)	**(KB)**	**(KB)**	**(KB)**	**(sec)**	**(sec)**
1	58	30	12	46	9.4	2.5
2	171	170	55	216	44.2	11.8
3	127	64	26	101	20.6	5.5
4	222	112	45	177	36.2	6.6
Total	678	376	138	540	110	25

the terrain and the physical well-being of the tourist. However, if we assume a normal pedestrian walking speed of 1.25 m/s (Knoblauch, Pietrucha, & Nitzburg, 1996) it can be seen that the tourist would have moved an additional 21 meters in the time it would have taken to just download the presentation if the wav format had been chosen. In the case of large tourist attractions that have a significant geographical footprint, this is not such a problem. However, that is frequently not the case, and it can be easily envisage that small specialised attractions such as sculptures could get overlooked. And it is in precisely bringing the tourist's attention to such attractions that offers such potential for improving their experience. In the next section, how this is achieved is considered.

CONTEXT-AWARE PRE-CACHING IN PRACTICE

In light of the previous discussion, there are two key elements that need to be reflected on when considering context-aware pre-caching. The first concerns the anticipation of, and the subsequent identification of, the subscriber's contextual state. The second concerns the generation of content, and its dissemination to the subscriber, in light of dynamic contextual states.

Anticipation of the Contextual State

To anticipate a contextual state arising, the necessary element(s) of context must be continuously observed, and some cues must be available to suggest a possible future contextual state. In the case of position, it is the availability of a physical environmental model that enables this. A position sensor allows position and direction be monitored. It is only in correlating this with an environmental

Figure 11. Specifying the trigger points is critical to ensuring the tourist receives the presentation when the most suitable context prevails

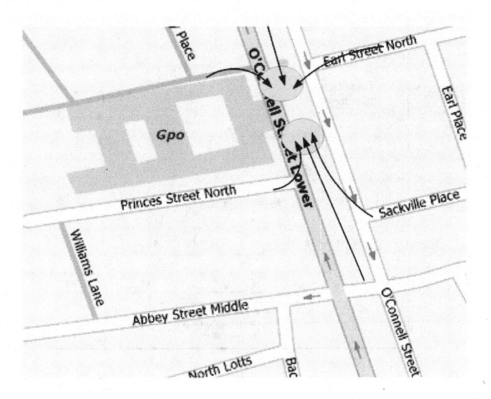

model (a map being the simplest implementation of this model), that meaningful contextual states can be identified, and possible future states envisaged.

Consider the case of a tourist approaching a historical building. They may approach it from different avenues; and even though they are obviously converging on the building, there is a risk that their trajectory may change. This risk is omnipresent and must be acknowledged, but the nearer the tourist is to the building, the less chance of it occurring. To maximise context identification, the building must be modelled. In certain cases, a single geographic position denoting the centre, and an approximate radius is sufficient. In complex cases, spatial objects may be utilised. One effective but simple approach is to model the building in terms of key points in which it can be approached from. Using the GPO as an example, it can be seen from Figure 11 that there are two such points. These points are trigger points and

represent the optimum positions from which a presentation on the GPO should be initiated; or in other words, they represent those points at which it is envisaged that the prevailing contextual situation will be most suitable for information presentation. At this point, the presentation must be available irrespective of delivery model engaged. It can pre-cached on the server for access by Pull, or a Push mechanism can be commenced if a streaming technology is used. But for pre-caching the content on the device, the outstanding challenge is how to identify when the process must commence such that the content is completely pre-cached when the tourist reaches the trigger point.

Four elements - data rates, content payload, walking speed and distance from trigger point are fundamental to identifying that moment for beginning the pre-caching process. Using walking speed and distance, an approximate time can be calculated. The inherent error in GPS is a source of

Figure 12. Once the tourist diverges from the trigger point, the presentation will commence provided that they are still with the predefined distance of the Point of Interest

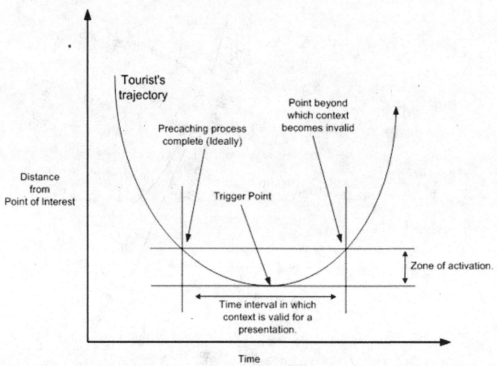

uncertainty in the calculation, but can be averaged. Though the walking speed is also an average, this may be regarded as a conservative value as in practice as there will almost invariably be delays due to window shopping, waiting at pedestrian lights and so on. How the content payload may be adjusted is discussed in the next section; however, the payload can be constructed on the fly, in response to the contextual situation at hand, or a number of potential candidate payloads be constructed, pre-cached on the networked node and the most suitable one dispatched to the device. Data rates represent the key problem as the number of users on a network determines the effective data rate. In principle, there should be a lower boundary, but it is the authors' experience that network operators will not commit to this. Thus, an average may be identified based on observation. The appropriate content payload is then dispatched for pre-caching on the device in an-

ticipation that it will be available for access in a timely manner.

Final responsibility for identifying the appropriate contextual state for rendering the content will usually reside on the remote device, as will responsibility for bringing the content to the subscriber's attention. In practice, there will be time interval over which the contextual state will remain valid. Due to the position error, this has to be assumed. A useful heuristic concerns the subscriber's behaviour in the vicinity of the trigger point. They will converge on this and then diverge (Figure 12). Hence, a distance can be specified that defines a zone of activation in which the contextual state (at least from a position perspective!) remains valid.

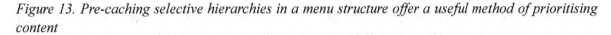

Figure 13. Pre-caching selective hierarchies in a menu structure offer a useful method of prioritising content

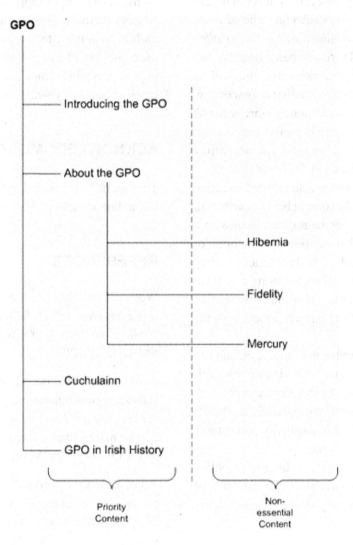

Content Refinement

In light of the previous discussion, the challenge is to reduce the amount of content transmitted such that it is guaranteed to reach the subscriber prior to the envisaged contextual situation arising, yet is adequate for a satisfactory experience. A solution to this lies in prioritization of the constituent elements in the content, and through the use of policies specified by the subscriber or service provider.

Recall from Section \ref{genie-media} that the menu structure described was one-dimensional, and that the content was prioritised within this according to mandatory items and the cultural interests. A nested menu hierarchy is also supported. The purpose behind this is to enable subscribers, should their interest be aroused, to request further information. As an illustration, consider the hierarchy illustrated in Figure 13. In this case, the item *About the GPO* has been augmented with addition material which is accessed by a separate menu structure. By selecting any of the items, further information is given. Though useful, this information is not a priority; thus, it is not urgent that it be pre-cached. On selecting one of these items, the necessary multimedia files can be *Pulled* down immediately. There will be a time delay, but because the subscriber is motivated, this will be perceived as tolerable, provided it is not excessive. In summary: an appropriate menu hierarchy can be harnessed to structure and prioritise the content, realizing a partial pre-caching solution, which may be viewed as a hybrid Push-Pull model.

Specifying policies are a simple but effective method for limiting the content being distributed. A content provider may negotiate a deal with a network operator that restricts the amount of content they can push at certain times, or may charge a premium rate for transmitting content at other times, for example. Thus the policies that they adopt must reflect their agreement with the operators.

Similarly, a subscriber may define certain policies when subscribing to the service, after negotiating with the service provider. For example, they may request that content be pre-cached in 512KB chunks, and that they will explicitly request any further content that they require.

In essence, parameters resulting from policy specification are effectively further elements of context that must be considered in the delivery of the service.

CONCLUSION

Delivering multimedia-enriched services in situations of fluctuating context raises particular difficulties for service providers. In the case of mobile subscribers, the situation is exacerbated due to the limited computational and communication capacity of the average mobile device. Augmenting the traditional Pull/Push dissemination approaches with appropriate context parameters offers great potential for customising and personalising services. In cases of highly dynamic contextual situations, a context-aware pre-caching approach is advocated. Such an approach offers an effective strategy for minimising the inherent limitations of mobile computing technologies while enhancing the capability of content providers to take advantage of prevailing contextual conditions, even in cases of highly dynamic circumstances.

ACKNOWLEDGMENT

This work is supported by Science Foundation Ireland under grant 07/CE/I1147

REFERENCES

W3C. (2010). *Synchronized Multimedia Integration Language (SMIL 3.0)*. Retrieved January 4, 2010, from http://www.w3.org/TR/2008/REC-SMIL3-20081201/

Acharya, S., Franklin, M., & Zdonik, S. (1997). Balancing push and pull for data broadcast. In *Proceedings of the 1997 ACM sigmod international conference on management of data (Sigmod '97)* (pp. 183-194). New York: ACM.

Afonso, A. P., & Silva, M. J. (2004). Dynamic information dissemination to mobile users: Mobility in databases and distributed systems: Summing up achievements of the past decade. *Mobile Networks and Applications*, *9*(5), 529–536.. doi:10.1023/B:MONE.0000034706.03412.38

Barbara, D. (1999). Mobile computing and databases-a survey. *IEEE Transactions on Knowledge and Data Engineering*, *11*(1), 108–117.. doi:10.1109/69.755619

Barish, G., & Obraczke, K. (2000). World wide web caching: trends and techniques. *IEEE Communications Magazine*, *38*(5), 178–184.. doi:10.1109/35.841844

Bhide, M., Deolasee, P., Katkar, A., Panchbudhe, A., Ramamritham, K., & Shenoy, P. (2002). Adaptive push-pull: disseminating dynamic web data. *IEEE Transactions on Computers, 51*(6), 652–668..doi:10.1109/TC.2002.1009150

Cao, J., Zhang, Y., Cao, G., & Xie, L. (2007). Data consistency for cooperative caching in mobile environments. *IEEE Computer, 40*(4), 60–66.

Chen, R., Toran-Marti, F., & Ventura-Traveset, J. (2003). Access to the egnos signal in space over mobile-ip. *GPS Solutions, 7*(1), 16–22.

Cheverst, K., Mitchell, K., & Davies, N. (2002). Exploring context-aware information push. *Personal and Ubiquitous Computing, 6*(4), 276–281..doi:10.1007/s007790200028

Chow, C.-Y., Leong, H. V., & Chan, A. (2004). Peer-to-peer cooperative caching in mobile environments. In *Proceedings of the 24th International Conference on Distributed Computing Systems Workshops* (pp. 528-533).

Enge, P., Walter, T., Pullen, S., Kee, C., Chao, Y.-C., & Tsai, Y.-J. (1996). Wide area augmentation of the global positioning system. *Proceedings of the IEEE, 84*(8), 1063–1088..doi:10.1109/5.533954

3GPP. (2008). User *Equipment (UE) positioning in Universal Terrestrial Radio Access Network (UTRAN); Stage 2 (TS No 25.305). 3rd Generation Partnership Project (3GPP)*. Retrieved from http://www.3gpp.org/ftp/Specs/html-info/25305.htm

Hightower, J., & Borriello, G. (2001, August). Location systems for ubiquitous computing. *IEEE Computer, 34*(8), 57–66.

Imielinski, T., & Badrinath, B. R. (1994). Mobile wireless computing: challenges in data management. *Communications of the ACM, 37*(10), 18–28..doi:10.1145/194313.194317

ITU-T. (2001). *Arrangement of digits, letters and symbols on telephones and other devices that can be used for gaining access to a telephone network*. Geneva, Switzerland: International Telecommunications Union.

Kobsa, A., Koenemann, J., & Pohl, W. (2001). Personalised hypermedia presentation techniques for improving online customer relationships. *The Knowledge Engineering Review, 16*(2), 111–155..doi:10.1017/S0269888901000108

Lee, D. L., Xu, J., Zheng, B., & Lee, W.-C. (2002). Data management in location-dependent information services. *IEEE Pervasive Computing / IEEE Computer Society* and *IEEE Communications Society, 1*(3), 65–72. doi:.doi:10.1109/MPRV.2002.1037724

Lee, K. C. K., Leong, H. V., & Si, A. (1999). Semantic query caching in a mobile environment. SIGMOBILE Mob. *Computer Communication Review, 3*(2), 28–36..doi:10.1145/584027.584029

Lin, Y.-W., & Lin, C.-W. (2004). An intelligent push system for mobile clients with wireless information appliances. *IEEE Transactions on Consumer Electronics, 50*(3), 952–961..doi:10.1109/TCE.2004.1341706

NMEA. (2008). *NMEA 0183, The Standard for Interfacing Marine Electronics*. Severna Park, MD: NMEA.

Ren, Q., & Dunham, M. H. (2000). Using semantic caching to manage location dependent data in mobile computing. In *Proceedings of the 6th annual international conference on mobile computing and networking (Mobicom '00)* (pp. 210-221). New York: ACM.

Shen, H., Kumar, M., Das, S. K., & Wang, Z. (2005). Energy Efficient data caching and prefetching for mobile devices based on utility. *Mobile Networks and Applications, 10*(4), 475–486..doi:10.1007/s11036-005-1559-8

Toran-Marti, F., & Ventura-Traveset, J. (2004). *The esa egnos project: The First step of the European contribution to the global navigation satellite system (gnss)*. Paper presented at the Navigare conference.

Ubisense. (2010). *Class leading precision Location - Factsheet*. Retrieved January 4, 2010, from http://www.ubisense.net/pdf/fact-sheets/products/software/Precise-Location-EN090624.pdf

Yin, L., & Cao, G. (2004, September). Adaptive power-aware prefetch in wireless networks. *IEEE Transactions on Wireless Communications, 3*(5), 1648–1658..doi:10.1109/TWC.2004.833430

Zhao, Y. (2002, July). Standardization of mobile phone positioning for 3g systems. *IEEE Communications Magazine, 40*(7), 108–116..doi:10.1109/MCOM.2002.1018015

Zheng, B., Xu, J., & Lee, D. L. (2002). Cache invalidation and replacement strategies for location- dependent data in mobile environments. [f]. *IEEE Transactions on Computers, 51*(10), 1141–1153..doi:10.1109/TC.2002.1039841

This work was previously published in International Journal of Ambient Computing and Intelligence, Volume 2, Issue 3, edited by Kevin Curran, pp. 19-39, copyright 2010 by IGI Publishing (an imprint of IGI Global).

Chapter 14
Simplicity, Consistency, Universality, Flexibility and Familiarity:
The SCUFF Principles for Developing User Interfaces for Ambient Computer Systems

Rich Picking
Glyndwr University, UK

Vic Grout
Glyndwr University, UK

John McGinn
Glyndwr University, UK

Jodi Crisp
Glyndwr University, UK

Helen Grout
Glyndwr University, UK

ABSTRACT

This paper describes the user interface design, and subsequent usability evaluation of the EU FP6 funded Easyline+ project, which involved the development of ambient assistive technology to support elderly and disabled people in their interaction with kitchen appliances. During this process, established usability design guidelines and principles were considered. The authors' analysis of the applicability of these has led to the development of a new set of principles, specifically for the design of ambient computer systems. This set of principles is referred to as SCUFF, an acronym for simplicity, consistency, universality, flexibility and familiarity. These evaluations suggest that adoption of the SCUFF principles was successful for the Easyline+ project, and that they can be used for other ambient technology projects, either as complementary to, or as an alternative to more generic and partially relevant principles.

DOI: 10.4018/978-1-4666-0038-6.ch014

Copyright © 2012, IGI Global. Copying or distributing in print or electronic forms without written permission of IGI Global is prohibited.

INTRODUCTION AND MOTIVATION FOR RESEARCH

We have developed user interfaces situated in modified familiar home devices, specifically television sets, mobile devices and interactive digital photographic frames, as part of the EU FP6 IST Easyline+ project (Low Cost Advanced White Goods for a Longer Independent Life of Elderly People).

Sensors using radio frequency identification (RFID), ZigBee, powerline communication and infra-red technologies enable the Easyline+ system to interact with the home environment. Human activity is monitored by an intelligent server, which we call the *e-servant*. The e-servant recognizes and adapts to changing needs as the user grows less able over time.

A simple example of an Easyline+ interaction is the scenario of a cooker hob being left on either with no pan on it or after a pan has been removed. The message *Hob left on with no* pan is conveyed to the user (wherever they may be in the home). The precise nature of the interaction and the range of options available to the user are adaptive, flexible and dependent on their level of ability, which can be assessed on a number of scales. However, the essence of the dialogue in this case would be that the user could turn off the hob remotely or respond: *Yes, I know; leave it on* (if they are permitted to according to their profile). Other scenarios include: *Food has expired in the fridge, The washing cycle has finished, This food cannot be microwaved,* and so forth. Additionally, a standalone RFID reader advises the user what to do with an item of food or clothing, an innovation particularly useful for visually impaired people. To support the international dimension, a range of European languages is also supported. The system is also adaptive in that it can modify the user interface for changing physical and cognitive abilities.

During the project's development, a number of user-centred exercises and events were undertaken to tune the design requirements, including workshops, focus groups, interviews, and evaluation sessions (Picking et al., 2009). We also employed personas (Cooper, 2004; Blythe & Dearden, 2009) to help us stay focused on the expectations of the end users. Summative testing of the ranges of devices and interface designs took place in a purposely developed usability laboratory, which simulated an elderly/disabled person's living space.

Satisfying the user and functional requirements are of course critical in any computer system development project, and good design augments these by referencing design principles relevant to the domain of enquiry. This paper describes the rationale for how we framed our user interface design decisions, and how this framing provided us with a structure which we propose here as a set of principles specifically for user interface design practice in the domain of ambient computer systems.

USER INTERFACE DESIGN GUIDELINES AND PRINCIPLES

The process of user interface design can be highly complex, as typically there are many competing variables involved. We could describe those variables as the *who* (the user population), the *where* (the environment the proposed system will be used in), the *how* (the style of user interaction, and the design of the tasks), and the *what* (the technological nature of the devices as well as the software/hardware constraints). Most user interface designers champion the *who* as the most important of the four variables, and consequently advocate a user-centred approach to their work.

To support designers in their consideration of users, a number of guidelines have been published over many years. Such guidelines aim to steer designers by keeping them on the track of developing quality, consistent user interfaces that conform to the standards expected by the *owners* of

Table 1. Shneiderman's eight golden rules of interface design

Principle	Description
S1. Strive for consistency	Consistent sequences of actions should be required in similar situations; identical terminology should be used; consistent commands should be employed.
S2. Enable frequent users to use shortcuts	As the frequency of use increases, so do the user's desires to reduce the number of interactions and to increase the pace of interaction. Abbreviations, function keys, hidden commands, and macro facilities are very helpful to an expert user.
S3. Offer informative feedback	For every operator action, there should be some system feedback.
S4. Design dialog to yield closure	Sequences of actions should be organized into groups with a beginning, middle, and end.
S5. Offer simple error handling	As much as possible, design the system so the user cannot make a serious error. If an error is made, the system should be able to detect the error and offer simple, comprehensible mechanisms for handling the error.
S6. Permit easy reversal of actions	This feature relieves anxiety, since the user knows that errors can be undone; it thus encourages exploration of unfamiliar options.
S7. Support internal locus of control	Experienced operators strongly desire the sense that they are in charge of the system and that the system responds to their actions. Design the system to make users the initiators of actions rather than the responders.
S8. Reduce short-term memory load	The limitation of human information processing in short-term memory requires that displays be kept simple, multiple page displays be consolidated, window-motion frequency be reduced, and sufficient training time be allotted for codes, mnemonics, and sequences of actions.

the guidelines. Examples of these include Apple's I-phone Human Interface Guidelines (Apple Inc., 2010) and Microsoft's Inductive User Interface Guidelines (Microsoft Corporation, 2001). As they tend to be for specific styles of interaction, for known types of devices, and for tasks that take place in typical environments (in other words the *how's*, *what's* and *where's* are predictable), such guidelines are always highly detailed.

At a further level of abstraction, design principles seek to cover a wide range of applications and application domains. Most sets of design principles are relatively short, comprising typically between six and ten individual principles. A well-known example is Shneiderman's eight golden rules of design (Shneiderman, 1999), summarized in Table 1.

During our initial consideration of user interface design guidelines and principles for ambient computing systems, we quickly determined that detailed guidelines were not applicable as they are too specific for the wide range of ambient computing applications, their users, and their environments. However, such guidelines may be developed for individual projects or platforms.

Rather, our concern centred on whether design principles, such as those of Shneiderman's, could easily be mapped onto the ambient subset of generic interactive computing applications. In order to do this, we looked at two further well-known sets of principles (Constantine & Lockwood, 1999; Nielsen, 2005) to determine their common features, possible differences, and whether any of them were appropriate for an ambient computing project. These are summarized in Table 2 and Table 3.

Table 2. Constantine and Lockwood's user interface design principles

Principle	Description
C1. The structure principle	Your design should organize the user interface purposefully, in meaningful and useful ways based on clear, consistent models that are apparent and recognizable to users, putting related things together and separating unrelated things. The structure principle is concerned with your overall user interface architecture.
C2. The simplicity principle	Your design should make simple, common tasks simple to do, communicating clearly and simply in the user's own language, and providing good shortcuts that are meaningfully related to longer procedures.
C3. The visibility principle	Your design should keep all needed options and materials for a given task visible without distracting the user with extraneous or redundant information.
C4. The feedback principle	Your design should keep users informed of actions or interpretations, changes of state or condition, and errors or exceptions.
C5. The tolerance principle	Your design should be flexible and tolerant, reducing the cost of mistakes and misuse by allowing undoing and redoing, while also preventing errors wherever possible.
C6. The reuse principle	Your design should reuse internal and external components and behaviors, maintaining consistency with purpose rather than merely arbitrary consistency, thus reducing the need for users to rethink and remember.

COMPARISON AND SYNTHESIS OF PRINCIPLES

We now move on to consider how the aforementioned usability principles apply to user interfaces for ambient computer systems. Each principle has been given a unique code in this paper for ease of cross referencing and discussion. Shneiderman's set is defined as {**S1...S8**}, Constantine and Lockwood as {**C1...C6**}, and Nielsen as {**N1...N10**}.

Our methodology uses a simple form of theme analysis, where we identify the common themes that run through each of the sets, and then assess that theme's applicability to the domain of ambient systems. We then synthesize them to propose our own set of principles for this domain.

Shneiderman's first principle S1, Strive for consistency marks clearly the theme of *consistency*, which is repeated in C1, C6 and N4. Ambient computer systems are no different from any other in this respect. The user interfaces should always be consistent.

The principle of *simplicity* is also evident throughout, specifically in Constantine and Lockwood's second principle C2, The simplicity principle. This principle is also evident in the descriptions of S8, N6 and N8, where advice is given of not overwhelming users' cognitive abilities by over-complication of the interface. Maximizing the system's visibility is also highlighted in C3 and N1. This is clearly a fundamental principle for most interactive computer systems, yet one might argue that for ambient systems, where the computer system often *disappears*, this might cause some confusion. The user interface itself is the one thing that may remain visible, but not always. For example, in a smart home environment, the interface may be embedded within a room's familiar fixtures and fittings, and the system status is evident in the environment, not in the interface. The same argument applies to the principles of feedback and closure, which are highlighted by S3, S4 and C4. We are not arguing here that visibility, feedback and closure are not important. Rather, for the specific domain of ambient computer systems

Table 3. Nielsen's usability heuristics

Principle	Description
N1. Visibility of system status	The system should always keep users informed about what is going on, through appropriate feedback within reasonable time.
N2. Match between system and the real world	The system should speak the users' language, with words, phrases and concepts familiar to the user, rather than system-oriented terms. Follow real-world conventions, making information appear in a natural and logical order.
N3. User control and freedom	Users often choose system functions by mistake and will need a clearly marked "emergency exit" to leave the unwanted state without having to go through an extended dialogue. Support undo and redo.
N4. Consistency and standards	Users should not have to wonder whether different words, situations, or actions mean the same thing. Follow platform conventions.
N5. Error prevention	Even better than good error messages is a careful design which prevents a problem from occurring in the first place. Either eliminate error-prone conditions or check for them and present users with a confirmation option before they commit to the action.
N6. Recognition rather than recall	Minimize the user's memory load by making objects, actions, and options visible. The user should not have to remember information from one part of the dialogue to another. Instructions for use of the system should be visible or easily retrievable whenever appropriate.
N7. Flexibility and efficiency of use	Accelerators -- unseen by the novice user -- may often speed up the interaction for the expert user such that the system can cater to both inexperienced and experienced users. Allow users to tailor frequent actions.
N8. Aesthetic and minimalist design	Dialogues should not contain information which is irrelevant or rarely needed. Every extra unit of information in a dialogue competes with the relevant units of information and diminishes their relative visibility.
N9. Help users recognize, diagnose, and recover from errors	Error messages should be expressed in plain language (no codes), precisely indicate the problem, and constructively suggest a solution.
N10. Help and documentation	Even though it is better if the system can be used without documentation, it may be necessary to provide help and documentation. Any such information should be easy to search, focused on the user's task, list concrete steps to be carried out, and not be too large.

where the environment itself is often the *output device* for want of a better term, these principles become less prominent. Consequently, we propose that they can be absorbed into the overall principle of *simplicity*.

Constantine and Lockwood's sixth principle C6, The reuse principle is interesting to discuss from an ambient perspective. As ambient systems interact with humans in their environments, it is highly likely that more than one instance of a user interface will exist. For example, there may be a user interface in several rooms in a smart home or workplace, and there may be mobile interfaces owned by each person within that environment. This principle of reuse not only applies to the internal components of a user interface, but should also be adhered to for alternative user interfaces and their platforms. In other words, the user interface should be universally the same (as far as possible) for all platforms and all devices. We term this principle of external consistency *universality*, and we regard it to be specifically important for ambient systems.

The nature of the disappearing computer in ambient computer systems leads us next to concentrate on Nielsen's second principle N2, Match between system and the real world. Clearly, ambient systems are very closely linked with the *real world*, and so particular attention on this principle is warranted. To this end, user interface metaphors have been successfully applied in ambient user interface design (Adam et al., 2008). Many ambient user interfaces are embedded within the environment, and often in familiar devices (appliances, televisions for example). Also, their users expect their interaction with the ambient computer system to be natural and familiar, and in some cases the interaction itself is invisible to the user (for example, where lights are switched on when a room is entered). We term this principle *familiarity*.

Nielsen's seventh principle N7, Flexibility and efficiency of use reminds us of the requirement that ambient computer systems should be personalizable. This principle is also referred to in S2, where frequent or expert users should be provided with faster ways to achieve their goals. Ambient systems are also often adaptive and intelligent enough to know who their user is, so this principle of *flexibility* is clearly fundamental to this domain.

A number of the previously published principles focus on error handling, and error recovery (S5, C5, N5, N9, S6, C5, N3). These principles are of course crucial for all typical interactive systems. For ambient systems with typical user interfaces, the same applies, although we argue that for an interface to be truly ambient, errors should be either avoided at all costs, or if not then not critical, and easily rectified by a user's subsequent action. In other words, the environment would behave in a manner familiar to the user as if they were not actually using a computer system. In the

same respect, the concept of *undo* is unnatural, conflicting with the principle of *familiarity*.

Two further established principles recommend that the user should feel in control and be the initiator of dialogues (S7, N3). This is clearly true for traditional computer applications, but in ambient systems, the system itself often initiates a dialogue, and also often controls that dialogue by responding to human behavior and environmental situations.

The only principle not yet discussed is Nielsen's tenth N10, Help and documentation. We agree with Nielsen that it is better that a system can be used without help or documentation. Ambient systems especially should be intuitive and encourage natural behaviour. Whilst all systems will be supported by some form of documentation, we consider this principle to be peripheral to the fundamental principles of user interfaces for ambient computer systems.

Now that all the published principles have been discussed, we can reflect on the themes identified. This analysis has provided us with five principles, derived from those themes: Simplicity, Consistency, Universality, Flexibility, and Familiarity – re-arranged now to give us the SCUFF acronym.

In the following section, we describe how we applied the SCUFF principles to a real ambient system design project and the subsequent evaluation of its user interface.

APPLICATION AND EVALUATION OF THE SCUFF PRINCIPLES

Interface devices implemented in the Easyline+ project include the television, interactive digital photo frames (DPFs) and hand-held (or worn) mobile devices (MDs). The television was selected as the central point of control in the home, an observation corroborated by initial user surveys and the narrative workshops. This *simplicity* and *familiarity* of the user interface device conforms to the SCUFF principles, and is also supported by research into elderly users' views of interaction with technology (Davidoff et al., 2005; Nygard, 2008).

DPFs can be positioned in any room of the home for immediate notification (when not in use, they display conventional photos) and MDs can be used for emergencies and other forms of mobile interaction – in the garden, for example. It could be argued that MDs are not popular with the current generation of elderly people; however, this is changing quickly as such devices become more ubiquitous. All devices present an identical display, to provide external consistency of use (the *universality* principle).

The *consistency* principle is assured throughout the interface design with consistent presentation of the display layout, placement of menus, use of colour, text, graphics and icons. Dialogue with users was also designed to be consistent and appropriate for the user.

Flexibility was enabled as this dialogue could be adapted for the user's individual needs. We employed three levels of cognitive adaption, three levels of visual adaption, and three of aural adaption. The latter two physical factors are also adaptable by providing users with larger and louder physical display devices. Blind users are supported as the interface is usable in aural display only. However, a suitable tactile input device is required for these users.

The *familiarity* principle informed our selection of remote input devices for the TV, based on the four-colour (red, green, yellow and blue) buttons of a typical television remote-control. This four-colour menu style of interaction was also employed on devices not associated with the TV such as DPFs and MDs, allowing for complete *universality* of device appearance and operation.

An example of the final interface design, maintaining adherence to the SCUFF principles, is given in Figure 1.

USABILITY EVALUATION

To test our designs, and indirectly the value of the SCUFF principles, we conducted between-groups laboratory-based usability studies with heterogeneous groups of users, including elderly and disabled users, people with learning difficulties, as well as with 'healthy' adults. We were interested in evaluating the latter group for two reasons. Firstly, it has been documented that elderly and vulnerable participants in usability studies may react differently than they normally would, for example by being over-positive due to their involvement in the study (Park & Schwartz, 2000; Eisma et al., 2004). Comparing their results with what might be termed a control group would potentially identify issues of this nature. Secondly, our earlier evaluations suggested that the product might be suitable for time-impoverished people (for example, stressed parents with babies in the home), not just elderly and disabled people (Picking et al., 2009).

We selected a total of 27 participants for this evaluation exercise, comprising nine elderly users, nine with learning difficulties, and nine from the 'control' group. Each group was given a set of scenarios to follow (for example loading the refrigerator, baking food, and doing laundry), which involved interaction with the kitchen appliances and the user interface, which for this study was provided on a television screen and an MD. Participants' activities were recorded in the laboratory, and were subsequently analyzed. They were also asked to complete a usability experience questionnaire comprising 20 semantically-rated questions, which were categorized according to usability, design and layout, functionality, user satisfaction, and expected future use.

The aggregated results for every category and for all groups indicated a positive outcome for the usability experience questionnaire. An Analysis of Variance (ANOVA) revealed that there were no significant differences in the responses provided by the three groups ($F = 1.52$; $p < 0.05$), apart from

Figure 1. Interface design screen example

one question which asked whether they felt embarrassment at using the system - some members of the learning difficulties group were uncomfortable with it from this point of view. The control group performed expectedly better in general, and the only observed usability issues involved elderly users' difficulty in using a standard remote control handset and the small-screened MD, both of which were easily rectified by selecting alternative input and output devices.

CONCLUSION

It is very well-documented that we are experiencing an increase in the number of elderly people and a reduction of younger people to care for them as they lose their independence in later years. Our evaluation of the Easyline+ project suggests that it has made a small but valuable contribution towards helping elderly and disabled people remain independently in their own homes for longer, something that is popular with those people, as well as potentially tempering future increases in elderly healthcare spending. The design of the user interfaces was informed not only by our close work with our user population, but also by the SCUFF principles we employed.

For future projects of this nature, where ambient technologies are embedded in human environments, adherence to the SCUFF principles should help designers focus on the unique factors that must be considered for user interface design in this domain.

ACKNOWLEDGMENT

This research was supported through the European Union Framework Six (FP6) Information Society Technologies (IST) programme (No. 045515) EASYLINE+, 'Low Cost Advanced White Goods for a Longer Independent Life of Elderly People'.

REFERENCES

Adam, S., Mukasa, K. S., Breiner, K., & Trapp, M. (2008). An apartment-based metaphor for intuitive interaction with ambient assisted living applications. In *Proceedings of 23rd BCS Conference on People and Computers, British Computer Society*, Liverpool, UK (pp. 67-75).

Apple Inc. (2010). *I-phone human interface guidelines*. Retrieved March 31, 2010, from http://developer.apple.com/iPhone/library/documentation/UserExperience/ Conceptual/MobileHIG

Blythe, M., & Dearden, A. (2009). Representing older people: towards meaningful images of the user in design scenarios. *Universal Access in the Information Society*, 8, 21–32.. doi:10.1007/s10209-008-0128-x

2000Cognitive aging: A primer. InPark, D., & Schwarz, N. (Eds.), *Psychology Press* (p. 238). New York: Taylor and Francis.

Constantine, L. L., & Lockwood, L. A. D. (1999). *Software for use: a practical guide to the models and methods of usage-centered design*. Reading, MA: Addison-Wesley.

Cooper, A. (2004). *The inmates are running the asylum* (2nd ed.). Upper Saddle River, NJ: Sams Publishing.

Davidoff, S., Bloomberg, C., Li, I. A. R., Mankoff, J., & Fussell, S. R. (2005). The book as user interface: lowering the entry cost to email for elders. In *Proceedings of CHI '05 extended abstracts on Human factors in computing systems* (pp. 1331-1334).

Eisma, R., Dickinson, A., Goodman, J., Syme, A., Tiwari, L., & Newell, A. (2004). Early user involvement in the development of Information Technology-related products for older people. *Universal Access in the Information Society*, 3(2), 131–140.. doi:10.1007/s10209-004-0092-z

Microsoft Corporation. (2001). *Microsoft Inductive User Interface Guidelines*. Retrieved March 31, 2010, from http://msdn.microsoft.com/en-us/library/ms997506.aspx#iuiguidelines_topic2

Nielsen, J. (2005). *Ten usability heuristics*. Retrieved March 31, 2010, from http://www.useit.com/papers/heuristic /heuristic_list.html

Nygard, L. (2008). The meaning of everyday technology as experienced by people with dementia who live alone. *Dementia (London)*, 7(4), 481–502.. doi:10.1177/1471301208096631

Picking, R., Robinet, A., Grout, V., McGinn, J., Roy, A., Ellis, S., & Oram, D. (2009). A case study using a methodological approach to developing user interfaces for elderly and disabled people. *The Computer Journal*. doi:.doi:10.1093/comjnl/bxp089

Schneiderman, B. (1999). *Designing the user interface* (3rd ed.). Reading, MA: Addison-Wesley.

This work was previously published in International Journal of Ambient Computing and Intelligence, Volume 2, Issue 3, edited by Kevin Curran, pp. 40-49, copyright 2010 by IGI Publishing (an imprint of IGI Global).

Chapter 15
A Low-Cost Multi-Touch Surface Device Supporting Effective Ergonomic Cognitive Training for the Elderly

Vasiliki Theodoreli
Athens Information Technology, Greece

Theodore Petsatodis
Athens Information Technology, Greece

John Soldatos
Athens Information Technology, Greece

Fotios Talantzis
Athens Information Technology, Greece

Aristodemos Pnevmatikakis
Athens Information Technology, Greece

ABSTRACT

The emerging surface computing trend is a key enabler for a wide range of ergonomic interfaces and applications. Surface computing interfaces are considered appropriate toward facilitating elderly interaction with ICT devices and services. In this paper, the authors present the development of an innovative low-cost multi-surface device and its application in elderly cognitive training. The multi-touch device has been designed and implemented as a cost-effective motivating environment for elderly cognitive training. Along with the implementation of the device and the bundled services, this paper also presents a number of cognitive training exercises that have been developed on the device.

DOI: 10.4018/978-1-4666-0038-6.ch015

Copyright © 2012, IGI Global. Copying or distributing in print or electronic forms without written permission of IGI Global is prohibited.

1. INTRODUCTION

Surface computing technologies (including multi-touch devices & surfaces) are increasingly leading to perceptive innovative ergonomic interfaces, which support natural interactivity and motivating environments for a number of different applications (Moscovich & Hughes, 2008; Murray-Smith et al., 2008). Recent applications enable faster and easier task completion, which overall results in productivity improvements (Kristensson et al., 2008; Muto & Diefenbach, 2008). The applications span typically various domains including information displays for public sectors applications and banking, as well as motivating interactive environments for gaming and ambient assisted living. A prominent application domain for surface computing is cognitive training of older adults suffering from normal cognitive decline, as well as mild dementia. Recent studies have concluded that multi-touch surface interfaces are ergonomic and highly acceptable by the elderly (Gamberini et al., 2006). Note that surface computing based cognitive training exercises could have a high societal impact given their importance towards alleviating the different forms of dementia. It is estimated that by 2030 an approx. 20% of the population will suffer from dementia, while by 2020, 40 million people will be affected by Alzheimer's disease (AD) worldwide (Petersen et al., 2001; Alzheimer's Association, 2009). At the same time, the average cost for the AD illness (from the diagnosis to death) is in the range of few hundred dollars. Cognitive training based on surface computing interfaces (including multi-touch interfaces) is promising to alleviate the above problems, which underpins the importance of surface computing technology.

Tabletops are the workspaces we regularly use in the daily life. In the home environment, we switch between tables to proceed with different types of work or amusement, such as reading/writing of documents and card games. With the help of an interactive surface we can enable a natural interface for controlling the technologies of a smart environment and playing cognitive games.

As a result of the growing momentum of surface computing applications, several technologies (including both research prototypes and commercial products) have emerged. In the research field, we have witnessed frameworks for (multi-touch) surface computing (e.g., Natural User Interface Group, 2009), which include APIs (Application Programming Interfaces) towards leveraging multi-touch events and accordingly binding them to applications. As part of research projects, there are also perceptive components' libraries (e.g., for finger/gesture) tracking, which can be used in conjunction with specialized middleware in order to map low-level events from the tracker(s) to high-level application events suitable for authoring and developing applications (Peltonen et al., 2008; Vandoren et al., 2008). At the same time, several commercial-off-the-shelf (COTS) frameworks for multi-touch surface computing have emerged. A prominent example is Microsoft's Microsoft Surface product (http://www.microsoft.com/surface/), which represents the state of the art in surface computing. Microsoft Surface supports sophisticated robust multi-touch functionality, along with the possibility of (tag-based) object identification. Another example of commercial technology is Diamond Touch, a technology for creating touch-sensitive input devices which allow multiple, simultaneous users to interact in an intuitive fashion (Dietz & Leigh, 2001). Diamond Touch technology was originally developed at Mitsubishi Electric Research Labs (MERL) and is now exploited by company Circle Twelve Inc. It is a very intuitive technology, yet it requires a projector to be mounted on the ceiling. These commercial platforms provide high-quality ergonomics and extremely versatile programming environments at a relatively high cost.

In this paper, we introduce a new multi-touch surface platform, along with a pool of applications for elderly cognitive training. Our multi-touch surface platform is a low-cost device when compared to commercial multi-touch devices, without however any essential loss of functionality and programmability. This cost-effective nature of the introduced device can potentially lower the cost of its widespread deployment. The platform relies on a novel robust visual finger tracking algorithm, which is presented in the paper along with the main software components of the multi-touch platform.

On top of the platform several cognitive training games for elderly suffering from cognitive decline have been developed. The games are ergonomic, easy to use and feature interfaces tailored to the elderly needs. Furthermore, they are pleasant and relevant to the elderly lives. The design and employment of the games is based on extensive user-studies and response evaluation from questionnaires. 68 elderly participated in a survey organized by Instituto Gerontologico Matia in Spain in order to define their expectations and reactions from an interactive surface and computer-based cognitive training. Surprisingly 63% of the participants felt comfortable using an interactive device for gaming as long as it has a simple user interface and allows them to use their hands.

The games constitute realistic proof-of-concept applications, which have been successfully deployed over the surface platform. Specifically, they leverage most of the capabilities of the surface platform in order to maximize usability and acceptance by the end-users. Results from early expert evaluations of the games have confirmed their potential therapeutic value. The games manifest the maturity of the multi-touch surface platform. It is envisaged that the platform could be used in other application domains as well.

The presented work falls in the scope of the HERMES project (Facal et al., 2009; Buiza et al., 2009), an EC co-funded research project on ICT and ageing well, which focus of cognitive training through conventional gaming experiences (such as puzzles, mazes, sudokus etc.) that are implemented over a multi-touch surface.

Among the key innovations of the HERMES gaming environment is that the games/exercises are supported by data associated with the elderly daily life, which permits memory simulation for incoming events through directly addressing the end-users daily situation. Prior to presenting the HERMES multi-touch platform and associated games, the paper introduces several other relevant research projects. The rest of the paper is structured as follows: Section 2 following this introduction reviews recent projects using surface computing for elderly cognitive training. Section 3 describes the HERMES multi-touch platform, illustrating its main components. Accordingly, Section 4 presents a number of cognitive games which have been developed and deployed over the HERMES platform. Section 5 discusses the programming model of the HERMES multi-touch platform i.e., what is the development workflow for a new surface application. Finally, section 7 concludes the paper.

2. RELATED WORK

Several projects have strived to employ advanced ICT based interaction mechanisms in order to boost the elderly cognitive abilities, as well as in order to create added value assistive systems for senior citizens (Stanford, 2002). These projects have developed and evaluated systems that employ ICT in order to enhance the effectiveness of conventional techniques, programs and interventions in terms of their ability to alleviate cognitive (e.g., memory) problems. Several applications have been developed in the scope of device-oriented projects, which aim at delivering suitable devices for people with dementia. Devices are typically used to support human-centric services such as time orientation and reminders for medication (Duff & Dolphin, 2007), facilitation of social interaction (Meiland et al., 2007), as well as health monitoring in mobility scenarios (Guerri et al., 2009). Likewise wearable systems are also used for elderly activity monitoring (Hong et al., 2008). An alternative approach to device oriented and wearable systems are provided by smart spaces, which provide a less obtrusive solution for acquiring and processing the elderly context (Dimakis et al., 2008). Smart spaces applications for elderly care include a number of context-aware homes (Abowd et al., 2002; Meyer & Rakotonirainy, 2003). Some projects have also developed systems for monitoring the elderly activities in a domestic environment (Kasteren & Kröse, 2007; Potamianos et al., 2008). It should be noted that smart spaces systems are likely to employ various ergonomic devices (e.g., Tablet PCs, touch-screens, surface computers) in order to interact with the elderly users.

More recent projects have adopted multi-touch surfaces in order to support elderly cognitive training. Specifically:

- The ElderGames (CN 034552) project (Gamberini et al., 2006), has developed a table surface, which is used for as a motivating game environment for the Elderly.
- The ICT PSP SOCIABLE project (Pantelopoulos, 2010), employs surface computing interfaces in order to support cognitive training and social interaction applications for the elderly.
- Silverfit (http://silverfit.nl/en/index.htm) and Softkinetic (http://www.softkinetic. net/) have recently partnered for the development of natural multi-touch interfaces to facilitate rehabilitative games for the elderly.

It should be noted that recent clinical studies have proven that ICT based cognitive exercises could essentially improve cognitive performance. A recent study was conducted among 85 healthy adult participants who trained on forty (40) online exercises/games. The online exercises used were those of HAPPYneuron Inc. (http://www.happy-neuron.com) (Dunning, 2008), which targeted

the five main cognitive areas of the brain. The results manifested that regardless of age, gender and educational level, the summary scores of the study participants increased significantly across all five major cognitive domains after participation in online cognitive training.

The HERMES multi-touch platform and cognitive games are totally in-line with the above wave of surface computing and cognitive training applications. HERMES has however the distinct advantage of being a low-cost solution, when compared to the above solutions. Furthermore, the HERMES surface computing devices integrates with the ontologies/databases of the HERMES pervasive computing system (also developed within the project), which acquire, contain and analyze contextual information about the elderly user of the system. As a result, several HERMES cognitive training applications are executed over data of the elderly daily life, which boosts their user-friendliness and overall acceptance.

3. THE HERMES MULTI-SURFACE PLATFORM

Figure 1 illustrates the architecture of the multi-surface device, which was designed and contracted in the scope of the HERMES project.

The figure depicts the main components comprising the platform including multi-touch hardware, the finger tracker algorithm, the flosc communication server, the TUIO framework, as well as the client applications built over the device. The following paragraphs described each one of these components.

3.1 Hardware

The introduced platform was designed for use by elderly people. Hence, the platform was designed and implemented for users who are not expected to be familiar with technology or be able to interact with a complex human-computer interface. Thus,

Figure 1. The interconnected HERMES Multi-Surface Platform architecture

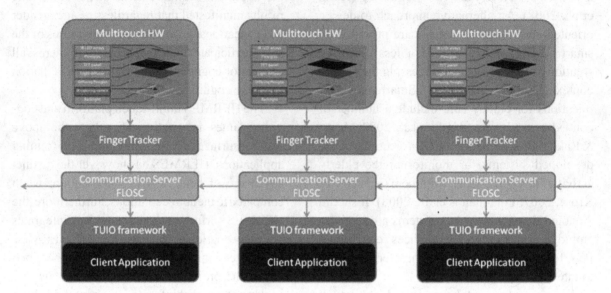

a special multi-touch surface interface has been designed, based on hand-gestures that humans are already familiar with. This enhances interaction simplicity and makes games more appealing to elders. A surface with multi-touch functionality also allows scientists to implement games with complex requirements. The surface is designed to be able to be embedded on a typical table. This is expected to enhance the interaction quality of the user with the device and the cognitive games.

Using interfaces that require users to familiarize with several devices (e.g., the combination of a keyboard, mouse and computer monitor) could result to confusion and a demanding learning curve. An interactive surface can integrate such a design on the same physical device. Given this requirement, a TFT computer monitor has been modified in order to operate both as system input and output. Monitor layers have been separated so that we take advantage of the transparency of TFT panels when subjected to infrared (IR) illumination. Figure 2 shows the components of the interactive surface.

An acrylic panel is placed on top of the TFT panel, the edges of which are illuminated by four IR-Light Emitting Diode (LED) arrays emitting at 940nm. Due to the Frustrated Total Internal Reflection (FTIR) effect, a finger touch on the surface of the acrylic panel generates lighting blobs. This is due to the fact that the refractive index of skin is higher than that of the air.

The basic principle of operation can be seen in Figure 3. The position of blobs that manage to penetrate the TFT panel is captured by a USB camera through an Ultraviolet /Visual (UV/VIS) cut optical filter at 790nm. The camera feed captured is then fed into the tracker.

It is also worth noting that the amount of IR illumination emitted by the fluorescent lamps of the TFT often masked out the finger blobs. To overcome this problem the backlight has been replaced by cool-white LEDs whose IR emission does not cover the intensity of the blobs. Also, several layers of light diffusers have been used in order to generate a smooth background illumination for the TFT panel.

Figure 2. Multi-touch system layers

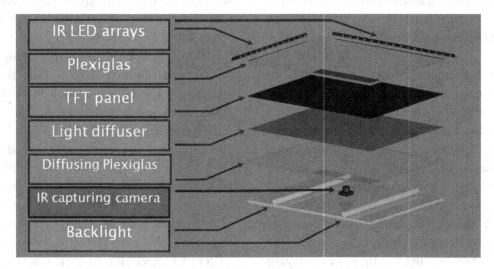

Figure 3. FTIR principle of operation

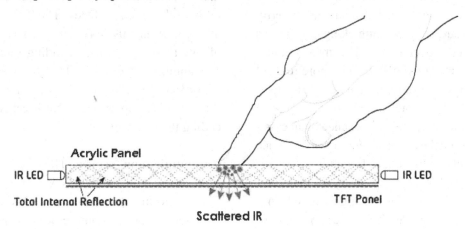

3.2 Software Components

In this section we describe the software platform which supports cognitive training games within the HERMES project. The platform comprises several software entities, namely the Finger Tracker that processes the input from the multi-touch device, the Communication Server that delivers gesture information from the Finger Tracker to the application layer and the Client (cognitive games). In the sequel we elaborate on each of these software components.

Finger Tracker: The interactive surface designed yields very good quality images of the moving fingertips, hence a simple contact-based tracker is utilized for propagating the location of the fingertips across time. This results in an algorithm of low computational complexity. According to this approach, the frames from the NIR camera are processed to extract the objects to track. We hence avoid the more elaborate approach of likelihood tracking (Stone et al., 1999). We initiate a Kalman filter (Kalman, 1960) per detected fingertip, hence handling each fingertip independently, avoiding the complexity of joint target tracking (Blackman & Popoli, 1999).

The images captured from the NIR camera are binarized using a constant threshold, due to the absence of adverse illumination effects, ensured by the hardware design. The resulting active pixels are grouped into objects using 4-way connectivity. These objects are the pool of two types of contacts: those used for track initialization, and those used at the measurement update stage of the Kalman tracker(s). The initialization contacts are selected based on strict size and aspect ratio criteria. This minimizes false positives, at the risk of delaying the initialization of a track in two cases: when originally a fingertip touches the surface too lightly (small object size) or more than the fingertip touches the surface producing elongated objects (large object aspect ratio). The measurement update contacts are selected using more relaxed size and aspect ratio criteria. This is safe as these contacts do not generate false positives and on the other hand facilitate the maintenance of an existing track should the fingertip temporarily produce erratic objects on the binary frames.

During the tracking cycle, every Kalman filter first updates the state of all targets based on a constant velocity model. The states comprise of two-dimensional position and velocity. Consequently, all the updated states are associated to measurement update contacts using an optimal greedy algorithm, the Hungarian (or Munkres) algorithm (Blackman & Popoli, 1999), which minimizes the overall Euclidean distance between the targets and the contacts. The associated contacts are used for the measurement update stage of the Kalman filters. Any states without contacts associated to them are kept active using the constant velocity updates for up to a third of the second. If in that interval there is no association, the track is terminated. The associated measurement update contacts are then removed from the pool of objects and the initialization contacts are selected from the remaining objects using the stricter criteria. These initialize new Kalman filters with a unique track ID.

At every frame, the fingertip tracking system reports the IDs and the positions of all active tracks (fingertips). The tracker in action on the binarized NIR images is shown in Figure 4.

The tracking system is very fast; Indicatively 300 frames can be processed per second on a 2.5 GHz Intel Penryn processor. Regarding implementation, the IPP and OvenCV libraries have been used in order to optimize the performance of the tracker software. The coordinates of each fingertip are communicated to the server using TUIO (A Protocol for Tangible User Interfaces) protocol standards. TUIO is an open framework that defines a common protocol and API for tangible multi-touch surfaces. The TUIO protocol allows the transmission of an abstract description of interactive surfaces, including touch events and tangible object states. This protocol encodes control data from the tracker application and sends it to any client application that is capable of decoding the protocol.

Communication Server: The Communication server implemented as part of the software platform is based on the FLOSC Java built server that can communicate with anything that uses the Open Sound Control protocol. The server sends and receives OSC packets via UDP, translates bi-directionally between binary OSC packets and an XML encoding of OSC packets, and sends and receives XML entities via TCP in a way that's compatible with Flash's XMLSocket feature. The communication Server acts as a gateway between OSC and Flash, allowing messages to go in both directions. It can accept simultaneous input from multiple OSC connections and Flash clients, and can broadcast messages to multiple Flash clients. This enables for development of networked cognitive games that give the ability to HERMES users to

Figure 4. Typical operation of the finger tracking system for five simultaneous contacts. Contacts and tracks are shown.

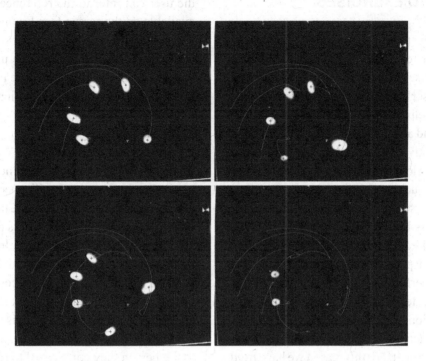

interact with each other through multiplayer cognitive games.

Client Applications: The client applications developed (cognitive training games) are based on the TUIO decoding framework that is implemented in Actionscript 3.0 by NUI Group (Natural User Interface Group) modified accordingly to support the different needs of each cognitive training game (different gestures, multiplayer option, communication with the central database of HERMES system).

Programming Model

Building an application over the multi-touch platform is facilitated through the use of the TUIO framework that provides a starting point for creating objects with multi-touch capabilities. Initially, we have to identify the specific needs of the application we want to develop, in terms of interactivity with the user. This implies specifying which gestures we want to support and by which objects.

The next step is to implement and test the desired behavior either based on the TUIO framework or by customizing it in order to provide additional functionality. For example an object that rotates can be implemented by using the existing Rotatable class in TUIO, but if we want to implement an object that rotates only to specific degrees, then we have to extend the existing class and write the extra code for this specific case.

Finally, after having implemented the behaviors we want our objects to support we build the application itself by combining those various objects and integrating them in a complete graphical user interface.

4. COGNITIVE TRAINING GAMES AND EXERCISES

The main objective of the cognitive games developed so far for the multi-touch platform is to stimulate the user's memory via simple tasks that relate to the user's everyday life. Employing such king of data helps the users feel more engaged to the process and also helps illustrate the use of the specific cognitive exercise.

Moreover a lot of attention is given on exploiting the multi-touch capabilities of the surface, thus engaging the user in bilateral hand movements whenever possible. In all games the user can select the desired level; at the end of each round the system may propose a level change according to the user's performance.

One of the desired aspects of the games is to avoid frustration of the user, in particular when it comes to interacting with the multi-touch interface and the objects on it. For this reason we have tried to model most of the objects in such a way that they resemble real objects on a table. This means that the users can move them around and change their size according to their liking, so the overall user interface has more flexibility and extends the classic notion of static computer graphical user interfaces. All the currently supported gestures (dragging, rotation, scaling of objects) are common in all games implemented so far, providing a common interaction framework to the user.

Finally, in all the games we have integrated a human-like helper that can provide information about the games, the use of the objects etc both in text as well as in audio. This is available both in text as well as in audio (text-to-speech).

Puzzle

In this game the user is presented with a number of pictures to manipulate (move around, rotate or resize). After the selection of a specific image as well as the desired level of difficulty, the user is presented with a number of puzzle tiles to reassemble the image. At any point during the game the user can refer to the reference image that is available on the screen (see Figure 5).

The implementation of a puzzle game over a multi-touch surface permits the user to interact with the puzzle pieces in a more natural way allowing use of both hands as with a real puzzle.

Who is Who

The Who is Who game aims at helping the user remember the names of familiar people by providing textual clues about them (like their job, where they live etc). Initially the user is presented with a number of photos as well as clues (the actual number depends on the selected difficulty) and is asked to drag and drop the clues to the correct person. When all the clues are correctly matched to the appropriate photos, the user is presented with a number of name clues and has to attach them to the person they correspond to (see Figure 6).

In order to complete the game the user can use both hands when dragging and dropping clues and can manipulate the objects in order to move them around, magnify and rotate them at will. Once again, the freedom to manipulate the objects as if they were pieces of paper on a table provides a more realistic environment to the user placing the focus on the game's objective (memory reinforcement) rather than on how to cope with the game's controls.

Maze

The maze game is designed in order to help the user remember appointments like going to the doctor or visiting a friend. At the beginning the user is asked to select two among a number of possibilities like a person's name and the date/time of the appointment with the specific person. After having selected the two required clues, a maze is generated, having two entry points and one target point somewhere inside. The two clues are placed in the entry points of the maze and the

Figure 5. Puzzle Game. The user can simultaneously move more than one piece.

Figure 6. Who Is Who Game. The user can resize the tags and the pictures.

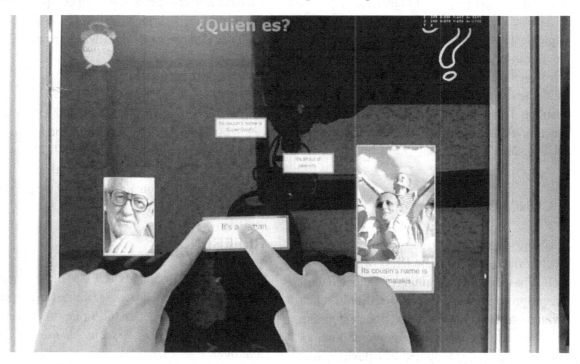

Figure 7. Maze Game. The user plays with both hands.

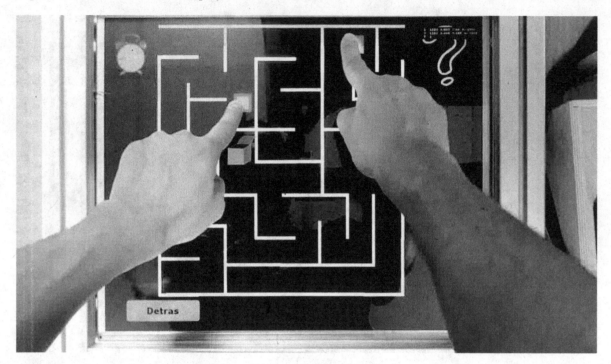

user has to move them simultaneously (one with each hand) and get them to meet each other in the designated target point (see Figure 7).

Such a version of a maze game can only be implemented on a multi-touch surface, given that the user is required to use both hands in order to drive each clue to the target. If the user lifts a hand, the corresponding clue returns to its initial position. This way the user trains his ability to synchronize his hands' movements in order to achieve some specific goal.

5. CONCLUSION

This paper has illustrated the potential of multi-touch surface computing, in terms of its benefits for ICT based cognitive training of senior citizens. Several projects have already adopted multi-touch surface interfaces towards the vision of enabling stimulating motivating and ergonomic interactions between the elderly and ICT devices. It is illustrated that early feedback from elderly users

manifests that the introduced approach is promising. As an example of practical implementation, we have also illustrated the main components of the multi-touch surface device which has been used in the scope of the HERMES project.

Acknowledgment

This work is part of the EU HERMES project (FP7-216709), partially funded by the European Commission in the scope of the 7th ICT Framework. The authors acknowledge valuable help and contributions from all partners of the project.

REFERENCES

Abowd, G. A., Bobick, I., & Essa, E. Mynatt, & Rogers, W. (2002). The Aware Home: Developing Technologies for Successful Aging. In *Proceedings of the American Association of Artificial Intelligence (AAAI) Conference.*

Alzheimer's Association. (2009). Alzheimer's Disease Facts and Figures. *Alzheimer's & Dementia, 5*(3).

Blackman, S., & Popoli, R. (1999). *Design and Analysis of Modern Tracking Systems*. Boston: Artech House.

Buiza, C., Soldatos, J., Petsatodis, T., Geven, A., Etxaniz, A., & Tscheligi, M. (2009). HERMES: Pervasive computing and cognitive training for ageing well. In S. Omatu et al. (Eds.), *Proceedings of the International Work-Conference on Artificial Neural Networks* (pp. 755-762).

Dietz, P., & Leigh, D. (2001). A Multi-User Touch Technology . In *Proceedings of User Interface Software and Technology* (pp. 219–226). DiamondTouch.

Dimakis, N., Soldatos, J., Polymenakos, L., Fleury, P., Curín, J., & Kleindienst, J. (2008). Integrated Development of Context-Aware Applications in Smart Spaces. *IEEE Pervasive Computing / IEEE Computer Society* [and]. *IEEE Communications Society, 7*(4), 71–79. doi:.doi:10.1109/MPRV.2008.75

Duff, P., & Dolphin, C. (2007). Cost-benefit analysis of assistive technology to support independence for people with dementia – Part 1: Development of a methodological approach to the ENABLE cost-benefit analysis. *Technology and Disability, 19*, 73–78.

Dunning, T. (2008). Neuron Launches Online Brain Games. *Activities, Adaptation and Aging, 31*(4), 59–60. .doi:10.1300/J016v31n04_05

Facal, D., Buiza, C., González, M. F., Soldatos, J., Petsatodis, T., Talantzis, F., et al. (2009). Cognitive Games for Healthy Elderly People in a Multi-touch Screen. In *Proceedings of International Congress on Digital Homes, Robotics and Telecare for All*.

Gamberini, L., Alcaniz, M., Barresi, G., Fabregat, M., Ibanez, F., & Prontu, L. (2006). Cognition, technology and games for the elderly: An introduction to ELDERGAMES Project. *PsychNology Journal, 4*(3), 285–308.

Guerri, J. G., Antón, A. B., Pajares, A., Monfort, M., & Sánchez, D. (2009). A mobile device application applied to low back disorders. *Multimedia Tools and Applications, 42*(3), 317–340. .doi:10.1007/s11042-008-0252-x

Hong, Y. J., Kim, I. J., Ahn, S. C., & Kim, H. G. (2008). Activity Recognition Using Wearable Sensors for Elder Care. In *Proceedings of the Second International Conference on Future Generation Communication and Networking* (pp.302-305).

Kalman, R. E. (1960). A new approach to linear filtering and prediction problems. *Journal of Basic Engineering, 82*(D), 35-45.

Kristensson, P. O., Arnell, O., Björk, A., Dahlbäck, N., Pennerup, J., Prytz, E., et al. (2008). InfoTouch: an explorative multi-touch information visualization interface for tagged photo collections. In *Proceedings of the Nordic Conference on Human-Computer Interaction.*

Mahmud, A. A., Mubin, O., Reny, J. R., Shadid, S., & Yeo, L. (2007). Affective Tabletop Game: A New Gaming Experience for Children. In *Proceedings of the Second Annual IEEE International Workshop on Horizontal Interactive Human-Computer System.*

Meiland, F. J. M., Reinersmann, A., Bergvall-Kareborn, B., Craig, D., Moelaert, F., & Mulvenna, M. D. (2007). *COGKNOW: Development and evaluation of an ICT device for people with mild dementia in Medical and Care Compunetics* (Bos, L., & Blobel, B., Eds.). Lansdale, PA: IOS Press.

Meyer, S., & Rakotonirainy, A. (2003). A survey of research on context-aware homes. In *Proceedings of the Australasian information security workshop conference on ACSW frontiers* (pp.159-168).

Moscovich, T., & Hughes, J. F. (2008). Indirect mappings of multi-touch input using one and two hands. In *Proceedings of the SIGCHI conference on Human factors in computing systems* (pp.1275-1284).

Murray- Smith. R., Williamson, J., Hughes, S., & Quaade, T. (2008). Stane: synthesized surfaces for tactile input. In *Proceedings of the SIGCHI conference on Human factors in computing systems* (pp. 1299-1302).

Muto, W., & Diefenbach, P. (2008). Applications of multi-touch gaming technology to middle-school education. In *Proceedings of the ACM SIGGRAPH 2008 Posters*.

Natural User Interface Group. (2009). *Touchlib: A Multi-Touch Development Kit*. Retrieved from http://www.nuigroup.com/touchlib

Pantelopoulos, S. (2010). SOCIABLE: a surface computing platform empowering more effective cognitive training interventions for healthy elderly and demented patients. In *Proceedings of the International Conference of Alzheimer's Disease International*.

Peltonen, P., Kurvinen, E., Salovaara, A., Jacucci, G., Ilmonenm, T., Evans, J., et al. (2008). It's mine, don't touch": Interactions at a large multi-touch display in a city Center. In *Proceedings of the SIGCHI conference on human factors in computing systems* (pp.1285-1294). New York: ACM Press.

Petersen, R. C., Stevens, J. C., Ganguli, M., Tangalos, E. G., Cummings, J. L., & DeKosky, S. T. (2001). *Practice parameter: Early Detection of dementia: Mild cognitive impairment (an evidence-based review). Report of the Quality Standards Subcommittee of the American Academy of Neurology*. Neurology.

Potamianos, G., Huang, J., Marcheret, E., Libal, V., Balchandran, R., Epstein, M., et al. (2008). Far-field multimodal speech processing and conversational interaction in smart spaces. In *Hands-Free Speech Communication and Microphone Arrays*.

Stanford, V. M. (2002). Pervasive computing: Applications - using pervasive computing to deliver elder care. *IEEE Distributed Systems Online, 3*(3).

Stone, L., Barlow, C., & Corwin, T. (1999). *Multiple Target Tracking*. Boston: Artech House.

van Kasteren, T. L. M., & Kröse, B. J. A. (2007). Bayesian Activity Recognition in Residence for Elders. In *Proceedings of the International Intelligent Environments Conference* (pp. 209-212).

Vandoren, P., Laerhoven, T. V., Claesen, L., Taelman, J., Raymaekers, C., & Reeth, F. V. (2008). IntuPaint: Bridging the Gap Between Physical and Digital Painting. In *Proceedings of TABLETOP* (pp. 71-78). Washington, DC: IEEE.

This work was previously published in International Journal of Ambient Computing and Intelligence, Volume 2, Issue 3, edited by Kevin Curran, pp. 50-62, copyright 2010 by IGI Publishing (an imprint of IGI Global).

Chapter 16
Exploring Multi-Path Communication in Hybrid Mobile Ad Hoc Networks

Roberto Speicys Cardoso
INRIA, France

Mauro Caporuscio
Politecnico di Milano, Italy

ABSTRACT

Ambient computing requires the integration of multiple mobile heterogeneous networks. Multi-path communication in such scenarios can provide reliability and privacy benefits. Even though the properties of multi-path routing have been extensively studied and a number of algorithms proposed, implementation of such techniques can be tricky, particularly when resource-constrained nodes are connected to each other through hybrid networks with different characteristics. In this paper, the authors discuss the challenges involved in implementing multipath communication on a middleware for hybrid mobile ad hoc networks. The authors present the PLASTIC middleware, several compelling applications of multi-path communication and the main issues concerning their implementation as a primitive middleware-provided communication.

INTRODUCTION

Ambient computing requires the seamless integration of heterogeneous networks. Resources in an environment may be available through independent networks using different technologies,

DOI: 10.4018/978-1-4666-0038-6.ch016

and users must be able to access them regardless of communication heterogeneity. For instance, a group of collocated resources (e.g., a printer and a projector) may be connected through a Bluetooth network while another remote resource is only accessible through WiFi (e.g., a file server). Fortunately, having multiple network interfaces embedded into a single mobile user device can

Copyright © 2012, IGI Global. Copying or distributing in print or electronic forms without written permission of IGI Global is prohibited.

Figure 1. A MANET and an HMANET

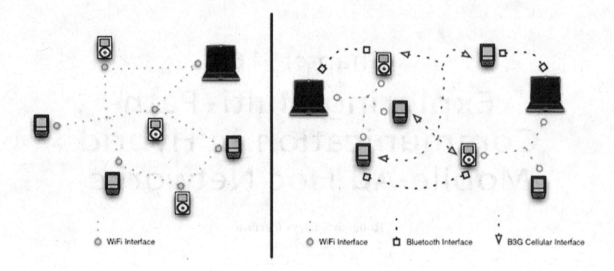

greatly simplify this task. Current cell phones featuring heterogeneous network interfaces (e.g., WiFi, Bluetooth and cellular 3G) can provide users with access not only to resources on networks directly connected to the device but also by forming ad hoc networks and accessing resources on remote networks through other mobile devices.

We call these mobile networks that use heterogeneous wireless technologies Hybrid Mobile Ad hoc NETworks (HMANETs). They are typically formed by independently managed networks connected to each other by multi-homed devices (also referred to as bridges). All nodes in such networks are potentially mobile (as opposed to wireless mesh networks (Akyildiz, Wang, & Wang, 2005)) and any two nodes may be directly connected by multiple different links (in opposition to traditional mobile ad hoc networks (MANETs) where any two nodes share at most one direct connection). More importantly, those connections use different technologies and present heterogeneous properties such as delay, throughput, security, energy consumption and cost. Figure 1 shows the differences between MANETs and HMANETs.

One consequence of the network interface diversity is that there are potentially multiple

paths, with different properties, between the source and destination nodes of a message. Applications can take advantage of this path redundancy by using multiple paths for a single communication. Nodes can send the same message through different paths to tolerate unpredictable connection failures, which is particularly important in networks that present unstable structures. Nodes can also send parts of a message through different links to enhance communication privacy and resistance against eavesdropping. Messages can be divided into shares in such a way that an attacker has to control a certain number of shares to reconstruct the whole message.

However interesting the multi-path approach might be, the implementation of point-to-point multi-path communication on an HMANET is complex. Our goal is to enable a node embedding multiple interfaces to establish a session with another node equipped with multiple interfaces, regardless of the IP addresses they use to communicate; messages that belong to the same session may have different source and destination IP addresses. The Internet Protocol suite, however, does not natively support such communication through multiple paths. It is not possible, for instance, to create a single unicast TCP session that spans multiple source and destination addresses. Even when using connection-less UDP, application-layer code is necessary to determine that packets containing different source and destination IP addresses are part of the same session. Multicast can be used to send the same message to several destination addresses through multiple paths, but it does not support sending from different source IP addresses or sending different parts of the same message to multiple destination addresses. Additionally, the topology of a HMANET changes frequently and multi-path communication must adapt dynamically to the properties of available connections.

Such characteristics call for a middleware approach for multi-path routing. By managing multi-path routes on a layer above the network, the middleware can profit from the routing protocols already implemented and running locally on each network and create an overlay network responsible for routing packets among hybrid networks. Multi-path routing on this overlay network is performed regardless of the IP addresses used as the message source or destination since the middleware can more easily manage sessions comprising different overlay connections between nodes on hybrid networks.

Moreover, the middleware can perform routing decisions, such as route selection, based on both network-layer information (e.g., delay and throughput) and higher-level information (e.g., trust or context). For instance, suppose that the middleware provides a reputation service such as the one propose by (Liu & Issarny, 2007) to establish the user trust on nodes forming the network. A multi-path routing protocol implemented at the middleware-layer can use that information to determine the route trust and to define the number of routes that must be redundantly used to minimize the risk of eavesdropping. The middleware can also use additional contextual information not provided by the network layer, such as the node location, to choose routes.

In this paper we reflect on the practical challenges involved in providing multi-path communication capabilities as part of a middleware for hybrid mobile ad hoc networks. Many research efforts studied the properties of multi-path routing in MANETs (Mueller, Tsang, & Ghosal, 2004) and proposed applications such as using multi-path routing for improving the quality of service (Liao, Wang, Sheu, & Tseng, 2002) and the use of multiple routes for load balancing (Pearlman, Haas, Peter, & Tabrizi, 2000). In this paper, however, we investigate scenarios where we are more interested in guaranteeing that a message will reach its destination reliably and privately. For this reason, we will focus on two types of multi-path communication applications: message redundancy to improve communication reliability and message sharing to improve communication privacy.

The paper is organized as follows. In the next section, we discuss related work in middleware-provided multi-path communication for mobile networks. After that, we present the PLASTIC middleware, which we will use as a case study for describing implementation issues. In the following section we discuss some applications of multi-path communications that are particularly compelling in HMANETs and after that we detail the issues concerning implementation of such features in the middleware layer. Finally, in the last section we present our conclusions and future perspectives.

RELATED WORK

In this paper we discuss the issues of implementing multi-path communication for HMANETs as a middleware-provided functionality. In particular, we discuss how the middleware can take into account both application and network requirements to provide multi-path communication primitives that increase message reliability and privacy. Others also suggested that network protocol concerns such as security and energy management in

MANETs are naturally cross-layer, and an effective solution for those issues requires the cooperation of different software layers (Conti, Maselli, Turi, & Giordano, 2004). Some advocate the cooperation between the routing and middleware layers to improve the performance of routing in overlay networks (Borgia, Conti, Delmastro, & Gregori, 2005). Those works, however, do not consider networks containing different technologies, nor the specific issue of multi-path communication.

Multi-path communication is discussed to a greater extent in the context of mesh networks. A protocol that uses multiple paths to increase the mesh network throughput is proposed by (Nandiraju, S., & Agrawal, 2006). This work explores the fact that most of the traffic on a mesh either goes to or comes from the Internet gateway, and proposes the use of multiple paths to increase throughput to those specific nodes. The work of (Sheriff & Belding-Royer, 2006) proposes a more general approach, where multiple paths are used to optimize throughput between any two nodes of the mesh. However, since those protocols are implemented at the network level, they are designed to optimize network-layer metrics such as bandwidth and packet loss and neglect other requirements such as energy consumption, security and cost. Most of existing works, however, considers multi-path communication in mobile networks as the combination of two independent problems: (1) multi-path traffic allocation and (2) multi-path routing. The mechanism for traffic allocation proposed by (Conti, Gregori, & Maselli, 2006) called REEF, assumes the existence of a multi-path routing protocol that provides the next hop and the number of hops of routes to the destination. Based on this restrict information, REEF estimates route reliability and enables source nodes to select the most reliable route among all available. Multiple routes are used as alternative paths to less reliable routes, but not simultaneously.

The approach presented in (Papadimitratos & Haas, 2003) on the other hand, simultaneously uses multiple paths to increase security of message transmission in MANETs. This protocol, called SMT, also relies on a multi-path routing protocol for route discovery. Having a set of paths to a destination, the source node can split a message into a number of shares and send them to the destination simultaneously using multiple paths. The security that SMT provides depends on the availability of multiple disjoint paths, which can be a strong requirement in HMANETs. Since the protocol is implemented at the transport layer, it only considers message transmission success rate for route selection and does not take into account higher layer requirements such as trust or application needs. SMT also assumes that all networks use the same technology and thus does not use network specific criteria for path selection such as security and cost.

Concerning multi-path routing, a number of works propose extensions to existing routing protocols for ad hoc networks. Multi-path extensions to AODV (Marina & Das, 2001; Lee & Gerla, 2000), DSR (Nasipuri & Das, 1999; Lee & Gerla, 2001) and OLSR (Yi, Cizeron, Hamma, & Parrein, 2008) exist on the literature, but they do not specifically handle multi-radio issues. Existing routing protocols designed for networks where nodes feature multiple radio interfaces like (Pirzada, Portmann, & Indulska, 2008) and (Draves, Padhye, & Zill, 2004) on the other hand, do not support multi-path route discovery.

Some of the multi-path extensions mentioned above attempt to optimize route discovery to reduce multi-path routing overhead, for instance by using additional routes only when the main route breaks, by discovering multiple routes only when the required bandwidth cannot be achieved through a single route or by favoring discovery of routes with better throughput. However, since those protocols are implemented at the transport layer, they do not take into account application and user needs, and the protocol-provided optimization may conflict with other more important requirements such as energy efficiency. For that reason, we propose multi-path communication to

Figure 2. PLASTIC Middleware

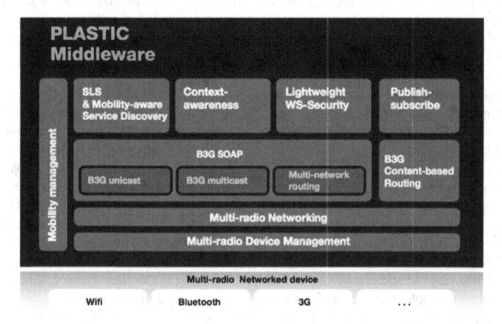

be provided by the middleware, which can perform routing decisions on behalf of the applications, taking into account user and application needs but also considering the current network status.

PLASTIC OVERVIEW

The PLASTIC project (www.ist-plastic.org) aims at developing a comprehensive provisioning platform for software services deployed over B3G networks. The project builds upon both Web services and standard component-based technologies and integrates methods and tools for service development, from design to validation, and a supporting middleware for service provisioning in B3G networks. In particular, the main objectives for the PLASTIC middleware are (1) allowing the deployment of services over a large diversity of terminals, including (mobile) wireless, resource-constrained ones and (2) supporting advanced functionalities for mobile adaptable services, i.e., context-aware service management, trust

and security management, SLA enforcement, and information dissemination.

Towards the first objective, the PLASTIC middleware (shown in Figure 2) builds upon the Web Service Architecture, so as to benefit from the pervasive nature of Web technologies that makes them available in most digital environments (B3G SOAP layer). The PLASTIC middleware assumes an all-IP environment but without global routing, and enables the effective exploitation of B3G networking capabilities by composing the various networks in reach to improve availability of services and to offer seamless mobility. This specifically calls for routing protocols for the B3G network (Multi-network routing), where routing should meet requirements associated with both the communication protocols used at the application level and the features of the underlying composed networks (B3G unicast and B3G multicast). Also, the middleware manages the various radio interfaces (Multi-radio Device Management) that are embedded on wireless devices, offering the abstraction of an integrated multi-radio interface to the software services of the upper layers (Multi-radio networking). Such abstraction increases the quality of service access by exploiting the underlying redundancy of B3G network connectivity that results from having distinct radio network links directly connecting two nodes in a transparent way for users.

With respect to the work presented in this paper, we are interested in the Multi-radio Networking layer. Its primary role is to enable the following core functionalities: (1) PLASTIC-Address management, (2) providing communication facilities and (3) interface activation and network selection. In order to identify an application in the network, nodes are assigned a PLASTIC-Address, a unique identifier that resolves into the actual set of IP addresses bound to the device hosting the application. Upper layers can use this address instead of the traditional IP-based addressing scheme. The PLASTIC-Address is automatically generated and managed by the Multi-radio Networking layer. This layer also provides two types of communication facilities: (i) synchronous unicast is used to read/write packets exchanged during the interaction between client and user applications, and (ii) asynchronous multicast allows the user application to send multicast packets to all members of a group. Finally, this layer also activates and selects the best possible networks (among those available) with respect to application- and user-required QoS level.

MULTI-PATH COMMUNICATION APPLICATIONS

As previously discussed, we assume an environment with multiple highly heterogeneous networks running the IP protocol, but without global IP routing. Devices featuring multiple network interfaces can independently form ad hoc networks and some of them may volunteer to route packets between different networks, creating an overlay network formed by bridges and heterogeneous wireless networks. This overlay network can provide various independent paths between a source and a destination, that can be explored to overcome connection instability.

The goal of the multi-path communication middleware component is to improve the existing PLASTIC single path communication with multi-path routing. Multi-path communication is used autonomously by the middleware based on user-defined criteria, and exposed to applications through a middleware API. This allows applications to use reliable or privacy-preserving communication for critical messages only, reducing the performance cost of multi-path routing.

Different types of route exist on a network. According to (Mueller, Tsang, & Ghosal, 2004) routes can be node-disjoint, that have no links or nodes in common, link-disjoint, that have no links in common and non-disjoint, that may have nodes and links in common. In HMANETs, however, we consider two different types of nodes: network nodes and bridge nodes. A route in a HMANET, then, alternates between bridge nodes and network nodes and as such we can have bridge-disjoint routes (do not have bridges in common), network-disjoint routes (do not have networks in common) and totally-disjoint routes. Even though totally-disjoint routes offer stronger reliability, network-disjoint and bridge-disjoint routes are also important. Networks on a HMANET are heterogeneous and present different levels of stability and network-disjoint paths help to establish a more reliable communication channel. Bridges are also unstable because they are voluntary and may move or cease to work as a bridge so bridge-disjoint paths are necessary to provide alternative routes.

To improve communication reliability, the middleware uses message redundancy. The goal of message redundancy is to send the same message across different paths to increase the probability that it will reach its destination. Based on the characteristics of available routes (such as reliability, latency or throughput) the middleware must decide how many additional routes are required to achieve a certain level of reliability. The middleware must also dynamically determine which type of route (bridge-disjoint, network-disjoint or totally-disjoint) is necessary to obtain a reliable communication channel.

Message sharing can enhance communication confidentiality and improve privacy. The idea of message sharing is to divide a message into multiple parts that can be sent through different communication channels in such a way that, to recover the contents of a message, an attacker must control a certain number of shares. By spreading those shares through channels with heterogeneous properties, attackers have to use more resources to access the contents of a message than in the traditional single-path communication model.

This property can be obtained through a *(M, N)* coding algorithm such as (Ayanoglu, Chih-Lin, Gitlin, & Mazo, 1993) where N is the total number of shares and M is the number of shares required to obtain the message. Coding algorithms have the advantage of causing a small overhead, because each coded share is smaller than the original message. However, each share reveals something about the whole message, and an adversary controlling X messages, $X < M$, can guess the $M - X$ remaining shares and recover the whole message, which is undesirable for privacy protection.

Another possibility is to use a *(t, n)* secret-sharing scheme (Shamir, 1979) where n is the total number of shares and t is the number of shares necessary to recover the whole message. Protocols such as (Lou, Liu, & Fang, 2004) that perform multi-path routing using traditional secret sharing schemes, however, incur on an excessive overhead because in those schemes each share must be at least as big as the message itself (Csirmaz, 1997). An attractive solution is to use a scheme with computational secrecy (Krawczyk, 1993) instead of a scheme with perfect secrecy. A secret sharing scheme with computational secrecy has the advantage of resulting in an overhead comparable to coding algorithms but still

providing secrecy against attacks from resource-bounded adversaries.

Whenever a message must be shared, the middleware has to decide which paths to use, in how many parts divide a message and how many shares will be necessary to recover the whole message. Path choice involves quality and reliability information, but can also take into account the software platform of each device or the technology of each network in the paths between the message source and its destination. Those parameters allow computation of paths that resist to attacks in different software platforms or network technologies (Desmedt, Wang, & Burmester, 2006). Since security vulnerabilities are usually platform-dependent, this strategy can assure that the communication remains private even in face of malicious attacks against vulnerable platforms.

IMPLEMENTATION CHALLENGES IN THE CONTEXT OF PLASTIC

Implementation of message redundancy and message sharing in hybrid mobile ad hoc networks presents many practical challenges. There are issues related to the physical wireless layer, for instance how to avoid interferences when simultaneously using multiple wireless interfaces or to the architecture such as the integration of multi-path routing with service discovery to rank results according to multi-path availability. In this section, however, we discuss the challenges related to the implementation of multi-path routing as a middleware-provided communication primitive.

Routing Protocol Each network integrated in a HMANET is autonomously organized and runs the routing protocol better adapted to its local requirements. As such, it is unfeasible to define a single routing protocol to be executed by all devices on a HMANET, including bridges. Rather, a more suitable solution to allow for packet routing among networks is to create an overlay network containing bridges that run a bridge-to-bridge routing protocol while local delivery on each network is performed using the network-specific protocol. To explore multi-path routing on the overlay network, thus, each bridge must learn from the routing protocol all available paths to a destination. Traditional MANET routing protocols, however, keep only a single path between nodes, more specifically the path with the smallest number of hops (Perkins & Royer, 1999; Johnson, Maltz, & Broch, 2001; Jacquet, Muhlethaler, Clausen, Laouiti, Qayyum, & Viennot, 2001). Multi-path extensions to those protocols exist, but some of them only use a secondary route if the main route breaks (Lee & Gerla, 2000; Marina & Das, 2001) or only compute network-disjoint routes (Nasipuri & Das, 1999) while our scenario requires discovery of network-disjoint, bridge-disjoint and totally-disjoint routes. Routing protocols specifically designed for providing multi-path routes in MANET do not focus on security or privacy issues (Ma & Ilow, 2003).

The routing protocol must also provide additional information about each network and each node such as available bandwidth, technology, security properties, and delay. Additionally, bridges must be able to define the whole path used by each packet to reach its destination. This is necessary to ensure that the packets will follow different routes. Protocols based on routing tables, hence, are not appropriate since each node keeps a local routing table and autonomously forwards packets to the next hop towards the packet destination; different packets to the same destination will always be forwarded to the same next hop. A more adequate technique to forward packets is source route (Johnson, Maltz, & Broch, 2001) where the source node includes in the packet header the whole path that the packet must follow to reach

the destination. As such, the source can define in the packet headers that two packets addressed to the same destination must traverse disjoint paths.

We designed a hybrid ad hoc routing protocol that uses source routes to forward packets and ensures that the path defined at the packet source will be respected during packet transmission. The protocol also proactively keeps the shortest route to every node on the network using the efficient flooding mechanism proposed by OLSR (Jacquet, Muhlethaler, Clausen, Laouiti, Qayyum, & Viennot, 2001) while multiple paths to a destination are discovered on demand by using a technique similar to DSR (Johnson, Maltz, & Broch, 2001). Route announcements contain not only connectivity information but also quality information such as network throughput, delay, software platform and cost. This protocol provides single-path routing without extra cost and reduces the overhead of multiple route discovery only to situations where a node requires this type of communication.

Multi-path Granularity There are two issues related to granularity in multi-path applications. The first issue, which is more often discussed in the literature, is traffic allocation granularity (Krishnan & Silvester, 1993; Lai, 1985), which defines the smallest traffic unit that can be assigned to each path. From the application standpoint, the smallest unit is a message. However, in the network layer, a message can originate a number of packets depending on its size and on the network's maximum transmission unit (MTU). Per message allocation enables different messages to follow different routes while in per packet allocation different packets from the same message can use different paths.

Implementing per message traffic allocation when devices feature multiple network interfaces is not straightforward. Messages from the same connection can arrive through different interfaces from distinct source IP addresses, but the Internet Protocol suite cannot keep a session across different source and destination addresses. In that case, the middleware must implement some type of session management mechanism, on top of the IP stack, to identify related messages and to deliver relevant messages to applications. Per packet allocation is trickier to implement, since different packets from the same message may arrive through different addresses to the destination. For TCP connections, this would require modifications on the IP stack. However, we can use UDP messages to encapsulate each packet and then use the same middleware layer on top of IP to reconstruct application messages.

The second issue is path selection granularity. Paths can be defined per connection, per message or per packet. Considering that nodes HMANETs are mobile, paths may change frequently. Routes found at the beginning of a connection may not be available towards its end depending on how often nodes move or how long the connection lasts. However, smaller granularities can cause unnecessary overhead. The best strategy, hence, is to select a set of paths when creating a connection, and reselect them after a pre-defined period of time or when a certain number of paths are disconnected.

Network Density Availability of multiple paths between two nodes is highly dependent on bridge location. Bridges connect different networks and can increase network density if conveniently deployed. Current PLASTIC strategies for bridge election only take into account resource availability. This strategy can be improved to incorporate the current network topology, for instance, to prioritize bridges that increase network density regardless of the resources they provide. The election algorithm can also consider properties such as stability and trust on networks and bridges to elect new bridges that provide alternative paths to untrusted or unreliable nodes.

Finally, bridges can be temporarily enabled to create a short-lived alternative route to a required destination. Whenever a node not acting as a bridge receives a route request for an alternative route, it may forward the route request to neighbor networks and become a bridge if it discovers an alternative route. An incentive mechanism could be used to stimulate nodes to share resources and act as bridges.

CONCLUSION

Multi-path communication can provide greater reliability and improve privacy of message transmissions. By simultaneously using multiple paths to send the same message, or parts of one message, applications can increase the probability that a message will reach its destination and make it harder for an attacker to read its contents. Those properties are particularly important in mobile and infrastructure-less networks with unstable topologies where untrusted user devices forward packets.

We propose the introduction of an additional layer to the PLASTIC middleware, responsible for handling multi-path communication issues. Figure 3 shows the position of the Multi-path Communication layer in the PLASTIC Middleware architecture. This layer uses functionalities provided by the Multi-radio Networking layer such as the ability to send packets through different interfaces or to resolve a PLASTIC Address into its corresponding set of valid IP addresses.

The Multi-path Communication layer, however, is optional: whenever a SOAP message must be sent through a single path, the B3G SOAP layer can dispatch it directly to the Multi-radio Networking layer. The multi-path routing component uses a hybrid routing protocol (proactive and reactive) to reduce routing overhead; multi-path routing messages are only transmitted when multi-path communication is necessary. The Message Sharing and the Path Selection components

Figure 3. Multi-path communication layer on PLASTIC middleware

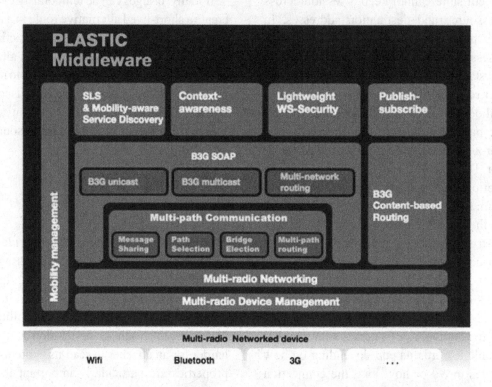

rely on information obtained by the Multi-path Routing component, and are also only used when the application requires stronger reliability or privacy.

We are now developing the Multi-path Communication layer. We plan to evaluate the processing and network overhead produced when simultaneously using different paths to transmit a message and we are now evaluating the energy cost imposed by the multi-path routing protocol described in the previous section when compared to traditional ad hoc routing protocols. Finally, we also intend to analyze the availability of multiple disjoint paths in HMANETs and to quantify the reliability and privacy benefits provided by the multi-path approach.

ACKNOWLEDGMENT

This work is part of the IST PLASTIC project and has been funded by the European Commission, FP6 contract number 026955.

REFERENCES

Akyildiz, I. F., Wang, X., & Wang, W. (2005). Wireless Mesh Networks: A Survey. *Computer Networks and ISDN Systems*, 445–487.

Ayanoglu, E., Chih-Lin, I., Gitlin, R. D., & Mazo, J. E. (1993, November). Diversity Coding for Transparent Self-Healing and Fault-Tolerant Communication Networks. *IEEE Transactions on Communications*, 1677–1686. doi:10.1109/26.241748

Borgia, E., Conti, M., Delmastro, F., & Gregori, E. (2005, August 22). Experimental Comparison of Routing and Middleware Solutions for Mobile Ad Hoc Networks: Legacy vs Cross-layer Approach. In *Proceedings of the 2005 ACM SIGCOMM Workshop on Experimental Approaches to Wireless Network Design and Analysis (E-WIND '05)* (pp. 82-87).

Conti, M., Gregori, E., & Maselli, G. (2006). Reliable and Efficient Forwarding in Ad Hoc Networks. *Ad Hoc Networks, 4*(3), 398–415.. doi:10.1016/j.adhoc.2004.10.006

Conti, M., Maselli, G., Turi, G., & Giordano, S. (2004). Cross-Layering in Mobile Ad Hoc Network Design. *Computer, 2*(37), 48–51.. doi:10.1109/MC.2004.1266295

Csirmaz, L. (1997, November). The Size of a Share Must Be Large. *Journal of Cryptology*, 223-231.

Desmedt, Y., Wang, Y., & Burmester, M. (2006, August 31). Revisiting Colored Networks and Privacy Preserving Censorship. In *Proceedings of the First International Workshop on Critical Information Infrastructures Security (CRITIS 2006)* (pp. 140-150).

Draves, R., Padhye, J., & Zill, B. (2004, September 26). Routing in Multi-radio, Multi-hop Wireless Mesh Networks. In *Proceedings of the 10th Annual International Conference on Mobile Computing and Networking (MobiCom '04)* (pp. 114-128).

Jacquet, P., Muhlethaler, P., Clausen, T., Laouiti, A., Qayyum, A., & Viennot, L. (2001, December 28). Optimized Link State Routing Protocol for Ad Hoc Networks. In *Proceedings of the IEEE International Multi Topic Conference. Technology for the 21st Century (INMIC 2001)* (pp. 62-68).

Johnson, D. B., Maltz, D. A., & Broch, J. (2001). DSR: the Dynamic Source Routing Protocol for Multihop Wireless Ad Hoc Network. In Perkins, C. E. (Ed.), *Ad Hoc Networking* (pp. 139–172). Boston: Addison-Wesley Longman Publishing Co.

Krawczyk, H. (1993, August 22). Secret Sharing Made Short. In *Proceedings of the 13th Annual International Cryptology Conference on Advances in Cryptology (CRYPTO '93)* (pp. 136-146).

Krishnan, R., & Silvester, J. A. (1993, March 28). Choice of Allocation Granularity in Multipath Source Routing Schemes. In *Proceedings of the Twelfth Annual Joint Conference of the IEEE Computer and Communications Societies (INFOCOM '93)* (pp. 322-329).

Lai, W. S. (1985). Bifurcated Routing in Computer Networks. *SIGCOMM Computer Communication Review, 15*(3), 28–49.. doi:10.1145/1015621.1015625

Lee, S.-J., & Gerla, M. (2000, September 23). AODV-BR: Backup Routing in Ad Hoc Networks. In *Proceedings of the Wireless Communications and Networking Conference (WCNC'00)* (pp. 1311-1316).

Lee, S.-J., & Gerla, M. (2001, November 6). Split Multipath Routing with Maximally Disjoint Paths in Ad Hoc Networks. In *Proceedings of the IEEE International Conference on Communications (ICC '01)* (pp. 3201-3205).

Liao, W.-H., Wang, S.-L., Sheu, J.-P., & Tseng, Y.-C. (2002). A Multi-Path QoS Routing Protocol in a Wireless Mobile Ad Hoc Network. *Telecommunication Systems, 19*(3-4), 329–347.. doi:10.1023/A:1013838304991

Liu, J., & Issarny, V. (2007, August). An Incentive Compatible Reputation Mechanism for Ubiquitous Computing Environments. *International Journal of Information Security*, 297–311. doi:10.1007/s10207-007-0029-7

Lou, W., Liu, W., & Fang, Y. (2004, November 22). SPREAD: Enhancing Data Confidentiality in Mobile Ad Hoc Networks. In *Proceedings of the Twenty-third Annual Joint Conference of the IEEE Computer and Communications Societies (INFOCOM 2004)* (pp. 2404-2413).

Ma, R., & Ilow, J. (2003, October 20). Reliable Multipath Routing with Fixed Delays in MANET Using Regenerating Nodes. In *Proceedings of the 28th Annual IEEE International Conference on Local Computer Networks* (pp. 719-725).

Marina, M. K., & Das, S. R. (2001, November 11). On-demand Multipath Distance Vector Routing in Ad Hoc Networks. In *Proceedings of the Ninth International Conference on Network Protocols* (pp. 14-23).

Mueller, S., Tsang, R. P., & Ghosal, D. (2004). Multipath Routing in Mobile Ad Hoc Networks: Issues and Challenges. In E. Gelenbe (Ed.), *Performance Tools and Applications to Networked Systems* (pp. 209–234). Berlin: Springer. doi:10.1007/978-3-540-24663-3_10

Nandiraju, N. S., & Agrawal, D. P. (2006, October 9). Multipath Routing in Wireless Mesh Networks. In *Proceedings of the IEEE International Conference on Mobile Adhoc and Sensor Systems* (pp. 741-746).

Nasipuri, A., & Das, S. R. (1999, November 10). On-demand Multipath Routing for Mobile Ad Hoc Networks. In *Proceedings of the Eighth IEEE International Conference on Computer Communications and Networks* (pp. 64-70).

Papadimitratos, P., & Haas, Z. J. (2003). Secure Message Transmission in Mobile Ad Hoc Networks. *Ad Hoc Networks*, 1(1), 193–209.. doi:10.1016/S1570-8705(03)00018-0

Pearlman, M. R., Haas, Z. J., Peter, S., & Tabrizi, S. S. (2000, August 11). On the Impact of Alternate Path Routing for Load Balancing in Mobile Ad Hoc Networks. In *Proceedings of the 1st ACM international symposium on Mobile ad hoc networking & computing (MobiHoc '00)* (pp. 3-10).

Perkins, C. E., & Royer, E. M. (1999, February 25). Ad-hoc On-Demand Distance Vector Routing. In *Proceedings of the Second IEEE Workshop on Mobile Computer Systems and Applications (WMCSA '99)* (pp. 90-100).

Pirzada, A. A., Portmann, M., & Indulska, J. (2008). Performance Analysis of Multi-radio AODV in Hybrid Wireless Mesh Networks. *Computer Communications*, 885–895. doi:10.1016/j.comcom.2007.12.012

Shamir, A. (1979). How to Share a Secret. *Communications of the ACM, 612–613.* doi:. doi:10.1145/359168.359176

Sheriff, I., & Belding-Royer, E. (2006, October 1). Multipath Selection in Multi-radio Mesh Networks. In *Proceedings of the 3rd International Conference on Broadband Communications, Networks and Systems* (pp. 1-11).

Yi, J., Cizeron, E., Hamma, S., & Parrein, B. (2008, March 31). Simulation and Performance Analysis of MP-OLSR for Mobile Ad Hoc Networks. In *Proceedings of the IEEE Wireless Communications and Networking Conference (WCNC '08)* (pp. 2235-2240).

This work was previously published in International Journal of Ambient Computing and Intelligence, Volume 2, Issue 4, edited by Kevin Curran, pp. 1-12, copyright 2010 by IGI Publishing (an imprint of IGI Global).

Chapter 17
Interoperable Semantic and Syntactic Service Discovery for Ambient Computing Environments

Sonia Ben Mokhtar
LIRIS CNRS, France

Pierre-Guillaume Raverdy
INRIA, France

Aitor Urbieta
IKERLAN-IK4, Spain

Roberto Speicys Cardoso
INRIA, France

ABSTRACT

The inherent heterogeneity of ambient computing environments and their constant evolution requires middleware platforms to manage networked components designed, developed, and deployed independently. Such management must also be efficient to cater for resource-constrained devices and highly dynamic situations due to the spontaneous appearance and disappearance of networked resources. For service discovery protocols (SDP), one of the main functions of service-oriented architectures (SOA), the efficiency of the matching of syntactic service descriptions is most often opposed to the fullness of the semantic approach. As part of the PLASTIC middleware, the authors present an interoperable discovery platform that features an efficient matching and ranking algorithm able to process service descriptions and discovery requests from both semantic and syntactic SDPs. To that end, the paper defines a generic, modular description language able to record service functional properties, potentially extended with semantic annotations. The proposed discovery platform leverages the advanced communication capabilities provided by the PLASTIC middleware to discover services in multi-network environments. An evaluation of the prototype implementation demonstrates that multi-protocols service matching supporting various levels of expressiveness can be achieved in ambient computing environments.

DOI: 10.4018/978-1-4666-0038-6.ch017

Copyright © 2012, IGI Global. Copying or distributing in print or electronic forms without written permission of IGI Global is prohibited.

1. INTRODUCTION

Ambient computing envisions the unobtrusive diffusion of computing and networking resources in physical environments, enabling users to access information and computational resources anytime and anywhere, and this in a user-centric way, i.e., where user interaction with the system is intuitive, pleasant and natural. Mobile users take part in these ambient computing environments by carrying around tiny personal devices that integrate seamlessly in the existing infrastructure. Such a setup is highly open and dynamic. Therefore, these environments must support ad hoc deployment and execution, integrating the available hardware and software resources at any given time and place. This dynamic merging is facilitated when organizing resources as autonomous, networked components. The Service-Oriented Architecture (SOA) computing paradigm is particularly appropriate for ambient computing systems. Indeed, in this architectural style, networked devices and their hosted applications are abstracted as loosely coupled services that can be integrated into larger systems. Service discovery (SD) is then an essential function within SOA, especially in the ambient computing environment, as it enables the runtime association to networked services. Three basic roles are identified for service discovery in SOA: (1) *Service provider* is the role assumed by a software entity offering a networked service; (2) *Service requester* is the role of an entity seeking to consume a specific service; (3) *Service repository* is the role of an entity maintaining information on available services and a way to access them. A service description formalism or language to describe the service functional properties complemented with a service discovery protocol enables service providers, requesters and repositories to interact with each other. A comprehensive service discovery solution for ambient computing environments must at once address a wide range of interoperability issues due to the environments' heterogeneity, and the fact that ambient software

services and potential software clients (assuming the role of service requester) are designed, developed and deployed independently.

Many research projects as presented in Section 2 have addressed some of the interoperability issues such as protocol interoperability, network interoperability, or semantics. In the context of the PLASTIC project[1], which aims to support the deployment and dynamic composition of mobile, adaptable applications in ambient computing environments, and in particular applications complying with Web-service standards, the PerSeSyn (*Pervasive Semantic Syntactic*) service discovery platform presented in Section 3 aims to address the above interoperability issues and provide a comprehensive SD solution for ambient computing environments. In this paper, we focus in particular on the challenges posed by enabling interoperable semantic-based discovery on top of heterogeneous, both syntactic and semantic-based SDPs. Towards this purpose, we introduce in Section 4 the *PerSeSyn Service Description Model* (PSDM), and, as its instantiation, the *PerSeSyn Service Description Language* (PDSL). PSDM is a conceptual model for enabling semantic mapping between heterogeneous service description languages. PSDL, which is an instantiation of PSDM, is not yet another service description language but a combination of emergent standards for service specification, namely SAWSDL[2] and WS-BPEL[3]. PSDL is then employed as the common representation for service descriptions and requests. Based on PSDM and PSDL, we define a set of conformance relations, as presented in Section 5, for matching heterogeneous service descriptions going from elementary syntactic service descriptions (e.g., given in SLP) to rich semantic service descriptions with associated conversations (e.g., given in OWL-S). Furthermore, we introduce a mechanism for ranking heterogeneous matching results towards efficient matching of service capabilities. We further evaluate in Section 6 the impact of introducing semantic based matching in addition to protocol interoperability realized through protocol translation. We finally summarize our contribution in Section 7.

2. RELATED WORK

Service discovery protocols enable services on a network to discover each other, express opportunities for collaboration, and compose themselves into larger collections that cooperate to meet an application's needs. Many academic and industry-supported SDPs have already been proposed such as UDDI or CORBA's Trading Service for the Internet, or SLP and Jini for local and ad hoc networks. Classifications for SDPs (Zhu, Mutka, & Ni, 2005) distinguish between pull-based and push-based protocols. In pull-based protocols, clients send a request to service providers (distributed pull-based mode) or to a third-party repository (centralized pull-based mode) in order to get a list of services compatible with the request attributes. In push-based protocols, service providers provide their service descriptions to all clients that locally maintain a list of the available networked services. Leading SDPs in ambient computing environments use a pull-based approach (Jini, SSDP), often supporting both the centralized and distributed modes of interaction (SLP, WS-Discovery). In centralized pull-based discovery protocols, one or a few repositories store the descriptions of the available services in the network, and their location is either well-known (e.g., UDDI) or dynamically discovered (e.g., Jini). Repositories are usually kept up to date by requiring explicit sign-off or by removing entries periodically. If multiple repositories exist, they cooperate to distribute the service registrations among them or to route requests to the relevant repository according to pre-established relationships.

Although many SDPs solutions with well-proven protocol implementations are now available, a number of challenging issues remain for the ambient computing computing environment, as outlined below.

Multi-protocols SD: Middleware heterogeneity raises interoperability issues between the different SDPs (e.g., SLP, SSDP, UDDI) active in the environment. Existing SDPs do not directly interoperate with each other as they employ incompatible formats and protocols for service descriptions or discovery requests, and also use incompatible data types or communication models. In any case, the diverse environment constraints and the de-facto standard status of some of the existing protocols make it unlikely for a new and unique SDP to emerge. Several projects have thus investigated interoperability solutions (Grace, Blair, & Samuel, 2003; Koponen & Virtanen, 2004; Nakazawa, Tokuda, Edwards, & Ramachandran, 2006), as requiring clients and service providers to support multiple SDPs is not realistic. SDP interoperability is typically achieved using intermediate common representations of service discovery elements (e.g., service description, discovery request) (Bromberg & Issarny, 2005) instead of direct mappings (Koponen & Virtanen, 2004), as the latter does not scale well with the number of supported protocols. Furthermore, the interoperability layer may be located close to the network layer (Bromberg & Issarny, 2005), and efficiently and transparently translate network messages between protocols, or may provide an explicit interface (Raverdy, Issarny, Chibout, & de La Chapelle, 2006) to clients or services so as to extend existing protocols with advanced features such as context management.

Context-aware SD: A major trend to handle the richness and heterogeneity of ambient computing environments is to rely on context information for inferring mobile users' needs and autonomously locate the most appropriate services (Lee & Helal, 2003). Context-aware SDPs aim to provide users with the best networked services based on their preferences, needs and runtime conditions (Chen & Kotz, 2002; Lee, Faratin, Bauer, & Wroclawski, 2004), sometimes focusing on location-awareness (Zhu, Mutka, & Ni, 2003) or QoS (Capra, Zachariadis, & Mascolo, 2005). The evaluation of context properties may be achieved through the evaluation of context rules (Raverdy, Riva, de la Chapelle, Chibout, & Issarny, 2006) or the maximization of a utility function (Capra et al., 2005), but commonly relies on strict syntactic matching between the information provided by the client and by the service. Context-aware SDPs therefore assume that all clients and service providers use the same terminology to identify the same contextual information. Such assumption is not realistic in ambient computing environments as, there, networked components are designed, developed and deployed independently.

Semantic SD: The matching of service requests and service advertisements is classically based on assessing the syntactic conformance of functional properties. However, an agreement on a common syntactic standard is hardly achievable in open environments. Thus, higher-level abstractions, independent of the low-level syntactic realizations specific to the technologies in use, should be employed for denoting service semantics (Ben Mokhtar, Kaul, Georgantas, & Issarny, 2006). A number of approaches for semantic service specification have been proposed, and in particular for semantic Web services such as OWL-S (Martin et al., 2004) or SAWSDL (Lausen & Innsbruck, 2006). SAWSDL annotates Web services with semantics by attaching references to concepts from ontologies (e.g., OWL) to WSDL input, output and fault messages, as well as to operations. METEOR-S (Patil,

Oundhakar, Sheth, & Verma, 2004) uses DAML+OIL ontologies (precursor to OWL) to add semantics to WSDL and UDDI so as to annotate the communication aspects between services. Other efforts (Srinivasan, Paolucci, & Sycara, 2004; Sycara, Paolucci, Ankolekar, & Srinivasan, 2003; Trastour, Bartolini, & Gonzalez-Castillo, 2001) started to take care of some of the ambiguity in service descriptions, which is suitable for the open ambient computing environment. EASY (Ben Mokhtar, Preuveneers, Georgantas, Issarny, & Berbers, 2008) provides efficient semantic service discovery, a key requirement for the resource-limited devices found in ambient computing environments, by encoding ontology concepts off-line and adequately classifying service descriptions in the repository based on these encoded concepts.

Multi-networks SD: Network heterogeneity leads to many independent networks being available to users at a location, which can be loosely interconnected with today's multi-radio mobile devices. Innovative solutions are then required for the efficient inter-network dissemination, filtering and selection of discovery requests and announcements (Raverdy et al., 2006). Several projects have investigated peering (gateways) or application-level (P2P) routing combined with intelligent filtering to provide efficient and scalable multi-networks service discovery. The mSLP (Zhao & Schulzrinne, 2005) protocol improves SLP efficiency and scalability by introducing mesh enhancements for the peering of registries as well as preference filters. INS/Twine (Balazinska, Balakrishnan, & Karger, 2002) proposes a scalable P2P architecture where resolvers (i.e., directory services) collaborate as peers to distribute resource information and to resolve queries. GloServ (Arabshian & Schulzrinne, 2004) is an ontology-based global service discovery architecture that operates in wide area as well as local area networks using a hybrid hierarchical and peer-to-peer architecture. MUSDAC (Raverdy et al., 2006) dynamically composes nearby networks through specific components providing application-level routing on multi-radio devices, which enables the dissemination of discovery requests in the environment. The key issue for multi-networks discovery is to accurately report the dynamic changes in the network without jeopardizing processing and network resources due to the potentially considerable amount of information to exchange and process.

Security and privacy in SD: Securing the exchange of service descriptions and discovery requests is crucial in ambient computing environments, especially when such information is laced with service- or user-related contextual information that may be correlated to gain detail knowledge of a person (Zhu, Mutka, & Ni, 2004). Many mechanisms have been proposed to secure the disclosure of service information, focusing either on encryption and access rights (Czerwinski, Zhao, Hodes, Joseph, & Katz, 1999) or the need to balance disclosure and privacy (Zhu et al., 2004).

Mobility in SD: Client and service mobility have rarely been investigated in the context of service discovery, as supporting mobility (nomadic or seamless) is primarily seen as an issue for service access (i.e., maintaining connectivity). Applying mobility patterns has however been investigated as a way to favor interaction between nodes that will remain in the network reach of each other for the whole duration of the session (Liu & Issarny, 2005).

While the essence of the above issues is well understood, and individual solutions have been proposed that may form the foundations of a com-

prehensive service discovery solution for ambient computing environments, a number of problems remain, or arise from such combination. First and foremost, syntactic-based and semantic-based solutions have mostly been considered separately. Indeed, interoperability solutions enabling multi-protocols SDP have focused on syntactic SDPs. At the same time, semantic-based SDPs neither manage protocol nor network heterogeneity, and context-aware SDPs assume the consistent use of a common ontology by all clients and providers. A better integration of the semantic and syntactic worlds is required, which is the focus of our paper. Lastly, mobility as well as security and privacy are transversal issues that need to be supported and reflected at all levels. While not detailed in this paper, these two issues are clearly addressed in the PLASTIC middleware by keeping track of the location and addresses associated to mobile devices hosting services (PLASTIC Project, 2007), and introducing ambiguity in service advertisements and requests to protect private information used in service discovery (Cardoso, Ben Mokhtar, Urbieta, & Issarny, 2007).

3. THE PERSESYN SERVICE DISCOVERY PLATFORM

The PerSeSyn (Pervasive Semantic & Syntactic) platform is part of the *service accessibility and composition* functionality of the PLASTIC middleware (PLASTIC Project, 2007). The ambient computing environment in PLASTIC is perceived as a dynamic set of loosely coupled, heterogeneous networks. As these networks are managed independently, global IP routing is not guaranteed. The PLASTIC middleware thus aims to: (i) enable the effective exploitation of ambient computing networking capabilities, essentially by composing the various networks in reach to improve availability of services, and by supporting both clients' and services' mobility; and (ii) enable the execution and coordination of

Figure 1. PLASTIC middleware overview

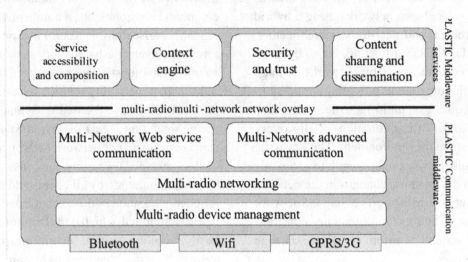

software services on mobile, wireless handheld terminals, i.e., dealing with application services deployed on the end-users' terminals, as opposed to services deployed in the core network. To achieve these goals, the PLASTIC middleware architecture, depicted in Figure 1, decomposes into two main layers:

1. The lower *PLASTIC communication middleware* layer deals with service provisioning in the multi-radio, multi-network environment. This layer first offers the abstraction of an integrated multi-radio network through the composition of the various networks in reach via the embedded radio interfaces of a mobile device. Application-level routing protocols are further offered on top of this *Multi-radio networking* layer: *Multi-Network Web-service communication* basically enriches traditional functionalities of a SOAP engine to allow for SOAP-based interaction in multi-radio multi-networks settings, while *Multi-Network advanced communication* protocols deal with P2P, group-based, and content-based communication in multi-networks.

2. The upper *PLASTIC middleware services* layer embeds advanced services that support effective service provisioning and adaptation for distributed applications. These functionalities are related to *accessibility and composition, context awareness, security and trust,* and *content sharing and dissemination*.

The PerSeSyn platform for interoperable, context-aware service discovery, which is part of the *Service accessibility and composition* functionality, uses a hierarchical approach for service discovery in multi-networks environments (see Figure 2). Indeed, a (logically) centralized *PerSeSyn Proxy* (PSS-P) coordinates service discovery within an independent network, while PSS-Ps in different networks communicate together in a fully distributed way to disseminate service information. PSS-Ps rely on the multi-network group communication feature of the underlying PLASTIC Communication middleware layer to disseminate service information across networks. This multi-network group communication is realized by *Multi-Radio Multi-Network Router* (MRMN-R) components deployed on devices connected to multiple networks, which implements the advanced routing protocols of PLASTIC.

Figure 2. Service Discovery Platform Architecture in PLASTIC

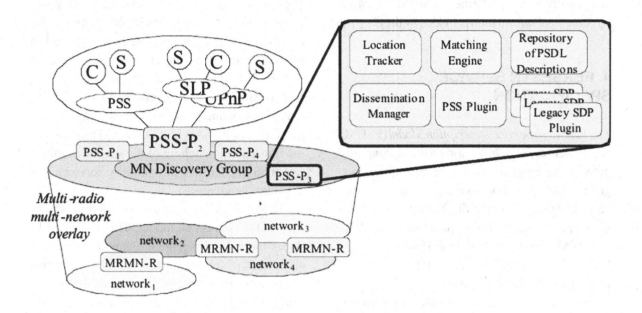

Interoperability is PerSeSyn is classically achieved through the use of a common representation for service descriptions and requests. However, interoperability between semantic-based and syntactic-based SDPs requires a higher level of abstraction, which is supported by the PSDM conceptual model (see Section 4 for a detailed description of PSDM and its instantiation PSDL).

PSS-Ps (see Figure 2) provide an explicit API supported by the *PSS Plugin* that enables clients (resp. providers) in a network to discover (resp. advertise) a service in the multi-network environment. It further enables clients and providers to benefit from all the platform's features (e.g., privacy, context-awareness) by directly issuing requests or advertisements in the PSDL format. Specific *Legacy SDP Plugins* register with the active SDPs in the network, and translate requests and advertisements in legacy formats to PSDL (e.g., SLP and UPnP in Figure 2).

Depending on the specific SDP, the legacy plugin either directly performs service discov-ery (i.e., pull-based only protocols) or registers for service advertisements (i.e., push-based and hybrid protocols). In the latter case, the PSDL description generated from a service announce-ment is sent to the *Repository* for storage. This repository also stores the PSDL descriptions issued by the PSS Plugin. The *Matching engine* combines various matching algorithms to support both syntactic-based and semantic-based service descriptions (i.e., requests and advertisements), and thus provides comprehensive interoperability between SDPs. When processing a service request, the matching engine forwards it to the active plugins for translation, and matches it against the repository. Finally, the *Dissemination Manager* controls the dissemination of local requests and the compilation of the results returned by distant PSS-Ps, while the *Location Tracker* collaborates with lower-level services in the PLASTIC Communication middleware to maintain the physical address of mobile services discovered in the environment. Context-awareness in PerSeSyn is primarily achieved by controlling the multi-network dissemination (Raverdy et al., 2006) of discovery requests (performed by MRMN-R based on contextual information provided by the PSS-P).

4. PERSESYN SERVICE SPECIFICATION

The *PerSeSyn Service Description Model* (PSDM) model serves as a basis for enabling mapping between heterogeneous service description languages including both syntactic and semantic-based languages. Specifically, service descriptions given using syntactic-based languages (e.g., UPnP, SLP, WSDL) and semantic-based languages (e.g., SAWSDL, OWL-S, WSMO) are translated by their respective plugin to PSDM-based descriptions. As a result, a service request may be matched using any of the existing descriptions stored in the repository, independently of the underlying original service description language.

4.1 PSDM: Model for Semantic and Syntactic Service Specification

The design of PSDM results from the analysis of many existing service description languages. Indeed, a first version of this model that supports only syntactic based languages has been introduced as part of the MUSDAC platform (Raverdy et al., 2006). This version of the model has been elaborated from the analysis of syntactic service description languages (e.g., UPnP, SLP and WSDL). It was used as a basis for enabling interoperability between protocols using these languages. In the EASY platform (Ben Mokhtar et al., 2008), we presented a model for the semantic specification of service capabilities. While the EASY platform presents a comprehensive semantic solution for specifying and matching service functional capabilities, it does not support syntactic and hybrid service specification and matching. This leads us to introduce PSDM that supports both syntactic-based and semantic-based service

descriptions, and related matching mechanisms. For instance, a service provider can either register a legacy syntactic-based service description using a legacy SPD, or decide to semantically enrich this description by further providing a distinct semantic description of the service. Furthermore, PSDM supports the incorporation of services that use existing semantic service description languages (e.g., SAWSDL, OWL-S) by enabling the transparent matching of the service capabilities with capabilities provided by services that use other languages.

The UML diagram depicted in Figure 3 shows the PSDM conceptual model. This model introduces the main conceptual elements that serve as a basis for matching service advertisements with service requests as further discussed in Section 5. Using this model, a service description is composed of two parts: a *profile*, and a *grounding*. The service profile is described as a non empty set of *capabilities* while the service grounding prescribes the way of accessing the service. A service capability is any functionality that may be provided by a service and sought by a client. It is described with its *Name*, a possibly empty set of *inputs*, a possibly empty set of *outputs,* and a potential *conversation*. Capabilities that do not have any associated input/output descriptions are those provided by legacy protocols that use names to characterize capabilities (e.g., a native SLP service). Inputs associated with a capability are the information necessary for the execution of the capability, while outputs correspond to the information produced by the capability. Input and outputs of capabilities are described with their *names*, *types* and a possible *semantic annotation* that is a reference to a concept in an existing ontology. Capabilities that do not have semantic annotations on the description of their inputs and outputs are those provided by legacy services without an enriched semantic interface (e.g., a native UPnP service). A conversation associated with a capability prescribes the way of realizing this capability through the execution of

Figure 3. PSDM

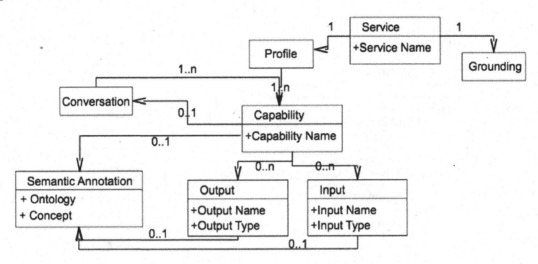

other capabilities. This conversation is described as a workflow of activities that may correspond either to elementary or composite capabilities. Elementary capabilities are those that do not have a conversation, while composite capabilities are those that are themselves composed of other capabilities.

Concretely, an elementary capability represents a basic interaction with a service. For instance, in the case of SLP services, it corresponds to the invocation of the whole service, whereas in the case of UPnP or WSDL services it corresponds to the invocation of one of the service operations.

4.2 PSDL: Language for Semantic and Syntactic Service Specification

In addition to the PSDM conceptual model, we further define the *PerSeSyn Service Description Language* (PSDL) as a concrete realization of this model. For the implementation of PSDL, we opted for an XML-based schema defining a container, which is combined with the two emergent standard service description languages namely SAWSDL and WS-BPEL. The PSDL description acts primarily as a top-level container for additional files

describing facets of the service. SAWSDL is used to describe the capability interfaces, while WS-BPEL is used to express conversations associated with capabilities. We employ SAWSDL for the definition of capability interfaces, as it supports both semantic and syntactic specification of service attributes (e.g., inputs, outputs). Thus, both legacy syntactic descriptions and rich semantic descriptions can be translated to SAWSDL. On the other hand, WS-BPEL is a comprehensive language for workflow specification, which is adequate for conversation specification. It has largely been adopted both in the industrial community and in academia. WS-BPEL supports only syntactic conversation specification, however, if combined with SAWSDL, semantic conversations can be defined. Furthermore, for the automated translation of service conversations we envision to build on the formal semantics of the existing languages (e.g., WS-BPEL (Cámara, Canal, Cubo, & Vallecillo, 2006), OWL-S (Narayanan & McIlraith, 2002)). Figure 4 shows an example of a PSDL description. In this example, the service is composed of two capabilities. The first capability has a complete functional description that comprises a reference to a SAWSDL file defining the

Figure 4. Example of a PSDL description

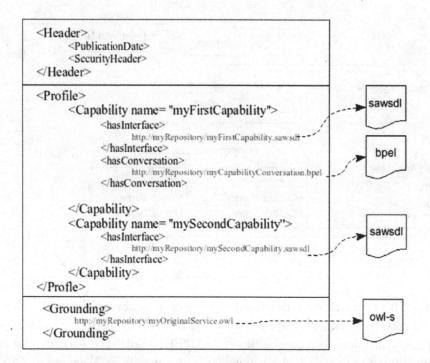

capability interface, and a WS-BPEL description that defines the conversation associated with the capability. The second capability of this service is only given with an interface description defined in a SAWSDL file.

5. MATCHING AND RANKING IN PERSESYN

Finding a service that exactly matches a client request is rather the exception than the rule in ambient computing environments. Thus, matching should be able to identify various degrees of conformance between services and clients, and rate services with respect to their suitability for a specific client request. We now present our set of conformance relations enabling interoperable matching of service capabilities in Section 4.1, and the associated service ranking mechanism in Section 4.2.

5.1 Interoperable Matching of Service Capabilities

Based on the PSDL language presented in Section 4, we present in this section a set of conformance relations for matching services in terms of their functional and non-functional properties. One of the particular features of PSDL is the support of heterogeneous service description languages. This is realized through the translation of the incoming heterogeneous service descriptions into PSDL descriptions. As described in our architecture (see Section 3), the repository of the PSS Proxy stores PSDL service descriptions generated by Legacy SD plugins from legacy descriptions (e.g., UPnP2PSD plugin), or directly provided by service providers using the PSS plugin interface. PSDL descriptions are used to assess the conformance with incoming service requests. Figure 5 gives an overview of how various legacy service descriptions are translated to PSDL. In this figure, five different scenarios are identified. The first scenario describes the case of a legacy service specified with the name of its provided functionality (e.g., a SLP service). In this case, the SLP2PSDL plugin translates the SLP description to a PSDL description. This description contains the SLP grounding information and links to a SAWSDL description that contains a single operation having as name the name of the SLP service without any input and output specification. The second scenario describes the case of a service that provides a list of operations described syntactically with their signatures, as it is the case for UPnP services or Web services. In this scenario, the corresponding plugin (e.g., UPnP2PSDL or WSDL2PSDL) translates the given description to a PSDL description, which links to a SAWSDL description that comprises a list of WSDL operations corresponding to the operations specified in the legacy description without semantic annotations. The third scenario describes the case of a service described as a set of semantically annotated operations (e.g., given as a SAWSDL description). In this case, the mapping is straightforward as it consists of linking the PSDL description to the given SAWSDL file or to map the terminology of the given file to SAWSDL if different.

The fourth scenario describes the case of a syntactic capability described with an associated conversation of operations (e.g., a service described as a WSDL operation that is realized through the execution of a WS-BPEL conversation). In this case the PSDL description contains the specification of both an interface and a conversation. The interface points to a SAWSDL description that contains a single operation without semantic specification and is used to describe the capability. On the other hand, the conversation links to a WS-BPEL description that describes the conversation associated with the operation. This WS-BPEL description uses itself another WSDL file that specifies the operations used in the conversation. The last scenario describes the case of a semantic capability having an associ-

ated conversation of semantic operations (e.g., an OWL-S service with a profile that describes the semantic capability and a process model that describes the associated conversation). In this case, the generated conversation also comprises both an interface and a conversation. However, compared with the previous case, the SAWSDL description used to describe the capability comprises semantic annotations of the capability elements (i.e., inputs, outputs). Furthermore, the WS-BPEL file describing the conversation associated with the capability uses another SAWSDL description in which the operations are also semantically annotated.

The conformance relations that we define in this paper depend on the scenarios introduced above. Indeed, the matching function used to assess the conformance of a service advertisement with a service request depends on the information contained in the request and the advertisement with respect to the above scenarios. For instance, comparing a service request described as a syntactic capability name (first scenario) with a rich semantic service description (third scenario), requires ignoring the semantic service annotations as well as input and output information and performing a syntactic comparison of the request with the capability names. The different cases of matching of heterogeneous service descriptions are outlined in Table 1. In this table a service request and a service advertisement can be described as: (1) a syntactic capability name; (2) a list of syntactic capabilities; (3) a list of semantic capabilities. Additionally, service advertisements can be further described as (4) a syntactic capability with an associated syntactic conversation and (5) a semantic capability with an associated semantic conversation. In this paper we do not consider the case where requests are specified with associated conversations. This may lead to a service composition process involving heterogeneous service advertisements, which we aim at addressing in our future work. The combination of the former scenarios gives fifteen cases for

Figure 5. Interoperability enabled by PSDL

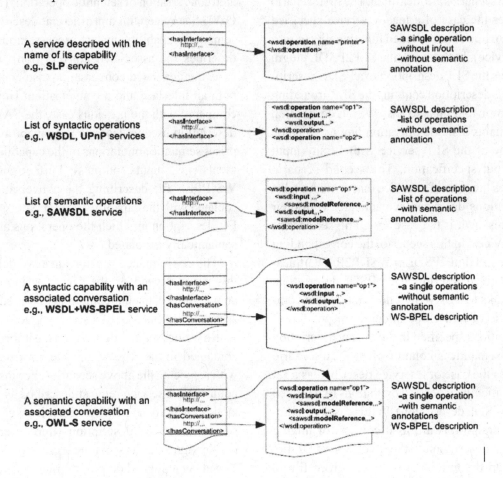

matching a service request with a service advertisement. Among these cases six cases are redundant in the table, which leads us to introduce the following six matching algorithms:

1. Syntactic matching of capability names, noted SynNameMatch(), consists of syntactically comparing the names of capabilities. However, as the syntactic matching has significant limitations such as false positive and false negative answers we rely on the function defined in (Seco, Veale, & Hayes, 2004) that uses the Wordnet[4] dictionary to evaluate the degree of similarity between two words of the dictionary. This similarity measure has a value in the interval [0,1].

Using this function, we define the function SyntacticDistance = *1-Wordnet similarity measure*, which we use with a threshold $\alpha \in$ [0,1] such that matching with distances above α are considered as failures. For instance, $\alpha=0$ implies that a matching holds only if the two words are synonyms with respect to the Wordnet dictionary. SynNameMatch() matching applies when either the request or the service are described as a syntactic capability name without an associated conversation (e.g., a SLP request with a SAWSDL service, a UPnP request with a SLP service). This function is defined as follows:

Table 1. Interoperable matching of services capabilities

		Request		
		Syntactic capability name	**List of syntactic capabilities**	**List of semantic capabilities**
Service	**Syntactic capability name**	SynNameMatch	SynNameMatch	SynNameMatch
	List of syntactic capabilities	SynNameMatch	SynSigMatch	SynSigMatch
	List of semantic capabilities	SynNameMatch	SynSigMatch	SemSigMatch
	Syntactic conversation	SynNameMatch + ExeConv	SynSigMatch + ExeConv	SynSigMatch + ExeConv
	Semantic conversation	SynNameMatch + ExeConv	SynSigMatch + ExeConv	SemSigMatch + ExeConv

SynNameMatch$(C_{adv}, C_{req})=$

SyntacticDistance$(C_{adv}.CapabilityName, C_{req}.CapabilityName) \leq \alpha$

2. Syntactic matching of capability names and conversation execution, noted SynNameMatch+ExeConv(), applies when the request is defined as a syntactic capability name and the service is either syntactic or semantic and has an associated conversation (e.g., an SLP request matched with an OWL-S service). In this case, we use the SynNameMatch() function defined above and if the matching holds the client executes the conversation associated with the matched capability.

3. Syntactic signature matching, noted SynSigMatch(), applies when the request is given as a list of syntactic capabilities and services are given as either a list of semantic capabilities or a list of syntactic capabilities. It applies also when a list of semantic capabilities is requested and only syntactic capabilities are provided by networked services. In the case of matching semantic capabilities with syntactic ones, the semantic annotations associated with capabilities' inputs and outputs are ignored. The SynSigMatch() function is defined as follows:

SynSigMatch$(C_{adv}, C_{req})=$

$\forall$ in $\in C_{adv}.In$, $\exists$ in' $\in C_{req}.In$:
SyntacticDistance$(in.Name, in'.Name) \leq \alpha$ and

$\forall$ out $\in C_{req}.Out$, $\exists$ out' $\in C_{adv}.Out$:
SyntacticDistance$(out.Name, out'.Name) \leq \alpha$

4. Syntactic signature matching and conversation execution, noted SynSigMatch+ExeConv(), applies when a service capability has an associated conversation either syntactically or semantically specified and the request is described as a list of capabilities, excluding the case where both of the request and the service are semantic-aware. In this case, we apply the SynSigMatch() matching defined above to assess the conformance of each requested capability with the provided ones, and if the matching holds, the client executes the associated conversation.

5. Semantic signature matching, noted SemSigMatch(), applies only when both the request and the advertisement are described as a set of semantic capabilities. While we previously defined a function for semantically matching service capabilities, this matching only supports fully semantically annotated capabilities (Ben Mokhtar et al., 2008). We thus improve this function with the support of hybrid matching of service

capabilities. Hybrid matching applies when services are not fully annotated, i.e., they may have both syntactic and semantic attributes, and is defined as follows:

SemSigMatch(C_{adv}, C_{req})=

$\forall$ in $\in C_{adv}.In$, $\exists$ *in'* $\in C_{req}.In$:

if (in.SemanticAnnotation$\neq$ null & in'.SemanticAnnotation$\neq$ null)

SemanticDistance(*in, in'*) $\leq \beta$ *Else*

SyntacticDistance(*in.Name, in'.Name*) $\leq \alpha$

and

$\forall$ out $\in C_{req}.Out$, $\exists$ *out'* $\in C_{adv}.Out$

if (out.SemanticAnnotation$\neq$ null & out'.SemanticAnnotation$\neq$ null)

SemanticDistance(*out, out'*) $\leq \beta$ *Else*

SyntacticDistance(*out.Name, out'.Name*) $\leq \alpha$

Where SemanticDistance() is a function used to check whether two concepts are related in an ontology (i.e., if one is more generic than the other) and returns the number of levels that separate these two concepts in the ontology hierarchy. We also use this function with a threshold β, which indicates the maximal number of levels that separate two concepts in an ontology above which the matching is considered as a failure.

6. Semantic signature matching and conversation execution, noted SemSigMatch+ExeConv(), applies in the only case where a request described as a set of semantic capabilities is matched with a service described as a semantic capability with an associated conversation. In this case, we use the SemSigMatch()

function to assess the conformance between semantic capabilities and the client has to execute the service conversation.

5.2 Ranking Heterogeneous Matching Results

We present in this section our mechanism for ranking service advertisements with respect to a service request. First, according to the degree of expressiveness of the service request, results coming from the various matching algorithms employed to assess the conformance of a service advertisement with the request, are ranked according to Table 2. For instance, for a request described as a list of semantic capabilities, ranking is performed according to the following expression:

SemSigMatch() > SemSigMatch+ExeConv() > SynSigMatch() >

SynSigMatch+ExeConv() > SynNameMatch() > SynNameMatch+ExeConv()

This means that results of semantic matching functions are preferred to results of syntactic matching functions. Furthermore, capabilities that do not have associated conversations are preferred to capabilities that require the execution of the corresponding service conversation by the client. Finally, results coming from the weakest matching function (i.e., syntactic matching of capability names) are given the least scores compared to the others.

On the other hand, the results of each of these matching functions are themselves classified according to their degree of conformance to the given request. The degree of conformance between a service request and a service advertisement is evaluated using the function ServiceDistance() which sums the results of SyntacticDistance() and SemanticDistance() functions used in the matching phase. If many provided capabilities have the same degree of conformance to a requested capability

Table 2. Ranking heterogeneous matching results

Request type	Preferred matching functions
Syntactic capability name	*SynNameMatch>SynNameMatch+ExeConv*
List of syntactic capabilities	*SynSigMatch>SynSigMatch+ExeConv>SynNameMatch > SynNameMatch+ExeConv*
List of semantic capabilities	*SemSigMatch>SemSigMatch+ExeConv>SynSigMatch>SynSigMatch+ExeConv>SynNameMatch > SynNameMatch+ExeConv*

we envision using non-functional properties (e.g., QoS) to select the most appropriate one (Ben Mokhtar et al., 2008).

6. PROTOTYPE IMPLEMENTATION AND PERFORMANCE EVALUATION

We have implemented a prototype of the PerSeSyn discovery platform using Java 1.6. To evaluate the efficiency of PerSeSyn, we evaluate the processing time to create PSDL requests and descriptions as a result of the translation of a legacy request/description. We also evaluate the processing time of matching various combinations of requests and descriptions. Tests are performed on a Windows XP PC with a 2.6GHz processor and 512 MB of memory. Results presented below are the average of 1000 tests. The standard deviation for the results presented below is negligible (less than 1%). As presented in (Raverdy et al., 2006), providing interoperability on top of simple, limited SDPs such as SLP may incur a significant overhead (i.e., overhead of over 200 milliseconds for a native discovery time of less than 1 millisecond for a similar configuration). It was analyzed that this overhead was by and large (two-thirds or almost 140 milliseconds) triggered by the SOAP-based interface of the interoperability service. This overhead however becomes negligible when interoperating with other SDPs such as UDDI that have a native discovery time between 1 and 6 seconds.

For the PerSeSyn prototype, the processing time for the translation of service descriptions

(requests and advertisements) from selected legacy SDPs to PSDL descriptions are provided in Table 3. The first line of this table represents the time to process a discovery request using SLP, UPnP and WSDL excluding the time to parse XML descriptions. The second line represents the time to process a discovery request in addition to the time to translate the request to PSDL. Finally, the third line represents the overhead of the translation. In this experiment times are given in microseconds. As it can be observed, this time increases with the complexity of the original description, and in particular the complexity and size of the original XML data to process. Overall, the translation time is not significant (tens to hundreds of microseconds) compared to the overall discovery time.

In Table 4, the processing time of the matching algorithms for the different combination of service requests and advertisements is provided. From the results of this experiment we can notice that the time to parse service and request descriptions is almost the same, because they are all PSDL descriptions (1865 microseconds on average with less than 2% of standard deviation). Additionally, syntactic matching based on capability names (SLP advertisement and request) is the most efficient, which is due to the fact that there is less information to compare (only capability names). Finally, thanks to the optimized semantic matching defined in (Ben Mokhtar et al., 2008) semantic matching of capabilities (SAWSDL advertisement and request) is as efficient as syntactic matching of capabilities (WSDL, UPnP advertisements and requests). Regarding other semantic-based languages (e.g., WSMO, OWL-S), we

Table 3. Legacy to PSDL translation (micro-seconds)

	SLP	UPnP	WSDL
Discovery request	22.8	32.4	243
Discovery Request + Translation to PSDL	23.4	85.1	287
Overhead of the Translation	0.6	52.7	44

expect the semantic matching of service capabilities to be performed as efficiently as SAWSDL matching as the descriptions are to be translated to PSDL.

Overall, it can be concluded that parsing and matching PSDL descriptions is also negligible when compared to the total discovery time (and in particular the processing time for SOAP communication).

Finally in Figure 6 we present an evaluation of the scalability of our semantic-syntactic service matching performed in a PerSeSyn service repository. In this experiment we increase the number of services in the repository from 1 to 128 services of different types (SLP, UPnP, WSDL and SAWSDL) and we perform the matching between a service request and services of the same type. All the times are in milli-seconds and do not include the time for parsing service descriptions.

In this experiment, semantic services (i.e., described using SAWSDL) are organized into graphs of similar capabilities as presented in (Ben Mokhtar et al., 2008). In this experiment we have been interested in two extreme scenarios of repository organization: the case where all the semantic services are semantically deferent from each other, i.e., the repository is not organized (curve SAWSDL Worst) and the case where all the services are semantically equivalent to each other, i.e., there is a single graph, with a single node that contains all the service capabilities (curve SAWSDL Best). A case where the repository is partially grouped (real case scenario) would be represented with a curve between these two extreme curves.

From this experiment we can notice that matching cost increases substantially when repository holds more than 100 services for the cases of UPnP, WSDL and unorganized semantic services (SAWSDL worst case). Nevertheless, when semantic services are related to each other (SAWSDL best case), thanks to the clustering of services, the scalability of the semantic matching is similar to the scalability of SLP based matching.

7. CONCLUSION

The ambient computing vision is increasingly enabled by the large success of wireless networks and devices. In ambient computing environments, heterogeneous software and hardware resources

Table 4. Syntactic-semantic parsing and matching processing time (micro-seconds)

		REQUESTED SERVICE							
		PSDL SLP		PSDL UPnP		PSDL WSDL		PSDL SAWSDL	
		Parsing	Matching	Parsing	Matching	Parsing	Matching	Parsing	Matching
ADVER-TISED SER-VICE	PSDL SLP	1798	**9.2**	1844	**9.0**	1832	**8.9**	1894	**11.3**
	PSDL UPnP	1907	**10.7**	1868	**18.0**	1859	**16.9**	1923	**18.8**
	PSDL WSDL	1882	**10.3**	1829	**18.1**	1822	**17.4**	1896	**19.0**
	PSDL SAWSDL	1888	**10.9**	1851	**19.3**	1841	**18.8**	1910	**21.3**

Figure 6. Scalability of PerSeSyn repository

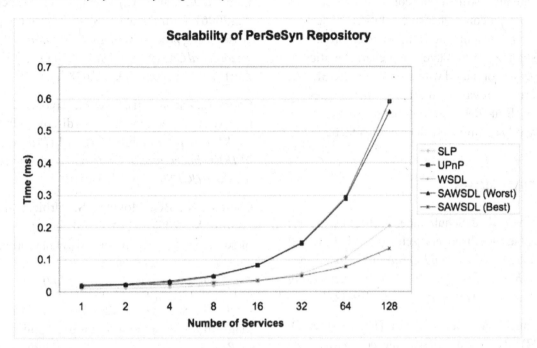

may be discovered and integrated transparently towards assisting the performance of users' daily tasks. An essential requirement towards the realization of such a vision is the availability of mechanisms enabling the discovery of resources that best fit the client applications' needs among the heterogeneous resources that populate the ambient computing environment. Following on

prior innovative solutions primarily addressing context-aware service discovery for multinetworks environments (MUSDAC) and for the semantic Web (EASY), we have introduced a conceptual model for service description as well as conformance relations for the efficient intermix of both syntactic-based and semantic-based SDPs. We have developed the PerSeSyn platform that

Table 5. PerSeSyn service discovery characteristics

	MUSDAC	EASY	PerSeSyn
Multi-protocol	Yes	No	Yes
Context-aware	Yes	Yes (context and QoS)	Yes (content, QoS, and mobility)
Semantic	No	Yes	Yes (hybrid Sem-Syn)
Multi-network	Yes	No	Yes
Mobility support	No	No	Yes
Security and Privacy	No	No	Yes
Service Description	Proprietary	Meta model for customized description language generation	Meta model for customized description language generation
SDP API	Client only API	Client and service APIs	Client and service API
Resource-aware	Yes (limited bridging overhead)	Yes (encoded ontologies for matching and classification)	Yes (both at the bridging and computing levels)

implements this model and conformance relations to provide a comprehensive solution for service discovery in ambient computing environment. We summarize in Table 5 the characteristics of PerSeSyn compared with EASY and MUSDAC. Performance evaluation of PerSeSyn validates our approach and demonstrates that semantics can be efficiently combined with legacy syntactic SDPs.

REFERENCES

Arabshian, K., & Schulzrinne, H. (2004). GloServ: Global service discovery architecture. In *Proceedings of the First Annual International Conference on Mobile and Ubiquitous Systems: Networking and Services (Mobiquitous)* (pp. 319-325).

Balazinska, M., Balakrishnan, H., & Karger, D. (2002). INS/Twine: A scalable peer-to-peer architecture for intentional resource discovery. In *Proceedings of the International Conference on Pervasive Computing 2002*.

Ben Mokhtar, S., Kaul, A., Georgantas, N., & Issarny, V. (2006). Efficient semantic service discovery in pervasive computing environments. In *Proceedings of the ACM/IFIP/USENIX, 7th International Middleware Conference Middleware 2006* (pp. 240-259).

Ben Mokhtar, S., Preuveneers, D., Georgantas, N., Issarny, V., & Berbers, Y. (2008). EASY: Efficient SemAntic service DiscoverY in pervasive computing environments with QoS and context support. *Journal of Systems and Software, 81*(5), 785–808.

Bromberg, Y., & Issarny, V. (2005). INDISS: Interoperable discovery system for networked services. In *Proceedings of the ACM/IFIP/USENIX, 6th International Middleware Conference Middleware 2005* (pp. 164-183).

Cámara, J., Canal, C., Cubo, J., & Vallecillo, A. (2006). Formalizing WSBPEL business processes using process algebra. *Electronic Notes in Theoretical Computer Science, 154*(1), 159–173.. doi:10.1016/j.entcs.2005.12.038

Capra, L., Zachariadis, S., & Mascolo, C. (2005). Q-CAD: QoS and context aware discovery framework for adaptive mobile systems. In *Proceedings of IEEE International Conference on Pervasive Services (ICPS05)* (pp. 453-456).

Cardoso, R., Ben Mokhtar, S., Urbieta, A., & Issarny, V. (2007). EVEY: Enhancing privacy of service discovery in pervasive computing. In *Proceedings of the International Middleware Conference 2007 (Middleware 2007)*.

Chen, G., & Kotz, D. (2002). Solar: An open platform for context-aware mobile applications. In *Proceedings of the 1st International Conference on Pervasive Computing (Pervasive 2002)*, Switzerland.

Czerwinski, S. E., Zhao, B. Y., Hodes, T. D., Joseph, A. D., & Katz, R. H. (1999). An architecture for a secure service discovery service. In *Proceedings of the 5th Annual ACM/IEEE International Conference on Mobile Computing and Networking (MobiCom '99)*, Seattle, WA (pp. 24-35).

Grace, P., Blair, G. S., & Samuel, S. (2003). ReM-MoC: A reflective middleware to support mobile client. In Proceedings of the *On the Move to Meaningful Internet Systems 2003: CoopIS, DOA, and ODBASE - OTM Confederated International Conferences, CoopIS, DOA, and ODBASE 2003* (pp. 1170-1187).

Koponen, T., & Virtanen, T. (2004). A service discovery: A service broker approach. In *Proceedings of the 37th Annual Hawaii International Conference on System Sciences*.

Lausen, H., & Innsbruck, D. (2006). *Semantic annotations for WSDL (SAWSDL)*. Retrieved September 28, 2006, from http://www.w3.org/TR/sawsdl/

Lee, C., & Helal, S. (2003). Context attributes: An approach to enable context-awareness for service discovery. In *Proceedings of the 2003 Symposium on Applications and the Internet* (p. 22).

Lee, G., Faratin, P., Bauer, S., & Wroclawski, J. (2004). A user-guided cognitive agent for network service selection in pervasive computing environments. In *Proceedings of the Second IEEE International Conference on Pervasive Computing and Communications (PerCom'04)* (p. 219).

Liu, J., & Issarny, V. (2005). Signal strength based service discovery (S3D) in mobile ad hoc networks. In *Proceedings of the 16th Annual IEEE International Symposium on Personal Indoor and Mobile Radio Communications (PIMRC'05)*, Berlin, Germany.

Martin, D., Burstein, M., Hobbs, J., Lassila, O., McDermott, D., McIlraith, S., et al. (2004). OWL-S: Semantic markup for web services. *W3C Member Submission.*

Nakazawa, J., Tokuda, H., Edwards, W. K., & Ramachandran, U. (2006). A bridging framework for universal interoperability in pervasive systems. In *Proceedings of the 26th IEEE International Conference on Distributed Computing Systems* (p. 3).

Narayanan, S., & McIlraith, S. A. (2002). Simulation, verification and automated composition of web services. In *Proceedings of the 11th International Conference on World Wide Web (WWW '02)*, Honolulu, HI (pp. 77-88).

Patil, A. A., Oundhakar, S. A., Sheth, A. P., & Verma, K. (2004). Meteor-s web service annotation framework. In *Proceedings of the 13th International Conference on World Wide Web (WWW '04)*, New York (pp. 553-562).

PLASTIC Project. (2007). *Middleware specification and architecture*. Retrieved from http://www-c.inria.fr:9098/plastic/test-1/m12/plastic_d3_1.pdf/download

Raverdy, P. G., Issarny, V., Chibout, R., & de La Chapelle, A. (2006). A multi-protocol approach to service discovery and access in pervasive environments. In *Proceedings of the 3rd Annual International Conference on Mobile and Ubiquitous Systems: Networks and Services (MOBIQUITOUS 2006)*, San Jose, CA.

Raverdy, P. G., Riva, O., de la Chapelle, A., Chibout, R., & Issarny, V. (2006). Efficient context-aware service discovery in multi-protocol pervasive environments. In *Proceedings of the 7th International Conference on Mobile Data Management (MDM'06)* (p. 3).

Seco, N., Veale, T., & Hayes, J. (2004). An intrinsic information content metric for semantic similarity in WordNet. In *Proceedings of the European Conference on Artificial Intelligence, 16*, 1089.

Srinivasan, N., Paolucci, M., & Sycara, K. (2004). Adding OWL-S to UDDI, implementation and throughput. In *Proceedings of the 1st Intl. Workshop on Semantic Web Services and Web Process Composition (SWSWPC 2004)* (pp. 6-9).

Sycara, K., Paolucci, M., Ankolekar, A., & Srinivasan, N. (2003). Automated discovery, interaction and composition of semantic web services. *Journal of Web Semantics, 1*(1), 27–46..doi:10.1016/j.websem.2003.07.002

Trastour, D., Bartolini, C., & Gonzalez-Castillo, J. (2001). A semantic web approach to service description for matchmaking of services. In *Proceedings of the International Semantic Web Working Symposium (SWWS)*.

Zhao, W., & Schulzrinne, H. (2005). Enhancing service location protocol for efficiency, scalability and advanced discovery. *Journal of Systems and Software, 75*(1-2), 193–204..doi:10.1016/j.jss.2004.04.011

Zhu, F., Mutka, M., & Ni, L. (2003). Splendor: A secure, private, and location-aware service discovery protocol supporting mobile services. In *Proceedings of the First IEEE International Conference on Pervasive Computing and Communications* (p. 235).

Zhu, F., Mutka, M., & Ni, L. (2004). PrudentExposure: A private and user-centric service discovery protocol. In *Proceedings of the Second IEEE Annual Conference on Pervasive Computing and Communications (PerCom 2004)* (p. 329).

Zhu, F., Mutka, M. W., & Ni, L. M. (2005). Service discovery in pervasive computing environments. *IEEE Pervasive Computing / IEEE Computer Society* and *IEEE Communications Society, 4*(4), 81–90. doi:10.1109/MPRV.2005.87

ENDNOTES

[1] http://www.ist-plastic.org/

[2] SAWSDL: Semantic Annotations for WSDL. http://www.w3.org/2002/ws/sawsdl/

[3] WS-BPEL: Web Services Business Process Execution Language. http://www.oasisopen.org/

[4] Wordnet dictionary: http://wordnet.princeton.edu/

This work was previously published in International Journal of Ambient Computing and Intelligence, Volume 2, Issue 4, edited by Kevin Curran, pp. 13-32, copyright 2010 by IGI Publishing (an imprint of IGI Global).

Chapter 18
Leveraging the Web Platform for Ambient Computing:
An Experience

Fabio Mancinelli
XWiki SAS, France

ABSTRACT

This paper explores the idea of what can be achieved by using the principles and the technologies of the web platform when they are applied to ambient computing. In this paper, the author presents an experience that realizes some of the goals of an Ambient Computing system by making use of the technologies and the common practices of today's Web Platform. This paper provides an architecture that lowers the deployment costs by maximizing the reuse of pre-existing components and protocols, while guaranteeing accessibility, interoperability, and extendibility.

INTRODUCTION

Pervasive and Ambient computing propose a paradigm where devices present in a physical environment collaborate in order to support people in carrying out their daily tasks (Satyanarayanan, 2001). Though many technologies have been introduced in order to implement this paradigm (Román, Hess, Cerqueira, Ranganathan, Camp-

bell, & Nahrstedt, 2002), there are still a lot of open issues that must be addressed and solved. In particular many of these issues concern the *"ubiquitousness"* of these solutions and their interoperability with the multitude of heterogeneous devices that might interact with such a kind of systems. In this paper we explore a very simple idea: what can be achieved by using the principles and the technologies of the Web Platform when they are applied to Ambient Computing? This idea is motivated by the fact the by leveraging the Web

DOI: 10.4018/978-1-4666-0038-6.ch018

Copyright © 2012, IGI Global. Copying or distributing in print or electronic forms without written permission of IGI Global is prohibited.

Platform we can address interoperability issues by relying on a uniform platform that has a well defined set of protocols and semantics. This is very important because different solutions must inter-operate in order to provide a better experience to the end-users. By using the Web Platform as a common ground, and by building on top of it, many of the interoperability issues are solved forefront. In this paper, basically, we took the Web Platform as the reference platform, and built on top of it a simple system that follows the Ambient Computing principles. Our aim was to describe the experience we did in building an actual system and to present the advantages that, in our opinion, derive from following such a kind of approach.

In the remainder of the paper we will introduce our reference platform (i.e., the Web Platform) and its characteristics; then we will present our architecture and we detail all the aspects that are addressed and how they are addressed by our system. Finally we present conclusions with final remarks.

THE WEB PLATFORM

In this section we will briefly introduce the Web Platform and what it consists of. With the term "Web Platform" we refer to the ensemble of the protocols and standards the World Wide Web is built upon. The term "Web Platform" has been circulating for a while in the Web community, and has gained more and more importance after that Google organized its first "Google I/O" conference (Google Inc., 2008a) whose aim was that of "*Advancing the Web as a Platform*". The term *platform* is crucial because nowadays developers are using the Web, its architecture and the technologies it is based on, as an actual platform for engineering, developing and deploying their applications. This is basically something similar to what happened with the Java Platform (Sun Microsystems, 2008), with the introduction of the Java language, its standard libraries and all

their extensions like the "Enterprise Edition" or the "Micro Edition". The idea of the Web as a platform is also corroborated by all the companies that are producing advanced tools and solutions for easily building complex application without taking care of all the low-level details (Ruby, Thomas, & Hansson, 2008) (Google Inc., 2008b)

The Web Platform has an architecture that is based on a well defined set of principles and constraints (Fielding, 2002) that are implemented by a set of standard and widely deployed communication protocols (Fielding, Gettys, Mogul, Frystyk, Masinter, Leach, & Berners-Lee, 1999), and makes use of commonly used data formats for exchanging information (IANA).

A key element in this architecture is the concept of *resource* and its associated *representations* (i.e., how a resource, which can be also a physical resource, is represented for being used and manipulated in a digital context). The term *"resource"* is highly generic but, as stated in Richardson and Ruby (2007), we can say that a resource is *"anything that is important enough to be referenced as a thing in itself"*. Representations are not the resources themselves, but are the means for retrieving and manipulating actual resources. For example, an image or an XML file might represent a physical person. By manipulating those representations we can change the way the physical person is "used" in the digital system, though without "modifying" the actual person.

The most important principles and constraints described in Fielding (2002) that are relevant for the purpose of this paper are:

- *Addressability*: Every resource must be addressable by a well-defined resource identifier.
- *Uniform interface*: A single interface, with a well-defined semantics, must be used for accessing and manipulating all the resources.
- *Hypermedia as the engine of application state*: By leveraging addressability, the

execution of the application is obtained by following hypermedia links to resources that represent the "next state" of the application.

These principles are implemented in the Web Platform in the following way: *addressability* is given by using Uniform Resource Identifiers (URIs) that provide a *"simple and extensible way for identifying an abstract or physical resource"* (Berners-Lee, Fielding, & Masinter, 1998). URIs are used extensively in order to address any resource, and to operate on their representations. URIs also enables hypermedia features that are used as the primary mechanism to make applications change their state. By providing links embedded in resource representations, applications may evolve by "visiting" those links and discovering new or related application states.

The *uniform interface* is provided by the HTTP protocol with its five standard methods and their well-defined semantics for interacting with resources. These methods are the well known GET, HEAD, PUT, DELETE, POST, and some other less known ones: OPTIONS, TRACE and CONNECT. Though the semantics for these methods is well defined, POST is an exception because its actual semantics depends on what is specified in the body of the corresponding HTTP request.

The HTTP protocol is a very simple request-response protocol that exchanges messages consisting of a set of headers and a body. Headers contain meta-information for further describing the HTTP message; the body contains data to be associated to HTTP messages depending on their nature. HTTP headers are essential for making messages self-descriptive and amenable to advanced pre/post processing (e.g., by enabling transparent representation transformation to a desired format or caching)

Response codes are another important aspect of the HTTP protocol. Each HTTP request comes with a response containing a code used to communicate the result of the request. There are several response codes, grouped in classes: *meta, success, redirection, client-side error* and *server-side error* classes. For the purpose of this paper, the redirection class will have a particular relevance, as it will be described below. A redirect response makes the client issue another equivalent request to a different resource instead of the original one. This mechanism is crucial for transparently coping with a fluid and dynamic environment, such as the one taken into account by Ambient Computing where resources might disappear or simply be reorganized.

To conclude this section we would like to point out that the most important part of the Web Platform consists of all the standard format, languages and clients that are used to create leverage for the web applications. In particular the XML (Bray, Paoli, Sperberg-McQueen, Maler, & Yergeau, 2006) and XHTML formats, the JavaScript (ECMA International, 1999) language and the standard-compliant Web browsers. These elements, of course, will be central in the experience presented in this paper.

ARCHITECTURE

In Ambient Computing, there are several issues that should be addressed in order to build an effective system. First of all there should be a way for defining, discovering and identifying what is available in the surroundings and, of course, there should be a way for interacting with the found entities.

These requirements entail several others that can be summarized as the following:

- *Networking:* How can the entities that are present in a given environment exchange information among them?
- *Environment partitioning:* How the surrounding environment is organized and this organization can be defined and identified?

- *Addressing:* How can we address entities that are in a given environment?
- *Management:* How can an entity providing a service declare itself, and how other entities can be aware of it?
- *Interaction:* How can entities co-operate, and what kind of interaction entities can have in order to fulfill a given task?

The proposed architecture is presented in Figure 1. Devices (i.e., the clients) and service device (i.e., the devices providing some kind of service to the others) populate an *environment*. An *environment manager* takes care of providing the necessary connectivity and maintaining the logical organization of the environment itself. Spaces are used as a means for further partitioning devices into classes using some criteria. We point out that the *environment manager* is where most of the support is centralized. On real deployment it could be a server connected to a WiFi router that provides connectivity for a local area network where all the devices and service devices are part of. It's the *environment manager* that contains all the logic for enabling devices and service devices to discover each other, as it will be described later. Service devices and devices are mobile wireless devices that take advantage of the *environment manager* connectivity in order to communicate among them.

By having in mind the previous list, in the following sections we will detail our architecture and explain how these requirements are met.

Networking

For our architecture we need a flexible networking infrastructure that should be widely supported and easy to manage. The choice is to use TCP/IP networking on top of WiFi connectivity. Basically the target infrastructure will consist of TCP/IP (private) networks that are pervasively available on a physical environment through WiFi hotspots. A hotspot defines an *environment* that logically regroups all the devices connected through the hotspot.

This choice might seem restrictive because it presupposes, in order to be compatible with the infrastructure, the availability of built-in WiFi support on the devices. However many current-generation smart-phones, PDAs, and appliances have already this support built-in and in the future this support will become more and more widespread.

Since we want to deploy the architecture on top of the Web Platform, another assumption we are making is that the devices should be equipped at least with a *Web browser*, i.e., a component capable of understanding the HTTP protocol. This again should not be too restrictive: a WiFi-equipped device surely has a browser built-in (or installable as a third party software), so we can suppose that if a device is able to connect to the WiFi infrastructure, it will also able to *"browse"*, using the HTTP protocol, what is available on that infrastructure as well. Of course the browser could be complemented with additional programs that provide more Ambient-Computing oriented interfaces: for example a bar-code scanner that uses the device's camera for reading data encoded as URLs and feed it directly to the browser instead of making the user type them.

Finally we don't make any assumption on the capabilities of the browser, unless for the fact that it should support basic XHTML capabilities like receiving and sending forms, and support *redirection*.

Environment Partitioning and Discovery

With the term *environment partitioning*, we refer to the definition of how a physical environment, i.e., the set of all the devices that are linked to a WiFi hotspot are organized. In order to do so we introduce the notion of space: a logical environment that is used to group devices that belong to the same "domain". The semantics of a domain

Figure 1. The system architecture

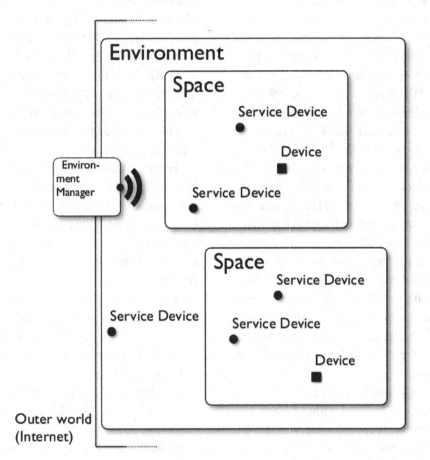

is defined by an administrator and can, for example, reflect the organization of the physical environment (i.e., each space might correspond to a physical room), or to some administrative partitioning (i.e., a space for the Computer Science Department).

The entry-point of the system, from the point of view of a device, is the WiFi hotspot where it connects. Once it is connected, an IP address is assigned to it and it can start to communicate with other entities present on the same network. The problem now is how can this device discover the partitioning that is defined for a given environment? Discovery protocols such as SLP (Guttman, Perkins, Veizades, & Day, 1999) or SSDP used in the Universal Plug and Play framework (Goland, Cai, Leach, Gu, & Albright, 1999), use the under-

lying network topology for delivering multicast packets containing announcement information about the device that are present in the network. This announcement also contains information about the actual logical or physical location of a given resource (e.g., printer-location: 'Room 3').

This approach has two consequences: first, a program listening for packets on a given multicast port should run on the mobile device; and second, the device should embed some logic in order to understand the messages and, for example, filter only the messages that refer to devices in "Room 3". Since these messages are completely arbitrary, an ad-hoc application is needed for this.

In our architecture we would like to impose the least requirements on the devices using the infrastructure (i.e., only they should be equipped only with a Web browser), so the previous approach is not suitable.

When a device wants to interact with the infrastructure it has to obtain an IP address from one of the available WiFi hotspots. This is usually done using the DHCP protocol (Droms, 1997) that configures the device's gateway, DNS and so on. So the idea is to configure the WiFi network for hosting a *transparent proxy* that will redirect all the traffic generated by the browser to a given server that can provide despite of the actual address the user typed in her browser, an XHTML page that represents the entry point for all the environments registered at that hotspot.

This is basically the role of the *Environment Manager* pictured in Figure 1. What this representation actually contains and how it is built will be detailed in following sections. Of course the content of this page will reflect the logical partitioning of the devices that are available in the environment.

This setup implements a transparent discovery mechanism that can be used without using any additional software. We would like to point out that what is discovered here is an entry point that will give directions, by means of hypermedia links, on how to reach actual devices, while in SLP the target devices are directly discovered. Therefore, our approach implies that there is a central authority, i.e., the Environment Manager that is behind the WiFi hotspot, that should keep track, in a centralized way, of all the device that are present in a given environment. The procedure for doing so will be described in the Management Section.

Addressing

When we reason about addressing the first thing to decide is what are the resources in our domain that needs to be addressed, and how these addresses are structured. In our architecture we will address two kinds of resources: spaces and service devices. The first ones are basically containers used for the logical organization of devices, in order to reflect their actual organization in physical places or in administrative domains; the second ones are devices that provide the actual services. As we are leveraging the Web Platform, we will use URIs for addressing resources, and the address template has the following form, which is an URI template as defined in Gregorio, Hadley, Nottingham, and Orchard (2008): http://environment/{space}/{device}

From the address template it is clear that it is not possible to specify space nesting. In fact, in our architecture, an address like http://campusbuilding/hall/room/printer would not be recognized. However we allow the definition of a logical hierarchy of spaces by associating to each space a parent addressable using the special address http://environment/{space}/parent. The request for a representation of this resource will result in a response that will redirect the client to the actual parent of the space contained in the address template.

The fact that service devices can be addressed using an URI implies that every service device must have a web proxy that can be used in order to interact with it. This web proxy, that can be located on the devices itself or somewhere else, is used to provide representations of the actual service that can be manipulated by clients in order to realize the interaction with the service. Usually, as we will show in the Interaction Section, this representation will consist of an XHTML page containing a form with all the relevant service attributes exposed by the device.

Management

In order to organize the partitioning of an *environment*, service devices need to be able to perform two sets of operations: logical *space* creation/removal/re-parenting, and device registration/un-registration/re-parenting (i.e., assignment to another *space*) in a given *environment*.

All these operation are carried out by leveraging the HTTP protocol.

Space operations are quite straightforward: a *space* is created or re-parented by PUTting the space name and the (optional) parent name to the *environment* entry-point, whose location is given by http://environment. Re-parenting is done in the case where the *space* already exists.

DELETEing the space address removes a space.

The current means by which they are performed are XHTML forms that are presented in documents that are served by the *environment manager*. These forms provide the interface for performing the previous operations, and are available as resources at well-defined URIs, that are http://environment/registration, and http://environment/{space}/registration for registering *spaces* and *service devices* respectively. The attributes for identifying the *space* name and parent are arbitrary since they are provided through the form by the same entity (i.e., the *environment* entry point) that will re-interpret them when they will be received as POSTed data. This is fine if the POSTer is a human who fills out the form, however if we imagine automating this process, then these attributes should be well defined and immutable.

The attentive reader might notice that XHTML forms only supports the GET and POST methods (This limitation will be overcome in XHTML5, but it will take some time before this standard will be widely adopted). However it is possible to overload the POST method by specifying the actual HTTP method in a hidden field of the form. In this way the POST request will be treated as if it were a request that used the HTTP method specified in the POSTed data.

Device registration, un-registration and re-parenting are done in a similar way. What changes is the set of attributes that are contained in the POSTed data. The device relevant attributes are: its name, the optional logical *space* where it is located, and the URI for its representation.

Figure 2. Environment entry point

Interaction

In this section we will present a classic interaction of a device with the system. This description is based on a real case study that we have implemented as a proof of concept.

A user enters a space and with its mobile phones looks for WiFi hotspots that are available. Once she has found a suitable one, she connects to it and opens her browser.

At this point she doesn't know what address to type in the address bar, however no matter what she will type the *Environment Manager* will intercept all her requests and reply as if they were addressed to it. Since many browsers have a predefined home page that is displayed when the browser is opened, this operation will be totally transparent for the user and what she will see after connecting to the hotspot is just the *environment* entry point as presented in Figure 2. Of course this means that the user will not be able to reach the "outer" Internet; however this interception mechanism could be put in place only for the first user request. In this way the user will be able to bookmark the environment entry point page, and will be free to use the Internet as usual afterwards.

From the environment entry point, the user can navigate the structure of the *environment* by following hyperlinks; for example she might go to the room she is currently.

Once the *space* page is displayed, the user has a view of all the devices that are present in the

Figure 3. A space accessible from an environment

Figure 4. A service device accessible from a space

given *space* (Figure 3). A *service device* called "MP3-player" is available for playing music in the current room. Clicking on the *service device* will present the user an interface for operating the player. Actually it is the web proxy associated to the MP3-player that serves this a representation in the form of a user interface built using an XHTML page containing a form for submitting data to the player.

We point out that the actual web proxy could be located everywhere in the network. For example, it could be running on the data centers of the campus (i.e., in the "outer world" pictured in Figure 1). What happens when a device requests an http://environment/{space}/{device} address is that the *Environment Manager* redirects the device to a new address that is the one of the actual web proxy for the *service device*. This is possible because the HTTP protocol supports, as described in the Web Platform section, redirection response codes.

Once the user has the device interface displayed on her mobile phone, she can select an MP3 file from her collection and send it to the *service device* for playing it. Again, this is done by leveraging the HTTP protocol that allows the user to POST data to a given address (i.e., the one of the *service device*). Figure 4 and Figure 5 show this interaction whose effect is that of having the (local) MP3 file streamed to the player in the room: the user can then enjoy her favorite music on the HiFi system's speakers in the room.

We would like to point out also the fact that since all the resources are directly addressable, the user has the possibility of bookmarking them for later usage. So, instead of following the link-chain from the *environment* entry point to the current *space* and then to the *service device*, she can directly jump to one or the other.

Finally, the user might also register a *service device* by using the registration interface provided by the *environment manager*. This interface, which is presented in Figure 7, allows the user to bind, in a given *space* a *service device* to a given web-proxy by giving its address. HTTP already provides authentication mechanisms that can be used to restrict this "administrative" task only to the users that are allowed to perform it (Figure 6).

Conclusion

In this paper we have presented an experience in building a system for Ambient Computing that

Figure 5. Device communication

Figure 6. Authentication

Figure 7. Service device registration

made use of the Web Platform as its reference architecture. What we presented in this paper is related to previous work presented in (Kindberg & Barton, 2001) and (Edwards, Newman, & Sedivy, 2001). In fact there is a big overlap with CoolTown which proposes an infrastructure that is based on the Web Platform, exposes devices through XHTML interfaces, and uses URIs as the mean for identifying them.

In our system we wanted to stick to basic features available in the Web Platform, without relying on any additional logic to devices. For example, in CoolTown, extra hardware is used for "sensing" device addresses provided by beacons, and to input them in the web browser (though these addresses might also be directly typed)

The principle we wanted to follow was to stick to the semantics of the HTTP protocol, that provide the uniform interface for accessing every device in the environment, and to build on top of it all the necessary infrastructure for manipulating and accessing the resources provided by these devices.

The experience has proven that this approach is very effective: our system has been built on top of reusable components (i.e., the Web Browser and the transparent proxy implemented using by a Squid web caching proxy, and a 20 lines PHP script for URI redirection), an *Environment Manager* that consists of less than 500 lines of code and a simple 10 lines Ruby script for implementing the MP3 Player proxy.

Of course our system is very limited at the moment, even when compared to the more advanced CoolTown one; however, it is already good enough for a simple Ambient Computing environment.

The future work will consist in experimenting in two directions: by integrating other Web technologies and standards in this "base system", and to investigate how the Web Platform could be extended in order to meet the additional requirements that are peculiar of Ambient Computing environments. The aim is to build a service-oriented middleware that is based on the principles described in Fielding (2000) and that will be inter-operable with the existing and widely deployed Web Platform.

REFERENCES

W3C HTML Working Group. (2002). *XHTML 1.0 the extensible hypertext markup language* (2nd ed.). Retrieved December 13, 2008, from http://www.w3.org/TR/2002/REC-xhtml1-20020801

Berners-Lee, T., Fielding, R., & Masinter, L. (1998). *Uniform resource identifiers (URI): Generic syntax.* Retrieved December 13, 2008, from http://www.ietf.org/rfc/rfc2396.txt

Bray, T., Paoli, J., Sperberg-McQueen, C. M., Maler, E., & Yergeau, F. (2006). *Extensible markup language (XML) 1.0* (4th ed.). Retrieved December 13, 2008, from http://www.w3.org/TR/2006/REC- xml- 20060816

Droms, R. (1997). *Dynamic host configuration protocol.* Retrieved December 13, 2008, from http://www.ietf.org/rfc/rfc2131.txt

ECMA International. (1999). *ECMAScript language specification.* Retrieved December 13, 2008, from http://www.ecma-international.org/publications /standards/Ecma-262.htm

Edwards, W. K., Newman, M. W., & Sedivy, J. Z. (2001). *The case for recombinant computing* (Tech. Rep.). Retrieved from http://www.parc.com/research/projects/obje

Fielding, R. (2002). *Architectural Styles and the Design of Network-based Software Architectures.* Unpublished doctoral dissertation, University of California, Irvine, CA.

Fielding, R., Gettys, J., Mogul, J., Frystyk, H., Masinter, L., Leach, P., & Berners-Lee, T. (1999). *Hypertext transfer protocol – HTTP/1.1.* Retrieved December 13, 2008, from http://www.ietf.org/rfc/ rfc2616.txt

Goland, Y. Y., Cai, T., Leach, P., Gu, Y., & Albright, S. (1999). *Simple service discovery protocol/1.0: Operating without an arbiter.* Retrieved from http://www.upnp.org/ draft_cai_ssdp_v1_03.txt

Google Inc. (2008a). *Google Web Toolkit.* Retrieved December 13, 2008, from http://code.google.com/webtoolkit

Google Inc. (2008b). *Google I/O.* Retrieved December 13, 2008, from http://code.google.com/events/io/

Gregorio, J., Hadley, M., Nottingham, M., & Orchard, D. (2008). *Uri template.* Retrieved December 13, 2008, from http://tools.ietf.org/html/draft-gregorio-uritemplate-03

Guttman, E., Perkins, C., Veizades, J., & Day, M. (1999). *Service location protocol, version 2.* Retrieved December 13, 2008, from http://www.ietf.org/rfc/rfc2165.txt

IANA. (2008). *Internet Assigned Numbers Authority: MIME media types.* Retrieved December 13, 2008, from http://www.iana.org/assignments/media-types

Kindberg, T., & Barton, J. (2001). A web-based nomadic computing system. *Computer Networks, 35*(4), 443–456.. doi:10.1016/S1389-1286(00)00181-X

Richardson, L., & Ruby, S. (2007). *RestFul Web Services.* New York: O'Reilly.

Román, M., Hess, C. K., Cerqueira, R., Ranganathan, A., Campbell, R. H., & Nahrstedt, K. (2002). Gaia: A Middleware Infrastructure to Enable Active Spaces. *IEEE Pervasive Computing / IEEE Computer Society* and *IEEE Communications Society,* 74–83. doi:10.1109/MPRV.2002.1158281

Ruby, S., Thomas, D., & Hansson, D. H. (2008). *Agile Web Development with Rails* (3rd ed.). Pragmatic Programmers.

Satyanarayanan, M. (2001). Pervasive computing: vision and challenges. *IEEE Personal Communications, 8*(4), 10–17.. doi:10.1109/98.943998

Sun Microsystems. (2008). *Java SE technologies at a glance.* Retrieved December 13, 2008, from http://java.sun.com/ javase/technologies/

This work was previously published in International Journal of Ambient Computing and Intelligence, Volume 2, Issue 4, edited by Kevin Curran, pp. 33-43, copyright 2010 by IGI Publishing (an imprint of IGI Global).

Chapter 19
Reducing Blocking Risks of Atomic Transactions in MANETs Using a Backup Coordinator

Joos-Hendrik Böse
International Computer Science Institute Berkeley, USA

Jürgen Broß
Freie Universität Berlin, Germany

ABSTRACT

In this paper, the authors present a probabilistic model to evaluate the reliability of the atomic commit for distributed transactions in mobile ad-hoc networks (MANETs). This model covers arbitrary MANET scenarios as well as strict and semantic transaction models. The authors evaluate the approach to integrate a backup coordinator to reduce blocking risks. For the purpose of showing an example of a MANET scenario, the authors illustrate how the considered blocking probability is very low.

1. INTRODUCTION

To provide for robustness and reliability of applications deployed to volatile environments such as MANETs, transaction processing is a key concept. Atomic transactions guarantee consistency of data and system states. Our belief is that MANETs are a fundamental building block of ambient computing environments. Several types of applications in ambient computing environments demand for atomicity guarantees, e.g., trading applications require money and goods atomicity when virtual goods, for example a music file, are exchanged for virtual money with persons nearby. Guaranteeing atomicity of such a distributed transaction requires agreement among transaction participants on the outcome of the transaction. This is typically achieved by an atomic commit protocol (ACP). It is generally known that in the presence of node or communication failures such protocols cannot avoid blocking (Skeen & Stonebraker, 1983). While in fixed networks such situations are rare

DOI: 10.4018/978-1-4666-0038-6.ch019

Copyright © 2012, IGI Global. Copying or distributing in print or electronic forms without written permission of IGI Global is prohibited.

due to low probabilities of site and communication failures, ambient computing scenarios are a more challenging environment.

Generally, a blocking situation arises when participants can no longer terminate their transaction branch independently, but are forced to wait until they can learn about the global transaction decision. Compared to ACPs tailored to MANETs like (Böse et al., 2005; Gruenwald & Banik, 2001), the use of a backup coordinator (BC) (Reddy & Kitsuregawa, 1998) is a more lightweight strategy to compensate for blocking. However, it is unclear whether the use of a BC is generally beneficial in a MANET scenario, as it introduces an additional source of failure. In this article we provide an in-depth analysis of the BC scheme for MANETs. We present a calculation model to answer the question whether blocking is a relevant problem in a specific MANET and transaction scenario and thus may require use of a BC. Additionally, the model then allows predicting to which degree blocking is reduced.

The remainder of this article is structured as follows: Section 2 introduces our system and failure model as well as the strict and semantic transaction model used within later sections. For both transaction models the integration of a backup coordinator is described. Section 3 presents an example MANET scenario and derives node and communication failure probabilities for this scenario. In Section 4 we describe a calculation model to estimate the risk of blocking situation caused by a node failure of the transaction coordinator and enhance the model to estimate the reduction of this risk if a backup coordinator is used in strict and semantic transaction models. Finally, Section 5 summarizes and concludes the article.

2. SYSTEM AND TRANSACTION MODEL

2.1 System and Failure Model

A MANET A is established between nodes located in a specific area. Due to node and communication failures, we do not assume that A is fully connected. For each node a chance exists to completely leave the area and thus to disconnect from A. We describe the probability for this event to happen until time t by the cumulative distribution function (cdf) $FL(t)$. We assume that a multi-hop routing protocol, such as AODV or DSDV, is used. Although message delays in A depend on the hop count of communication paths, for sake of simplicity, we assume an average message delay δm for all messages.

Communication characteristics of A are captured by the cdf $Fc(t)$, describing the probability that a communication path breaks until time t. In the following we refer to this time as *path duration*. The according probability density function (pdf) is denoted by $fc(t)$. Note that in this article we do not consider the case that a link may recover. In addition to communication failures, a node may suffer from exhausted energy resources or general technical failures. For these events we assume cdfs $FE(t)$ and $FT(t)$. Given the assumptions above, the proposed probabilistic failure model covers the following two types of failures:

Node Failures denote all events that cause a node to disconnect from A. Hence, $FN(t)$, the cdf of a node failure until time t, is given by the probability that a node leaves A, exhibits exhausted energy resources or suffers from a technical failure until t. $FN(t)$ is calculated by considering complementary probabilities:

$$FN(t) = 1 - ((1 - FL(t))(1 - FE(t))(1 - FT(t))).$$

Communication Failures cause the break of a communication path that was functional before. The failure of the link is induced by mobility or by node failures of relaying nodes. The cdf for a communication failure is denoted by $Fc(t)$. We show in Section 3 that $Fc(t)$ depends on the initial hop distance of communication partners.

By $F(t)$ we denote the cdf for the general failure that either a communication or a node failure occurs until t.

2.2 Distributed Transaction Models

The basic model we consider is the flat ACID transaction model. We assume that ACID is guaranteed locally on every node and transactions are only aborted due to node or communication failures. Following the X/Open DTP model (X/Open, 1996) a transaction consists of a set of operations that are issued by an *application*. All operations received by a *participant* constitute a local transaction branch of the global transaction. To avoid the need for initially choosing a *coordinator*, we assume that the application process and the transaction coordinator are co-located. In order to detect node and communication failures each execution of an operation is acknowledged by the participant. If an acknowledgment is not received during timeout Δop, the transaction is globally aborted.

We distinguish between *processing* and *decision phase* of a distributed transaction. The processing phase begins at time *ts*, when the transaction is initiated and ends at time *tp*, when the acknowledgment of the last operation of the global transaction is received by the coordinator.

A participant i receives the last operation of its transaction branch at some random time *to*. For each participant, the random variable *to* is distributed within the interval $[ts, tp]$ according to the cdf $O(to)$. Here, we assume $O(to)$ to be uniformly distributed. If no failure is detected during $[ts, tp]$, the decision phase is initiated by starting an ACP at time *tp*. The strict and semantic transaction models are based on this general model.

2.2.1 Strict Transaction Model

The strict transaction model requires that *strict atomicity* as for example defined in (Bernstein et al., 1987) is guaranteed. We assume that this is achieved by the use of the well-known two-phase commit protocol (2PC) (X/Open, 1996). Due to its popularity, we omit a detailed presentation of the protocol here.

Blocking Risk with Strict Atomicity

In 2PC a participant enters its so called *window of uncertainty* if it answers a commit-request of the coordinator with a positive vote. During this period the participant cannot autonomously proceed until it learns the global decision (i.e., it is blocked).

The decision phase begins at time *tp* (i.e., the ACP is started at *tp*). In fact, we assume that all *commit-request* messages are sent at *tp*. The coordinator awaits a timeout of Δvo for the participant's votes. Hence, the length of the critical window ΔU, when a participant is vulnerable to a coordinator's node failure, is at minimum $\Delta Umin = 2\delta m$ and at maximum $\Delta Umax = 2\delta m + \Delta vo$. In case that no undetected participant failure has occurred, ΔU has length $\Delta Umin$. Otherwise the coordinator has to await timeout Δvo, so that ΔU increases to $\Delta Umax$.

In the following we discuss how a BC can be integrated into 2PC. We present the basic idea and the additional blocking risk that is introduced by the use of a BC. For a more detailed description we refer to (Reddy & Kitsuregawa, 1998).

Integration of a Backup Coordinator

The *BC* is integrated into 2PC between *commit-request* and *commit* phase. If the main coordinator (*MC*) learns that all participants voted *yes*, it sends a *decided_commit* message to the BC. The *BC* saves the decision to stable log and acknowledges with a *recorded_commit* message. Then the *MC* initiates the commit phase of 2PC. If the *MC* learns that the transaction needs to be aborted, it directly informs the participants without contacting the *BC*. The *BC* possesses a veto right to abort the transaction until it writes a commit decision to its log. In case a participant is blocked, it contacts the *BC*. Depending on its local state, the *BC* either answers with a *commit* message or makes use of its veto right and aborts the transaction. If the *BC* has aborted the transaction it answers the *decided_commit* request of the *MC* with an *aborted* message. In effect transaction commit requires both coordinators, while the decision to abort a transaction can be made autonomously by one of the coordinators.

The added redundancy of coordinators is assumed to lower the risk of blocking due to a node failure, but it also introduces a new blocking situation: By issuing a *decided_commit* message, the *MC* hands over transaction control to the *BC*. Until a *recorded_decision* or *aborted* message is received, the *MC* remains uncertain and cannot conclude the transaction. To reduce this risk, the *MC* may perform a *reachability test* at *tp* by pinging the *BC* before issuing a *decided_commit* message. If it is unsuccessful, the transaction is aborted.

We distinguish between *early* and *late selection* of the *BC*. In *early selection*, the *BC* is chosen with transaction initiation, while with the *late selection* it is chosen right before *tp* and participants learn about the *BC* with the commit-request messages of the coordinator. In either case, participants know about the *BC before* they become uncertain. A reachability test is only required in case of early *BC* selection.

2.2.2 Semantic Transaction Model

In the semantic model a local transaction branch is committed as soon its last operation is successfully processed. This weaker atomicity notion called *semantic atomicity* (Korth et al., 1990) is maintained by means of compensating transactions, which semantically undo the effects of an already committed branch. An associated compensation transaction has to be executed in the case that a local commit conflicts with the global decision.

Hence, as long as a participant is uncertain about the global decision it has to maintain conditions that allow for compensation. A general problem here is that effects of the committed branch are visible to other transactions and compensation must consider these so called *dependent transactions*, e.g., the correctness criterion *soundness* introduced in (Korth et al., 1990) may require dependent transaction to be rejected, thus hindering the overall progress. Another negative effect is that uncertainty about the global decision possibly leads to non-optimal behavior. For instance, in trading applications, a participant that is uncertain about the global decision cannot use money or goods affected by the transaction in doubt, in other transactions.

Blocking Risk with Semantic Atomicity

Within the semantic model, processing and decision phase are not strictly separable: While in strict atomicity ΔU is the same for all participants, with semantic atomicity ΔU is individual for each participant. This is due to the fact that a participant *i* commits its local transaction branch right after successfully executing its last operation at time *to*, moving into uncertainty afterward. We assume that participants know which operation is the last one. The ack of this operation is an implicit *yes* vote to the coordinator. The coordinator later derives the global decision, without requiring an additional vote from this participant. In this model we define that the processing phase ends at *t'p*, which is the time the coordinator sends the last operation to the last participant denoted by *PAlast*. The coordinator derives the global decision at

$$tu = t'p + 2\delta m + \Delta ex,$$ where Δex is a constant time required by *PAlast* for the execution of the last operation.

The size of the uncertainty window is generally wider with semantic atomicity. If no participant failure occurs, the individual uncertainty period begins at $ti0$ and ends with $tu + \delta m$. If a participant failure is detected at tf, two cases have to be distinguished: In case $ti0 \leq tf$, the phase of uncertainty is described by the interval $[ti0, tf + \delta m]$. For $ti0 > tf$ the participant is never uncertain, as it receives the coordinator's decision before moving into uncertainty (abort during processing phase). In semantic atomicity a participant does not block as in strict atomicity. Analogous to blocking in strict atomicity, we denote this situation as *extended uncertainty*.

Note that semantic atomicity only allows for early selection of the *BC*, as no explicit commit-request messages are sent.

3. FAILURE PROBABILITIES IN MANETS

While for the calculation model presented in Section 4 it is non-relevant how failure probabilities are derived, the main intention of this section is to prove that derivation of the probabilities assumed in the system model is generally possible for MANETs.

We demonstrate their derivation for an example MANET scenario. In this scenario we assume that 15 mobile nodes move within a city area of 500*500m according to the Random Waypoint (RWP) mobility model at 2.0–5.0mps, relaying messages for each other using AODV. Mobile nodes are assumed to be equipped with 802.11a compliant radio adapters providing a transmission range of approx. 100m. Nodes use an electronic currency to trade electronic goods such as mp3 files. The exchange of goods and money has to happen in an atomic manner to ensure fairness: either both money and good are exchanged or nothing at all. Batteries of nodes are assumed to deliver 2h of service, while each node is expected to remain within the area for 30min before moving away. While the RWP model does not consider nodes to leave the MANET area, this behavior is described using the Area Graph-based mobility model (Bittner et al., 2005). However, nodes are expected to enter and leave the MANET at the same rate resulting in a constant number of nodes connected to the MANET. The mean time to failure due to a technical failure is assumed to be 500h.

It has been observed that the path duration (described by $Fc(t)$) is mainly influenced by the hop distance of nodes at transaction start (called *initial hop distance* (ihd)). We distinguish between ihd>2 (*case 2+ ihd*) and ≤ 2 (*case 1-2 ihd*), because resulting path durations mainly influences the probability of transaction abort (Böse, 2008).

3.1 Probability of Node Failures

Node failures cause a disconnection of a node from the MANET. In our example MANET setting a node's battery capacity is expected to hold for 2h and a technical failure is expected after 500h. Hence, $FE(t)$ describing the remaining battery capacity of a random node is uniformly distributed in $[1s, 7200s]$. The probability for technical failures $FT(t)$ is assumed to be exponentially distributed with $\lambda T = 1/18 \cdot 10^5$. The distribution of *sojourn times* $FL(t)$ depends on the individual node behavior. For simplicity we assume an exponential distribution, here with parameter $\lambda L = 1/1800$, as the expected sojourn time is 0.5h. The derived probability for a node failure is low for small periods, e.g., $FN(10s) = 0.0069$. Communication failures are more likely in the scenario, as shown in the following.

3.2 Probability of Communication Failures

The cdf $Fc(t)$ is primarily influenced by *node density*, *radio range*, *node mobility*, and *routing scheme* of the given MANET scenario. $Fc(t)$ additionally depends on the hop count of the path at initiation time. Due to the complexity in modeling the numerous dependent events, most scholars propose a statistical analysis of this problem, e.g., in (Sadagopan et al., 2003; Bai et al., 2003) it is shown that for the common mobility models RWP, Manhattan and Freeway mobility the path duration in case 2+ ihd can be approximated by exponential distributions. In contrast to the work cited above, we explicitly address case 1-2 ihd. To derive $Fc(t)$ for both cases in our example MANET setting we did a simulation study using the ns2 network simulator and a statistical analysis of its results.

The results of (Sadagopan et al., 2003; Bai et al., 2003) towards path durations for case 2+ ihd could be confirmed by fitting an exponential distribution with $\lambda=0.051$ to the measured data. However, for case 1-2 ihd path durations are better fit by a log-normal distribution, here with $\mu=3.53$ and $\sigma=0.67$. Thus, the important observation is that short after link initiation, for case 1-2 ihd a communication failure is unlikely, whereas exponentially distributed path durations always show the same failure rate. As average message delay δm we measured 180ms in the example scenario. We refer to our technical report (Böse, 2008) for a detailed description of the simulation study.

4. CALCULATION MODEL AND RESULTS

In this section, we derive a calculation model that allows estimating blocking probabilities that are caused by a node failure of the coordinator. The formulae we present have to be interpreted from a participant's perspective, i.e. they describe the probability for an individual participant to block. The individual participant is denoted by PA, the set of the other n-1 participants is denoted by $PAother$.

4.1 Preliminary Considerations

In many cases we calculate the probability that an event happens during an interval $[t1, t2]$. In the following we use the notation $F(t1..t2)$ for this probability (with F being a probability distribu-

tion function). We generally neglect events that occur in intervals $[t1, t2]$ of size $\leq \delta m$.

An important factor is the probability that a transaction enters the decision phase. The decision phase is not entered, if the transaction is aborted before, because the coordinator detects a participant's failure. A participant's failure is only detected if it occurs in $[ts, to]$, since then the coordinator would observe a missing ack. The probability $Po{>}f(tp)$ denotes that a participant's failure is detected within interval $[ts, tp]$ and is given by $P_{o>f}(t_p) = \int_0^{t_p} \int_0^{t_o} o(t_o)f(t_f)dt_f dt_o$ (with $ts=0$). The subscript $o{>}f$ indicates that this probability only considers failures that happen before acknowledgment of the last operation. Analogous the probability that a failure is not detected, is calculated by $P_{o<f}(t_p) = \int_0^{t_p} \int_{t_o}^{t_p} o(t_o)f(t_f)dt_f dt_o$.

4.2 Strict Atomicity

In the following we derive the blocking probability with and without use of a BC. For lack of space, the calculations of blocking risk with a single coordinator are described only briefly. A more detailed description is presented in (Böse & Broß, 2008; Böse 2008).

The basic idea to derive the blocking risk with a single coordinator (denoted $Pu(tp)$) is to calculate the probability that an uncertainty window either of size $\Delta Umax$ or $\Delta Umin$ is entered (the probabilities are called $PUmax(tp)$ and $PUmin(tp)$ respectively) and that the coordinator experiences a node failure during this period. For a transaction with n participants $PUmax(tp)$ is given by

$$P_{U\max}(t_p) = (1 - P_{o<f}(t_p))^{n-1} - (1 - F(t_p))^{n-1},$$

while $P_{U\min}(t_p) = (1 - F(t_p))^{n-1}$. We denote the probability of a coordinator's node failure within interval [*tp*, *tp*+Δ*Umin*] by *CUmin(tp)*. It is given by *Fn(tp..tp*+Δ*Umin)*. *CUmax(tp)* is defined analogously. The probability that *PA* does not encounter any failure until *tp*+Δ*Umin*, given by 1−*F(tp*+Δ*Umin)*, is denoted by *PAUmin(tp)*. Analogously we define *PAUmax(tp)*. Blocking occurs, if the coordinator suffers from a node failure during Δ*U*.

4.2.1 Backup Coordinator with Early Selection

Here, the BC is chosen at *ts* as a node that lies within 1-2 hop distance from all participants and the coordinator. A reachability test is executed as described in Subsection 2.2. We distinguish between standard blocking situations due to a coordinator failure and the additional situation where the MC is alive, but blocked. Four cases may lead to a standard blocking situation:

At least one unrecognized failure of a node in *PAother* occurred until *tp*. Then *PA* is blocked if MC and BC are unreachable at recovery time (the last point in time the global decision can arrive: *tp*+Δ*Umax*). As MC must have survived until *tp*, only a node failure within [*tp, tp*+Δ*Umax*] needs to be considered. The link between BC and *PA* may have been broken within [*ts, tp*+Δ*Umax*]. Then *BC1(tp)* describes the probability that *PA* blocks:

$$BC1(t_p) = P_{U\max}(t_p) \cdot C_{U\max}(t_p) \cdot F(t_p + \Delta U_{\max}) \quad (1)$$

2. No node in *PAother* fails, but BC encounters a communication failure with MC until *tp*. In this case the reachability test fails and MC decides on abort at *tp*+Δ*Umax*. Participant *PA* is blocked if MC fails in

[*tp, tp*+Δ*Umax*] and additionally, BC fails within [*tp, tp*+Δ*Umax*] or its link to *PA* brakes in [*ts, tp*+Δ*Umax*]. This probability is given by:

$$BC2(t_p) = (1 - F(t_p))^{n-1} \cdot F_C(t_p) \cdot C_{U\max}(t_p) \\ \cdot \left[F_n(t_p..t_p + \Delta U_{\max}) + F_C(t_p + \Delta U_{\max}) \right] \quad (2)$$

No node in *PAother* fails, but BC encounters a node failure until *tp*. Again, the reachability test fails and the transaction is aborted. A node failure of MC leads to blocking of *PA*, as the BC has already failed and is not reachable:

$$BC3(t_p) = (1 - F(t_p))^{n-1} \cdot F_n(t_p) \cdot C_{U\max}(t_p) \quad (3)$$

Neither a node in *PAother* nor the BC fails until *tp*. A coordinator's node failure in [*tp, tp*+2δ*m*] leads to a blocking situation in the case that also BC has suffered from a failure in this interval given by *BC4(tp)*:

$$BC4(t_p) = (1 - F(t_p))^{n-1} \cdot F_n(t_p..t_p + 2\delta_m) \quad (4)$$

The MC is blocked, if the *recorded_decision* message of the BC is awaited, but not received. A presumption for this to happen is that no failure of any node has occurred until *tp*. We distinguish two cases that actually lead to blocking of the MC. In the first case *A*, the BC encounters a node failure after sending the ack of the reachability test and before sending its *recorded_decision* message ([*tp*+δ*m, tp*+3δ*m*]). Then, the MC gets blocked and the BC is not reachable for *PA*. In case *B*, the BC suffers from a communication failure with MC in [*tp*+2δ*m, tp*+4δ*m*]. If additionally the communication link between BC and *PA* breaks until *tp*+Δ*Umax*, MC is blocked and *PA* cannot reach BC. Since *A* and *B* are not independent, probability has to be computed as *P(A)+P(B)-P(A)*P(B)*:

$$BC5(t_p) = (1 - F(t_p))^{n-1} \cdot (1 - F_n(t_p + \Delta U_{\max})) \\ \cdot \Big[F_n(t_p + \delta_m..t_p + 3\delta_m) + F_C(t_p + 2\delta_m..t_p + 4\delta_m) \\ \cdot F_C(t_p + \Delta U_{\max}) - F_n(t_p + \delta_m..t_p + 3\delta_m) \\ \cdot F_C(t_p + 2\delta_m..t_p + 4\delta_m) \cdot F_C(t_p + \Delta U_{\max}) \Big] \quad (5)$$

The probability of blocking with early selection of a BC is then given by:

$$P_{u,BCe}(t_p) = PA_{U\max}(t_p) \cdot$$
$$\left[BC1(t_p) + BC2(t_p) + BC3(t_p) \right.$$
$$\left. +BC5(t_p) \right] + PA_{U\min}(t_p) \cdot BC4(t_p)$$
$$(6)$$

4.2.2 Backup Coordinator with Late Selection

Here, the BC is chosen at *tp*, thus a working communication path is now required to last for ΔU only. The increased probability that BC and *PA* can communicate has the greatest influence on the end result. The computation of the blocking probability is analogous to 4.2.1. Cases (ii) and (iii) from above are not considered, as the BC is guaranteed to be available at *tp*. In the other formulae, intervals have to be adjusted, as no reachability test is executed. Line (1) of the following formula considers case (i) from above, line (2) considers case (iv) and line (3–4) describe the situation when MC is blocked:

$$P_{u,BCl}(t_p) = PA_{U\max} \cdot P_{U\max}(t_p) \cdot C_{U\max}(t_p) \cdot F(\Delta U_{\max})$$
$$+ PA_{U\min} \cdot P_{U\min}(t_p) \cdot F_n(t_p \ldotp \Delta U_{\min})$$
$$+ PA_{U\max} \cdot \left[F_n(2\delta_m) + F_C(2\delta_m) \cdot F_C(4\delta_m) \right.$$
$$\left. -F_n(2\delta_m) \cdot F_C(2\delta_m) \cdot F_C(4\delta_m) \right]$$
$$(7)$$

Figure 1(a) compares the blocking probabilities as computed by *Pu(tp)*, *Pu,BCe(tp)* and *PuBCl(tp)* for our example scenario with *n*=3 and Δvo=1s. We assume only transactions with 1–2 ihd (all *Fc(t)* are log-normal distributed), as the abort rate for 2+ ihd is unacceptable (Böse 2008). The important observation is that the risk of blocking caused by a coordinator's node failure is generally low in our scenario (*Pu(tp)*<0.0003). The scheme with early BC selection (*Pu,BCe(tp)*) shows to be

even more susceptible for blocking than a single coordinator. Only for very short transactions with *tp*<9s a reduction of the blocking risk is observed. However, this reduction is explained by an increased abort rate caused by unsuccessful reachability tests. For *tp*>9s the risk of the additional blocking situations overcompensates the benefit of the increased coordinators availability. In case late integration of the BC is used, the blocking risk is significantly reduced for 5s<*tp*<60s compared to a single coordinator.

4.3 Semantic Atomicity

We examine the probability of extended uncertainty from the perspective of *PA* that is not *PAlast*. The probability of *PA* to suffer from extended uncertainty due to a node failure of the (single) coordinator is called *P'u(t'p)*. For lack of space we omit a detailed description of how *P'u(t'p)* is derived and refer to (Böse & Broß, 2008; Böse, 2008).

4.3.1 Backup Coordinator with Early Selection

Extended uncertainty caused in [*ts*, *t'p*] can be healed by the BC if it is reachable for *PA* at *tu*+δm. For this event the probability is given by:

$$BC'1(t'_p) = P'_u(t'_p) \cdot F(t_u + \delta_m)$$
$$(8)$$

In [*t'p*, *tu*], the reachability test has to be taken into account. The MC checks reachability of BC at *t'p*. An answer is awaited until *t'p*+2δm+Δex. Thus, at *tu* MC knows the global decision as well if the reachability test was successful. To derive the desired probability for interval [*t'p*, *tu*], multiple situations for both outcomes of the reachability test must be considered. Like in Subsection 4.2.1 we distinguish between standard extended uncertainty and the situation where the MC is reachable but blocked. We first consider the standard cases:

Figure 1. Probability of blocking caused by a node failures of the coordinator

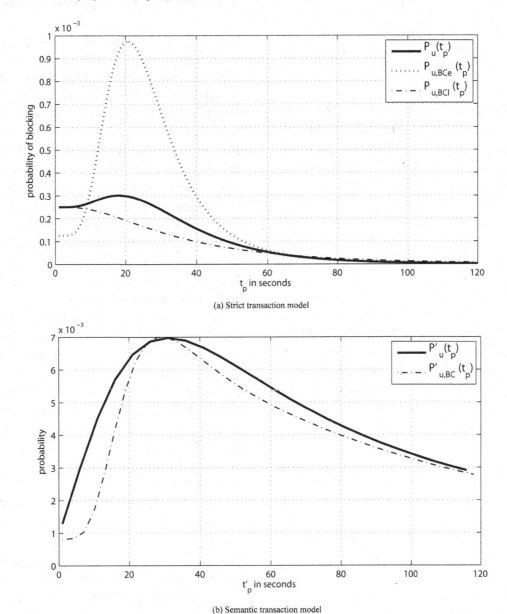

(a) Strict transaction model

(b) Semantic transaction model

If the reachability test fails, because the BC suffers from a node failure during $[ts, t'p+\delta m]$, *PA* remains uncertain if the MC suffers from a node failure in interval $[t'p, tu+\delta m]$:

$$BC'2(t'_p) = (1 - P_{o>f}(t'_p))^{n-1} \cdot F_n(t'_p + 2\delta_m) \cdot F_n(t'_p..t_u + \delta_m) \qquad (9)$$

In case the reachability test fails due to a communication failure in $[ts, t'p+2\delta m]$, *PA* remains uncertain if MC suffers from a node failure in interval $[t'p, tu+\delta m]$ and the BC is not reachable due to a node failure of BC in $[t'p, tu+\delta m]$ or a communication failure in $[ts, tu+2\delta m]$:

$$BC'3(t_p') = (1 - P_{o>f}(t_p'))^{n-1} \cdot$$
$$F_n(t_p' + \delta_m) \cdot F_n(t_p'..t_u + \delta_m)$$
$$\cdot \left[F_n(t_p'..t_u + \delta_m) + F_C(t_u + 2\delta_m) \right]$$

$$(10)$$

3. If no failure occurs until *t'p*, *PA* remains uncertain, if MC suffers from a node failure in [*t'p, tu*] and the BC is not reachable because of a node failure in [*t'p, tu*] or a communication failure with *PA* in [*ts, tu+2δm*]:

$$BC'4(t_p') = (1 - P_{o>f}(t_p'))^{n-1} \cdot$$
$$F_n(t_p'..t_u) \cdot \left[F_n(t_p'..t_u) + F_C(t_u + \delta_m) \right]$$

$$(11)$$

The situation, when *PA* remains uncertain although it can reach the MC, but the MC is blocked is derived by similar considerations that led to Formula (5) with different interval bounds. For lack of space we omit a detailed discussion of the derived Formula *BC'5(t'p)* here.

$$BC'5(t_p') = (1 - P_{o>f}(t_p'))^{n-1} \cdot$$
$$\left[F_n(t_p' + \delta_m..t_u) + F_C(t_p' + 2\delta_m..t_u) \right.$$
$$\cdot F_C(t_u) - F_n(t_p' + \delta_m..t_u) \cdot F_C(t_p' + 2\delta_m..t_u) \cdot F_C(t_u) \right]$$

$$(12)$$

The probability for *PA* to remain uncertain if a BC is used is now given by:

$$P_{u,BC}'(t_p') = BC'1(t_p') + (1 - F(t_u)) \cdot$$
$$\left[BC'2(t_p') + BC'3(t_p') + BC'4(t_p') + BC'5(t_p') \right]$$

$$(13)$$

Figure 1(b) plots the reduction of blocking risk achieved by a BC in the semantic model. For the example scenario of this work, a BC only slightly reduces blocking risks. Like in Subsection 4.2, a log-normal cdf for all *Fc(t'p)* is assumed.

5. SUMMARY AND CONCLUSION

In this article we presented an in-depth analysis of the use of a BC in MANETs. We developed a probabilistic model to predict the expected reduction of blocking risk in case a BC is used. Using the proposed model, we demonstrated the benefit of BC integration in transaction processing for an example MANET scenario. It showed that the time of BC selection is critical. In the strict model only late selection of the BC leads to a reduction of blocking risk, while early selection even increases blocking probability. In the semantic model the risk for blocking is generally higher, as uncertainty periods of participants are larger. Here, a BC reduces the blocking risk only slightly for the example scenario.

We argue that for strict transactions early selection of a BC is generally not feasible, while for semantic transactions such a general statement cannot be made. The provided calculation allows identifying critical scenarios, where the blocking risk reaches considerably high values and the use of a recovery strategy such as a BC is indicated. However, we argue that for most standard MANET scenarios the discussed blocking risk is low and negligible for most applications.

The calculation model presented is especially important as it showed that integration of a BC is not necessarily beneficial in every situation, but may increase blocking risks. In addition, our probabilistic model allows for easy integration of individual failure probabilities of BCs, i.e., using especially reliable BCs can be considered for scenarios where a base station can be used as BC.

While in this article we did not presented any simulation results supporting the calculation model presented, we refer to (Böse, Broß, & Schweppe, 2008) for ns2 simulation results supporting the abstractions made by our system and failure model.

REFERENCES

Bai, F., Sadagopan, N., & Helmy, A. (2003). *Important: a framework to systematically analyze the impact of mobility on performance of routing protocols for ad hoc networks.*

Bernstein, P. A., Hadzilacos, V., & Goodman, N. (1987). *Concurrency control and recovery in database systems.* Boston: Addison-Wesley Longman Publishing Co.

Bittner, S., Raffel, W.-U., & Scholz, M. (2005). The area graph-based mobility model and its impact on data dissemination. In *Proceedings of the 3rd IEEE international conference on pervasive computing and communication workshops (PERCOMW '05)* (pp. 268-272).

Böse, J.-H. (2008). *Abort and blocking risk of atomic transactions in mobile ad-hoc networks* (Tech. Rep. No. B-08-07). Berlin: Freie Universität Berlin. Retrieved from ftp://ftp.inf.fu-berlin.de/pub/reports/tr-b-08-7.pdf

Böse, J.-H., Böttcher, S., Gruenwald, L., Obermeier, S., Schweppe, H., & Steenweg, T. (2005). An integrated commit protocol for mobile network databases. In *Proceedings of the 9th International Database Engineering & Application Symposium (IDEAS'05)* (pp. 244-250). Washington, DC: IEEE Computer Society.

Böse, J.-H., & Broß, J. (2008). Predicting the blocking risk of atomic transactions in manets induced by coordinator failures. In *Proceedings of the IADIS International Conference Wireless Applications and Computing.*

Böse, J.-H., Broß, J., & Schweppe, H. (2008). A probabilistic model for blocking risks of atomic transactions in p2p networks. In *Proceedings of the International Workshop on Databases, Information Systems, and Peer-to-Peer Computing (DBISP2P)*, Auckland, New Zealand.

Gruenwald, L., & Banik, S. (2001). *A power-aware technique to manage realtime database transactions in mobile ad-hoc networks.*

Korth, H. F., Levy, E., & Silberschatz, A. (1990). A formal approach to recovery by compensating transactions. In D. McLeod, R. Sacks-Davis, & H.-J. Schek (Eds.), *Proceedings of the 16th International Conference on Very Large Data Bases* (pp. 95-106). San Francisco, CA: Morgan Kaufmann.

Reddy, P., & Kitsuregawa, M. (1998). Reducing the Blocking in Two-Phase Commit Protocol Employing Backup Sites. In *Proceedings of the 3rd IFCIS International Conference on Cooperative Information Systems* (pp. 406-416).

Sadagopan, N., Bai, F., Krishnamachari, B., & Helmy, A. (2003). *Paths: analysis of path duration statistics and their impact on reactive manet routing protocols.*

Skeen, D., & Stonebraker, M. (1983). A formal model of crash recovery in a distributed system. *IEEE Transactions on Software Engineering, 9*(3), 219–228. .doi:10.1109/TSE.1983.236608

X/Open. (1996). *Distributed transaction processing: Reference model* (version 3). Retrieved from http://www.opengroup.org/bookstore /catalog/ g504.htm

This work was previously published in International Journal of Ambient Computing and Intelligence, Volume 2, Issue 4, edited by Kevin Curran, pp. 44-54, copyright 2010 by IGI Publishing (an imprint of IGI Global).

Chapter 20
Schedule–Aware Transactions for Ambient Intelligence Environments

Vasileios Fotopoulos
University of Ioannina, Greece

Apostolos V. Zarras
University of Ioannina, Greece

Panos Vassiliadis
University of Ioannina, Greece

ABSTRACT

In this paper, the authors investigate the concept of designing user-centric transaction protocols toward achieving dependable coordination in AmI environments. As a proof-of-concept, this paper presents a protocol that takes into account the schedules of roaming users, which move from one AmI environment to another, avoiding abnormal termination of transactions when users leave an environment for a short time and return later. The authors compare the proposed schedule-aware protocol against a schedule-agnostic one. Findings show that the use of user-centric information in such situations is quite beneficial.

INTRODUCTION

The rapid emergence of novel technologies in the fields of mobile computing and networking fostered the transition from conventional distributed systems to mobile computing systems that consist of fixed and mobile devices (such as PDAs, Pocket PCs, smart-phones), which collaborate through wireless networking infrastructures. Going one

DOI: 10.4018/978-1-4666-0038-6.ch020

step further, the vision of *Ambient Intelligence (AmI)* investigates the possibility of realizing mobile computing environments that are aware and responsive to the presence of people (Aarts, Harwig, & Schuurmans, 2003; Weber et al., 2003). AmI is based on Weiser's pioneer work on ubiquitous computing (Weiser, 1991), which evolved later on to the concept of pervasive computing. Pervasive computing aims at a digital world, consisting of interconnected electronic devices that support the quotidian activities of people. AmI is

Copyright © 2012, IGI Global. Copying or distributing in print or electronic forms without written permission of IGI Global is prohibited.

particularly concerned by the users' experience in such a digital world. In other words, AmI puts a specific focus on the users and targets the development of *user-centric digital environments* that account for the users' needs, habits and satisfaction, while offering support that allows them to perform their everyday activities.

The vision of AmI motivates research towards coordination protocols that involve both mobile and fixed entities. In this paper, we particularly investigate the need for designing *user-centric transaction protocols* to achieve dependable coordination in AmI environments. *User-centric information can be exploited while coordinating a set of transaction participants towards avoiding abnormal transaction terminations.*

In this context, we focus on the abnormal ending of a transaction that takes place within an AmI environment, due to the fact that *one or more participating users leave the environment.* Leaving the environment means that the users' devices are no longer reachable, via the networking infrastructure that supports the transaction coordination. The idea behind our approach is that *if there is a certain level of knowledge behind the schedule of each participating user (i.e., the way the user moves from one environment to another), then we can exploit it to avoid abnormal transaction terminations, where a roaming user leaves the environment for short, only to return later.*

Taking a simple example, consider a conference that takes place in a number of conference rooms. Several researchers attend a technical session in conference room A (i.e., environment A). In this situation, a number of colleagues want to arrange a meeting for dinner or work after the technical session. One of them browses, using his Pocket-PC, information regarding available meeting places. His goal is to book a place at a certain time and insert a dinner meeting in the agenda applications that execute on his colleagues' laptops or Pocket-PCs. Obviously, setting up the dinner meeting involves performing a distributed transaction amongst the mobile devices that host

the agenda applications. The transaction requires each participant's agenda application to execute a local transaction and verify that there are no other obligations of the participant at the meeting time. This task might take a certain amount of time to complete. Assume now that during this time period, one of the participants leaves the gathering before the transaction completes, because his talk starts at conference room B (i.e., environment B). In such a situation, typical transaction protocols would abort the transaction, wasting thus the energy resources that were spent up to this point. Nevertheless, the transaction may have a chance for successful completion if we consider that the colleagues shall reunite after the coffee break. Hence, if the transaction protocol could be enriched with such kind of user-centric information (i.e., the users schedules) and reason with respect to this information, all the work that has been performed for fixing the dinner meeting would not be wasted.

Based on the previous discussion, *the contribution of this paper consists of designing a schedule-aware protocol and comparing it against a schedule-agnostic one.* Specifically, in Section 2 we present the necessary background and state-of-the art for this paper. In Section 3 we detail the proposed protocol. In Section 4, we present our experimental results. Finally, in Section 5 we summarize our contribution and provide insights for future work.

1. RELATED WORK AND BACKGROUND

The overall idea of user-centric transaction protocols and the particular protocol discussed in this paper fall in the general field of mobile transactions (Pitoura & Samaras, 1998; Serano-Alvarado, Roncancio, & Adiba, 2004). Until now there have been various approaches for mobile transactions that can be classified with respect to the system model that they assume into 3 different categories

(Serano-Alvarado et al., 2004). In all of them the transaction initiator is a mobile host and the entities that comprise the data, processed during the transaction execution are fixed hosts. Moreover, Serano-Alvarado et al. (2004) further identified the following more generic execution models:

1. In the first system model, transactions are initiated by mobile hosts and they aim at processing data located on other mobile hosts.
2. The second system model is the most generic one, where the execution of mobile transactions is distributed amongst several mobile and fixed hosts.

A few years ago, the previous execution models were considered as too ambitious but interesting (Serano-Alvarado et al., 2004). Nowadays, these models fit perfectly to the case of AmI environments. Until now, some interesting approaches have been proposed for dealing with transactions in the context of the aforementioned execution models. For instance, Bobineau, Pucheral, and Abdallah (2000), proposed a one-phase commit protocol for transactions involving mobile and fixed hosts, where the voting phase is eliminated and the master announces its own decision to the transaction participants; the decision is taken based on the master's perception on the successful execution of the individual transaction steps. Kumar, Prabhu, Dunham, and Seydim (2002), proposed TCOT where the master employs timeouts towards deciding about the outcome of a particular transaction. Younas, Chao, Wang, and Huang (2007) dealt with mobile host disconnections in transactions that involve several mobile and fixed hosts by a protocol that discovers alternative mobile hosts that may replace the disconnected ones. Nouali, Doucet, and Drias (2005) proposed a protocol for transactions that span across several mobile hosts, which may move across different interconnected network cells. The main idea is to use participant-agents (i.e. proxies to participants

that move to different network cells) to provide relocation transparency and timeouts to handle participant disconnections. Alternatively, Le and Nygard (2005) proposed the use of a data sharing space. Finally, Böttcher, Gruenwald, and Obermeier (2006) discuss a protocol that aims at reducing aborts and blocking time. In this paper, we go one step further by investigating the issue of using user-centric information towards designing distributed transaction protocols for AmI environments.

The protocol that we investigate in this paper relies on the combination of two classical protocols: (a) the presume-abort 2-phase-commit protocol (Mohan, Lindsay, & Obermark, 1986) and (b) the strict 2-phase-locking protocol (Eswaran, Gray, Lorie, & Traiger, 1976).

In general, the execution of a transaction involves (1) an entity that initiates it (hereafter we use the term *master* to refer to the transaction initiator) and (2) entities that comprise data, processed during the transaction execution (hereafter we use the term *cohort* to refer to these entities). Typically, the transaction execution consists of an *initiation* state, during which the master invites the cohorts to participate in the transaction and the cohorts accept or deny the invitation. If all goes well, the *initiation* state is followed by an *executing* state, during which the master processes data that may be of his own, or of the participating cohorts. At the time when the master decides to complete the transaction, the presume-abort protocol takes place amongst the participants (see Figure 1). Briefly, the presume-abort protocol comprises the two phases of the classical 2-phase-commit protocol. During the first phase, the master of the transaction sends to all cohorts a PREPARE message. Upon the reception of this message the cohorts should respond with their votes concerning the outcome of the transaction. The voting messages may be either to commit or to abort the transaction.

After the voting the transaction gets into a *prepared* state and the cohorts wait for the final decision for the outcome of the transaction. The

Figure 1. State diagram for a master completing a transaction under the a 2-phase commit protocol

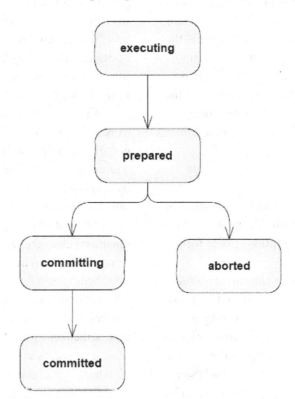

second phase of the protocol starts after the reception of all votes sent by the cohorts. If a negative vote exists, the master decides to abort the transaction, notifies accordingly all cohorts, and releases all information concerning the transaction (i.e., the transaction gets into an *aborting/aborted* state). Otherwise, if all votes were positive the master decides to commit the transaction, notifies accordingly all cohorts and waits for their acknowledgment (the transaction gets into a *committing* state). Upon the reception of the acknowledgments, the master releases all information concerning the transaction and the transaction get into a *committed* state. The presume-abort protocol further conforms to the following basic principle: *if a transaction participant tries to find out about whether a transaction was finally committed or aborted and there is no information available about this transaction, the transaction*

participant derives the conclusion that the transaction was aborted.

The strict 2-phase-locking protocol that we assume is a variant of the classical 2-phase-locking protocol, whose fundamental principle states that *no locks can be released until all necessary locks have been acquired from the transaction.* In the strict 2-phase-locking variant, *all locks are released at the end of the transaction.*

2. A SCHEDULE-AWARE PROTOCOL FOR AMI ENVIRONMENTS

In this section we discuss the issue of user-centric transactions in the context of AmI environments. The problem we wish to handle concerns the abnormal ending of the transaction due to the fact that a mobile user / transaction participant leaves the AmI environment where the transaction takes place. The idea behind our approach is that if there is a certain level of knowledge behind the schedule of the user, then we can exploit it to avoid the abnormal transaction termination. Based on this idea, we present a schedule-aware transaction protocol. Before presenting the protocol's internals, in Section 3.1, we start with preliminary concepts, foundations and assumptions for our problem.

2.1 Preliminaries

In this section we provide a formal definition of the entities that participate in the AmI environment, along with any assumptions made for the purpose of this paper.

In our modeling, an AmI environment is a set of cooperating nodes N. We deal with AmI environments as logical-level constructs that group nodes in a workgroup where they cooperate towards achieving a common goal. Depending on the case, this workgroup can be mapped to physical-level facilities (e.g., the AmI environment can be defined with respect to an area bounded by the connectivity range of a conventional networking infrastructure --e.g., a typical IEEE 802.11 network). More nodes can later join the environment and existing nodes can leave the environment. In the context of this paper, the terms 'join' and 'leave' the environment refer to a logical level participation to the AmI environment and not a physical one; in fact, the particularities of these actions at the physical level are orthogonal to the proposed protocol.

Our overall system model consists of a set of distinct AmI environments. Communication between nodes of N_i, N_j, for all $i, j \mid i \neq j$ is not possible.

The formation of the workgroup can be done by gathering the mobile nodes around a static, fixed point of reference (e.g., a standard access point in a building), or by arranging an ad-hoc network of mobile peers. In both of these cases, two kinds of nodes participate: (a) *fixed nodes* that are constantly part of their environment and (b)

mobile nodes, corresponding to users that move over the set of AmI environments. At any given time point, each environment comprises its fixed nodes and a (possibly empty) set of mobile nodes that happen to be part of the environment at that moment. Each node n has (a) a unique node id and (b) a finite set of *records*, or *variables*, denoted as $var(n)$, which are either read or updated in the context of a (possibly distributed) transaction. Moreover, each mobile node is characterized by a schedule that specifies its movement from one environment to another. A node's schedule is a finite list of pairs of the form (*environment, duration*) characterizing how long the node will remain in each environment. In Figure 2, we depict he schedule of a node which is going to stay for 20 time points in environment N_1, then move to environment N_2 where it will remain for 30 time points, then return to environment N_1 for a duration of 40 time points and finally move to environment N_3 where it will stay for 44 time points.

All nodes issue flat distributed transactions, i.e., transactions composed of tasks that are executed at different nodes, with the extra assumption that each node who is requested to perform such a task can execute this task locally without issuing another (nested) transaction. Also, we assume that each transaction is executed within the context of a single environment (still, this particular assumption can be relaxed with straightforward enhancements in the proposed protocol.).

Formally, each transaction is defined as the following tuple:

$$T = (TID, NID, MID, \{Steps\})$$

where *TID* is a unique identifier for the transaction, *NID* is the identifier of the environment within which the transaction must be executed, *MID* is the node identifier for the master node of the transaction and *Steps* is a finite list of steps (to be defined right away). Each Step is defined as a set of *actions*, with each action being a request

Figure 2. Exemplary schedule of a mobile node

N_1	20
N_2	30
N_1	40
N_3	44

to read or write a cohort's variable. An action is, thus, defined as the following tuple:

$$A = (CID, Action, Variable)$$

where *CID* is the node identifier of the cohort node that executes the action, *Action* belonging to the set {*READ, WRITE*} and *Variable* being the variable being read or written.

For reasons that will be apparent in the sequel, we would like to point out that it is easy to infer whether a node is mobile or fixed by its node id.

2.2 The Freeze on Leave Protocol

The main thrust of our contribution lies in the exploitation of the schedules of the mobile nodes. Assume that a mobile node is about to leave an environment where it participates as a cohort to a distributed transaction. In this case, a typical transaction protocol would simply abort the transaction. Following a different direction, we build on the idea on requiring the node to notify the transaction's master on its intention to leave, instead of sending an abort message. The crux of the proposed protocol is that the master tries to find *a rendezvous, i.e., a time point and a subsequent interval where all the participants of the transaction will meet again in the same environment*. If this is feasible, then the transaction is frozen, its state is recorded at the master and it will be defrozen again when the master's clock reaches the starting point of the rendezvous that the master

has calculated. Due to this mechanism, we call this protocol *Freeze on Leave* (FOL).

Assume a transaction that takes place in environment N_1 and involves a fixed master and two mobile cohorts, m_1 and m_2. Assume that at time point τ the master receives a message from cohort m_1 that the latter is leaving environment N_1. The schedules of the two cohorts at time point τ are depicted in Figure 3. The master, can calculate that, according to the cohorts' schedules, cohort m_1 will be back at the environment N_1 for the time interval [51-90] and cohort m_2 will also be back for the time interval [71-90]. The overlap of the two schedules can serve as a "rescue" interval for the successful completion of the transaction.

Interestingly, the protocol does not guarantee successful completion of the transaction. The risks of failure are primarily two: (a) a cohort violates its schedule and misses the rendezvous for the frozen transaction's defreeze, or (b) the transaction cannot be completed in the common time interval of the cohorts. In both of the aforementioned cases the protocol guarantees that the transaction shall be aborted.

In the rest of this section, we organize the discussion of the internals of the Freeze on Leave protocol in two parts: first we assume that the master is fixed and following we examine the case where the master is mobile. In both cases, the reaction of the master is also dependent upon the state in which it is in.

If the master of the transaction is fixed, then it does not need to worry about its own schedule, since it will continuously be present at the environment where the transaction takes place. As already mentioned, we are particularly interested in the case where a mobile cohort sends a message *LEAVE* to the master, signifying the cohort's intention to leave the environment. Whenever the master receives such a message it checks its state. If the master is in any state before *executing*, then it assumes that no work has actually been done (and therefore worth saving) and aborts the transaction. On the other hand, if the master is in

Figure 3. Schedules for mobile nodes at the time of departure of m_1

N_3	20
N_2	30
N_1	40
N_3	44
Schedule for m_1	

N_1	30
N_3	40
N_1	20
N_3	10
Schedule for m_2	

an *executing* or *prepared* state, it understands that there is a chance of salvaging the work that has been performed so far. The actions of the master depend upon its state.

A cohort leaves and the master is in executing state: In this case, when the master receives the LEAVE message from the cohort, it initiates the procedure for finding *a rendezvous, i.e., a common time point and a subsequent interval where all the mobile cohorts will be back in the environment again*. In case there is no such interval, the transaction is aborted as usually. If, on the other hand, such an interval exists, the master proceeds as following:

○ First, the master checks whether there are steps that can be executed without the leaving cohort. If the next step requires the departing cohort, then the master node proceeds as follows:

○ *it notifies all cohorts about the rendezvous* by sending to them a FREEZE message;

○ if the master has received acknowledgements from the last step (i.e., read or write actions), it assumes a *hung up* state – else it assumes an *ack hung up* state until all acknowledgements arrive;

○ If there are steps that can be executed without the departing cohort, then the master proceeds as follows:

○ *it notifies the departing cohort* about the rendezvous by sending to it a FREEZE message;

○ it assumes a *temp executing* state;

○ it waits for a step that requires the presence of an absent cohort to signal a *FREEZE* message *to all the cohorts* and moves to a state of *hung up* or *ack hung up*.

At the same time, when a cohort receives a FREEZE message, it moves to a *hung up* state.

The execution of the transaction continues interactively. Whenever a participating cohort returns to the environment, the master node tries to execute the next step of the transaction. If the execution of the next step is possible the master passes in a *temp executing* state and keeps up with the execution of the transaction until a step that requires a missing node; otherwise it remains in its previous state.

The overall defreeze of the transaction takes place when the rendezvous point arrives. At this point, the master checks if every cohort is present. If the rendezvous is missed, the master aborts the transaction and notifies all cohorts that are present accordingly. The cohorts that missed the rendezvous are aware of this situation; when the

Figure 4. State diagram for the master, when a cohort leaves and the master is in prepared state

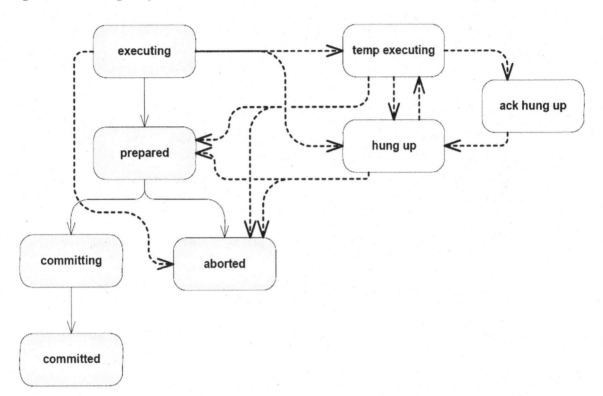

rendezvous is missed each one of them considers the transaction aborted.

Observe Figure 4 depicting the state diagram for the master in this case. The darker nodes correspond to the typical presume-abort 2-phase-commit protocol and the white nodes present the proposed extension.

A cohort leaves and the master is in prepared state: If the master receives a *LEAVE* message when it is in *prepared* state, it also needs to check whether it is possible to find *a rendezvous*. If such a rendezvous can not be found the transaction is aborted. Otherwise, the master (a) sends a FREEZE message *to the cohort leaving the environment* and (b) assumes a *vote hung up* state, waiting for the remaining cohorts' votes. When the master can reach a decision for the transaction, there are two cases:

- ◦ If the transaction is to be aborted, the master notifies all cohorts that are present about the decision and assumes a *partially abort* state, until the rendezvous point. At this point, the master sends an *ABORT* message to the returning cohorts and moves to an *aborted* state. Note that some cohorts may miss the rendezvous. These cohorts can not be notified by the master about the outcome of the transaction. However, since they are aware of the missed rendezvous, they shall abort the transaction by themselves.
- ◦ If the transaction is to be committed, the master moves to the *partially commit* state, until the rendezvous. At this point, the master checks if every cohort is present. If the rendezvous is missed, the master assumes an *abort-*

Figure 5. State diagram for the master, when a cohort leaves and the master is in prepared state

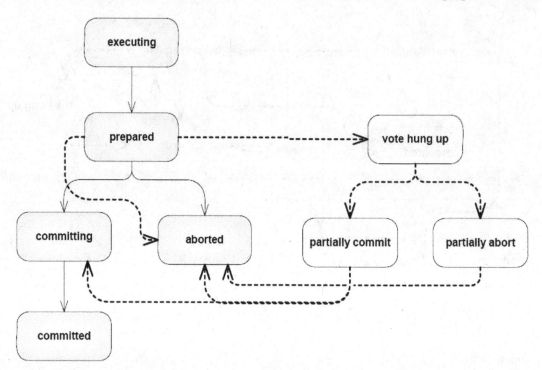

ed state. As previously, the cohorts that missed the rendezvous abort the transaction by themselves. If the rendezvous is met by all cohorts the master assumes a *committing* state.

Observe Figure 5 depicting the state diagram for the master in this case. The darker nodes correspond to the typical presume-abort 2-phase-commit protocol and the white nodes present the proposed extension.

If the master of the transaction is mobile, the overall behavior of the protocol is quite similar with what has been discussed for the case where the master is fixed. Nevertheless, below we summarize the main differences that exist in the case of the mobile master:

- Whenever the master tries to calculate a rendezvous, it takes into account *its own schedule along with the schedules of the participating cohorts.*

- If the master has to leave the environment while being in the *executing* or in the *prepared* state, there is nothing particularly different from the case of a mobile cohort leaving the environment. Nevertheless, due to the fact that the master needs to organize its departure and calculate the rendezvous, the master arranges *to send a LEAVE message to itself somewhat earlier than its departure.*

2.3 Discussion: Risks and Opportunities of the FOL Protocol

In this section we discuss possible risks and opportunities for improvement of the proposed protocol and explain some of our design choices.

Security and Privacy. A clear concern for the proposed protocol has to do with the fact that the cohorts' schedules must be released to the master resulting in a breach of privacy for the cohorts. *We should make clear that the proposed protocol operates under the assumption that the master is trusted.* If the master is not trusted by even one of the cohorts, then clearly, the transaction execution falls back to a schedule-agnostic mode. Also, it is not necessary to submit the full agenda of a cohort to the master; it is only sufficient to release a reasonably small subset of it for the context of a transaction. This can be achieved via a negotiation step during the handshake phase between the master and the cohorts. It is also possible to devise further optimizations, such as the anonymization of sensitive parts and the disclosure only of the case where the cohort will be back in the master's environment. Exploring these posibilities is an issue orthogonal to the protocol *per se*, especially since all of them result in the identification (or not) of common interval during which all the cohorts will be present in the same environment. So, for simplicity, in our deliberations we assume the simplest case, where all the cohorts automatically release their agendas to the master.

Concerning security, the transmission of the schedule to the master can be encrypted and even locally stored in an encrypted scheme; still, this is a topic for the implementing middleware to resolve and falls outside the scope of the paper.

Strictness of schedules. What happens if a node does not stick to its schedule? This is a realistic question that has to be answered by the protocol. There are mainly two cases:

1. A cohort is late in its rendezvous. In this case, the master initiates an abort message and the late cohort presumes by default that an abort will occur. A simple extension of the protocol can even give some extra time after the rendezvous as a buffering period for latecomers; in fact this buffering

period can even be calculated at the determination of the rendezvous time point. Still, this is a simple engineering extension to the protocol without significant implications.

2. A cohort is early in its rendezvous. This is no problem per se, if the cohort intends to stick to its previous schedule for the rest of its tasks. At the same time, this also presents an opportunity if *all* cohorts arrive early. It is possible to devise schemes to take this case into consideration; in our case we considered this to be a rare case and opted for a simpler protocol.

Other possible directions involve the monitoring of cohorts progress with respect to their registered schedule and the adaptation of the rendezvous point. We believe that the protocol should stick to *local scope principle*, in the sense that each master should only be interested in what happens in its specialized purview without global coordination or monitoring back-stage activities. Still, it is possible that in specialized situations, this could be performed with significant gains of committed transactions –at the expense, of course, of simplicity.

Opportunities for improvements. It is possible for the skeptical reader to raise questions related to the assumptions made in this paper. A simple example involves the role of environments in the whole setting: for example, if two different environments are close in terms of wireless transmission, or, if they have direct connection of their fixed nodes, is it possible to take advantage of this fact and improve the protocol? So far, we have assumed that an environment is an area within which the mobile nodes can communicate with each other, so, strictly speaking, as long as there is network connectivity among the involved nodes we should still consider that they are in the same environment. Still, it is possible to consider situations where an environment is bounded by geographical and connectivity constraints. Mesh networks, each employing a dedicated gateway node could possibly be considered in such a scenario and a cooperative scheme between them could be devised. We consider this opportunity as a topic for future research.

A second possibility has to do with the mobility of the nodes. Improvements of the protocol could be explored for the case that the nodes move groupwise, in a 'herd' fashion (Musolesi & Mascolo, 2007) as well in cases of other mobility models derived based on real-world observations (e.g., Bittner, Raffel, & Scholz, 2005; Tian, Haehner, Becker, Stepanov, & Rothermel, 2002). In general, a restriction of our model is that the nodes must return to the initiating environment to complete the transaction. It is possible to think of schemes where the nodes complete the transaction in another environment. Nevertheless, adopting such an approach would require total, detailed knowledge of all the schedules (against the aforementioned comments for privacy issues) and the environments and would result in a *global scope rendezvous* protocol. For practical purposes of efficiency and simplicity, we believe that a *local*, or at best, a *limited horizon scope* must be adopted, in which the rendezvous are considered without total knowledge of the network structure or the nodes' schedules. In other words, there is a trade-off between network and schedule knowledge, protocol simplicity and speed vs. the percentage of committed transactions. This trade-off is a function of the extent of the horizon that should be considered and its intricacies suggest another topic for future research.

3. EXPERIMENTS

To assess the idea of designing user-centric transaction protocols for AmI environments we implemented a simulator and performed a number of experiments. The goal of our experimental evaluation was to compare the FOL protocol we proposed in Section 3 against a schedule-agnostic protocol. The schedule-agnostic protocol relies on the following principle: whenever the designated time interval for the staying of a mobile node at a certain environment expires, the node (a) sends a message that aborts all the transactions to which it participates, and (b) leaves the environment (possibly to join the next environment in its schedule). The main metrics for our study were the percentages of aborted and committed transactions in the case of each protocol.

Concerning our experimental setup, we assumed 3 different AmI environments, each one of which comprised 30 fixed nodes. Given these environments we performed 4 different sets of experiments where the number of mobile nodes varied as follows: 10, 15, 20 and 25 mobile nodes. The overall number of variables for the fixed nodes was 640, while the overall number of variables for the mobile nodes was 320. The variables were equally distributed among the fixed and the mobile nodes.

The schedule of each mobile node was randomly generated with respect to the overall simulation time which was set to 1000 time units. The average visiting time of each node in a particular environment was 50 time units (i.e., it was randomly generated in the range [40, 60] with a uniform distribution). Therefore, each mobile node performed on average 25 visits in the 3 AmI environments.

The set of transactions used in our experiments was also randomly generated. In particular the number of steps of each transaction varied uniformly in the range of [1, 20]. The number of actions performed on each step was uniformly distributed in the range [1, 3]. Each action had a

Figure 6. FOL vs. a schedule-agnostic protocol: Percentage of aborted transactions

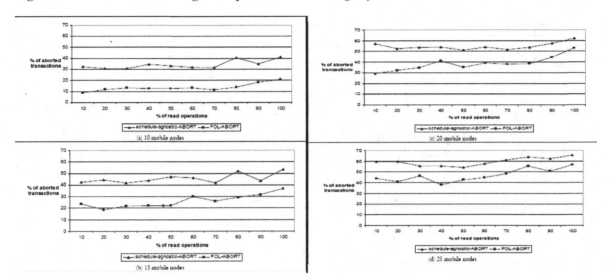

probability of 0.5 to be performed on a variable that belonged to a mobile node. Given that for each action a node is randomly selected with a uniform distribution, the number of nodes involved in the transactions was bounded by the number of steps that constituted the transactions. In each one of the 4 different sets of experiments that we performed we varied the percentage of read actions over the total number of actions from 10% to 100%. The percentage of read operations influences the contention for locks within each node, since read operations can read-lock the same variable simultaneously, whereas write operations lock the variables exclusively. Finally, in all our experiments, transactions were initiated in the AmI environments according to a Poisson distribution; on average, 2 transactions were initiated every 10 time units.

Figure 6 summarizes the results we obtained. More specifically, Figure 6 gives the percentages of aborted transactions resulted by the use of the two protocols in the 4 different configurations of our environments. In all cases, we can observe that the schedule-aware protocol exhibits a much better behavior; the percentages of aborted transactions in the case of the schedule-agnostic

protocol are much higher than the percentages of aborted transactions in the case of the schedule-aware protocol. Nevertheless, as we increase the number of mobile nodes involved in the 3 AmI environments the difference between the two protocols decreases given that the probability of finding rendezvous decreases.

Concerning the percentages of committed transactions (see Figure 7), we have also measured the effect of the number of mobile nodes and the composition of transactions with respect to reads and writes. The percentage of committed transactions is not the complement of the percentage of aborted transactions: this is due to the fact that due to strict locking of resources, starvations occur and some transactions never start. In this case we consider the transaction cancelled. If too many write operations take place, then the possibilities for concurrencies are reduced and many cancellations take place. Moreover, due to this fact, the schedule-aware and the schedule-agnostic protocols behave similarly. Still, as the number of read operations increases, more transactions can operate concurrently; the experiments show that (a) cancellations decrease (and the percentage of committed transactions increases) and (b) the

Figure 7. FOL vs. a schedule-agnostic protocol: Percentage of committed transactions

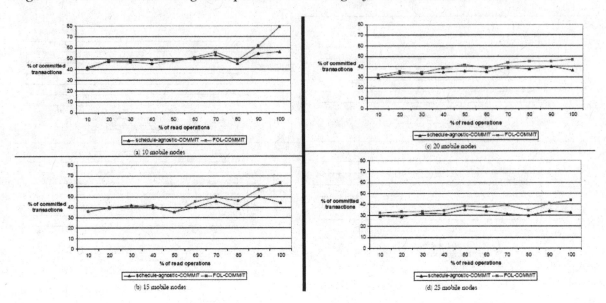

schedule-aware protocol performs better than the schedule-agnostic one. Moreover, the difference between the two protocols becomes clearer as we increase the number of mobile nodes involved in the environments.

4. CONCLUSION AND FUTURE WORK

In this paper we discussed our general position that concerns the need for designing user-centric transaction protocols towards achieving dependable coordination in AmI environments. We proposed such a protocol that takes into account the schedules of roaming users that move from one AmI environment to another, to avoid abnormal terminations of transactions when the users leave an environment for short, only to return later. We compared the proposed schedule-aware protocol against a schedule-agnostic one. Our findings showed that the use of user-centric information in such situations is quite beneficial. Our results motivate further investigation of the issue of user-centric transaction protocols. Currently we focus on more stochastic approaches for defining and

exploiting user centric information (e.g., probabilistic schedules, or schedules based on fuzzy sets). Privacy is also an interesting issue involved. Moreover, our research is oriented towards the design of customizable protocols where the outcome of transactions shall be decided with respect to user-defined context rules. Finally, we envision the provisioning of middleware support for user-centric transaction protocols, which consequently involves several issues including the specification of interoperable schedules and monitoring the availability of nodes in a particular environment.

ACKNOWLEDGMENT

We would like to thank the reviewers of earlier versions of this paper for their valuable comments that significantly improved the clarity of the paper.

REFERENCES

Aarts, E., Harwig, R., & Schuurmans, M. (2001). The Invisible Future: The Seamless Integration of Technology into Everyday Life . In Denning, P. J. (Ed.), *Ambient Intelligence* (pp. 235–250). New York: McGraw-Hill.

Bittner, S., Raffel, W.-U., & Scholz, M. (2005, March 8-12). The Area Graph-based Mobility Model and its Impact on Data Dissemination. In *Proceedings of the PerCom 2005 Workshops, the 3rd International Conference on Pervasive Computing and Communications*, Kauai Island, HI (pp. 268-272).

Bobineau, C., Pucheral, P., & Abdallah, M. (2000). A Unilateral Commit Protocol for Mobile and Disconnected Computing. In *Proceedings of the 12th International Conference on Parallel and Distributed Computing Systems (PDCS'00)*, Las Vegas, NV.

Böttcher, S., Gruenwald, L., & Obermeier, S. (2006, July 18-20). Reducing Sub-transaction Aborts and Blocking Time within Atomic Commit Protocols. In *Proceedings of the 23rd British National Conference on Databases (BNCOD 23)*, Belfast, Northern Ireland, UK.

Eswaran, K. P., Gray, J. N., Lorie, R. A., & Traiger, I. L. (1976). The Notions of Consistency and Predicate Locks in a Database System. *Communications of the ACM*, *19*(11), 624–633. .doi:10.1145/360363.360369

Kumar, V., Prabhu, N., Dunham, M. H., & Seydim, A. Y. (2002). TCOT- A Timeout-based Mobile Transaction Commitment Protocol. *IEEE Transactions on Computers*, *51*(10), 1212–1218. .doi:10.1109/TC.2002.1039846

Le, H. N., & Nygard, M. (2005, August 22-26). Mobile Transaction System for Supporting Mobile Work. In *Proceedings of the 16th IEEE International Workshop on Database and Expert Systems Applications, DEXA Workshops 2005*, Copenhagen, Denmark (pp. 1090-1094). Washington, DC: IEEE Computer Society.

Mohan, C., Lindsay, B., & Obermarck, R. (1986). Transaction Management in the R Distributed Database Management System. *ACM Transactions on Database Systems*, *11*(4), 378–396. .doi:10.1145/7239.7266

Musolesi, M., & Mascolo, C. (2007). Designing Mobility Models Based on Social Network Theory. *ACM SIGMOBILE Mobile Computing and Communications Review*, *11*(3), 59–70. .doi:10.1145/1317425.1317433

Nouali, N., Doucet, A., & Drias, H. (2005). A Two-Phase Commit Protocol for Mobile Wireless Environment. In *Proceedings of the Sixteenth Australasian Database Conference, Database Technologies 2005*, Newcastle, Australia (pp. 135-143).

Pitoura, E., & Samaras, G. (1998). *Data Management for Mobile Computing*. Dordrecht, The Netherlands: Kluwer Academic Publishers.

Serrano-Alvarado, P., Roncancio, C., & Adiba, M. (2004). A Survey of Mobile Transactions. *Distributed and Parallel Databases*, *16*(2), 193–230. .doi:10.1023/B:DAPD.0000028552.69032.f9

Tian, J., Haehner, J., Becker, C., Stepanov, I., & Rothermel, K. (2002). Graph-based Mobility Model for Mobile Ad Hoc Network Simulation. In *Proceedings of the 35th Annual Simulation Symposium Annual Simulation Symposium*, San Diego, CA (pp. 337-344). Washington, DC: IEEE Computer Society.

Weber, W., Braun, C., Glaser, R., Gsottberger, Y., Halik, M., Jung, S., et al. (2003). Ambient Intelligence - Key Technologies in the Information Age. In *Proceedings of the IEEE International Electron Devices Meeting (IEDM'03)* (pp. 1.1.1-1.1.8).

Weiser, M. (1991). The Computer of the Twenty-First Century. *Scientific American, 135,* 94–104. .doi:10.1038/scientificamerican0991-94

Younas, M., Chao, K.-M., Wang, P., & Huang, C.-L. (2007). QoS-aware Mobile Service Transactions in a Wireless Environment. *Concurrency and Computation, 19*(8), 1219–1236. .doi:10.1002/cpe.1157

This work was previously published in International Journal of Ambient Computing and Intelligence, Volume 2, Issue 4, edited by Kevin Curran, pp. 55-69, copyright 2010 by IGI Publishing (an imprint of IGI Global).

Compilation of References

(n.d.). *The Hand*. Retrieved from http://32feet.net/library/.

2000Cognitive aging: A primer . InPark, D., & Schwarz, N. (Eds.), *Psychology Press* (p. 238). New York: Taylor and Francis.

3GPP. (2008). User *Equipment (UE) positioning in Universal Terrestrial Radio Access Network (UTRAN); Stage 2 (TS No 25.305). 3rd Generation Partnership Project (3GPP)*. Retrieved from http://www.3gpp.org/ftp/Specs/html-info/25305.htm

Aarts, E., & Marzano, S. (2003). The new everyday: Visions of ambient intelligence. Rotterdam, The Netherlands: 010 Publishing.

Aarts, E. (2005). Foreword . In Cai, Y., & Abascal, J. (Eds.), *Ambient Intelligence in Everyday Life - State of the Art Survey* (p. vii). New York: Springer.

Aarts, E., Harwig, R., & Schuurmans, M. (2001). The Invisible Future: The Seamless Integration of Technology into Everyday Life . In Denning, P. J. (Ed.), *Ambient Intelligence* (pp. 235–250). New York: McGraw-Hill.

Abowd, G. A., Bobick, I., & Essa, E. Mynatt, & Rogers, W. (2002). The Aware Home: Developing Technologies for Successful Aging. In *Proceedings of the American Association of Artificial Intelligence (AAAI) Conference*.

Abowd, G., & Mynatt, E. (2000). Charting past, present, and future research in ubiquitous computing. *Transactions on Computer-Human Interaction (TOCHI), 7*(1).

Acharya, S., Franklin, M., & Zdonik, S. (1997). Balancing push and pull for data broadcast. In *Proceedings of the 1997 ACM sigmod international conference on management of data (Sigmod '97)* (pp. 183-194). New York: ACM.

Adam, S., Mukasa, K. S., Breiner, K., & Trapp, M. (2008). An apartment-based metaphor for intuitive interaction with ambient assisted living applications. In *Proceedings of 23rd BCS Conference on People and Computers, British Computer Society*, Liverpool, UK (pp. 67-75).

Adler, A., & Davis, R. (2004). Speech and Sketching for Multimodal Design. In *Proceedings of the 9th International Conference on Intelligent User Interfaces* (pp. 214-216).

Afonso, A. P., & Silva, M. J. (2004). Dynamic information dissemination to mobile users: Mobility in databases and distributed systems: Summing up achievements of the past decade. *Mobile Networks and Applications, 9*(5), 529–536. .doi:10.1023/B:MONE.0000034706.03412.38

Agarwal, N., & Liu, H. (2008). Blogosphere: research issues, tools, and applications. *SIGKDD Explorations Newsletter, 10*(1).

Akyildiz, I. F., Wang, X., & Wang, W. (2005). Wireless Mesh Networks: A Survey. *Computer Networks and ISDN Systems*, 445–487.

Allen, J. (1983). Maintaining knowledge about temporal intervals. *Communications of the ACM, 26*, 832–843. doi:. doi:10.1145/182.358434

Alonso, R., Tapia, D., & Corchado, J. (2011). SYLPH: A platform for integrating heterogeneous wireless sensor networks in ambient intelligence systems. *International Journal of Ambient Computing and Intelligence, 3*(2), 1–15.

Alzheimer's Association. (2009). Alzheimer's Disease Facts and Figures. *Alzheimer's & Dementia, 5*(3).

Amant, R., Dinardo, M., & Buckner, N. (2003). Balancing efficiency and interpretability in an interactive statistical assistant. In *Proceedings of the 8th international conference on Intelligent user interfaces (IUI '03)*. New York: ACM Press.

Amft, O., Lombriser, C., Stiefmeier, T., & Tröster, G. (2007) Recognition of user activity sequences using distributed event detection. In *Proceedings of the European Conference on Smart Sensing and Context (EuroSSC)* (pp. 126-141). Berlin: Springer.

AMIGO. (2009). The Amigo Project. Retrieved October 27, 2009, from http://www.hitech-projects.com/euprojects/amigo

Apple Inc. (2010). *I-phone human interface guidelines*. Retrieved March 31, 2010, from http://developer.apple.com/iPhone/library /documentation/UserExperience/Conceptual/MobileHIG

Arabshian, K., & Schulzrinne, H. (2004). GloServ: Global service discovery architecture. In *Proceedings of the First Annual International Conference on Mobile and Ubiquitous Systems: Networking and Services (Mobiquitous)* (pp. 319-325).

Ark, W., & Selker, T. (1999). A look at human interaction with pervasive computers. *IBM Systems Journal, 38*(4). .doi:10.1147/sj.384.0504

Arvidsson, D. (2009). *Physical activity and energy expenditure in clinical settings using multi-sensor activity monitors (Tech. Rep.)*. Gothenburg, Sweden: University of Gothenburg, Sahlgrenska Academy.

Asuncion, A., & Newman, D. (n.d.). *UCI Machine Learning Repository*. Retrieved October 20, 2009, from http://www.ics.uci.edu/~mlearn /MLRepository.html

Augusto, J., & Nugent, C. (2004). The use of temporal reasoning and management of complex events in smart homes. In Proceedings of ECAI-04, Valencia, Spain (pp. 778-782).

Augusto, J. C., & McCullagh, P. (2007). Ambient Intelligence: Concepts and Applications. *International Journal of Computer Science and Information Systems, 4*(1), 1–28. .doi:10.2298/CSIS0701001A

Ayanoglu, E., Chih-Lin, I., Gitlin, R. D., & Mazo, J. E. (1993, November). Diversity Coding for Transparent Self-Healing and Fault-Tolerant Communication Networks. *IEEE Transactions on Communications*, 1677–1686. doi:10.1109/26.241748

Aztiria, A., Augusto, J., Izaguirre, A., & Cook, D. (2008). Learning accurate temporal relations from user actions in intelligent environments. In Proc. 3rd Symposium of Ubiquitous Computing and Ambient Intelligence.

Bai, F., Sadagopan, N., & Helmy, A. (2003). *Important: a framework to systematically analyze the impact of mobility on performance of routing protocols for ad hoc networks*.

Baker, C. L., Saxe, R., & Tenenbaum, J. B. (2009). Action understanding as inverse planning. Cognition.

Balazinska, M., Balakrishnan, H., & Karger, D. (2002). INS/Twine: A scalable peer-to-peer architecture for intentional resource discovery. In *Proceedings of the International Conference on Pervasive Computing 2002*.

Baldauf, M., Dustdar, S., & Rosenberg, F. (2007). A survey on context-aware systems. *International Journal of Ad Hoc Ubiquitous Computing, 2*(4), 263–277. .doi:10.1504/IJAHUC.2007.014070

Bannach, D., Amft, O., & Lukowicz, P. (2009). Automatic Event-Based Synchronization of Multimodal Data Streams from Wearable and Ambient Sensors. In *Proceedings of the European Conference on Smart Sensing and Context (EuroSSC)* (pp 135-148).

Bao, L. (2003). *Physical Activity Recognition from Acceleration Data under Semi-Naturalistic Conditions*. Cambridge, MA: MIT.

Barbara, D. (1999). Mobile computing and databases-a survey. *IEEE Transactions on Knowledge and Data Engineering, 11*(1), 108–117. .doi:10.1109/69.755619

Barish, G., & Obraczke, K. (2000). World wide web caching: trends and techniques. *IEEE Communications Magazine, 38*(5), 178–184. .doi:10.1109/35.841844

Barnard, P., May, J., Duke, D., & Duce, D. (2000). Systems, interactions, and macrotheory. *Transactions on Computer-Human Interaction (TOCHI), 7*(2).

Basten, T., Geilen, M., & de Groot, H. (2003). *Ambient intelligence: Impact on embedded system design*. Boston, MA: Kluwer Academic Publishers.

Beattie, J. (2009). Improving food quality and preventing disease. *Rowett Research Institute Newsletter, 10*(1), 1–3.

Beier, B., & Vaughan, M. (2003). The bull's-eye: a framework for web application user interface design guidelines. In *Proceedings of the SIGCHI conference on Human factors in computing systems (CHI '03)*. New York: ACM Press.

Bellotti, V., Back, M., Edwards, W. K., Grinter, R., Henderson, A., & Lopes, C. (2002). Making sense of sensing systems: five questions for designers and researchers. In *Proceedings of the SIGCHI conference on Human factors in computing systems: Changing our world, changing ourselves (CHI '02)*. New York: ACM Press.

Ben Mokhtar, S., Kaul, A., Georgantas, N., & Issarny, V. (2006). Efficient semantic service discovery in pervasive computing environments. In *Proceedings of the ACM/IFIP/USENIX, 7th International Middleware Conference Middleware 2006* (pp. 240-259).

Ben Mokhtar, S., Preuveneers, D., Georgantas, N., Issarny, V., & Berbers, Y. (2008). EASY: Efficient SemAntic service DiscoverY in pervasive computing environments with QoS and context support. *Journal of Systems and Software, 81*(5), 785–808.

Bennett, F., Clarke, D., Evans, J. B., Hopper, A., Jones, A., & Leask, D. (n.d.). *Piconet, Embedded Mobile Networking*. Cambridge, UK: Cambridge University.

Benyon, D. (2004). *Designing Interactive Systems*. Reading, MA: Addison-Wesley.

Berners-Lee, T., Fielding, R., & Masinter, L. (1998). *Uniform resource identifiers (URI): Generic syntax*. Retrieved December 13, 2008, from http://www.ietf.org/rfc/rfc2396.txt

Bernstein, M., Kleek, M., Schraefel, M., & Karger, D. (2007). Management of personal information scraps. In *Proceedings of the extended abstracts on Human factors in computing systems (CHI '07)*. New York: ACM Press.

Bernstein, P. A., Hadzilacos, V., & Goodman, N. (1987). *Concurrency control and recovery in database systems*. Boston: Addison-Wesley Longman Publishing Co.

Bhide, M., Deolasee, P., Katkar, A., Panchbudhe, A., Ramamritham, K., & Shenoy, P. (2002). Adaptive push-pull: disseminating dynamic web data. *IEEE Transactions on Computers, 51*(6), 652–668. .doi:10.1109/TC.2002.1009150

Bio Trainer. (n.d.). *Bio Trainer Clinical Studies*. Retrieved from http://www.biotrainerusa.com/clinical.asp

Bishop, C. M. (2006). *Pattern Recognition and Machine Learning*. New York: Springer.

Bittner, S., Raffel, W.-U., & Scholz, M. (2005, March 8-12). The Area Graph-based Mobility Model and its Impact on Data Dissemination. In *Proceedings of the PerCom 2005 Workshops, the 3rd International Conference on Pervasive Computing and Communications*, Kauai Island, HI (pp. 268-272).

Blackman, S., & Popoli, R. (1999). *Design and Analysis of Modern Tracking Systems*. Boston: Artech House.

Blackwell, A. (2006). The reification of metaphor as a design tool. *Transactions on Computer-Human Interaction (TOCHI), 13*(4).

Bluetooth, S. I. G. (2001a). Generic Object Exchange Profile. *Bluetooth Specification 1.1* (Chapter 10, pp. 310-338).

Bluetooth, S. I. G. (2001c). Serial Port Profile. *Bluetooth Specification 1.1* (Chapter 5, pp. 172-196).

Bluetooth, S. I. G. (2001d). *Service Discovery Application profile. Bluetooth Specification 1.1* (Chapter 2, pp. 64-98).

Bluetooth. (n.d.). *Bluetooth Basics*. Retrieved from http://www.bluetooth.com/Bluetooth /Technology/ (2009)

Bluetooth, S. I. G. (2001b). *Technical Note, Bluetooth Tutorial*. Bluetooth.

Blythe, M., & Dearden, A. (2009). Representing older people: towards meaningful images of the user in design scenarios. *Universal Access in the Information Society, 8*, 21–32. . doi:10.1007/s10209-008-0128-x

Bobineau, C., Pucheral, P., & Abdallah, M. (2000). A Unilateral Commit Protocol for Mobile and Disconnected Computing. In *Proceedings of the 12th International Conference on Parallel and Distributed Computing Systems (PDCS'00)*, Las Vegas, NV.

Boehner, K., DePaula, R., Dourish, P., & Sengers, P. (2005). Affect: from information to interaction. In *Proceedings of the 4th decennial conference on Critical computing: between sense and sensibility (CC '05)*. New York: ACM Press.

Borgia, E., Conti, M., Delmastro, F., & Gregori, E. (2005, August 22). Experimental Comparison of Routing and Middleware Solutions for Mobile Ad Hoc Networks: Legacy vs Cross-layer Approach. In *Proceedings of the 2005 ACM SIGCOMM Workshop on Experimental Approaches to Wireless Network Design and Analysis (E-WIND '05)* (pp. 82-87).

Böse, J.-H. (2008). *Abort and blocking risk of atomic transactions in mobile ad-hoc networks* (Tech. Rep. No. B-08-07). Berlin: Freie Universität Berlin. Retrieved from ftp://ftp.inf.fu-berlin.de/pub/reports/tr-b-08-7.pdf

Böse, J.-H., & Broß, J. (2008). Predicting the blocking risk of atomic transactions in manets induced by coordinator failures. In *Proceedings of the IADIS International Conference Wireless Applications and Computing.*

Böse, J.-H., Böttcher, S., Gruenwald, L., Obermeier, S., Schweppe, H., & Steenweg, T. (2005). An integrated commit protocol for mobile network databases. In *Proceedings of the 9th International Database Engineering & Application Symposium (IDEAS'05)* (pp. 244-250). Washington, DC: IEEE Computer Society.

Böse, J.-H., Broß, J., & Schweppe, H. (2008). A probabilistic model for blocking risks of atomic transactions in p2p networks. In *Proceedings of the International Workshop on Databases, Information Systems, and Peer-to-Peer Computing (DBISP2P)*, Auckland, New Zealand.

Böttcher, S., Gruenwald, L., & Obermeier, S. (2006, July 18-20). Reducing Sub-transaction Aborts and Blocking Time within Atomic Commit Protocols. In *Proceedings of the 23rd British National Conference on Databases (BNCOD 23)*, Belfast, Northern Ireland, UK.

Bourguet, M., & Ando, A. (1998, April 18-23). Synchronization of speech and hand gestures during multimodal human-computer interaction. In *Proceedings of CHI '98*, Los Angeles (pp. 241-242).

Bovermann, T. (2010). Tangible Auditory Interfaces: Combining Auditory Displays and Tangible Interfaces. PhD thesis, Faculty of Technology, Bielefeld University, Germany.

Bovermann, T., Groten, J., de Campo, A., & Eckel, G. (2007). Juggling Sounds. In Proceedings of the 2nd International Workshop on Interactive Sonification, York, UK.

Bovermann, T., Hermann, T., & Ritter, H. (2006). Tangible Data Scanning Sonification Model. In Proceedings of the International Conference on Auditory Display (ICAD 2006), London, UK (pp. 77-82).

BoxLab. (2009). *Making Home Activity Datasets a Shared Resource*. Retrieved November 11, 2009, from http://boxlab.wikispaces.com/

Brachman, R., & Levesque, H. (2004). *Knowledge Representation and Reasoning (The Morgan Kaufmann Series in Arti□cial Intelligence)*. San Francisco: Morgan Kaufmann.

Bracke, W., Puers, R., & Hoof, C. V. (2007). *Ultra Low Power Capacitive Sensor Interfaces*. New York: Springer.

Brandes, M., & Rosenbaum, D. (2003). Correlations between the step activity monitor and the DynaPort ADL-monitor. *Clinical Biomechanics (Bristol, Avon), 19*, 91–94. PubMed doi:10.1016/j.clinbiomech.2003.08.001

Brave, S., & Dahley, A. (1997). inTouch: a medium for haptic interpersonal communication. In Proceedings of the Conference on Human Factors in Computing Systems (pp. 363-364).

Brave, S., Ishii, H., & Dahley, A. (1998). Tangible interfaces for remote collaboration and communication. In Proceedings of the 1998 ACM Conference on Computer Supported Cooperative Work (pp. 169-178).

Bray, T., Paoli, J., Sperberg-McQueen, C. M., Maler, E., & Yergeau, F. (2006). *Extensible markup language (XML) 1.0* (4th ed.). Retrieved December 13, 2008, from http://www.w3.org/TR/2006/REC- xml- 20060816

Bricon-Souf, N., & Newman, C. (2007). Context awareness in healthcare: A review. International Journal of Medical Informatics, 76(1), 2–12. PubMed doi:10.1016/j.ijmedinf.2006.01.003

Bromberg, Y., & Issarny, V. (2005). INDISS: Interoperable discovery system for networked services. In *Proceedings of the ACM/IFIP/USENIX, 6th International Middleware Conference Middleware 2005* (pp. 164-183).

Bromuri, S., & Stathis, K. (2007). Situating Cognitive Agents in GOLEM. In Engineering Environment-Mediated Multi-Agent Systems (LNCS 5049, pp. 115-134).

Bromuri, S., & Stathis, K. (2009). Distributed Agent Environments in the Ambient Event Calculus. In DEBS '09: Proceedings of the 3rd International Conference on Distributed Event-Based Systems (pp. 1-12). New York: ACM Publishing.

Brumitt, B., & Cadiz, J. J. (2001.) *Let There Be Light! Comparing Interfaces for Homes of the Future.* Paper presented at the 2001 IFIP TC.13 Conference on Human Computer Interaction (Interact 2001).

Buchanan, R. (1998). Branzi's Dilemma: Design in contemporary culture. *Design Issues, 14*(1). .doi:10.2307/1511825

Buiza, C., Soldatos, J., Petsatodis, T., Geven, A., Etxaniz, A., & Tscheligi, M. (2009). HERMES: Pervasive computing and cognitive training for ageing well. In S. Omatu et al. (Eds.), *Proceedings of the International Work-Conference on Artificial Neural Networks* (pp. 755-762).

Cai, Y. (2007). Instinctive Computing. In Pantic, M. (Ed.), *Human Computing (LNAI 4451).* New York: Springer.

Calvary, G., Thevenin, D., & Coutaz, J. (2003). *A Reference Framework for the Development of Plastic User Interfaces.* Retrieved June 20, 2008, from http://iihm. imag.fr/publs/ 2003/MuiBook03.pdf

Cámara, J., Canal, C., Cubo, J., & Vallecillo, A. (2006). Formalizing WSBPEL business processes using process algebra. *Electronic Notes in Theoretical Computer Science, 154*(1), 159–173. .doi:10.1016/j.entcs.2005.12.038

Cao, J., Zhang, Y., Cao, G., & Xie, L. (2007). Data consistency for cooperative caching in mobile environments. *IEEE Computer, 40*(4), 60–66.

Capra, L., Zachariadis, S., & Mascolo, C. (2005). Q-CAD: QoS and context aware discovery framework for adaptive mobile systems. In *Proceedings of IEEE International Conference on Pervasive Services (ICPS05)* (pp. 453-456).

Carbonell, N. (2006). Ambient Multimodality: towards Advancing Computer Accessibility and Assisted Living. *International Journal on Universal Access in the Information Society (UAIS)*, 18-26.

Cardoso, R., Ben Mokhtar, S., Urbieta, A., & Issarny, V. (2007). EVEY: Enhancing privacy of service discovery in pervasive computing. In *Proceedings of the International Middleware Conference 2007 (Middleware 2007).*

Cardou, P., & Angeles, J. (2007). Simplectic Architectures for True Multi-axial Accelerometers: A Novel Application of Parallel Robots. In *Proceedings of the IEEE International Conference on Robotics and Automation,* Italy.

Card, S. K., Moran, T. P., & Newall, A. (1983). *The psychology of human-computer interaction.* Mahwah, NJ: Lawrence Erlbaum Associates.

Card, S. K., Moran, T., & Newell, A. (1980). The keystroke-level model for user performance time with interactive systems. *Communications of the ACM, 23*(7). .doi:10.1145/358886.358895

Carmona, J., Atserias, J., Cervell, S., Márquez, L., Martí, M. A., Padró, L., et al. (1998). *An Environment for Morphosyntactic Processing of Unrestricted Spanish Text.* Paper presented at LREC'98, Granada, Spain.

Carnegie Mellon University Quality of Life Technology Centre. (2008). *Grand Challenge* project. Retrieved October 26, 2009, from http://www.cmu.edu/qolt/Research /projects/grand-challenge.html

Carroll, J. M., & Kellogg, W. A. (1989). Artifact as theory-nexus: hermeneutics meets theory-based design. In, *Proceedings of the SIGCHI conference on Human factors in computing systems: Wings for the mind (CHI '89)* (Vol. 20).

Carroll, J. M. (Ed.). (1991). *Designing interaction: psychology at the human-computer interface.* New York: Cambridge University Press.

Carroll, J. M., & Rosson, M. B. (1992). Getting around the task-artifact cycle: how to make claims and design by scenario. [TOIS]. *ACM Transactions on Information Systems, 10*(2). .doi:10.1145/146802.146834

Cassens, J., & Kofod-Petersen, A. (2007). *Explanations and Case-Based Reasoning in Ambient Intelligent Systems*. Retrieved November 26, 2007, from http://ceur-ws.org

de Man, H. (2003). Foreword. In T. Basten, M. Geilen, & H. de Groot (Eds.), *Ambient Intelligence: Impact on Embedded System Design* (p. vii). New York: Kluwer.

Castelfranchi, C. (2005). ToM and BIC: Intentional behavioral communication as based on the theory of mind. In Proceedings of the AISB Symposium on Social Virtual Agents (pp. 37).

Castelfranchi, C. (2006). SILENT AGENTS: From Observation to Tacit Communication. In J. Simão Sichman, H. Coelho, & S. O. Rezende (Eds.), Advances in Artificial Intelligence - Proceedings of IBERAMIA-SBIA 2006 (LNCS 4140). ISBN 3-540-45462.

Centers for Disease Control and Prevention. (n.d.). *Overweight and Obesity*. Retrieved from http://www.cdc.gov/obesity/defining.html

Chang, Y., Lim, Y., & Stolterman, E. (2008). Personas: from theory to practices. In *Proceedings of the 5th Nordic conference on Human-computer interaction: building bridges (NordiCHI '08)*. New York: ACM Press.

Chen, G., & Kotz, D. (2002). Solar: An open platform for context-aware mobile applications. In *Proceedings of the 1st International Conference on Pervasive Computing (Pervasive 2002)*, Switzerland.

Chen, H., Finin, T., & Joshi, A. (2005). The SOUPA ontology for pervasive computing. In Ontologies for Agents: Theory and Experiences (pp. 233-258). Basel, Switzerland: Birkhäuser Basel.

Chen, H. (2003). Creating Context Aware Software Agents. In *Innovative Concepts for Agent-Based Systems*. Berlin, Germany: Springer. doi:10.1007/978-3-540-45173-0_15

Chen, R., Toran-Marti, F., & Ventura-Traveset, J. (2003). Access to the egnos signal in space over mobile-ip. *GPS Solutions, 7*(1), 16–22.

Cheverst, K., Mitchell, K., & Davies, N. (2002). Exploring context-aware information push. *Personal and Ubiquitous Computing, 6*(4), 276–281. .doi:10.1007/s007790200028

CHIL. (2009). The CHIL project. Retrieved October 27, 2009, from http://chil.server.de

Chow, C.-Y., Leong, H. V., & Chan, A. (2004). Peer-to-peer cooperative caching in mobile environments. In *Proceedings of the 24th International Conference on Distributed Computing Systems Workshops* (pp. 528-533).

Christensen, E., Curbera, F., Meredith, G., & Weerawarana, S. (2001). Web service denition language (wsdl). Retrieved from http://www.w3.org/TR/wsdl

Chua, S.-L., Marsland, S., & Guesgen, H. (2009). Spatio-temporal and context reasoning in smart homes. In Proceedings of the COSIT-09 Workshop on Spatial and Temporal Reasoning for Ambient Intelligence Systems, Aber Wrac'h, France (pp. 9-20).

Clark, H. H., & Brennan, S. E. (1991). Grounding in communication . In Levine, J., Resnick, L. B., & Behrand, S. D. (Eds.), *Shared Cognition: Thinking as Social Practice* (pp. 127–149). Washington, DC: APA Books. doi:10.1037/10096-006

Constantine, L. L., & Lockwood, L. A. D. (1999). *Software for use: a practical guide to the models and methods of usage-centered design*. Reading, MA: Addison-Wesley.

Conti, M., Gregori, E., & Maselli, G. (2006). Reliable and Efficient Forwarding in Ad Hoc Networks. *Ad Hoc Networks, 4*(3), 398–415. .doi:10.1016/j.adhoc.2004.10.006

Conti, M., Maselli, G., Turi, G., & Giordano, S. (2004). Cross-Layering in Mobile Ad Hoc Network Design. *Computer, 2*(37), 48–51. .doi:10.1109/MC.2004.1266295

Cook, D. (2006). Health monitoring and assistance to support aging in place. *Journal of Universal Computer Science, 12*(1), 15–29.

Cook, D., Schmitter-Edgecombe, M., Crandall, A., Sanders, C., Davies, B., Siewiorek, N., & Sukthankar, R. (2008). Activity-Based Computing. *IEEE Pervasive Computing / IEEE Computer Society* [and]. *IEEE Communications Society, 7*(2), 20–21. doi:.doi:10.1109/MPRV.2008.26

Cooper, A. (2004). *The inmates are running the asylum* (2nd ed.). Upper Saddle River, NJ: Sams Publishing.

Csibra, G., & Gergely, G. (2006). 'Obsessed with goals': Functions and mechanisms of teleological interpretation of actions in humans. Acta Psychologica, 124, 60–78. PubMed doi:10.1016/j.actpsy.2006.09.007

Csirmaz, L. (1997, November). The Size of a Share Must Be Large. *Journal of Cryptology*, 223-231.

Cuijpers, R. H., van Schie, H. T., Koppen, M., Erlhagen, W., & Bekkering, H. (2006). Goals and means in action observation: A computational approach. Neural Networks, 19, 311–322. PubMed doi:10.1016/j.neunet.2006.02.004

Curran, K., McFadden, D., & Devlin, R. (2011). The role of augmented reality within ambient intelligence. *International Journal of Ambient Computing and Intelligence*, 3(2), 16–33.

Czerwinski, S. E., Zhao, B. Y., Hodes, T. D., Joseph, A. D., & Katz, R. H. (1999). An architecture for a secure service discovery service. In *Proceedings of the 5th Annual ACM/IEEE International Conference on Mobile Computing and Networking (MobiCom '99)*, Seattle, WA (pp. 24-35).

Dahlbäck, N., & Jönsson, A. (1992). *An empirically based computationally tractable dialogue model.* Paper presented at COGSCI'92.

Dahlbäck, N., & Jönsson, A. (1997). *Integrating Domain Specific Focusing in Dialogue Models.* Paper presented at EuroSpeech-97, Rhodes, Greece.

Dahlbom, B., & Mathiassen, L. (1997). The future of our profession. *Communications of the ACM, 40*(6). .doi:10.1145/255656.255706

Dalsgaard, P., & Hansen, L. (2008). Performing perception—staging aesthetics of interaction. *Transactions on Computer-Human Interaction (TOCHI), 15*(3).

Dam, A. (1997). Post-WIMP user interfaces. *Communications of the ACM, 40*(2).

Das, S., & Cook, D. J. (2004). Smart Home Environments: A Paradigm Based on Learning and Prediction. In *Wireless Mobile and Sensor Networks.* New York: Wiley.

Davidoff, S., Bloomberg, C., Li, I. A. R., Mankoff, J., & Fussell, S. R. (2005). The book as user interface: lowering the entry cost to email for elders. In *Proceedings of CHI '05 extended abstracts on Human factors in computing systems* (pp. 1331-1334).

Davidson, D. (2006). *The Essential Davidson.* New York: Oxford University Press.

Davis, M. (2008). Toto, I've Got a Feeling We're Not in Kansas Anymore.... *Interaction, 15*(5). .doi:10.1145/1390085.1390091

Desmedt, Y., Wang, Y., & Burmester, M. (2006, August 31). Revisiting Colored Networks and Privacy Preserving Censorship. In *Proceedings of the First International Workshop on Critical Information Infrastructures Security (CRITIS 2006)* (pp. 140-150).

Dey, A. K., Salber, D., Futakawa, M., & Abowd, G. D. (1999). The conference assistant: Combining context-awareness with wearable computing. *Proceedings of the 3rd International Symposium on Wearable Computers* (ISWC '99), October 20-21, 1999, (pp. 21-28).

Dey, A., & Abowd, G. (2000). Towards a Better Understanding of Context and Context- Awareness. Paper presented at the CHI 2000 Workshop on the What, Who, Where, When, and How of Context-Awareness.

Dey, A. K., Abowd, G. D., & Salber, D. A. (2001). A conceptual framework and a toolkit for supporting the rapid prototyping of context-aware applications. *Human-Computer Interaction, 16*(2), 97–166. .doi:10.1207/S15327051HCI16234_02

Dietz, P., & Leigh, D. (2001). A Multi-User Touch Technology . In *Proceedings of User Interface Software and Technology* (pp. 219–226). DiamondTouch.

Dimakis, N., Soldatos, J., Polymenakos, L., Fleury, P., Curín, J., & Kleindienst, J. (2008). Integrated Development of Context-Aware Applications in Smart Spaces. *IEEE Pervasive Computing / IEEE Computer Society* [and]. *IEEE Communications Society, 7*(4), 71–79. doi:. doi:10.1109/MPRV.2008.75

Dirgahayu, T., Quartel, D., & Sinderen, M. (2008). Designing interaction behaviour in service-oriented enterprise application integration. In *Proceedings of the 2008 ACM symposium on Applied computing (SAC '08)*. New York: ACM Press.

Dong, H., Keates, S., & Clarkson, P. J. (2002). Accommodating older users' functional capabilities. In Brewster, S., & Zajicek, M. (Eds.), *HCI BCS London* (pp. 10–11).

Dourish, P. (2006). Implications for design. In *Proceedings of the SIGCHI conference on Human Factors in computing systems (CHI '06).* New York: ACM Press.

Dourish, P. (2007). Responsibilities and implications: further thoughts on ethnography and design. In *Proceedings of the 2007 conference on Designing for User eXperiences (DUX '07)*. New York: ACM Press

Dourish, P., & Bellotti, V. (1992). Awareness and coordination in shared workspaces. In *Proceedings of the 1992 ACM conference on Computer-supported cooperative work (CSCW '92)*.

Draves, R., Padhye, J., & Zill, B. (2004, September 26). Routing in Multi-radio, Multi-hop Wireless Mesh Networks. In *Proceedings of the 10th Annual International Conference on Mobile Computing and Networking (MobiCom '04)* (pp. 114-128).

Droms, R. (1997). *Dynamic host configuration protocol.* Retrieved December 13, 2008, from http://www.ietf.org/rfc/rfc2131.txt

Dubberly, H., Pangaro, P., & Haque, U. (2009). What is interaction? are there different types? *interactions, 16*(1).

Ducatel, K., Bogdanowicz, M., Scapolo, F., Leijten, J., & Burgelman, J. C. (2001). *ISTAG Scenarios for Ambient Intelligence in 2010.* Tech. Rep.

Ducatel, K., Bogdanowicz, M., Scapolo, F., Leijten, J., & Burgelman, J. C. (2001). *Scenarios for ambient intelligence in 2010.* Brussels, Belgium: ISTAG.

Duda, R. O., Hart, P. E., & Stork, D. G. (2000). *Pattern classification.* New York: John Wiley & Sons.

Duff, P., & Dolphin, C. (2007). Cost-benefit analysis of assistive technology to support independence for people with dementia – Part 1: Development of a methodological approach to the ENABLE cost-benefit analysis. *Technology and Disability, 19*, 73–78.

Duke University. (2003). *Duke Smart Home Program.* Retrieved October 23, 2009, from http://www.smarthome.duke.edu/home/

Dunning, T. (2008). Neuron Launches Online Brain Games. *Activities, Adaptation and Aging, 31*(4), 59–60. .doi:10.1300/J016v31n04_05

Duong, T., Bui, H., Phung, D., & Venkatesh, S. (2005). Activity recognition and abnormality detection with the switching hidden semi-Markov model. In. *Proceedings of, CVPR-05*, 838–845.

ECMA International. (1999). *ECMAScript language specification.* Retrieved December 13, 2008, from http://www.ecma-international.org/publications /standards/Ecma-262.htm

Edwards, W. K., Newman, M. W., & Sedivy, J. Z. (2001). *The case for recombinant computing* (Tech. Rep.). Retrieved from http://www.parc.com/research/projects/obje

Eisma, R., Dickinson, A., Goodman, J., Syme, A., Tiwari, L., & Newell, A. (2004). Early user involvement in the development of Information Technology-related products for older people. *Universal Access in the Information Society, 3*(2), 131–140. .doi:10.1007/s10209-004-0092-z

Ellis, C., Gibbs, S., & Rein, G. (1991). Groupware: some issues and experiences. *Communications of the ACM, 34*(1). .doi:10.1145/99977.99987

Elting, C., Rapp, S., Möhler, G., & Strube, M. (2003). *Architecture and Implementation of Multimodal Plug and Play.* Paper presented at the 5th International Conference on Multimodal Interfaces, Vancouver, British Columbia, Canada.

EMHF. (n.d.). Tackling Overweight and Obesity in Men in Europe. *European Men's Health Forum.*

Engelmore, R., & Mogan, T. (1988). *Blackboard Systems.* Reading, MA: Addison-Wesley.

Enge, P., Walter, T., Pullen, S., Kee, C., Chao, Y.-C., & Tsai, Y.-J. (1996). Wide area augmentation of the global positioning system. *Proceedings of the IEEE, 84*(8), 1063–1088. .doi:10.1109/5.533954

Essl, G., & O'Modhrain, S. (2004). Scrubber: an interface for friction-induced sounds. In *Proceedings of the 2005 Conference on New Interfaces for Musical Expression (NIME '05)*, Singapore, Singapore (pp. 70-75).

Eswaran, K. P., Gray, J. N., Lorie, R. A., & Traiger, I. L. (1976). The Notions of Consistency and Predicate Locks in a Database System. *Communications of the ACM, 19*(11), 624–633. .doi:10.1145/360363.360369

European Association for the Study of Obesity. (2004). Retrieved from http://www.easo.org/ working_groups_childhood_3.htm

Facal, D., Buiza, C., González, M. F., Soldatos, J., Petsatodis, T., Talantzis, F., et al. (2009). Cognitive Games for Healthy Elderly People in a Multi-touch Screen. In *Proceedings of International Congress on Digital Homes, Robotics and Telecare for All*.

Fallman, D. (2003). Design-oriented human-computer interaction. In *Proceedings of the SIGCHI conference on Human factors in computing systems (CHI '03)*. New York: ACM Press.

Fellbaum, C. (1998). *WordNet: An Electronic Lexical Database (Language, Speech, and Communication)*. Cambridge, MA: MIT Press.

Fielding, R. (2002). *Architectural Styles and the Design of Network-based Software Architectures*. Unpublished doctoral dissertation, University of California, Irvine, CA.

Fielding, R., Gettys, J., Mogul, J., Frystyk, H., Masinter, L., Leach, P., & Berners-Lee, T. (1999). *Hypertext transfer protocol – HTTP/1.1*. Retrieved December 13, 2008, from http://www.ietf.org/rfc/ rfc2616.txt

Filipe, P., & Mamede, N. (2005). *Towards Ubiquitous Task Management*. Retrieved January 14, 2008, from http://www.inesc-id.pt/ficheiros/publicacoes/2166.pdf

Firstbeat Technologies. (2007). *An Energy Expenditure Estimation Method Based on Heart Rate Measurement*. Firstbeat Technologies Ltd.

Fitzmaurice, G. W., Ishii, H., & Buxton, W. (1995). Bricks: Laying the Foundations for Graspable User Interfaces. In Proceedings of CHI 1995 (pp. 442-449).

Flycht-Eriksson, A., & Jönsson, A. (2003). *Some empirical findings on dialogue management and domain ontologies in dialogue systems - Implications from an evaluation of BirdQuest*. Paper presented at the Workshop on Discourse and Dialogue, Sapporo, Japan.

Forlizzi, J., & Battarbee, K. (2004). Understanding experience in interactive systems. In *Proceedings of the 5th conference on Designing interactive systems: processes, practices, methods, and techniques (DIS '04)*. New York: ACM Press.

Freksa, C. (1992). Temporal reasoning based on semi-intervals. *Artificial Intelligence, 54*, 199–227. doi:. doi:10.1016/0004-3702(92)90090-K

Frøkjær, E., & Hornbæk, K. (2008). Metaphors of human thinking for usability inspection and design. *Transactions on Computer-Human Interaction (TOCHI), 14*(4).

Gajos, K. Z. (2008). *Automatically Generating User Interfaces*. Unpublished doctoral dissertation, University of Washington, Seattle, WA. Retrieved July 30, 2009, from http://www.cs.washington.edu/ ai/puirg/papers/ kgajos-dissertation.pdf

Gajos, K. Z., Weld, D. S., & Wobbrock, J. O. (2008). Decision-Theoretic User Interface Generation. In *Proceedings of AAAI'08, NECTAR paper track*, Chicago, IL.

Gamberini, L., Alcaniz, M., Barresi, G., Fabregat, M., Ibanez, F., & Prontu, L. (2006). Cognition, technology and games for the elderly: An introduction to ELDER-GAMES Project. *PsychNology Journal, 4*(3), 285–308.

Georgantas, N., & Issarny, V. (2010). Ad-hoc ambient computing. *Special Issue on Ad hoc Ambient Computing* [IJACI]. *International Journal of Ambient Computing and Intelligence, 2*(4), iii–iv.

Georgia Institute of Technology. (2000). *Aware Home Research Initiative*. Retrieved October 23, 2009, from http://awarehome.imtc.gatech.edu/

Giardini, F., & Castelfranchi, C. (2004). Behavior Implicit Communication for Human-Robot Interaction. In Proceedings of the AAAI Fall Symposium 2004 on the Intersection of Cognitive Science and Robotics: From Interfaces to Intelligence) (pp. 91-96).

Goland, Y. Y., Cai, T., Leach, P., Gu, Y., & Albright, S. (1999). *Simple service discovery protocol/1.0: Operating without an arbiter*. Retrieved from http://www.upnp.org/ draft_cai_ssdp_v1_03.txt

Goldhaber, M. H. (1997). The Attention and the Net. *First Monday, 2*(4).

Goldhaber, M. H. (2006). How (Not) to Study the Attention Economy: A Review of The Economics of Attention: Style and Substance in the Age of Information. *First Monday, 11*(11).

Google Inc. (2008a). *Google Web Toolkit*. Retrieved December 13, 2008, from http://code.google.com/webtoolkit

Google Inc. (2008b). *Google I/O*. Retrieved December 13, 2008, from http://code.google.com/events/io/

Gopalratnam, K., & Cook, D. (2004). Active LeZi: An incremental parsing algorithm for sequential prediction. *International Journal of Artificial Intelligence Tools, 14*(1-2), 917–930. doi:.doi:10.1142/S0218213004001892

Gould, J., & Lewis, C. (1985). Designing for usability: key principles and what designers think. *Communications of the ACM, 28*(3). PubMed doi:10.1145/3166.3170

Grace, P., Blair, G. S., & Samuel, S. (2003). ReMMoC: A reflective middleware to support mobile client. In Proceedings of the *On the Move to Meaningful Internet Systems 2003: CoopIS, DOA, and ODBASE - OTM Confederated International Conferences, CoopIS, DOA, and ODBASE 2003* (pp. 1170-1187).

Grassé, P. P. (1959). La Reconstruction du Nid et les Coordinations Inter-individuelles chez Bellicosoitermes Natalensis et Cubitermes. La Théorie de la Stigmergie: Essai d'Interprétation du Comportement des Termites Constructeurs. *Insectes Sociaux, 6*, 41–81. .doi:10.1007/BF02223791

Greenfield, A. (2006). *Everyware: The dawning age of ubiquitous computing*. Berkeley, CA: Peachpit Press.

Gregorio, J., Hadley, M., Nottingham, M., & Orchard, D. (2008). *Uri template*. Retrieved December 13, 2008, from http://tools.ietf.org/html/draft-gregorio-uritemplate-03

Gruenwald, L., & Banik, S. (2001). *A power-aware technique to manage realtime database transactions in mobile ad-hoc networks.*

Guerri, J. G., Antón, A. B., Pajares, A., Monfort, M., & Sánchez, D. (2009). A mobile device application applied to low back disorders. *Multimedia Tools and Applications, 42*(3), 317–340. .doi:10.1007/s11042-008-0252-x

Guttman, E., Perkins, C., Veizades, J., & Day, M. (1999). *Service location protocol, version 2*. Retrieved December 13, 2008, from http://www.ietf.org/rfc/rfc2165.txt

Hainer, V., Frelut, M., & Seidell, J. (2002). *Obesity in Europe, The Case for Action*. International Obesity Taskforce & European Association for the Study of Obesity.

Häkkilä, J., & Mäntyjärvi, J. (2006). Developing design guidelines for context-aware mobile applications. In *Proceedings of the 3rd international conference on Mobile technology, applications & systems (Mobility '06)*. New York: ACM Press.

Hawthorn, D. (2000). Possible implications of aging for interface designers. *Interacting with Computers, 12*, 507–528. .doi:10.1016/S0953-5438(99)00021-1

Health and Fitness Institute. com. (n.d.). *Medical Reasons for Obesity*. Retrieved from http://healthandfitnessinstitute.com/medical-reasons-for-obesity.htm

Healthy People 2010 Operational Definition. (n.d.). *Operational Definition: Objective* (pp. 22-2).

Heidegger, M. (1927). Sein und Zeit. Halle A. D. S: Niemeyer.

Heim, S. (2007). *The Resonant Interface – HCI Foundations for interaction design*. Reading, MA: Addison-Wesley.

Hermann, T., & Ritter, H. (1999). Listen to your Data: Model-Based Sonification for Data Analysis. In Proceedings of the Advances in Intelligent Computing and Multimedia Systems, Baden-Baden, Germany (pp. 189–194).

Hermann, T., Bovermann, T., Riedenklau, E., & Ritter, H. (2007). Tangible Computing for Interactive Sonification of Multivariate Data. In Proceedings of the 2nd Interactive Sonification Workshop.

Hermann, T., Krause, J., & Ritter, H. (2002). Real-Time Control of Sonification Models with an Audio-Haptic Interface. In Proceedings of the International Conference on Auditory Display 2002 (pp. 82-86).

Hermann, H., & Hunt, A. (Eds.). (2005). *IEEE Multimedia, Special Issue Interactive Sonification*. Washington, DC: IEEE.

Hightower, J., & Borriello, G. (2001, August). Location systems for ubiquitous computing. *IEEE Computer, 34*(8), 57–66.

Hinckley, K., Pierce, J., Sinclair, M., & Horvitz, E. (2000). Sensing techniques for mobile interaction. In *Proceedings of the 13th annual ACM symposium on User interface software and technology (UIST '00)*. New York: ACM Press.

Hindmarsh, J., Fraser, M., Heath, C., Benford, S., & Greenhalgh, C. (2000). Object-focused interaction in collaborative virtual environments. *Transactions on Computer-Human Interaction (TOCHI), 7*(4).

Hollan, J., Hutchins, E., & Kirsh, D. (2000). Distributed cognition: toward a new foundation for human-computer interaction research. *Transactions on Computer-Human Interaction (TOCHI), 7*(2).

Hollingsed, T., & Novick, D. (2007). Usability inspection methods after 15 years of research and practice. In *Proceedings of the 25th annual ACM international conference on Design of communication (SIGDOC '07)*. New York: ACM Press.

Hommel, B., Musseler, J., Aschersleben, G., & Prinz, W. (2001). The theory of event coding (TEC): A framework for perception and action planning. [PubMed]. *The Behavioral and Brain Sciences, 24*, 849–878. doi:10.1017/S0140525X01000103

Hong, Y. J., Kim, I. J., Ahn, S. C., & Kim, H. G. (2008). Activity Recognition Using Wearable Sensors for Elder Care. In *Proceedings of the Second International Conference on Future Generation Communication and Networking* (pp.302-305).

Hornecker, E., & Buur, J. (2006). Getting a grip on tangible interaction: a framework on physical space and social interaction. In *Proceedings of the SIGCHI conference on Human Factors in computing systems (CHI '06)*. New York: ACM Press.

Hub, A., Diepstraten, J., & Ertl, T. (2004). Design and development of an indoor navigation and object identification system for the blind. In Assets '04: Proceedings of the 6th International ACM SIGACCESS Conference on Computers and Accessibility (pp. 147-152). New York: ACM Publishing.

Hughes, J., Randall, D., & Shapiro, D. (1992). Faltering from ethnography to design. In *Proceedings of the 1992 ACM conference on Computer-supported cooperative work (CSCW '92)*. New York: ACM Press.

Hughes, J., King, V., Rodden, T., & Andersen, H. (1995). The role of ethnography in interactive systems design. *Interaction, 2*(2). .doi:10.1145/205350.205358

Hydra. (2009). The Hydra project. Retrieved October 27, 2009, from http://www.hydramiddleware.eu

Iacoboni, M. (2008). *Mirroring people: The new science of how we connect with others*. New York: Farrar, Straus and Giroux.

IANA. (2008). *Internet Assigned Numbers Authority: MIME media types.* Retrieved December 13, 2008, from http://www.iana.org/assignments/media-types

Ihnatko, A. (2011, July 11). MacBook Air is where the iCloud lives. *ComputerWorld*. Retrieved from http://www.computerworld.com/s/article /9218293/MacBook_Air_is_where_ the_iCloud_lives?taxonomyId=15

Imielinski, T., & Badrinath, B. R. (1994). Mobile wireless computing: challenges in data management. *Communications of the ACM, 37*(10), 18–28. .doi:10.1145/194313.194317

Intille, S. S. (2009). *Developing Shared Home Behavior Datasets to Advance HCI and Ubiquitous Computing Research*. Retrieved November 11, 2009, from http://web.mit.edu/datasets/Home.html

Intille, S. S., Larson, K., Munguia Tapia, E., Beaudin, J., Kaushik, P., Nawyn, J., & Rockinson, R. (2006). Using a live-in laboratory for ubiquitous computing research . *Pervasive computing*, 349-365.

Ishii, H., & Ullmer, B. (1997). Tangible bits: towards seamless interfaces between people, bits and atoms. In *Proceedings of the SIGCHI conference on Human factors in computing systems (CHI '97)*. New York: ACM Press.

Ishii, H. (2008). Tangible User Interfaces, MIT Media Laboratory . In Sears, A., & Jacko, J. A. (Eds.), *The human-Computer Interaction Handbook, Fundamentals, Evolving Technologies and Emerging Applications*. New York: CRC Press.

ITU-T. (2001). [*Arrangement of digits, letters and symbols on telephones and other devices that can be used for gaining access to a telephone network*. Geneva, Switzerland: International Telecommunications Union.]. *E (Norwalk, Conn.)*, 161.

IUFoST. (2007). *Obesity*. International Union of Food Science and Technology.

Jacob, R. (2006). What is the next generation of human-computer interaction? In *Proceedings of the extended abstracts on Human factors in computing systems (CHI '06)*. New York: ACM Press.

Jacob, R. J. K., Girouard, A., Hirshfield, L. M., Horn, M. S., Shaer, O., Solovey, E. T., & Zigelbaum, J. (2008). Reality-based interaction: a framework for post-WIMP interfaces.

Jacob, R., Deligiannidis, L., & Morrison, S. (1999). A software model and specification language for non-WIMP user interfaces. *Transactions on Computer-Human Interaction (TOCHI), 6*(1).

Jacquet, P., Muhlethaler, P., Clausen, T., Laouiti, A., Qayyum, A., & Viennot, L. (2001, December 28). Optimized Link State Routing Protocol for Ad Hoc Networks. In *Proceedings of the IEEE International Multi Topic Conference. Technology for the 21st Century (INMIC 2001)* (pp. 62-68).

Jaimes, A., & Sebe, N. (2007). Multimodal human-computer interaction: A survey. *Computer Vision and Image Understanding. Special Issue on Vision for Human-Computer Interaction, 108*(1-2), 116–134.

Jakkula, V., & Cook, D. (2008). Anomaly detection using temporal data mining in a smart home environment. [PubMed]. *Methods of Information in Medicine, 47*(1), 70–75.

Jeffries, R., Miller, J., Wharton, C., & Uyeda, K. (1991). User interface evaluation in the real world: a comparison of four techniques. In *Proceedings of the SIGCHI conference on Human factors in computing systems (CHI '91)*. New York: ACM Press

Jeong, K., Won, J., & Bae, C. (2008). User activity recognition and logging in distributed Intelligent Gadgets. In *Proceedings of the IEEE International Conference on Multisensor Fusion and Integration for Intelligent Systems* (pp. 683-686).

Johnson, D. B., Maltz, D. A., & Broch, J. (2001). DSR: the Dynamic Source Routing Protocol for Multihop Wireless Ad Hoc Network . In Perkins, C. E. (Ed.), *Ad Hoc Networking* (pp. 139–172). Boston: Addison-Wesley Longman Publishing Co.

Jorge, J. (2001). Adaptive Tools for the Elderly. *New Devices to cope with Age-Induced Cognitive Disabilities*.

Kalman, R. E. (1960). A new approach to linear filtering and prediction problems. *Journal of Basic Engineering, 82*(D), 35-45.

Karat, C., Halverson, C., Horn, D., & Karat, J. (1999, May 15-20). Patterns of entry and correction in large vocabulary continuous speech recognition systems. In *Proceedings of CHI'99*, Pittsburgh, PA (pp. 568-575).

Kawaguchi, A. (2003). Capturing and analyzing requirement: in case of software and applying to hardware. In *Proceedings of the 2003 conference on Asia South Pacific design automation (ASPDAC)*. New York: ACM Press.

Keinonen, T. (2008). User-centered design and fundamental need. In *Proceedings of the 5th Nordic conference on Human-computer interaction: building bridges (NordiCHI '08)*. New York: ACM Press.

Khanna, G. (2005). *Building Bluetooth Applications on the Windows CE 5.0 and Windows Mobile Platforms*. Microsoft.

Kilander, F., & Lönnqvist, P. (2002). A Whisper in the Woods: An Ambient Soundscape for Peripheral Awareness of Remote Processes. In Proceedings of the International Conference on Auditory Display 2002.

Kindberg, T., & Barton, J. (2001). A web-based nomadic computing system. *Computer Networks, 35*(4), 443–456. . doi:10.1016/S1389-1286(00)00181-X

Klemmer, S., Hartmann, B., & Takayama, L. (2006). How bodies matter: five themes for interaction design. In *Proceedings of the 6th conference on Designing Interactive systems (DIS '06)*. New York: ACM Press.

Kobsa, A., Koenemann, J., & Pohl, W. (2001). Personalised hypermedia presentation techniques for improving online customer relationships. *The Knowledge Engineering Review, 16*(2), 111–155. .doi:10.1017/S0269888901000108

Kolehmainen, K., Hongisto, M., & Kanstrén, T. (2008). Optimizing dynamic performance scaling for user interface performance. In *Proceedings of the International Conference on Mobile Technology, Applications, and Systems (Mobility '08)*.

Koponen, T., & Virtanen, T. (2004). A service discovery: A service broker approach. In *Proceedings of the 37th Annual Hawaii International Conference on System Sciences*.

Korth, H. F., Levy, E., & Silberschatz, A. (1990). A formal approach to recovery by compensating transactions. In D. McLeod, R. Sacks-Davis, & H.-J. Schek (Eds.), *Proceedings of the 16th International Conference on Very Large Data Bases* (pp. 95-106). San Francisco, CA: Morgan Kaufmann.

Kosta, E., Pitkänen, O., Niemelä, M., & Kaasinen, E. (2010). Mobile-centric ambient intelligence in health and homecare - Anticipating ethical and legal challenges. *Science and Engineering Ethics*, *16*(2), 303–323. doi:10.1007/s11948-009-9150-5

Kramer, G. (Ed.). (1994). *Auditory Display*. Reading, MA: Addison-Wesley.

Krawczyk, H. (1993, August 22). Secret Sharing Made Short. In *Proceedings of the 13th Annual International Cryptology Conference on Advances in Cryptology (CRYPTO '93)* (pp. 136-146).

Krishnamurthy, B., Gill, P., & Arlitt, M. (2008). A few chirps about twitter. In *Proceedings of the first workshop on Online social networks (WOSP '08)*. New York: ACM Press.

Krishnan, R., & Silvester, J. A. (1993, March 28). Choice of Allocation Granularity in Multipath Source Routing Schemes. In *Proceedings of the Twelfth Annual Joint Conference of the IEEE Computer and Communications Societies (INFOCOM '93)* (pp. 322-329).

Kristensson, P. O., Arnell, O., Björk, A., Dahlbäck, N., Pennerup, J., Prytz, E., et al. (2008). InfoTouch: an explorative multi-touch information visualization interface for tagged photo collections. In *Proceedings of the Nordic Conference on Human-Computer Interaction*.

Kumar, V., Prabhu, N., Dunham, M. H., & Seydim, A. Y. (2002). TCOT- A Timeout-based Mobile Transaction Commitment Protocol. *IEEE Transactions on Computers*, *51*(10), 1212–1218. .doi:10.1109/TC.2002.1039846

Kweon, S., Cho, E., & Kim, E. (2008). Interactivity dimension: media, contents, and user perception. In *Proceedings of the 3rd international conference on Digital Interactive Media in Entertainment and Arts (DIMEA '08)*. New York: ACM Press.

Lai, W. S. (1985). Bifurcated Routing in Computer Networks. *SIGCOMM Computer Communication Review*, *15*(3), 28–49. .doi:10.1145/1015621.1015625

Lal, R. (2008). *Measurement of Energy Expenditure*. School of Biological, Chemical and Environmental Sciences.

Lausen, H., & Innsbruck, D. (2006). *Semantic annotations for WSDL (SAWSDL)*. Retrieved September 28, 2006, from http://www.w3.org/TR/sawsdl/

Le, H. N., & Nygard, M. (2005, August 22-26). Mobile Transaction System for Supporting Mobile Work. In *Proceedings of the 16th IEEE International Workshop on Database and Expert Systems Applications, DEXA Workshops 2005*, Copenhagen, Denmark (pp. 1090-1094). Washington, DC: IEEE Computer Society.

Lee, C., & Helal, S. (2003). Context attributes: An approach to enable context-awareness for service discovery. In *Proceedings of the 2003 Symposium on Applications and the Internet* (p. 22).

Lee, G., Faratin, P., Bauer, S., & Wroclawski, J. (2004). A user-guided cognitive agent for network service selection in pervasive computing environments. In *Proceedings of the Second IEEE International Conference on Pervasive Computing and Communications (PerCom'04)* (p. 219).

Lee, S.-J., & Gerla, M. (2000, September 23). AODV-BR: Backup Routing in Ad Hoc Networks. In *Proceedings of the Wireless Communications and Networking Conference (WCNC'00)* (pp. 1311-1316).

Lee, S.-J., & Gerla, M. (2001, November 6). Split Multipath Routing with Maximally Disjoint Paths in Ad Hoc Networks. In *Proceedings of the IEEE International Conference on Communications (ICC '01)* (pp. 3201-3205).

Lee, D. L., Xu, J., Zheng, B., & Lee, W.-C. (2002). Data management in location-dependent information services. *IEEE Pervasive Computing / IEEE Computer Society* [and]. *IEEE Communications Society*, *1*(3), 65–72. doi:. doi:10.1109/MPRV.2002.1037724

Lee, I., & Chen, S. (2009). Trends in ubiquitous multimedia computing. *International Journal of Multimedia and Ubiquitous Engineering*, *4*(2).

Lee, K. C. K., Leong, H. V., & Si, A. (1999). Semantic query caching in a mobile environment. SIGMOBILE Mob. *Computer Communication Review, 3*(2), 28–36. .doi:10.1145/584027.584029

Lenat, D. B. (1995). CYC: A large-scale investment in knowledge infrastructure. *Communications of the ACM, 38*(11), 33–38. .doi:10.1145/219717.219745

Lenat, D. B., Guha, R. V., Pittman, K., Pratt, D., & Shepherd, M. (1990). CYC: Toward programs with common sense. *Communications of the ACM, 33*(8), 30–49. .doi:10.1145/79173.79176

Liao, W.-H., Wang, S.-L., Sheu, J.-P., & Tseng, Y.-C. (2002). A Multi-Path QoS Routing Protocol in a Wireless Mobile Ad Hoc Network. *Telecommunication Systems, 19*(3-4), 329–347. .doi:10.1023/A:1013838304991

Lim, Y-K., Stolterman, E., & Tenenberg, J. (2008). The anatomy of prototypes: Prototypes as filters, prototypes as manifestations of design ideas. *Transactions on Computer-Human Interaction (TOCHI), 15*(2).

Lin, Y.-W., & Lin, C.-W. (2004). An intelligent push system for mobile clients with wireless information appliances. *IEEE Transactions on Consumer Electronics, 50*(3), 952–961. .doi:10.1109/TCE.2004.1341706

Liu, J., & Issarny, V. (2005). Signal strength based service discovery (S3D) in mobile ad hoc networks. In *Proceedings of the 16th Annual IEEE International Symposium on Personal Indoor and Mobile Radio Communications (PIMRC'05)*, Berlin, Germany.

Liu, J., & Issarny, V. (2007, August). An Incentive Compatible Reputation Mechanism for Ubiquitous Computing Environments. *International Journal of Information Security*, 297–311. doi:10.1007/s10207-007-0029-7

Li, X., Feng, L., Zhou, L., & Shi, Y. (2009). Learning in an Ambient Intelligent World: Enabling Technologies and Practices. *IEEE Transactions on Knowledge and Data Engineering, 21*(6), 910–924. .doi:10.1109/TKDE.2008.143

Loadstone. (2009). Loadstone Project. Retrieved October, 28, 2009, from http://www.loadstone-gps.com/

Logan, B., Healey, J., Philipose, M., Tapia, M. E., & Intille, S. (2007). A long-term evaluation of sensing modalities for activity recognition. In *Proceedings of the International Conference on Ubiquitous Computing* (pp. 483-500). Berlin: Springer.

Lombriser, C., Bharatula, N. B., Roggen, D., & Tröster, G. (2007). On-Body Activity Recognition in a Dynamic Sensor Network. In *Proceedings of the Second International Conference on Body Area Networks (BodyNets)* (No. 17).

Löndahl, C. (2007). *Obesity - A Threat to a Public Health?* Swedish Council for Working Life and Social Research.

Lopez-de-Ipina, D., Vazquez, J. I., & Abaitua, J. (2007). *A Web 2.0 Platform to Enable Context-Aware Mobile Mash-ups*. Retrieved November 3, 2008, from http://paginaspersonales.deusto.es/dipina /publications/SentientGraffitiAml07.pdf

Lou, W., Liu, W., & Fang, Y. (2004, November 22). SPREAD: Enhancing Data Confidentiality in Mobile Ad Hoc Networks. In *Proceedings of the Twenty-third Annual Joint Conference of the IEEE Computer and Communications Societies (INFOCOM 2004)* (pp. 2404-2413).

Lugmayr, A., Risse, T., Stockleben, B., Kaario, J., & Laurila, K. (2008). *Semantic Ambient Media Expereinces SAME 2008 (NAMU Series)*. Retrieved October 28, 2008, from Newell, A. F. (2008). Commentary on Computers and People with Disabilities: Accessible Computing – Past Trends and Future Suggestions. *Transactions on Accessible Computing, 1*(2), 9.1-9.7.

Ma, R., & Ilow, J. (2003, October 20). Reliable Multipath Routing with Fixed Delays in MANET Using Regenerating Nodes. In *Proceedings of the 28th Annual IEEE International Conference on Local Computer Networks* (pp. 719-725).

Mahmud, A. A., Mubin, O., Reny, J. R., Shadid, S., & Yeo, L. (2007). Affective Tabletop Game: A New Gaming Experience for Children. In *Proceedings of the Second Annual IEEE International Workshop on Horizontal Interactive Human-Computer System*.

Mamdani, A., Pitt, J., & Stathis, K. (1999). Connected Communities from the standpoint of Multi-agent Systems. *New Generation Computing, 17*(4), 381–393. .doi:10.1007/BF03037244

Mao, J.-Y., Vredenburg, K., Smith, P., & Carey, T. (2005). The state of user-centered design practice. *Communications of the ACM, 48*(3). .doi:10.1145/1047671.1047677

Marchionini, G., & Sibert, J. (1991). An agenda for human-computer interaction: science and engineering serving human needs. *SIGCHI Bulletin, 23*(4).

Marina, M. K., & Das, S. R. (2001, November 11). On-demand Multipath Distance Vector Routing in Ad Hoc Networks. In *Proceedings of the Ninth International Conference on Network Protocols* (pp. 14-23).

Martin, D., Burstein, M., Hobbs, J., Lassila, O., McDermott, D., McIlraith, S., et al. (2004). OWL-S: Semantic markup for web services. *W3C Member Submission.*

Marx, M., & Schmandt, C. (1996, April 13-18). MailCall: Message presentation and navigation in a nonvisual environment. In *Proceedings of CHI'96,* Vancouver, British Columbia, Canada (pp. 165-172).

Massie, T. H., & Salisbury, J. K. (1994). The PHANTOM Haptic Interface: A Device for Probing Virtual Objects. In Proceedings of the ASME Winter Annual Meeting, Symposium on Haptic Interfaces for Virtual Environment and Teleoperator Systems.

Mateas, M., Salvador, T., Scholtz, J., & Sorensen, D. (1996). Engineering Ethnography in the Home. In *CHI 96 Conference Companion* (pp. 283-284).

Mazé, R. (2007). *Occupying time: design, technology and the form of interaction.* Stockholm, Sweden: Axl Books.

McCarthy, J. (1960). *Physical Activity. European Opinion Research Group EEIG* (pp. 183–186). Special Eurobarometer.

McCartney, J. (2002). Rethinking the computer music language: SuperCollider. *Computer Music Journal, 26*(4), 61–68. .doi:10.1162/014892602320991383

McClelland, I. (2005). 'User experience' design a new form of design practice takes shape. In *Proceedings of CHI '05 extended abstracts on Human factors in computing systems.* New York: ACM Press.

Meghdadi, T., & Arts, S. (2003, September). *Symbol Selects Socket Connection Solution Using Bluetooth® Wireless Technology for PPT 8800 Mobile Terminal.* Chicago: Frontline Supply Chain Week.

Meiland, F. J. M., Reinersmann, A., Bergvall-Kareborn, B., Craig, D., Moelaert, F., & Mulvenna, M. D. (2007). *COGKNOW: Development and evaluation of an ICT device for people with mild dementia in Medical and Care Compunetics* (Bos, L., & Blobel, B., Eds.). Lansdale, PA: IOS Press.

Melanson, J. R., & Freedson, P. (1994). Validity of the Computer Science and Applications, Inc. (CSA) activity monitor. *Journal of the American College of Sports Medicine.*

Metcalf, B. S., Voss, L. D., & Wilkin, T. J. (2002). Accelerometers identify inactive and potentially obese children (EarlyBird 3). *Archives of Disease in Childhood, 87,* 166–167. PubMed doi:10.1136/adc.87.2.166

Meyer, H., & Kuropka, D. (2006). Requirements for automated service composition. In Proceedings of the Business Process Management Workshops (pp. 447-458).

Meyer, S., & Rakotonirainy, A. (2003). A Survey of Research on Context-Aware Homes. *Conferences in Research and Practice in Information Technology Series, 21, 158–168.*

Microsoft Corporation. (2001). *Microsoft Inductive User Interface Guidelines.* Retrieved March 31, 2010, from http://msdn.microsoft.com/en-us/library/ms997506. aspx#iuiguidelines_topic2

Miller, C. (1997). Computational approaches to interface design: what works, what doesn't, what should and what might. In *Proceedings of the 2nd international conference on Intelligent user interfaces (IUI '97).* New York: ACM Press.

Miller, M. (2001). *Discovering Bluetooth.* USA: SYBEX Inc.

Milward, D., & Beveridge, M. A. (2004, July 19-21). *Ontologies and the Structure of Dialogue.* Paper presented at CATALOG, 8th Workshop on the Semantics and Pragmatics of Dialogue, Barcelona, Spain.

Mitra, S., & Acharya, T. (2007). Gesture Recognition: A Survey. *IEEE Transactions on Systems, Man and Cybernetics. Part C, Applications and Reviews, 37*(3), 311–324. .doi:10.1109/TSMCC.2007.893280

Mohan, C., Lindsay, B., & Obermarck, R. (1986). Transaction Management in the R Distributed Database Management System. *ACM Transactions on Database Systems*, *11*(4), 378–396. .doi:10.1145/7239.7266

Montoro, G., Haya, P. A., & Alamán, X. (2004). *Context adaptive interaction with an automatically created spoken interface for intelligent environments*. Paper presented at INTELLCOMM 04, Bangkok, Thailand.

Montoro, G., Haya, P. A., Alamán, X., López-Cózar, R., & Callejas, Z. (2006). A proposal for an XML definition of a dynamic spoken interface for ambient intelligence. In *Proceedings of the International Conference on Intelligent Computing (ICIC 06),* Kunming, China (pp. 711-716).

Moscovich, T., & Hughes, J. F. (2008). Indirect mappings of multi-touch input using one and two hands. In *Proceedings of the SIGCHI conference on Human factors in computing systems* (pp.1275-1284).

Mozer, M. C. (2005). Lessons from an adaptive house . In Cook, D., & Das, R. (Eds.), *Smart environments: Technologies, protocols, and applications* (pp. 273–294). Hoboken, NJ: J. Wiley & Sons. doi:10.1002/047168659X.ch12

MRC. (2009). Moderate obesity takes years off life expectancy, though not as many as smoking. *Medical Research Council Media Release*. msdn. (n.d.). *About Bluetooth*. Retrieved from http://msdn.microsoft.com/en-us/library/aa362761(VS.85).aspx msdn. (n.d.). *About Bluetooth*. Retrieved from http://www.palowireless.com/bluetooth/

Mueller, S., Tsang, R. P., & Ghosal, D. (2004). Multipath Routing in Mobile Ad Hoc Networks: Issues and Challenges. In E. Gelenbe (Ed.), *Performance Tools and Applications to Networked Systems* (pp. 209–234). Berlin: Springer. doi:10.1007/978-3-540-24663-3_10

Mukerjee, A., & Joe, G. (1990). A qualitative model for space. In Proceedings of AAAI-90, Boston (pp. 721-727).

Muller, M., & Kuhn, S. (1993). Participatory design. *Communications of the ACM, 36*(6). .doi:10.1145/153571.255960

Munguia Tapia, E., Intille, S. S., & Larson, K. (2004). *Activity recognition in the home using simple and ubiquitous sensors*. Paper presented at Pervasvie 2004, Vienna, Austria.

Munguia, E. T., Intille, S. S., Lopez, L., & Larson, K. (2006). The design of a portable kit of wireless sensors for naturalistic data collection. In [Berlin: Springer.]. *Proceedings of the PERVASIVE, 2006*, 117–134.

Murphy, K. P. (2002). Dynamic Bayesian networks: Representation, inference and learning. Unpublished doctoral dissertation, University of California, Berkeley.

Murphy, T. (2009, September 10). STOP Obesity Alliance Issues Recommendations to Ensure Health Reform Successfully Addresses Obesity Epidemic. *Medical News Today*. Retrieved from http://www.medicalnewstoday.com/ articles/163443.php

Murray- Smith. R., Williamson, J., Hughes, S., & Quaade, T. (2008). Stane: synthesized surfaces for tactile input. In *Proceedings of the SIGCHI conference on Human factors in computing systems* (pp. 1299-1302).

Musolesi, M., & Mascolo, C. (2007). Designing Mobility Models Based on Social Network Theory. *ACM SIGMOBILE Mobile Computing and Communications Review*, *11*(3), 59–70. .doi:10.1145/1317425.1317433

Muto, W., & Diefenbach, P. (2008). Applications of multitouch gaming technology to middle-school education. In *Proceedings of the ACM SIGGRAPH 2008 Posters.*

Mylopoulos, J., Chung, L., & Yu, E. (1999). From object-oriented to goal-oriented requirements analysis. *Communications of the ACM, 42*(1). PubMed doi:10.1145/291469.293165

Mynatt, E. D., Back, M., Want, R., & Frederick, R. (1997). Audio Aura: Light-weight audio augmented reality. In *Proceedings of ACM UIST'97,* Banff, Alberta, Canada (pp. 211-212).

Nagao, K., & Rekimoto, J. (1995). Ubiquitous talker: Spoken language interaction with real world objects. In *Proceedings of IJCAI-95* (Vol. 2, pp. 1284-1290).

Nakazawa, J., Tokuda, H., Edwards, W. K., & Ramachandran, U. (2006). A bridging framework for universal interoperability in pervasive systems. In *Proceedings of the 26th IEEE International Conference on Distributed Computing Systems* (p. 3).

Nandiraju, N. S., & Agrawal, D. P. (2006, October 9). Multipath Routing in Wireless Mesh Networks. In *Proceedings of the IEEE International Conference on Mobile Adhoc and Sensor Systems* (pp. 741-746).

Narayanan, S., & McIlraith, S. A. (2002). Simulation, verification and automated composition of web services. In *Proceedings of the 11th International Conference on World Wide Web (WWW '02)*, Honolulu, HI (pp. 77-88).

Nasipuri, A., & Das, S. R. (1999, November 10). On-demand Multipath Routing for Mobile Ad Hoc Networks. In *Proceedings of the Eighth IEEE International Conference on Computer Communications and Networks* (pp. 64-70).

Natural User Interface Group. (2009). *Touchlib: A Multi-Touch Development Kit*. Retrieved from http://www.nuigroup.com/touchlib

Nau, D., Cao, Y., Lotem, A., & Muftoz-Avila, H. (1999). Shop: Simple hierarchical ordered planner. In IJCAI'99: Proceedings of the 16th International Joint Conference on Artincial Intelligence (pp. 968-973). San Francisco: Morgan Kaufmann.

Newcomer, E. (2002). *Understanding Web Services: XML, WSDL, SOAP and UDDI*. Reading, MA: Addison-Wesley.

NHS. (n.d.). *Obesity (Silver Spring, Md.)*. Retrieved from http://www.nhs.uk/Conditions/Obesity /Pages/Introduction.aspx.

Nielsen, J. (2005). *Ten usability heuristics*. Retrieved March 31, 2010, from http://www.useit.com/papers/heuristic /heuristic_list.html

Nielsen, J., & Molich, R. (1990). Heuristic evaluation of user interfaces. In *Proceedings of the SIGCHI conference on Human factors in computing systems (CHI '90)*. New York: ACM Press.

NMEA. (2008). *NMEA 0183, The Standard for Interfacing Marine Electronics*. Severna Park, MD: NMEA.

Norman, D. A. (2002). *The Design of Everyday Things*. New York: Basic Books.

Nouali, N., Doucet, A., & Drias, H. (2005). A Two-Phase Commit Protocol for Mobile Wireless Environment. In *Proceedings of the Sixteenth Australasian Database Conference, Database Technologies 2005*, Newcastle, Australia (pp. 135-143).

Nygard, L. (2008). The meaning of everyday technology as experienced by people with dementia who live alone. *Dementia (London)*, 7(4), 481–502. . doi:10.1177/1471301208096631

Oh, Y., Schmidt, A., & Woo, W. (2007). *Designing, developing, and evaluating context-aware systems. MUE2007* (pp. 1158–1163). IEEE Computer Society.

Oliveira, R., & Rocha, H. (2005). Towards an approach for multi-device interface design. In *Proceedings of the 11th Brazilian Symposium on Multimedia and the web (WebMedia '05)*. New York: ACM Press.

O'Modhrain, S., & Essl, G. (2004). PebbleBox and CrumbleBag: tactile interfaces for granular synthesis. In Proceedings of the 2004 Conference on New Interfaces for Musical Expression (NIME '04), Singapore, Singapore (pp. 74-79).

Pantelopoulos, S. (2010). SOCIABLE: a surface computing platform empowering more effective cognitive training interventions for healthy elderly and demented patients. In *Proceedings of the International Conference of Alzheimer's Disease International*.

Papadimitratos, P., & Haas, Z. J. (2003). Secure Message Transmission in Mobile Ad Hoc Networks. *Ad Hoc Networks*, 1(1), 193–209. .doi:10.1016/S1570-8705(03)00018-0

Patil, A. A., Oundhakar, S. A., Sheth, A. P., & Verma, K. (2004). Meteor-s web service annotation framework. In *Proceedings of the 13th International Conference on World Wide Web (WWW '04)*, New York (pp. 553-562).

Patten, J., & Ishii, H. (2007). Mechanical constraints as computational constraints in tabletop tangible interfaces. In Proceedings of the SIGCHI Conference on Human Factors in Computing Systems (pp. 809-818).

Pearce, S. (2007, July). *Juice PAM Firmware Functional Specification*. Cambridge Consultants.

Pearl, J. (2000). *Causality: Models, Reasoning, and Inference*. Cambridge, UK: Cambridge University Press.

Pearlman, M. R., Haas, Z. J., Peter, S., & Tabrizi, S. S. (2000, August 11). On the Impact of Alternate Path Routing for Load Balancing in Mobile Ad Hoc Networks. In *Proceedings of the 1st ACM international symposium on Mobile ad hoc networking & computing (MobiHoc '00)* (pp. 3-10).

Peltonen, P., Kurvinen, E., Salovaara, A., Jacucci, G., Ilmonenm, T., Evans, J., et al. (2008). It's mine, don't touch": Interactions at a large multi-touch display in a city Center. In *Proceedings of the SIGCHI conference on human factors in computing systems* (pp.1285-1294). New York: ACM Press.

Pérez, G., Gabriel de Amores, J., & Manchón, P. A. (2006). Multimodal Architecture for Home Control by Disabled Users. In *Proceedings of the IEEE/Acl 2006 Workshop on Spoken Language Technology,* New York (pp. 134-137). Washington, DC: IEEE Computer Society.

Pérez, G., Amores, G., Manchón, P., Gómez, F., & González, J. (2006). Integrating OWL Ontologies with a Dialogue Manager. *Procesamiento del Lenguaje Natural, 37,* 153–160.

Perkins, C. E., & Royer, E. M. (1999, February 25). Ad-hoc On-Demand Distance Vector Routing. In *Proceedings of the Second IEEE Workshop on Mobile Computer Systems and Applications (WMCSA '99)* (pp. 90-100).

Petersen, R. C., Stevens, J. C., Ganguli, M., Tangalos, E. G., Cummings, J. L., & DeKosky, S. T. (2001). *Practice parameter: Early Detection of dementia: Mild cognitive impairment (an evidence-based review). Report of the Quality Standards Subcommittee of the American Academy of Neurology.* Neurology.

Petroski, H. (1994). *The Evolution of Useful Things: How Everyday Artifacts-From Forks and Pins to Paper Clips and Zippers-Came to be as They are.* New York: Vintage Books.

Pezzulo, G. (2008). Coordinating with the Future: The Anticipatory Nature of Representation. *Minds and Machines, 18,* 179–225. .doi:10.1007/s11023-008-9095-5

Picking, R., Robinet, A., Grout, V., McGinn, J., Roy, A., Ellis, S., & Oram, D. (2009). A case study using a methodological approach to developing user interfaces for elderly and disabled people. *The Computer Journal.* doi:.doi:10.1093/comjnl/bxp089

Pilgrim, C. (2008). Improving the usability of web 2.0 applications. In *Proceedings of the nineteenth ACM conference on Hypertext and hypermedia (HT '08).* New York: ACM Press.

Pinelle, D., Gutwin, C., & Greenberg, S. (2003). Task analysis for groupware usability evaluation: Modeling shared-workspace tasks with the mechanics of collaboration. *Transactions on Computer-Human Interaction (TOCHI), 10*(4).

Pirzada, A. A., Portmann, M., & Indulska, J. (2008). Performance Analysis of Multi-radio AODV in Hybrid Wireless Mesh Networks. *Computer Communications,* 885–895. doi:10.1016/j.comcom.2007.12.012

Pitoura, E., & Samaras, G. (1998). *Data Management for Mobile Computing.* Dordrecht, The Netherlands: Kluwer Academic Publishers.

PLASTIC Project. (2007). *Middleware specification and architecture.* Retrieved from http://www-c.inria.fr:9098/plastic/test-1/m12/plastic_d3_1.pdf/download

Plewe, D. (2008). Transactional arts: interaction as transaction. In *Proceeding of the 16th ACM international conference on Multimedia (MM '08).* New York: ACM Press.

Ponce, J., Berg, T., Everingham, M., Forsyth, D., Hebert, M., Lazebnik, S., et al. (2006). Dataset issues in object recognition. In *Proceedings of Toward Category-Level Object Recognition* (pp. 29-48).

Porzel, R., & Gurevych, I. (2002). *Towards Context-adaptive Utterance Interpretation.* Paper presented at the 3rd SIGDial Workshop on Discourse and Dialogue, Philadelphia.

Potamianos, G., Huang, J., Marcheret, E., Libal, V., Balchandran, R., Epstein, M., et al. (2008). Far-field multimodal speech processing and conversational interaction in smart spaces. In *Hands-Free Speech Communication and Microphone Arrays.*

Preuveneers, D., Van den Bergh, J., Wagelaar, D., Georges, A., Rigole, P., Tim Clerckx, T., et al. (2004). Towards an Extensible Context Ontology for Ambient Intelligence. In *Ambient Intelligence* (LNCS 3295, pp. 148-159).

Punie, Y. (2003). A Social and Technological View of Ambient Intelligence in Everyday Life: What Bends the Trend? In Proceedings of the *The European Media and Technology in Everyday Life Network, 2000-2003*. Retrieved November 27, 2007, from www.lse.ac.uk/collections/EMTEL/reports /punie_2003_emtel.pdf

Quesada, J. F., García, F., Sena, E., Bernal, J. A., & Amores, J. G. (2001). Dialogue Management in a Home Machine Environment: Linguistic Components over an Agent Architecture. *Procesamiento del Lenguaje Natural, 27*, 89–96.

Ramos, C., Augusto, J. C., & Shapiro, D. (2008). Ambient Intelligence - the Next Step for Artificial Intelligence. *IEEE Intelligent Systems, 23*(2), 15–18. .doi:10.1109/MIS.2008.19

Ran, L., Helal, S., & Moore, S. (2004). Drishti: An Integrated Indoor/Outdoor Blind Navigation System and Service. In PERCOM '04: Proceedings of the Second IEEE International Conference on Pervasive Computing and Communications (pp. 23).Washington, DC: IEEE Computer Society.

Randell, D., Cui, Z., & Cohn, A. (1992). A spatial logic based on regions and connection. In Proceedings of KR-92, Cambridge, MA (pp. 165-176).

Raverdy, P. G., Issarny, V., Chibout, R., & de La Chapelle, A. (2006). A multi-protocol approach to service discovery and access in pervasive environments. In *Proceedings of the 3rd Annual International Conference on Mobile and Ubiquitous Systems: Networks and Services (MOBIQUITOUS 2006),* San Jose, CA.

Raverdy, P. G., Riva, O., de la Chapelle, A., Chibout, R., & Issarny, V. (2006). Efficient context-aware service discovery in multi-protocol pervasive environments. In *Proceedings of the 7th International Conference on Mobile Data Management (MDM'06)* (p. 3).

Rayner, M., Lewin, I., Gorrell, G., & Boye, J. (2001, September). *Plug and Play Speech Understanding*. Paper presented at the 2nd SIGdial Workshop on Discourse and Dialogue.

Reddy, P., & Kitsuregawa, M. (1998). Reducing the Blocking in Two-Phase Commit Protocol Employing Backup Sites. In *Proceedings of the 3rd IFCIS International Conference on Cooperative Information Systems* (pp. 406-416).

Reithinger, N., Alexandersson, J., Becker, T., Blocher, A., Engel, R., Löeckelt, M., et al. (2003). *SmartKom - Adaptive and Flexible Multimodal Access to Multiple Applications*. Paper presented at the 5th International Conference on Multimodal Interfaces, Vancouver, British Columbia, Canada.

Remagnino, P., & Foresti, G. L. (2005). Ambient Intelligence: A New Multidisciplinary Paradigm. *IEEE Transactions on Systems, Man, and Cybernetics. Part A, Systems and Humans, 35*(1), 1–6. .doi:10.1109/TSMCA.2004.838456

Ren, Q., & Dunham, M. H. (2000). Using semantic caching to manage location dependent data in mobile computing. In *Proceedings of the 6th annual international conference on mobile computing and networking (Mobicom '00)* (pp. 210-221). New York: ACM.

Richardson, L., & Ruby, S. (2007). *RestFul Web Services*. New York: O'Reilly.

Riva, G., Vatalaro, F., Davide, F., & Alcaiz, M. (Eds.). (2005). *Ambient intelligence: The evolution of technology, communication and cognition towards the future of human-computer interaction*. Studies in New Technologies and Practices in Communication, vol. 6. Amsterdam, The Netherlands: IOS Press. Retrieved from: http://www.neurovr.org/emerging/volume6.html

Rivera-Illingworth, F., Callaghan, V., & Hagras, H. (2007). Detection of normal and novel behaviours in ubiquitous domestic environments. The Computer Journal.

Roche, J., & Hanlon, J. (2009, November 2).What is Bluetooth? *Cnet Australia*. Retrieved from http://www.cnet.com.au/what-is-bluetooth-240091501.htm?omnRef=NULL

Rohrhuber, J. (2008). Implications of Unfolding. In Paradoxes of Interactivity (pp.175-189).

Román, M., Hess, C. K., Cerqueira, R., Ranganathan, A., Campbell, R. H., & Nahrstedt, K. (2002). Gaia: A Middleware Infrastructure to Enable Active Spaces. *IEEE Pervasive Computing / IEEE Computer Society [and] IEEE Communications Society*, 74–83. doi:10.1109/MPRV.2002.1158281

Ross, D. A., & Blasch, B. B. (2000). Wearable interfaces for orientation and wayfinding. In Assets '00: Proceedings of the Fourth International ACM Conference on Assistive Technologies (pp. 193-200). New York: ACM Publishing.

Rowett Research Institute. (n.d.). Improving food quality and preventing disease. *Rowett Research Institute*.

Ruby, S., Thomas, D., & Hansson, D. H. (2008). *Agile Web Development with Rails* (3rd ed.). Pragmatic Programmers.

Ruthven, I. (2008). The context of the interface. In *Proceedings of the second international symposium on Information interaction in context (IIiX '08)*. New York: ACM Press.

Sadagopan, N., Bai, F., Krishnamachari, B., & Helmy, A. (2003). *Paths: analysis of path duration statistics and their impact on reactive manet routing protocols*.

Sadri, F., & Stathis, K. (2008). Ambient Intelligence . In Rabunal Dopico, J. R., Dorado, J., & Pazos, A. (Eds.), *Encyclopaedia of Artificial Intelligence*. Hershey, PA: Information Science Reference. doi:10.4018/978-1-59904-849-9.ch013

Salber, D., & Abowd, G. D. (1998). *The design and use of a generic context server.* Paper presented at Perceptual User Interfaces Conference (PUI'98).

Santofimia, M. J., Moya, F., Villanueva, F. J., Villa, D., & Lopez, J. C. (2008). Integration of intelligent agents supporting automatic service composition in ambient intelligence. In Proceedings of the IEEE/WIC/ACM International Conference on Web Intelligence and Intelligent Agent Technology (Vol. 2, pp. 504-507).

Satyanarayanan, M. (2001). Pervasive computing: vision and challenges. *IEEE Personal Communications*, 8(4), 10–17. . doi:10.1109/98.943998

Sauro, J., & Kindlund, E. (2005). A method to standardize usability metrics into a single score. In *Proceedings of the SIGCHI conference on Human factors in computing systems (CHI '05)*. New York: ACM Press.

Schilit, B., Adams, N., & Want, R. (1994). Context-Aware Computing Applications. In Proceedings of the IEEE Workshop on Mobile Computing Systems and Applications (pp. 85-90).

Schmandt, C., & Negroponte, N. (1994). *Voice communication with computers: conversational systems*. New York: Van Nostrand Reinhold.

Schmidt, A. (2005). Interactive Context-Aware Systems Interacting with Ambient Intelligence . In Riva, G., Vatalaro, F., Davide, F., & Alcaniz, M. (Eds.), *Ambient Intelligence, The Evolution of Technology, Communication and Cognition, Towards the Future of Human-Computer Interaction* (p. 164). Amsterdam: IOS Press.

Schmidt, A., Beigl, M., & Gellersen, H. W. (1999). There is more to context than location. *Computers & Graphics*, 23(6), 893–901. .doi:10.1016/S0097-8493(99)00120-X

Schneiderman, B. (1999). *Designing the user interface* (3rd ed.). Reading, MA: Addison-Wesley.

Searle, J. (1969). *Speech Acts*. London: Cambridge University Press.

Seco, N., Veale, T., & Hayes, J. (2004). An intrinsic information content metric for semantic similarity in WordNet. In [ECAI]. *Proceedings of the European Conference on Artificial Intelligence, 16*, 1089.

Serrano-Alvarado, P., Roncancio, C., & Adiba, M. (2004). A Survey of Mobile Transactions. *Distributed and Parallel Databases, 16*(2), 193–230. .doi:10.1023/B:DAPD.0000028552.69032.f9

Shadbolt, N. (2003). Ambient Intelligence. *IEEE Intelligent Systems, 18*(4), 2–3. .doi:10.1109/MIS.2003.1200718

Shamir, A. (1979). How to Share a Secret. *Communications of the ACM, 612–613*. doi:.doi:10.1145/359168.359176

Shapiro, D. (2005). Participatory design: the will to succeed. In *Proceedings of the 4th decennial conference on Critical computing: between sense and sensibility.* New York: ACM Press.

Shen, H., Kumar, M., Das, S. K., & Wang, Z. (2005). Energy Efficient data caching and prefetching for mobile devices based on utility. *Mobile Networks and Applications, 10*(4), 475–486. .doi:10.1007/s11036-005-1559-8

Sheriff, I., & Belding-Royer, E. (2006, October 1). Multipath Selection in Multi-radio Mesh Networks. In *Proceedings of the 3rd International Conference on Broadband Communications, Networks and Systems* (pp. 1-11).

Shnayder, V., Chen, B., Lorincz, K., Fulford-Jones, T. R. F., & Welsh, M. (2005). *Sensor networks for medical care* (Tech. Rep. No. 08-05). Cambridge, MA: Harvard University.

Simonsen, J., & Kensing, F. (1997). Using ethnography in contextual design. *Communications of the ACM, 40*(7). .doi:10.1145/256175.256190

Skeen, D., & Stonebraker, M. (1983). A formal model of crash recovery in a distributed system. *IEEE Transactions on Software Engineering, 9*(3), 219–228. .doi:10.1109/TSE.1983.236608

Souza, C., Prates, R., Barbosa, S., & Edmonds, E. (2000). Semiotic approaches to user interface design . In *CHI '00 extended abstracts on Human factors in computing systems*. New York: ACM Press. doi:10.1145/633292.633513

Srinivasan, N., Paolucci, M., & Sycara, K. (2004). Adding OWL-S to UDDI, implementation and throughput. In *Proceedings of the 1st Intl. Workshop on Semantic Web Services and Web Process Composition (SWSWPC 2004)* (pp. 6-9).

Stanford Encyclopedia of Philosophy. (2009). *Computer Information Ethics*. Retrieved September 10, 2009, from http://plato.stanford.edu/entries/ethics-computer

Stanford, V. M. (2002). Pervasive computing: Applications - using pervasive computing to deliver elder care. *IEEE Distributed Systems Online, 3*(3).

Stathis, K., & Toni, F. (2004). Ambient Intelligence using KGP Agents. In Proceedings of the 2nd European Symposium for Ambient Intelligence, Eindhoven, The Netherlands (pp. 351-362). Berlin, Germany: Springer-Verlang.

Stathis, K., Spence, R., Bruijn, O. D., & Purcell, P. (2005). Ambient Intelligence: Agents and Interaction in Connected Communities . In Purcell, P. (Ed.), *The Networked Neighbourhood*. Springer.

Steele, B., Holt, L., Ferris, S., Lakshminaryan, S., & Buchner, D. M. (2000). Physical Activity in COPD Using a Triaxial Accelerometer. *Chest, 117*, 1359–1367. PubMed doi:10.1378/chest.117.5.1359

STMicroelectronics. (2001). *BluetoothTM Profiles Overview*. STMicroelectronics.

Stone, L., Barlow, C., & Corwin, T. (1999). *Multiple Target Tracking*. Boston: Artech House.

Storf, H., & Becker, M. (2008). A Multi-Agent-based Activity Recognition Approach for Ambient Assisted Living. Retrieved from http//www.aal-europe.eu

Suchman, L. (1987). *Plans and Situated Actions: The Problem of Human-Machine Communication (Learning in Doing: Social, Cognitive and Computational Perspectives)*. New York: Cambridge University Press.

Suchman, L. (1995). Making work visible. *Communications of the ACM, 38*(9). .doi:10.1145/223248.223263

Suchman, L. (2006). *Human-Machine Reconfigurations*. Cambridge, UK: Cambridge University Press.

Sun Microsystems. (2008). *Java SE technologies at a glance*. Retrieved December 13, 2008, from http://java.sun.com/ javase/technologies/

Sutcliffe, A. (2000). On the effective use and reuse of HCI knowledge. *Transactions on Computer-Human Interaction (TOCHI), 7*(2).

Sutherland, I. E. (1963). Sketchpad, a man-machine graphical communication system. Unpublished doctoral dissertation, Massachusetts Institute of Technology, Cambridge, MA.

Sybase iAnywhere. (2009). *Bluetooth - A Technical Description of Blue SDK Profiles from Sybase iAnywhere*. Sybase.

Sycara, K., Paolucci, M., Ankolekar, A., & Srinivasan, N. (2003). Automated discovery, interaction and composition of semantic web services. *Journal of Web Semantics, 1*(1), 27–46. .doi:10.1016/j.websem.2003.07.002

Tapia, E. M., Intille, S. S., & Larson, K. (2004). Activity recognition in the home setting using simple and ubiquitous sensors. In [Berlin: Springer.]. *Proceedings of PERVASIVE, 2004*, 158–175. doi:10.1007/978-3-540-24646-6_10

Tavenard, R., Salah, A., & Pauwels, E. (2007). Searching for temporal patterns in ami sensor data. In. *Proceedings of Am, I2007*, 53–62.

Taylor, M. E., Matuszek, C., Klimt, B., & Witbrock, M. J. (2007). Autonomous classification of knowledge into an ontology. In Proceedings of the FLAIRS Conference (pp. 140-145).

Tetzlaff, L., Kim, M., & Schloss, R. J. (1995). Home Health Care Support. In *CHI 95 Conference Companion*.

Tham, Ng. A. (1998). *Equality service accessible for all citizens, in particular elderly and disabled: TIDE.*

The Future of Wireless Medical Devices. (n.d.). *Cambridge Consultants.*

This work was previously published in International Journal of Ambient Computing and Intelligence, Volume 2, Issue 4, edited by Kevin Curran, pp. 44-54, copyright 2010 by IGI Publishing (an imprint of IGI Global).

Tian, J., Haehner, J., Becker, C., Stepanov, I., & Rothermel, K. (2002). Graph-based Mobility Model for Mobile Ad Hoc Network Simulation. In *Proceedings of the 35th Annual Simulation Symposium Annual Simulation Symposium,* San Diego, CA (pp. 337-344). Washington, DC: IEEE Computer Society.

Toney, A., Mulley, B., Thomas, B., & Piekarski, W. (2003). Social weight: designing to minimize the social consequences arising from technology use by the mobile professional. *Personal and Ubiquitous Computing, 7*(5). .doi:10.1007/s00779-003-0245-8

Toran-Marti, F., & Ventura-Traveset, J. (2004). *The esa egnos project: The First step of the European contribution to the global navigation satellite system (gnss)*. Paper presented at the Navigare conference.

Trastour, D., Bartolini, C., & Gonzalez-Castillo, J. (2001). A semantic web approach to service description for matchmaking of services. In *Proceedings of the International Semantic Web Working Symposium (SWWS)*.

Tryon, W. W. (2008). Methods of Measuring Human Activity. *Journal of Behaviour Analysis in Health, Sports, Fitness and Medicine, 1*(2).

Tummolini, L., Castelfranchi, C., Ricci, A., Viroli, M., & Omicini, A. (2004). "Exhibitionists" and "Voyeurs" do it better: A Shared Environment for Flexible Coordination with Tacit Messages. In H. van Parunak & D. Weyns (Eds.), Proceedings of the Workshop on Coordination in Emergent Societies (E4MAS 2004).

Tummolini, L., Castelfranchi, C., Ricci, A., Viroli, M., & Omicini, A. (2004). What I See is What You Say: Coordination in a Shared Environment with Behavioral Implicit Communication. In G. Vouros (Ed.), Proceedings of the Workshop on Coordination in Emergent Societies (CEAS 2004).

Ubisense. (2010). *Class leading precision Location - Factsheet*. Retrieved January 4, 2010, from http://www.ubisense.net/pdf/fact-sheets/products/software/Precise-Location-EN090624.pdf

Ullmer, B., & Ishii, H. (2000). Emerging Frameworks For Tangible User Interfaces. *IBM Systems Journal, 39*(3-4), 915–931. .doi:10.1147/sj.393.0915

University of Cambridge. (2007, April). *Why are we so fat?* Retrieved from http://www.research-horizons.cam.ac.uk/ spotlight/why-are-we-so-fat-.aspx

University of Rochester. (2001). *Smart Medical Home*. Retrieved October 23, 2009, from http://www.future-health.rochester.edu /smart_home/

Urbieta, A., Barrutieta, G., Parra, J., & Uribarren, A. (2008). A survey of dynamic service composition approaches for ambient systems. In SOMITAS '08: Proceedings of the 2008 Ambi-Sys workshop on Software Organisation and MonIToring of Ambient Systems, Brussels, Belgium (pp. 1-8). ICST (Institute for Computer Sciences, Social-Informatics and Telecommunications Engineering).

van Kasteren, T. L. M., & Kröse, B. J. A. (2007). Bayesian Activity Recognition in Residence for Elders. In *Proceedings of the International Intelligent Environments Conference* (pp. 209-212).

van Loenen, E. J. (2003). On the role of Graspable Objects in the Ambient Intelligence Paradigm. In *Proceedings of the Media Interaction Group*, Philips Research Labs, Eindhoven, The Netherlands. Retrieved May 21, 2008, from http://www.minatec.com/grenoble-soc/proceedings03/ Pdf/Van%20Loenen.pdf

Vandoren, P., Laerhoven, T. V., Claesen, L., Taelman, J., Raymaekers, C., & Reeth, F. V. (2008). IntuPaint: Bridging the Gap Between Physical and Digital Painting. In *Proceedings of TABLETOP* (pp. 71-78). Washington, DC: IEEE.

Verma, D., & Rao, R. P. N. (2006). Planning and Acting in Uncertain Environments using Probabilistic Inference. In Proceedings of IROS (pp. 2382-2387).

Vian, K., Liebhold, M., & Townsend, A. (2006). The Many Faces of Context-Awareness: A Spectrum of Technologies, Applications and Impacts (Technology Horizons Program. Tech Rep. SR-1014). Retrieved from http://www.iftf.org

Villanueva, F. J., Villa, D., Santofimia, M. J., Moya, F., & Lopez, J. C. (2009). A framework for advanced home service design and management. Paper presented at the International Conference on Consumer Electronics.

Villanueva, F. J., Moya, F., Rincon, F., Santofimia, M. J., Villa, D., & Barba, J. (2009). Towards a unified middleware for ubiquitous and pervasive computing. *International Journal of Ambient Computing and Intelligence*, *1*(1), 53–63. doi:10.4018/jaci.2009010105

Vredenburg, K., Mao, J.-Y., Smith, P., & Carey, T. (2002). A survey of user-centered design practice. In *Proceedings of the SIGCHI conference on Human factors in computing systems: Changing our world, changing ourselves (CHI '02)*. New York: ACM Press.

W3C HTML Working Group. (2002). *XHTML 1.0 the extensible hypertext markup language* (2nd ed.). Retrieved December 13, 2008, from http://www.w3.org/TR/2002/REC-xhtml1-20020801

W3C. (2010). *Synchronized Multimedia Integration Language (SMIL 3.0)*. Retrieved January 4, 2010, from http://www.w3.org/TR/2008/REC-SMIL3-20081201/

Wahlster, W. (Ed.). (2006). *SMARTKOM: Foundations of Multimodal Dialogue Systems, Cognitive Technologies Series*. Berlin, Germany: Springer. doi:10.1007/3-540-36678-4

Walker, M. A., Fromer, J., Di Fabbrizio, G., Mestel, C., & Hindle, D. (1998, April 18-23). What can I say? Evaluating a spoken language interface to email. In *Proceedings of CHI'98*, Los Angeles (pp. 582-589).

Walker, M. A., Litman, D. J., Kamm, C. A., & Abella, A. (1997). *PARADISE: A framework for evaluating spoken dialogue agents*. Paper presented at the Thirty-Fifth Annual Meeting of the Association for Computational Linguistics.

Ward, J. A., Lukowicz, P., Troster, G., & Starner, T. E. (2006). Activity Recognition of Assembly Tasks Using Body-Worn Microphones and Accelerometers. *IEEE Transactions on Pattern Analysis and Machine Intelligence*, *28*(10), 1553–1567. PubMed doi:10.1109/TPAMI.2006.197

Ward, K., & Novick, D. G. (1995, May 7-11). Integrating multiple cues for spoken language understanding. In *Proceedings of CHI'95*, Denver, CO.

Warneke, B., Last, M., & Liebowitz, B. (2001). Smart Dust: Communicating with a Cubic-Millimetre. *IEEE Computing*, *31*(3), 44–51.

Warschauer, M. (2004). *Technology and Social Inclusion* (pp. 5-10). Cambridge, MA: MIT press. Retrieved from http://www./3s.de/web/upload/documents /1/SAME0820-lugmayr.pdf

Washington State University. (2009). *CASAS Smart Home Project*. Retrieved October 26, 2009, from http://ailab.wsu.edu/casas/

WayFinder. (2009). Wayfinder access. Retrieved October 28, 2009, from http://www.wayfinder.com

Weber, W., Braun, C., Glaser, R., Gsottberger, Y., Halik, M., Jung, S., et al. (2003). Ambient Intelligence - Key Technologies in the Information Age. In *Proceedings of the IEEE International Electron Devices Meeting (IEDM'03)* (pp. 1.1.1-1.1.8).

Weight-Control Information Network. (2003). Medical Care for Obese Patients. *National Institutes of Health*, 3-5335.

Weiser, M. (1991). The Computer of the Twenty-First Century. *Scientific American*, *135*, 94–104. .doi:10.1038/scientificamerican0991-94

Weiser, M. (1995). The computer for the 21st century . In *Human-computer interaction: Toward the year 2000* (pp. 933–940). San Francisco: Morgan Kaufmann.

Whittaker, S. (1996). Talking to strangers: an evaluation of the factors affecting electronic collaboration. In *Proceedings of the 1996 ACM conference on Computer supported cooperative work (CSCW '96)*. New York: ACM Press.

Whittaker, S., Swanson, J., Kucan, J., & Sidner, C. (1997). TeleNotes: managing lightweight interactions in the desktop. *Transactions on Computer-Human Interaction (TOCHI), 4*(2).

Whittaker, S., Terveen, L., & Nardi, B. (2000). Let's stop pushing the envelope and start addressing it: a reference task agenda for HCI. *Human-Computer Interaction, 15*, 75–106. .doi:10.1207/S15327051HCI1523_2

Wiberg, M. (2001). RoamWare: an integrated architecture for seamless interaction in between mobile meetings. In *Proceedings of the 2001 International ACM SIGGROUP Conference on Supporting Group Work (GROUP '01)*. New York: ACM Press.

Wigley, A., & Foot, D. (2007). *Microsoft Mobile Development Handbook*. Microsoft Press.

Wikipedia. (n.d.). *OBject EXchange*. Retrieved from http://en.wikipedia.org/wiki/OBEX

WISP. (2009). WISP Wiki. Retrieved from http://wisp.wikispaces.com/

X/Open. (1996). *Distributed transaction processing: Reference model* (version 3). Retrieved from http://www.opengroup.org/bookstore /catalog/g504.htm

Yang, A., Jarafi, R., Sastry, S., & Bajcsy, R. (2009). Distributed Recognition of Human Actions Using Wearable Motion Sensor Networks. *Journal of Ambient Intelligence and Smart Environments*.

Yankelovich, N. (1996). How do users know what to say? *Interactions (New York, N.Y.), 3*(6). .doi:10.1145/242485.242500

Yi, J., Cizeron, E., Hamma, S., & Parrein, B. (2008, March 31). Simulation and Performance Analysis of MP-OLSR for Mobile Ad Hoc Networks. In *Proceedings of the IEEE Wireless Communications and Networking Conference (WCNC '08)* (pp. 2235-2240).

Yin, L., & Cao, G. (2004, September). Adaptive power-aware prefetch in wireless networks. *IEEE Transactions on Wireless Communications, 3*(5), 1648–1658. .doi:10.1109/TWC.2004.833430

Younas, M., Chao, K.-M., Wang, P., & Huang, C.-L. (2007). QoS-aware Mobile Service Transactions in a Wireless Environment. *Concurrency and Computation, 19*(8), 1219–1236. .doi:10.1002/cpe.1157

Zhao, W., & Schulzrinne, H. (2005). Enhancing service location protocol for efficiency, scalability and advanced discovery. *Journal of Systems and Software, 75*(1-2), 193–204. .doi:10.1016/j.jss.2004.04.011

Zhao, Y. (2002, July). Standardization of mobile phone positioning for 3g systems. *IEEE Communications Magazine, 40*(7), 108–116. .doi:10.1109/MCOM.2002.1018015

Zheng, B., Xu, J., & Lee, D. L. (2002). Cache invalidation and replacement strategies for location- dependent data in mobile environments. [f]. *IEEE Transactions on Computers, 51*(10), 1141–1153. .doi:10.1109/TC.2002.1039841

Zhu, F., Mutka, M., & Ni, L. (2003). Splendor: A secure, private, and location-aware service discovery protocol supporting mobile services. In *Proceedings of the First IEEE International Conference on Pervasive Computing and Communications* (p. 235).

Zhu, F., Mutka, M., & Ni, L. (2004). PrudentExposure: A private and user-centric service discovery protocol. In *Proceedings of the Second IEEE Annual Conference on Pervasive Computing and Communications (PerCom 2004)* (p. 329).

Zhu, F., Mutka, M. W., & Ni, L. M. (2005). Service discovery in pervasive computing environments. *IEEE Pervasive Computing / IEEE Computer Society* [and]. *IEEE Communications Society, 4*(4), 81–90. doi:.doi:10.1109/MPRV.2005.87

Zimmerman, J., Forlizzi, J., & Evenson, S. (2007). Research through design as a method for interaction design research in HCI. In *Proceedings of the SIGCHI conference on Human factors in computing systems (CHI '07)*. New York: ACM Press.

About the Contributors

Kevin Curran, BSc (Hons), PhD, SMIEEE, FBCS CITP, SMACM, FHEA, is a Reader in Computer Science at the University of Ulster and group leader for the Ambient Intelligence Research Group. His achievements include winning and managing UK & European Framework projects and Technology Transfer Schemes. Dr. Curran has made significant contributions to advancing the knowledge and understanding of computer networking and systems, evidenced by over 700 published works. He is perhaps most well-known for his work on location positioning within indoor environments, pervasive computing, and internet security. His expertise has been acknowledged by invitations to present his work at international conferences, overseas universities, and research laboratories. He is a regular contributor to BBC Radio & TV news in the UK and is currently the recipient of an Engineering and Technology Board Visiting Lectureship for Exceptional Engineers and is an IEEE Technical Expert for Internet/Security matters. He is listed in the *Dictionary of International Biography,* Marquis *Who's Who in Science and Engineering,* and in *Who's Who in the World.* Dr. Curran was awarded the Certificate of Excellence for Research in 2004 by Science Publications and was named Irish Digital Media Newcomer of the Year Award in 2006. Dr. Curran has performed external panel duties for various Irish Higher Education Institutions. He is a fellow of the British Computer Society (FBCS), a senior member of the Association for Computing Machinery (SMACM), a senior member of the Institute of Electrical and Electronics Engineers (SMIEEE), and a fellow of the higher education academy (FHEA). Dr. Curran's stature and authority in the international community is demonstrated by his influence, particularly in relation to the direction of research in computer science. He has chaired sessions and participated in the organising committees for many highly-respected international conferences and workshops. He is the Editor in Chief of the *International Journal of Ambient Computing* and *Intelligence* and is also a member of 15 journal editorial committees and numerous international conference organising committees. He has authored a number of books and is the recipient of various patents. He has served as an advisor to the British Computer Society in regard to the computer industry standards and is a member of BCS and IEEE Technology Specialist Groups and various other professional bodies.

* * *

Xavier Alamán got his PhD in Computer Science (Universidad Complutense de Madrid - 1993), MSc. Artificial Intelligence (Univ. California Los Angeles - 1990), MSc. Computer Science (Universidad Politecnica de Madrid - 1987), MSc. Physics (Universidad Complutense de Madrid - 1985). He has served as the Dean of the School of Engineering, Universidad Autónoma de Madrid, from 2000 to 2004. He got the tenure in the same university in 1998, as professor of Computer Science. He previously was an IBM researcher for 7 years. His research interests include Ambient Intelligence, Knowledge Management cooperative tools, and multimedia systems. He has been main researcher in several R&D projects in these areas. He has contributed with more that 50 publications in journals, books and conferences.

Luca Benini is a Full Professor at the University of Bologna. He also holds a visiting faculty position at the Ecole Polytecnique Federale de Lausanne (EPFL). He received a Ph.D. degree in electrical engineering from Stanford University in 1997. Prof. Benini's research interests are in the fields of multi-processor and networks systems-on-chip, ambient intelligence systems design, energy-efficient smart sensors and sensor networks, biochips for the recognition of biological molecules, bioinformatics and advanced algorithms for in silicon biology. He has published more than 450 papers in peer-reviewed international journals and conferences, three books, several book chapters and two patents. He has been program chair and general chair of the Design Automation and Test in Europe conference. He is Associate Editor of the IEEE Transactions on Computer-Aided Design of Circuits and Systems and of the ACM Journal on Emerging Technologies in Computing Systems. He is a Fellow of the IEEE.

Tim Boucher is a writer working in technical theatre, as an assistant stage manager, stagehand, carpenter, electrician, scenic artist and occasional bit part actor. His first-hand experience in the production field provides a springboard for the crafting of a first-person folk historical narrative about traveling performers, artists, artisans and laborers in the service of culture and the business of entertainment.

Till Bovermann is a research associate at the Ambient Intelligence Group at the Cognitive Interaction Technology Center of Excellence at Bielefeld University (CITEC). He is also involved in the C5 project Alignment in AR-based cooperation of the CRC673-Alignment in Communication. Previously, he worked as a research assistant at the Neuroinformatics Group at Bielefeld University. He received a Ph.D. in Computer Science in 2010 from Bielefeld University (thesis: Tangible Auditory Interfaces). His current research interests are the integration of auditory displays and tangible interfaces to form an integral system for data emersion into the human life world. His arts-related interests are in media arts, especially interactive performances and just-in-time programming of media with a strong focus on sound.

Joos-Hendrik Böse is a postdoctoral fellow at the International Computer Science Institute Berkeley. He received his Ph.D. in computer science from Freie Universität Berlin for his work on data management in mobile environments and on stochastic failure models for atomic transactions. His research activities focus on scalable data management and data analysis in distributed environments.

Stefano Bromuri obtained his PhD at Royal Holloway University of London where he is currently working as a research assistant in the Department of Computer Science. He also holds a MSc in Information, Telecomunication and Computer Engineering and a BSc in Software Engineering from the University of Bologna. Previously he has been working as a Research Assistant for the ArguGRID project funded by the European Union under the FP6 framework. His research interests are: Multi-agent Systems, Logic Programming, Object Oriented Programming, Workflow Management Systems, GRID computing, Wireless Sensor Networks, Ambient Intelligence, Lego Robots and 3D engines.

Jürgen Broß received his B.Sc. from the Universität Duisburg-Essen and his M.Sc. from the Freie Universität Berlin. In his M.Sc. thesis he examined the applicability of Backup Coordinators for the reduction of transaction blocking risks. Since 2006 he is research staff at Freie Universität Berlin. His general research interests are management and analysis of unstructured data (e.g., text mining methods), as well as data management in volatile environments.

Mauro Caporuscio has currently a Post-Doc position at Politecnico di Milano, Italy. He received his Ph.D. in Computer Science from the University of L'Aquila, Italy (2006). He was Professional Research Assistant at the University of Colorado (2002), and Research Engineer at INRIA Paris-Rocquencourt (2006-2009). He has published various papers on the most important international journals and conferences and has served in the program committee of various international conferences. He also has been involved in different EU projects. His research interests mainly focus on the application of Software Engineering methodologies and techniques to the field of distributed systems. To this extent, particular attention is devoted to Event-based systems, Service Oriented Architecture and Pervasive Computing.

Roberto Speicys Cardoso is a systems engineer at INRIA Paris-Rocquencourt, where he works with the ARLES project-team on the design and implementation of a middleware for mobile environments. He obtained his PhD in 2009 from the University of Paris VI, France, with the thesis "A service-oriented middleware for privacy protection in pervasive systems". He is mainly interested in application adaptation in dynamic, mobile, and evolutionary environments (particularly concerning Quality of Service, Security and Privacy) and how Trust Management and Social Network data can improve application adaptation.

Cristiano Castelfranchi, senior research scientist at the Institute of Psychology of the Italian National Research Council, has been coordinator of the "Artificial Intelligence, Cognitive Models and Interaction" Unit, and of the "Social Psychology" Unit. His interests cover multi-agent systems research, cognitive modeling and social psychology. Dr. Castelfranchi has been the promoter of the Social Behavior Simulation Project at IP-CNR, and one of the pioneers of Distributed AI in Italy and Europe. He teachs "Cognitive Psychology" and "Artificial Intelligence" at the University of Siena. He has published extensively in cognitive psychology, in artificial intelligence, and in social theory and simulation. His books include Che figura! (1988) (about social emotions), Artificial Social Systems (1994), and Cognitive and Social Action (1995). He has been an invited speaker at IJCAI-97 where he gave a lecture on social reasoning for AI agents, and at SimSoc'97 about modeling social functions. Cristiano Castelfranchi is a professor of Cognitive Sciences at the University of Siena, Department of Communication Science, and director of ISTC-CNR, in Roma. A cognitive scientist with a background in linguistics and psychology, he is active in the Multi-Agent Systems, the Social Simulation, and the Cognitive Science communities. Fellow of ECCAI (European Coordinating Committee for AI); program chair of the First International Joint Conference on Autonomous Agents and Multi-Agent Systems (AAMAS-2002); chair of several international workshops in these fields (like ATAL and "Trust and Deception in Artificial Societies"), and advisory member of several international conferences and societies (like Cognitive Science; IFMAS). Participating in a number of research networks under the European IV and V Framework. Research fields of interest include: cognitive agent theory and architecture; multi-agent systems; agent-based social simulation; social cognition and emotions, with special focus on trust and deception. He published 4 books in English, and 11 in Italian; more than 200 conference and journal articles on cognitive, computational and formal-theoretical models of social interaction and social mind. Invited speaker at IJCAI'97 (and several other conferences and workshops in AI and cognitive studies); member of the editorial board of Autonomous Agents and MAS, Cognitive Science Quarterly, the MIT CogNet.

Rem W. Collier BSc, M.Sc., M.Phil., PhD, has been a lecturer in the Department of Computer Science in UCD since September 2003. His primary research area is Intelligent Software Agents and more specifically, agent-oriented programming languages and frameworks via the open source Agent Factory platform. Dr Collier has published 4 journal articles, 4 book chapters, and has 60+ conference and workshop publications. In addition to his primary research focus, Dr Collier also has interests in Information Retrieval and is currently working on the development of intelligent middleware for the Sensor Web.

Jodi Crisp obtained a BSc(Hons) in Computer Science from the University of Southampton in 2001 and an MSc in Human-Computer Interaction with Ergonomics from University College London in 2008. She has worked as a software engineer, integration engineer, senior test analyst and lexicographer before her role as a usability tester and developer on the EasyLine+ project at Glyndwr University. She has extensive experience of all aspects of the software development lifecycle, with a particular emphasis on usability.

Jonathan Doherty (BSc, PhD) is a research associate in the Intelligent Systems Research Centre at the University of Ulster. He has published and holds patents in the area of Song-Form Intelligent Self-Similarity K-Means Clustering to address gaps in streaming music over wireless networks. His research interests include Musical Information Retrieval, Network protocols, Multimedia and Ambient Assisted Living.

Vasileios Fotopoulos received his B.Sc. in Computer Science from the Department of Computer Science, University of Ioannina in 2005. He received his M.Sc. in Computer Science from the same department in 2008. His research interests include middleware and P2P networks.

Helen Grout graduated with honours in Environmental Studies from North East Wales Institute of Higher Education in 2004. After a brief period of working in industry she returned to academia, completing a PGCE at Glyndwr University in 2009. She then worked as a tester and developer on the EU funded Easyline+ project. From April 2010 Helen has been researching Phytophthora Pseudosyringea in Vaccinium myrtillus on Cannock Chase for a PhD at Staffordshire University. She is a Member of the Institute for Learning.

Vic Grout was awarded the BSc(Hons) degree in Mathematics and Computing from the University of Exeter in 1984 and the PhD degree in Communication Engineering ("Optimisation Techniques for Telecommunication Networks") from Plymouth Polytechnic in 1988. He has worked in senior positions in both academia and industry for over twenty years and has published and presented over 200 research papers. He is currently Professor of Network Algorithms at Glyndwr University, Wales, where he leads the Centre for Applied Internet Research. His research interests span several areas of computational mathematics, particularly the application of heuristic principles to large-scale problems in Internet design, management and control. Professor Grout is a Chartered Engineer, Electrical Engineer, Scientist,

Mathematician and IT Professional, a Fellow of the Institute of Mathematics and its Applications, British Computer Society and Institution of Engineering and Technology and a Senior Member of the Institute of Electrical and Electronics Engineers. He chairs the biennial international conference series on Internet Technologies and Applications (ITA 05, ITA 07, ITA 09 and ITA 11).

Hans Guesgen is a professor of computer science in the School of Engineering and Advanced Technology at Massey University in Palmerston North, New Zealand. He holds a diploma in computer science and mathematics of the University of Bonn, a doctorate in computer science of the University of Kaiserslautern, and a higher doctorate (Habilitation) in computer science of the University of Hamburg, Germany. He worked as a research scientist at the German National Research Center of Computer Science (GMD) at Sankt Augustin from 1983 to 1992. During this period he held a one-year post-doctoral fellowship at the International Computer Science Institute in Berkeley, California. In 1992 he joined the Computer Science Department of the University of Auckland, where he worked until moving to Massey University in 2007. His research interests include ambient intelligence and spatio-temporal reasoning.

Pablo A. Haya is a full–time teacher in the School of Engineering of the U.A.M. and a researcher of AmILab (ambient intelligence laboratory). His research interests currently focus on Human Computer Interaction over Intelligent Environments. He is member of the IEEE. He received his PhD in Computer Science and Telecommunications from the Universidad Autónoma of Madrid. Contact him at Amilab, EPS-UAM, C. Fco. Tomas y Valiente 11, 28049 Madrid Spain; pablo.haya@uam.es

Rosaleen Hegarty BSc (Hons) is a PhD student researching in the area of Ambient Intelligence in the School of Computing and Intelligent Systems, Faculty of Computing and Engineering at the University of Ulster, Magee College.

Thomas Hermann studied physics at Bielefeld University. From 1998 to 2001 he was a member of the interdisciplinary Graduate Program "Task-oriented Communication". He started the research on sonification and auditory display in the Neuroinformatics Group and received a Ph.D. in Computer Science in 2002 from Bielefeld University (thesis: Sonification for Exploratory Data Analysis). After research stays at the Bell Labs (NJ, USA, 2000) and GIST (Glasgow University, UK, 2004), he is currently assistant professor and head of the Ambient Intelligence Group within CITEC, the Center of Excellence in Cognitive Interaction Technology, Bielefeld University. His research focus is sonification, datamining, human-computer interaction and cognitive interaction technology.

Clemens Lombriser received his MSc ETH in information technology and electrical engineering-from ETH Zurich in 2005. He has since worked at the Wearable Computing Laboratory at ETH Zurich, where he received his Dr. sc. ETH (Ph.D) in 2009. His research interests lie in the recognition of human activities from miniaturized sensor nodes embedded into objects, worn on the body, or integrated in the environment. His contributions involve dynamic adaptation of distributed processing within sensor networks and algorithms for recognizing context information within networks of collaborating sensor nodes. During his work he has been involved in various projects to record data from ambient intelligence environments.

Juan Carlos Lopez received the MS and PhD degrees in Telecommunication (Electrical) Engineering from the Technical University of Madrid (UPM) in 1985 and 1989, respectively. From Sep 1990 to Aug 1992, he was a Visiting Scientist in the Department of Electrical and Computer Engineering at Carnegie Mellon University, Pittsburgh, PA (USA). His research activities center on computer-aided design of integrated circuits and systems. His work is focused on algorithms for automatic synthesis, co-design and embedded computing. From 1989 to 1999, he has been an Associate Professor of the Department of Electrical Engineering at UPM. Currently, Dr. L<F3>pez is a Professor of Computer Architecture and Dean of the School of Computer Science at the University of Castilla-La Mancha.

Tom Lunney BSc (Hons), MSc, P.G.C.E, PhD, MIEEE, MBCS received his degrees from Queen's University Belfast, and is now a Senior Lecturer in Computer Science in the University of Ulster. His research areas include concurrent and distributed systems, artificial intelligence and multi-modal computing. He has presented papers at a range of International Conferences and participated in the organising committees for a number of international conferences and workshops. He has taught at other educational institutions including Queens University, Belfast and The University of Pau, France. He is currently Course Director for postgraduate masters programmes in the University of Ulster.

Fabio Mancinelli is a Computer Science researcher and professional whose interests are mainly in the field of distributed systems and software architectures. His recent works are about software adaptability, software complexity and web-oriented architectures. Currently he is working for a small startup building next generation wiki software for the web.

Stephen Marsland is an associate professor in computer science and the postgraduate director in the School of Engineering and Advanced Technology at Massey University in Palmerston North, New Zealand. He has a degree in mathematics from Oxford University (1998) and a PhD from Manchester University (2002). Before moving to Massey University in 2004, he held postdoc positions in the UK, the USA, and Germany. His research interests are in mathematical computing, principally shape spaces, Euler equations, machine learning, and algorithms.

John McGinn graduated with first-class honours in Multimedia Computing from the North East Wales Institute of Higher Education (NEWI) in 2000. Since then he has worked as a lecturer, senior lecturer and research fellow at NEWI and Glyndwr University and, most recently, as the lead developer for the FP6 EU-funded programme: "Easyline+: Low Cost Advanced White Goods for a Longer Independent Life of Elderly People". John's research interests include network protocols and standards and distributed collaboration and visualization. He has published and presented a number of technical papers on topics from information visualization to traffic filters and routing. He is a member of the British Computer Society and the Institution of Engineering and Technology.

Sonia Ben Mokhtar is junior CNRS researcher (CR2) at the LIRIS laboratory since October 2009. Before that, she was a research associate at University College London, taking part in the Mobile Systems Special Interest Group from November 2007 to October 2009. She received her Ph.D. degree in December 2007 from Université Pierre et Marie Curie, Paris 6. During her Ph.D., Sonia was carrying out her research at the INRIA Paris-Rocquencourt research center as member of the ARLES research group. Her topics of interest include: Middleware for Pervasive Computing Environments, Pervasive Social Networks, Service Oriented Computing (SOC, SOA), Dynamic Service Discovery and Composition in Mobile Environments, Semantic Web, Ontologies, Folksonomies, QoS- and Context-awareness.

Germán Montoro received his PhD in Electrical and Computer Engineering (Universidad Autónoma de Madrid - 2005) and currently is full-time teacher at Universidad Autónoma de Madrid. He has been an invited researcher at the University of Miami and University of Ulster. His research interests are spoken dialogue systems and adaptive interfaces, focussed on ambient intelligence. He has contributed with numerous publications in journals, chapters of books and conferences.

Francisco Moya received his MS and PhD degrees in Telecommunication Engineering from the Technical University of Madrid (UPM), Spain, in 1996 and 2003 respectively. From 1999 he works as an Assistant Professor at the University of Castilla-La Mancha (UCLM). His current research interests include heterogeneous distributed systems and networks, electronic design automation, and its applications to large-scale domotics and system-on-chip design.

Maurice Mulvenna received his degrees from the University of Ulster, where he is a senior lecturer in computer science. He researches artificial intelligence and pervasive computing and serves on many program committees, including IEEE Pervasive Computing, IEEE Pervasive Computing and Applications, Pervasive Systems and Computing and IEEE-ACM Web Intelligence. He is a senior member of both the IEEE and Association for Computing Machinery (ACM), and is a chartered member of the British Computer Society (BCS).

Hayat Mushcab holds an MSc in Computing and Intelligent Systems from the University of Ulster in Northern Ireland as well as a BSc in Health Information Management and Technology from King Faisal University in Saudi Arabia. Her research interests in computer science include programming mobile devices, Internet Security and Medical Informatics.

Michael J. O'Grady is a researcher based in the School of Computer Science & Informatics at University College Dublin. His research interests include the applicability of intelligent systems in the pervasive and mobile computing domains. Currently, he is focusing on the engineering of Ambient Assisted Living systems that realize adaptive and autonomic behaviours. He was appointed to the permanent research staff of UCD in October 2008. Dr. O'Grady has published in a range of international journals and conferences, having 18 journal publications and over 50 publications in peer reviewed conferences and workshops. He has co-edited four conference proceedings and contributed to over 10 book chapters. Dr. O'Grady is a senior member of the ACM and IEEE.

Gregory M. P. O'Hare is an Associate Professor within the School of Computer Science & Informatics at UCD. He has published over 295 refereed publications in Journals and International Conferences, seven books and has won significant grant income (ca. €28.00M). His research interests are in the areas of Distributed Artificial Intelligence and Multi-Agent Systems (MAS), Robotics, Mobile and Ubiquitous Computing, Autonomic Systems and Wireless Sensor Networks. He has supervised some 16 Ph.D. and 29 M.Sc. students to completion in his career to date. Prof. O'Hare is a Fellow of the British as well as the Irish Computer Society, a member of the ACM, AAAI and a Chartered Engineer. He is the Chair of the European Research Consortium on Informatics and Mathematics (ERCIM) Working Group on Sensor Web. Currently, he is one of the Principal Investigators and founders of CLARITY: The Centre for Sensor Web Technologies (funded 2008-2013).

Theodoros Petsatodis obtained his BSc in Automation Engineering from Technological Educational Institute of Piraeus in March 2006. He holds a Masters of Science in Information and Telecommunications Technologies from Athens Information Technology (AIT). He is currently pursuing his PhD at Center for TeleInFrastruktur (CTiF) of Aalborg University (AAU) in Denmark, on Voice Activity Detection within Varying Environments.In the past he has worked as an Electronics Engineer, being responsible for system level architecture of gas-tank level GSM-telemetry applications operating within explosive areas, and for electronic & analog design of the corresponding prototypes. Since February 2008, he has been working as a researcher in the Autonomic and Grid Computing Group of AIT. His research interests focus in Signal Processing, and especially Voice Activity Detection and Bio-Signal Processing.

Giovanni Pezzulo is a researcher at the Istituto di Linguistica Computazionale "Antonio Zampolli" of the National Research Council of Italy, currently working in the Institute of Cognitive Sciences and Technologies, CNR, in Rome. He holds a degree in Philosophy of Science and a PhD in Cognitive Psychology. His research interests are both theoretical and computational. Topics include: anticipation and anticipatory behavior (see the EU funded project MindRACES); cognitive architectures (trying to bridge sensorimotor interaction with high-level cognitive capabilities such as practical reasoning); goal-oriented behavior; representation (theoretical and computational models); motivation (and their roles in determining behavior); decision making under uncertainty (theoretical and computational models, some experimental work), schema-based agent architectures (see the EU-funded project HUMANOBS), computational linguistics.

Rich Picking is a Reader in Human-Computer Interaction and Deputy Director of the Centre for Applied Internet Research at Glyndwr University, Wrexham, Wales. He completed his doctoral thesis in 1996 in interactive hypermedia and multimedia design, under the supervision of Professor Cliff McKnight at Loughborough University. Currently, he specializes in user interface design and evaluation for assisted living, and is the lead designer and technical manager for the FP6 EU-funded programme: "Easyline+: Low Cost Advanced White Goods for a Longer Independent Life of Elderly People". Dr. Picking has extensive experience in both academia and industry, and has worked as a user interface design expert on many projects in a wide range of industries, such as engineering, logistics, security, production control, healthcare, and e-commerce. He has published widely on these topics.

Aristodemos Pnevmatikakis is an associate professor at Athens Information Technology. His research interests span the areas of Signal Processing and Communications, focusing on pattern recognition, detection and tracking, multimedia processing, data conversion, signal processing for the physical layer and RF system level design. He is co-author of the book Delta-Sigma Modulators, Modeling, Design and Applications, (Imperial College Press, London, UK, 2003). His research outcomes have been featured on Greek national TV, radio and newspapers, have been demonstrated at national and international events and have been evaluated at international evaluation campaigns. He has been involved in numerous

EU and national funded research projects. He received his BSc in Physics from University of Patras, Greece in 1993 and his MSc and PhD from Imperial College, University of London in 1995 and 1999 respectively. Since July 2003, he is with AIT. He has been with Intracom (2001-2003) and Integrated Systems Development (1999-2001).

Pierre-Guillaume Raverdy is research engineer at INRIA (France). After his Ph.D. on load balancing in distributed systems, he went to Sony Research Labs in Tokyo and San Jose to investigate meta-programming, adaptive systems, and middleware support for mobile multimedia services. Now at INRIA, Dr. Raverdy has participated in several European research projects on service-oriented middleware for heterogeneous networks. His topics of interest include: Middleware for Pervasive Computing Environments, Mobile Web Services, Heterogeneous Networks Composition, Mesh Networks and Context-aware Service Discovery.

Maria Jose Santofimia received the degree of Technical Engineer in Computer Science in 2001 from the University of Córdoba (Spain); the Master's degree on Computer Security from the University of Glamorgan (Wales, UK) in 2003; and the degree of Engineer in Computer Science in 2006 from the University of Castilla-La Mancha (Spain). She is currently working towards her PhD as a member of the Computer Architecture and Networks Research Group (ARCO) at the Univeristy of Castilla-La Mancha. She is an assistant professor in the School of Computer Science in Ciudad Real.

Kostas Stathis is a Senior Lecturer in the Department of Computer Science at Royal Holloway, University of London. He has held posts in the Department of Computing, City University London, the Department of Computer Science, University of Pisa, and the Department of Imperial College London, where he also received his PhD. He has been the coordinator of the development effort for the agent platform PROSOCS, funded by the EU project SOCS and the GOLEM agent environment funded by the EU project ArguGRID. His research interests include: Social Computing; Cognitive & Autonomous Agents; Artificial Agent Societies; Agent Communication; Programmable Agents and Agent Platforms; Representation of Human-Computer (or Computer-Computer) Interaction as a Game. Applications of interest focus on Ambient Intelligence, Connected Communities, and Electronic Commerce. He is a member of ACM, IEEE, BCS and an associate practitioner of the UK Higher Education Academy.

John Soldatos, (born in Athens, Greece in 1973) is with Athens Information Technology (AIT) since March 2003, where he is currently an Associate Professor. Dr. Soldatos has had an active role (wp-leader, technical manager, project manager) in more than 20 EC (European Commission) and GSRT (Greek Secretariat for Research and Technology) co-funded research projects. Dr. Soldatos has also considerable experience (senior developer, IT systems architect, team leader, technical project manager) in enterprise IT projects, where he worked for leading Greek enterprises. As a result of his research activities he has co-authored more than 130 papers published in international journals and conference proceedings, while he has also co-edited two books and two journal special issues. His current research interests are in Pervasive and Autonomic Computing. Dr. Soldatos serves as a reviewer in major journals, as an evaluator for EU projects/proposals and business plans, while he has also served as organizing chair, tutorial chair, and TPC member in numerous conferences. Recently, he served as TPC co-chair of the "flagship" IEEE PIMRC conference (1200 participants).

Fotios Talantzis, obtained his BEng in Electronic and Computer Engineering in 2000. He followed this by an MSc (Telecommunications and Signal Processing) and a PhD on Acoustical Signal Processing in Imperial College London. His work during his studies dealt with creation of mathematical models that investigated the robustness of 3-D audio and hands-free telephony. In general, his research allowed for a series of journal and conference publications while in parallel he enriched his professional skills by working as a consultant in respectful Greek and UK companies. In 2004 he returned to Greece to join Athens Information Technology in which he works as an Assistant Professor. He also serves as a visiting academic in Imperial College London. His work now concentrates on development of technologies that enable creation of non-obtrusive environments. He has research interests that concentrate on acoustic source localization, blind source separation, adaptive signal processing, bioengineering and financial signal processing.

Vasiliki Theodoreli received her Diploma in Electric and Computer Enginnering from National Polytechnic University of Athens in 2007 and she is currently pursuing her MSc degree in Information Networking from the Carnegie Mellon University, in collaboration with Athens Information Technology. Along with her studies she is working as a research assistant in Autonomic and Intelligent Systems Laboratory in Athens Information Technology. Her research interests include among others Human Computer Interaction, Affective Computing and Artificial Intelligence.

Declan Traynor is a under-graduate Computer Science student at the University of Ulster in Northern Ireland. He has a wide range of interests in computing and is especially interested in Ambient Intelligence and networking.

Gerhard Tröster Prof. Gerhard Tröster (SM'93) received the M.Sc. degree in electrical engineering from the Technical University Karlsruhe, Karlsruhe, Germany, in 1978, and the Ph.D. degree in electrical engineering from the Technical University Darmstadt, Darmstadt, Germany, in 1984. During the eight years he spent at Telefunken Corporation, Germany, he was responsible for various national and international research projects focused on key components for ISDN and digital mobile phones. Since 1993 he has been a Professor and Head of the Wearable Computing Lab, Swiss Federal Institute of Technology (ETH) Zurich, Switzerland. His field of research includes wearable computing for healthcare and production, context awareness in ambient environment and in large socio-technical systems, smart textiles, sensor networks and electronic packaging.

Luca Tummolini (PhD) is a graduate in Cognitive Science from the University of Siena. His main interests are on normative multi-agent systems, coordination problems and institutions.

René Tünnermann is a research associate at the Ambient Intelligence Group at the Cognitive Interaction Technology Center of Excellence at Bielefeld University (CITEC). He studied science informatics at Bielefeld University. During his studies he worked as a student worker at the Neuroinformatics Group of Bielefeld University and the Alignment in AR-based cooperation project of the CRC673-Alignment in Communication. His research focus lies with tangible computing and interactive surfaces.

Aitor Urbieta is Ph.D. student at IKERLAN-IK4 (Spain). He is investigating the use of Preconditions- and Effects-based service representation models for services behaviour representation in intelligent environments. Besides, he is working on middleware issues for semantic and context-aware service discovery, composition and adaptation. He received his Bachelor in Computer Science from the University of Mondragon, he will finish his Ph.D. in 2010 and his topics of interest include: Middleware for Pervasive Computing Environments, Service Oriented Computing (SOC, SOA), Preconditions- and Effects-based Service Modeling, Service Discovery and Composition in Pervasive Environments, Context-aware service adaptation.

Visara Urovi is a PhD student and research assistant in the Department of Computer Science at Royal Holloway, University of London. Previously, she has been working as a reserach assistant for the EU project ArguGRID. Visara holds a MSc in Information, Telecomunication and Computer Engineering and a BSc in Software Engineering from the University of Bologna. Her research interests include Multi Agent Systems, Logic Programming, Semantic Web Services, Communication protocols and Distributed Systems. Currently, she is investigating Social Interaction in multi agent systems.

Panos Vassiliadis received his Ph.D. from the National Technical University of Athens in 2000. He joined the Department of Computer Science of the University of Ioannina as a lecturer in 2002. Currently, Dr. Vassiliadis is also a member of the Distributed Management of Data (DMOD) Laboratory (http://www.dmod.cs.uoi.gr/). His research interests include data warehousing, web services and database design and modeling. More information is available at http://www.cs.uoi.gr/~pvassil.

David Villa received his MS degree in Computer Engineering from the University of Castilla-La Mancha in 2002. Since then he works as a Teaching Assistant at the University of Castilla-La Mancha (UCLM). He is currently pursuing the PhD degree in Computer Science from UCLM. His current research interests include heterogeneous distributed systems, and distributed embedded system design.

Felix J. Villanueva received the Computer Eng. Diploma from the University of Castilla-La Mancha (UCLM) in 2001. In 1998 he joined the Computer Architecture and Networks Group at UCLM where he is now working as Teaching Assistant. He is currently pursuing the PhD degree in Computer Science from UCLM. His research interests include wireless sensor networks, ambient intelligence and embedded systems.

Mikael Wiberg, PhD is an associate professor at the department of Informatics at Umeå university in Sweden. Wiberg is also the Research Director for UID - Umeå Institute of Design (swe: "Designhögskolan") at Umeå University. Wiberg has published his work in a number of international journals, including ToCHI, BIT, IEEE Network, etc. and he has also published his work in books (including his role as editor for the book "The Interaction Society"). Currently Wiberg is also associate editor for ISJ - Information Systems Journal.

Ermai Xie is a graduate in Computer Science from the University of Ulster. He is currently studying for an MSc in Computing and Intelligent Systems at the University of Ulster. He has worked for many years in the IT industry both in China and the UK. He has published in the fields of medical and networking. He has worked on collaborative funded projects with the University of Ulster and hospitals in Northern Ireland. Currently, his research interests are in skeletal animation and neural networks.

Piero Zappi received its M.S. and Ph.D degrees in Electronic Engineering both from the universityof Bologna in 2005 and 2009 respectively. He won a prize for his M.S. thesis given by C.N.A.(National Confederation for arts and crafts). Since January 2009 he is working with the universityof Bologna as full collaborator. His research is mostly in the field of wireless sensor networks(WSN) and embedded systems. Main topics include: implementation of Zigbee based WSN, use of Pyroelectric InfraRed (PIR) detector for ambient monitoring, data management in redundant WSN, tangible interfaces and smart objects. He has been 6 month visiting research at ETH (Zurich) for ajoin research activity with the Wearable Lab at the institute of electronic.

Apostolos Zarras received his B.Sc. in Computer Science in 1994 from the Computer Science Department of the University of Crete. From the same department he received his M.Sc. in Distributed Systems and Computer Architecture. In 1999 he received his Ph.D. in Distributed Systems and Software Architecture from the University of Rennes I. Now he holds an Assistant Professor position at the Department of Computer Science of the University of Ioannina and he is a member of the Distributed Management of Data (DMOD) Laboratory (http://www.dmod.cs.uoi.gr/). His research interests include middleware, model-driven architecture development, quality analysis of software systems and pervasive computing. Further information can be found at http://www.cs.uoi.gr/~zarras.

Index